GEORGINA CAMPBELL'S

IRELAND

THE BEST OF THE BEST

The *very* best places to eat, drink and stay

Georgina Campbell Guides

Editor: Georgina Campbell

Epicure Press, PO Box 6173, Dublin 13, Ireland

website: www.ireland-guide.com

email: info@ireland-guide.com

Published 2018.

Updates and further information available from ireland-guide.com

▸ Front cover photograph: Mulranny Park Hotel, 'View From Nephin Restaurant'

▸ County Mayo introductory page image courtesy of David Loftus, Mayo.ie.
   Caption: Croagh Patrick & Clew Bay From Inishnakillew

▸ Food producers featured: Keem Bay Smoked Salmon; Mulranny Park Hotel Homemade Round Brown Soda Bread; Oilean Eadaigh Brewery, Throstle Preacher Pale Ale; Carrowholly Cheese

▸ Image of Restaurant Patrick Guilbaud courtesy of Barry McCall

City and county introductions © W.M. Nixon

Research and editorial assistance: Irish Food Writers' Guild members, especially Jeanne Quigley, Jillian Bolger and Anne Marie Carroll, and the assessment team.

Design and Artwork by Kandid Design - kandid-design.com

Printed and bound in Spain

First published 2018 by Georgina Campbell Guides Ltd.

ISBN 978-1-903164-341

GEORGINA CAMPBELL'S ireland

Editor's Introduction	5
ENTRIES: Republic of Ireland	
Dublin City	6
County Dublin	56
County Carlow	70
County Cavan	81
County Clare	87
Cork City	117
County Cork	133
County Donegal	187
County Galway	205
County Kerry	252
County Kildare	295
County Kilkenny	307
County Laois	321
County Leitrim	329
County Limerick	336
County Longford	350
County Louth	355
County Mayo	363
County Meath	390
County Monaghan	397
County Offaly	402
County Roscommon	409
County Sligo	414
County Tipperary	431
County Waterford	442
County Westmeath	455
County Wexford	466
County Wicklow	482
ENTRIES: NORTHERN IRELAND	
Belfast City	493
County Antrim	512
County Armagh	522
County Down	527
County Fermanagh	546
County Londonderry	550
County Tyrone	562

We would like to acknowledge the support of our Affiliated Sponsor **Hertz Ireland Car Hire** and the following regional bodies for their help and support in the development of this guide:

VISUAL
visualcarlow.ie
carlowtousism.com

Comhairle Chontae na Gaillimhe
Galway County Council

galwaygastronomy.ie

monaghantourism.ie

 @/MonaghanTourism

 /monaghantourism/

Comhairle Contae
Fhine Gall
Fingal County
Council

visitfingal.ie

Limerick
CITY & COUNTY
COUNCIL
Limerick - Explore, Discover
and Be Inspired

limerick.ie

Birr Castle Gardens &
Science Centre
birrcastle.com
visitoffaly.ie

Kerry County Council
kerrycoco.ie

VisitLongford.ie

visitlongford.ie

TIPPERARY
Time to take it all in

tipperary.com

Kilkenny
Living History, Loving Culture

www.visitkilkenny.ie

@LoveKilkenny

/visit kilkenny

MAYO.IE

mayococo.ie

WEXF☐RD
SO OLD, SO NEW
www.visitwexford.ie

visitwexford.ie
wexford.ie

EDITOR'S INTRODUCTION

It is over a decade since we published a new edition of 'The Best of the Best' and it has been an interesting journey.

In some ways Ireland seems much smaller now - improved infrastructure certainly makes it much easier and more enjoyable to get around this beautiful country than it ever has been, and the motorway system not only makes direct journeys faster and safer but it relieves the secondary roads of heavy traffic, allowing for more relaxing journeys for the leisurely traveller who can take time to enjoy the landscape and stop off at interesting little places along the way.

Yet in other ways it seems a far bigger country, as there is so much to engage the interest of the curious traveller, especially when to comes to food, drink and hospitality. When we made our choices for the last edition of 'Best of the Best' - a selection of the very best of their type taken, as this one is, from our much bigger, but also excellent, broad-based main collection of recommendations - it was relatively straightforward. 'Best' was generally seen as high-end and the vast majority of our much smaller selection tended to be well-established - and often famous - places in the upper price bracket.

But this book - which includes twice as many recommendations as the last 'Best' edition and, based on rising standards, could easily have many more - is testament to recent changes. There's now a special brand of excellence that covers a much broader spectrum and includes many very casual places to eat, drink and stay, so this selection reflects that changing perception, and the fact that 'best' experiences are accessible to all, regardless of taste or budget. A stay at a simple island B&B or converted horse truck, for example, can be at least as memorable as a break in a top hotel, or a casual meal in a beach shack might be the highlight of a holiday that also includes plenty of fine dining. And many of the establishments selected for this book have been included because they give visitors a particular opportunity to experience Irish culture and history as much as for the world-renowned hospitality of the people and outstanding food and drink.

New tourist regions, notably the *Wild Atlantic Way* (wildatlanticway.com) and *Ireland's Ancient East* (irelandsancienteast.com) are leading travellers to regional food experiences, often discovered through excellent local tourism groups such as County Clare's *Burren Food Trail*, the *Gourmet Greenway* in Mayo, and the *Boyne Valley Food Series* in Meath and Louth. Food tourism is a relatively new concept in Ireland but it is a uniquely interesting way to get to know a country and - thanks to the huge strides that have been made in artisan food production in recent years - engaging with the people who produce and prepare the good food that is now served in every corner of Ireland is a unique way of getting involved with local communities.

While we don't directly recommend food producers or retailers in this book, they are the foundation of our good food story and information on many of them is on our website. The kind of people who run our recommended establishments will lead you to them as you travel around, with personal suggestions of places that people who are interested in good food should visit - and also through the food they serve, and the often fascinating provenance stories that they share with their guests.

I hope you will enjoy using this book as much as we and our highly-valued assessment team always enjoy visiting the people featured in it - and wish you very happy and rewarding travelling in Ireland.

Georgina Campbell

Georgina Campbell, Editor

Malahide Castle
Co. Dublin

visitfingal.ie

COUNTY DUBLIN

Dublin County is divided into the three administrative "sub-counties" of **Dun Laoghaire-Rathdown** (dltourism.ie) to the southeast, **South Dublin** to the southwest, and the large 450sq.km territory of **Fingal** (visitfingal.ie) to the north. But although these regions are among the most populous and economically active in all Ireland, the notion of Greater Dublin being in four administrative parts is only slowly taking root. So if you feel that the frenetic pace of Dublin city is overpowering, you'll very quickly find that nearby, in what for many folk is still just County Dublin, there continue to be oases of a much more easy-going way of life waiting to be discovered.

Admittedly, the fact that the handsome Dublin Mountains overlook the city in spectacular style means that, even up in the nearby hills, you can be well aware of the city's buzz. But if you want to find a vigorous contrast between modern style and classical elegance, it can be found in an unusual form at Dun Laoghaire, setting for one of the world's largest artificial harbours, granite-built in meticulous Victorian style.

Northward beyond the city into **Fingal**, despite the proximity of the airport you'll quickly discover an away from-it-all sort of place of estuary towns, extensive farming, pleasant parkland, fishing and sailing ports, and offshore islands alive with seabirds, while South Dublin – which more accurately might be called "Southwest Dublin" - balances the other regions with its pleasant mixture of the urban and the intensely rural, with the feeling that "real Ireland" has in places managed to seep into the city - and thrive.

LOCAL ATTRACTIONS AND INFORMATION

>Balbriggan/Skerries - **Ardgillan Castle**
  www.ardgillancastle.ie | 01 849 2212

>Donabate - **Newbridge House** Park & Traditional Farm
  www.newbridgehouseandfarm.com | 01 843 6534

>Howth - **Howth Tourism** www.visithowth.ie

>Malahide - **Malahide Castle**
  www.malahidecastleandgardens.ie | 01 846 2184

DUBLIN
A TOWN FOR OUR TIMES

Dublin's commercial and creative energy is matched by the vibrancy of its everyday life and hospitality. It's an old town whose many meandering stories have interacted and combined to create today's busy riverside and coastal metropolis, an entertaining place well suited to the civilised enjoyment of life in the 21st Century.

Located beside a wide bay with some extraordinarily handsome hills and mountains near at hand, the city has long had the dictates of stylish living as an important part of its makeup. Yet most Dubliners wear their city's history lightly in an environment where the past lives with the present in ancient monuments, historic buildings, gracious squares and a fine old urban style that still manages to be gloriously alive. This if anything is emphasised by the city's modern architecture, seen particularly in the area around the Liffey in the former docklands in the International Financial Services Centre north of the river, and across the river around Grand Canal Dock.

It's a city of two names. *Baile Atha Cliath* - the official name in recent times - means nothing more exciting than "the townland of the hurdle ford". Ancient Ireland being an open-plan sort of place without towns, the site of the future city was no more than a river crossing between the territories of several comfortable monasteries.

But where the residents saw some inconvenience in the river, the Vikings sensed an opportunity. When they first brought their longships up the River Liffey around 837AD, they knew of a sheltered berth in a place which the locals of the hurdle ford called Dubh Linn - "the black pool". The Vikings settled along Wood Quay and around what is now Dublin Castle, created a major trading centre - and eventually went native.

As for the great seaport, it is still very much part of the city, and has never been busier. With forty major ship movements every day, sea and city are closely intertwined. However, Dublin Port is becoming a people-oriented transit focus, a giant ferry and cruise-liner port in the midst of residential, hospitality, administrative, business, service, entertainment and cultural centres.

In times past, the city's few large enterprises tended to be aimed at personal needs and the consumer market, rather than some aspiration towards heavy industry. Typical of them was Guinness's Brewery, founded in 1759. Today, its work-force may be much slimmed in every sense, but it still creates the black nectar, and if a new mash is under way up at the brewery and the wind is coming damply across Ireland from the west, the aroma of Guinness in the making will be wafted right into the city centre, the moist evocative essence of Anna Livia herself, while the imaginatively renovated Guinness Storehouse - with its interactive museums, restaurants and bars - provides Ireland's premier visitor centre.

LOCAL ATTRACTIONS AND INFORMATION

>**Dublin Castle** Dame Street 01 677 7129
>**Gaiety Theatre** South King Street 01 677 1717
>**Guinness Storehouse** 01 408 4800
>**Irish Tourist Board/Failte Ireland** Amiens Street 01 884 7700
>**Kilmainham Gaol** Kilmainham 01 4535984

>**National Gallery of Ireland** Merrion Square West 01 6615133
>**National Museum of Ireland** Collins Barracks 01 677 7444
>**Old Jameson Distillery** Smithfield Dublin 7 01 807 2355
>**Zoological Gardens** Phoenix Park 01 677 1425

CHAPTER ONE RESTAURANT

18/19 PARNELL SQUARE DUBLIN 1

01 873 2266 | info@chapteronerestaurant.com

www.chapteronerestaurant.com

EAT

Set in the arched basement beneath the Irish Writers' Museum, this atmospheric restaurant offers one of the country's finest dining experiences, focusing on Irish artisan produce and innovative techniques. Chef-patron Ross Lewis and a superb front-of-house team have earned an enviable reputation for outstanding modern Irish cooking and warm, engaging service. The cooking is classic French, lightly tempered by modern influences, and showcasing specialist Irish produce whenever possible. From lunch to an evening of culinary theatre at the Chef's Table, a meal here is always delicious and memorable.

★★

L Tue-Fri, 12.30-2, D Tue–Sat 7.30-10.30. Set L from €32, set Chef's table L €55. D Tasting menu €90. Set Chef's Table D €100. Closed L Sat, all Sun & Mon (Open Mon in Dec), 2 weeks Christmas, 2 weeks Aug. CC. **Directions:** Parnell Square north, beside Hugh Lane Gallery.

ELY BAR & BRASSERIE

CHQ IFSC DUBLIN 1   EAT I DRINK
01 672 0010 I elybrasserie@elywinebar.com
www.elywinebar.ie

Offering almost 100 wines by the glass, top-notch organic food (much of it from the Robson family's organic farm in Co Clare), great coffee and relaxed service, Erik and Michelle Robson's contemporary venue is a winner day or night. A younger sister to the original Ely wine bar on Ely Place, the stylish waterside atrium sits above spectacularly renovated 200-year-old wine vaults below. The décor is dashing, and includes a spacious heated outdoor terrace. The real star here, the wine list, runs to over 500 bottles and there's also a carefully selected beer list.

Seats 350 (+ 120 outdoors). Food Mon-Sat 12-late. L Mon-Fri 12-3. Brunch Sat 12-4, Sun to 6. Early D 5-6.30, from about €25. D Mon-Sat 5-late (early D 5-6.30). Closed Christmas. CC. **Directions:** IFSC quays, overlooking Georges Dock, 2 min Connolly Station or the Convention Centre.

FISH SHOP

6 QUEEN STREET DUBLIN 1   EAT
01 430 8594 | hello@fish-shop.ie
www.fish-shop.ie

Starting life as a fish and chip shack in Blackrock Market, Fish Shop is the latest incarnation by Londoner Jumoke Akintola and Tramore man Peter Hogan. The blink-and-you'll-miss-it restaurant just opposite Dice Bar, is low-key and unassuming, which makes dining here even more of a pleasant surprise. Each day they offer 4-6 courses based on the day's fresh catch, with matching wines available too. The pared-back décor, relaxed service, cool tunes, super ingredients and honest cooking make this tiny restaurant an absolute gem in the heart of Smithfield – and Fish Shop offers tremendous value for money.

Seats 16. Open Wed-Sat, 5-10. Set D from €39. Tasting D from €55. Closed Sun-Tue. **Also at:** 76 Benburb Street (Fish+Chip Shop & Wine Bar) **Directions:** North quays - just opposite Dice Bar.

MR FOX RESTAURANT

38/39 PARNELL SQUARE WEST DUBLIN 1   EAT | DRINK
01 874 7778 | info@mrfox.ie
www.mrfox.ie

On the west side of a busy Georgian square, this atmospheric sister to Stephen McAllister's Dublin 2 dining destination, The Pig's Ear, is in a smartly welcoming townhouse basement across from the Rotunda Hospital. Set in the original kitchen and adjoining areas, including a lovely bar and impressive outdoor courtyard, it's a tasteful and comfortable space equally suited to a business lunch, group celebration or romantic date. A short lunch and pre-theatre menu focuses on quality and interest while the à la carte is adventurous - all matched by excellent modern cooking and engaged service.

Seats 60. L Tue-Sat 12-2, D Tue-Sat 5-9.30. Pre-theatre 5-6, from about €22. Closed Sun, Mon, bank hols, 4 days Christmas, 1st week Jan. CC. **Directions:** West Parnell Square, opposite car exit from Rotunda Hospital.

VINTAGE TEA TOURS

MEETING POINT @ EPIC THE IRISH EMIGRATION MUSEUM
THE CHQ CUSTOM HOUSE QUAY DUBLIN 1
01 526 6961 (Mon-Fri) | info@vintageteatours.ie
www.vintageteatours.ie

If an Afternoon Tea bus tour of Dublin appeals, this should be just the ticket - traditional 3-tier afternoon tea fare served on a genuine 1961 Routemaster named Pauline. It's a fun atmosphere with everyone taking photos - of the food, themselves, the interior of the bus - but when they finally turn their attention to the outside, they find that Pauline, not surprisingly, is the centre of attention in the city streets. Children wave and passengers wave back, parents smile as everyone sits and nibbles while Pauline goes through the Phoenix Park, taking in Aras an Uachtarain and the American Ambassador's residence; she drives slowly through Georgian Dublin, O'Connell Street, and past the Jeanie Johnston sitting proudly in the Liffey...Magic.

Seats 38. Tours Wed-Sun, 11-12.30, 1.15-2.45, 3.30-5. Set afternoon tea menu, €40-€50 depending on seat booked. Children 6+ welcome.

THE WINDING STAIR

40 LOWER ORMOND QUAY DUBLIN 1   EAT

01 872 7320 | restaurant@winding-stair.com
www.winding-stair.com

Cosy, hip and bustling, Elaine Murphy's iconic restaurant overlooking the Ha'penny Bridge serves lip-smacking modern Irish food. Wooden floorboards, bentwood chairs and simple tables keep it cosy and relaxed while the menu sings with 'the organic and real', from seasonal signature dishes to outstanding renditions of Irish classics. The kind of place chefs come on their night off, the appealing menu is packed with top Irish artisan products. Once a beloved bookshop café, (the bookshop still operates downstairs) this first-floor dining room has a well-earned following.

Seats 60; L Mon-Fri 12-5. A la carte 12-10.30. D 5-10.30. Brunch Sat & Sun 12-4. Wine from €26. Closed 24-26 Dec, 1-2 Jan, Good Friday, 17 Mar. CC. **Directions:** On the north quays, opposite the Ha'penny bridge. **Also at:** The Washerwoman (see entry) the Woollen Mills (next door), and The Legal Eagle (www.thelegaleagle.ie).

AMUSE

22 DAWSON STREET DUBLIN 2   EAT
01 639 4889 | info@amuse.ie
www.amuse.ie

Combining the best of French techniques with Japanese and Irish ingredients, Conor Dempsey's fresh approach to cooking ensures Amuse is a star in Dublin's fine dining scene. Drawing on his cooking experience in some of Europe's top restaurants, Conor creates show-stopping food that will excite the most frequent of diners. The early dinner menu offers some of the best value in town (from about €34) with the Paris to Tokyo 5 or 9-course Tasting Menu the ultimate treat, especially when paired with wines. A high-end, intimate and original dining experience.

⭐

Seats 40. Open: L Tue-Sat, 12.30-2.30; set L from €24. Early D from €34. D Tue-Sat 6-9.30. Set D from €46. Tasting Menus: L about €40, D from €75. Closed Sun & Mon. Wheelchair access. CC. **Directions:** Top of Dawson Street.

777 RESTAURANT

7 CASTLE HOUSE SOUTH GREAT GEORGES STREET DUBLIN 2   EAT
01 425 4052 | info@777.ie
www.777.ie

Part Mexican cantina, part New York cool, 777 serves up authentic Mexican cooking alongside a dazzling array of over 80 tequilas and mescals. The rustic south-of-the-border Mexican fare includes tasty dishes such as the Asada de Carne, 24oz Ribeye sharing plate, prepared on a wood-burning grill - heftily-priced at about €65, but discounted to a more accessible level on Monday nights. Tables come with a selection of fiery sauces to up the heat and savvy owner John Farrell (proprietor of Dillingers and Butcher Grill in Ranelagh) has created a stylish and cool dining experience and a drinks list that includes cocktails, craft beer and cider - and the house ginger beer.

Seats about 40. Open Mon-Wed 5.30-10, Thu to 11, Fri & Sat 5-12, Sun 2-10. CC. **Directions:** Bottom of South Great Georges Street.

BEWLEY'S GRAFTON STREET

BEWLEY'S BUILDING GRAFTON ST DUBLIN 2   EAT
01 672 7720 | GraftonStreet@Bewleys.com
www.bewleys.com

Formerly Bewley's Oriental Café - as still proclaimed on the historic front façade - and Grafton Street's quintessential meeting place since 1840, this much-loved institution re-opened to acclaim in 2017 following a long closure and major refurbishment. Fans flocked back to see it, and check whether old favourites were still on the menu. It's brighter than it used to be, but the famous Harry Clarke windows and period fireplaces are looking their best, also proper café tables and bentwood chairs. But Bewley's is still all about best coffees and teas, and what to have with them. They do savoury food, of course, but it's the bakery that draws people back - the famous sticky buns, the coffee Opera cake and, of course, the Bewley's Mary Cake.

Open Mon-Sat 8am-8pm, Sun 10am-8pm. CC. **Directions:** prominent building on Dublin's premier shopping street.

BROOKS HOTEL & FRANCESCAS RESTAURANT

DRURY STREET DUBLIN 2   EAT | STAY
01 670 4000 | reservations@brookshotel.ie
www.brookshotel.ie

Minutes from Grafton Street this discreetly luxurious hotel is an oasis of calm in the city centre, offering excellent accommodation, quiet chill-out spaces and good breakfasts. The style is a pleasing combination of traditional with contemporary touches and the elegant Francesca's restaurant is a destination in itself. Overseen by head chef Patrick McLarnon, who sources mainly local ingredients with great care, the cooking is imaginative and there's a strong emphasis on fish and seafood.

Rooms 98 (8 shower only, 2 wheelchair friendly). Lift. Restaurant: D Sun-Thu 6-9.30 (Fri-Sat to 10). Set D from €29, also à la carte & vegetarian menus. Reservations advised. Jasmine Bar 12-10. Full wheelchair access. Fitness suite, sauna, in-house cinema. Open all year (closed to non-residents 24-25th Dec). CC. **Directions:** Near St Stephen's Green, between Grafton and Great St. Georges Streets; opposite Drury Street carpark.

CHAMELEON INDONESIAN RESTAURANT

1 LOWER FOWNES STREET TEMPLE BAR DUBLIN 2   EAT
01 671 0362 I book@chameleonrestaurant.com
www.chameleonrestaurant.com

Tucked away off the main cobbled thoroughfare of bustling Temple Bar, Carol Walsh and Kevin O'Toole's Chameleon Restaurant has been surprising locals and tourists alike since 1994 with its informal fun atmosphere and unique take on authentic Indonesian dining. Their speciality 'Rijst Tafel' (small plates of fragrant, spicy dishes for sharing) offers diners an evocative, sociable dining experience – and good value, as well as accomplished cooking (with great choices for vegetarians) and warm and welcoming service. Allow plenty of time to enjoy it.

D Wed-Sun from 4pm. Early D about €19, available Tue-Thu & Sun, 5-7pm, Fri & Sat 5-6.30pm. Set menus from about €25 (€29 with dessert). CC. **Directions:** Just off Wellington Quay.

THE CLARENCE & CLEAVER EAST

6-8 WELLINGTON QUAY DUBLIN 2   EAT I STAY
01 407 0800 I reservations@theclarence.ie
www.theclarence.ie

One of Dublin's most iconic hotels, the Arts & Crafts interior on the edge of Temple Bar is elegantly hip, with accommodation offering a combination of contemporary comfort and period style. Guests love the clubby Octagon Bar and the much talked about **Cleaver East** restaurant; created by high profile chef Oliver Dunne, it brings a slice of hipster New York to the heart of Temple Bar. Expect fine dining treats matched with edgy décor and smart cocktails. Also a popular destination for Brunch and the quirky 'Not Afternoon Tea'.

Rooms 49 (1 wheelchair friendly). Lift. Room rate about €340. Cleaver East: seats 90. Brunch Fri–Sun 12-3, D Mon-Sat 5.30-10.30, (Sun to 9.30). Food daily Octagon Bar (12-8), Liquor Rooms (5-10) & The Study Café (12-10.15). Restaurant closed 24 Dec-27 Dec. CC. **Directions:** Overlooking the River Liffey at Wellington Quay.

THE CLIFF TOWN HOUSE & URCHIN SEAFOOD BAR

22 ST STEPHEN'S GREEN DUBLIN 2   EAT | STAY
01 638 3939 | info@theclifftownhouse.com
www.theclifftownhouse.com

Sister-property to the celebrated Cliff House Hotel in Waterford, this elegant Georgian townhouse, overlooking St Stephen's Green, has nine stylish bedrooms and a handsome seafood restaurant and oyster bar. A contemporary basement bar, **Urchin**, also seafood focused, specialises in small plates of imaginative food and great cocktails, and the unique décor - think Alice's Beach-Hut in Wonderland with candy stripes and beach-brolly colours - keeps the mood lively. A fun dining option.

Rooms 9. Room rate from €240. L daily 12-2.15. D Mon-Sat from 5.15, Sun 6-8.45. Early D Mon-Sat from €25, also à la carte. Set Sun L 12-4, from €30. Bar food from 12. Oyster & Champagne Bar 12-2.30 & 5.30-10.30. Urchin: Mon-Sat from 12 noon-closing, Sun from 4. Closed 25 & 31 Dec, 1 Jan, Good Fri. CC. **Also at** Cliff at Lyons & Cliff House Hotel (see entries).

CONRAD DUBLIN & THE COBURG

EARLSFORT TERRACE DUBLIN 2   EAT | DRINK | STAY
01 602 8900 | dublininfo@conradhotels.com
www.conraddublin.com

Recently refurbished, this comfortable big-brand hotel is a business favourite and has real heart thanks to warm service, thoughtful details and the pleasantly contemporary guestrooms. The Conrad's stylish new brasserie, The Coburg, is definitely not an average hotel restaurant. From beautiful décor to an appetising menu, engaged service and delicious food it has really raised the game in hotel dining in Dublin. The fresh and exciting all-day menu features classic brasserie dishes, with top-notch cooking and well-chosen wines to match. Also interesting is Alfie Byrne's bar; operated by Galway Bay Brewery it specialises in craft drinks and informal dining.

Rooms 191 (1 wheelchair friendly). Lift. Room rate from about €240. Coburg Brasserie: open 6.30–11 daily. Wine from €29. Bar food daily 12-9. Res D only Dec 25. Hotel open all year. CC. **Directions:** opposite National Concert Hall.

CORNUCOPIA

19 WICKLOW STREET DUBLIN 2

01 677 7583 | info@cornucopia.ie

www.cornucopia.ie

EAT

Beloved of students, alternative diners and mainstream guests who never expected to enjoy vegetarian food so much, this long-established wholefood restaurant caters for all kinds of restrictive diets (gluten-free, dairy-free etc) with its home-cooked vegetarian offerings and has become a Dublin institution. It's very informal, especially during the day (when window seats are well placed for people-watching), and regulars like it for its simple wholesomeness. Vegetarian breakfasts are a speciality and ingredients are organic, as far as possible.

Seats 48. Mon 8.30-9, Tue-Sat to 10, Sun & Public Hols 12-9. A la carte (menu changes daily). Closed 25-26 Dec. 1 Jan, Easter Sun/Mon, Oct bank hol Sun/Mon. CC. **Directions:** Off Grafton St. Turn at Brown Thomas.

DAX RESTAURANT

23 UPPER PEMBROKE STREET DUBLIN 2

01 676 1494 I olivier@dax.ie

www.dax.ie

EAT

Despite its popularity since it first opened in an intimate Georgian basement in Pembroke Street in 2004, Dax manages to feel delightfully exclusive, like a well-kept secret amongst foodie friends. In 2017 the dream team of chef Graham Neville and restaurateur Olivier Meisonnave reunited 12 years after first working together in Thornton's, giving Dax a whole new energy. Outstanding modern Irish cooking, using the finest seasonal Irish produce, is matched by charming service and a top wine selection, ensuring Dax's future as one of the finest and most exciting restaurants in Dublin.

⭐

Seats 65. L Tue-Fri, 12.30-2. Set L from about €28, also à la carte. Early D Tue-Fri 6-6.45 from €32. D Tue-Sat 6-9.30 (Fri-Sat to 10) à la carte. Surprise Menu €90. Vegetarian menu. Reservations recommended. Closed Sat L, Sun, Mon, 25 Dec-4 Jan, 1/2 weeks Aug.

THE DEAN

33 HARCOURT STREET DUBLIN 2
01 607 8110 | info@thedean.ie
www.deanhoteldublin.ie

EAT | DRINK | STAY

More like the home of a creative 30-something than an hotel, this recent addition to Dublin's accommodation has a distinctive New York-vibe. Behind the smart Georgian façade you'll find moody lighting, poured concrete, parquet floors, chrome tables and cleverly designed bedrooms with lovely touches. The rooftop is home to Sophie's, a modern Italian restaurant, and a large terrace, perfect for cocktails with a view.

Busy by night, weekend DJs draw a sophisticated crowd.

Room only from about €105. Sophie's Restaurant: breakfast: 7-11. Brunch: Sat, Sun & bank hol Mon 11-3. L Mon-Fri 12-3. D daily 5 -'late'. Set menu for groups from €45. Wine from about €26. Rotisserie L & short daily menu available in the Dean Bar. Late bar Fri & Sat, 11pm-'late'. CC.
Directions: Off the south-west corner of St Stephen's Green.

DELAHUNT

39 CAMDEN STREET LOWER DUBLIN 2
01 598 4880 | delahuntcamden@gmail.com
www.delahunt.ie

EAT

Delahunt is a thing of rare beauty – a modern restaurant in an old building that looks beautiful and serves beautiful food. Owner Darren Free has put thought into everything, from the beautiful refurbishment of this landmark Victorian grocers, to the carefully constructed menu, wine list and well trained staff. Expect great modern Irish cooking of choice ingredients by head chef Dermot Staunton - who has led the kitchen

team since opening in 2015 - and you won't be disappointed. Relaxed and reliable, a great resurrection of a Victorian landmark.

Restaurant: D Tue-Sat & bank hol Sun 5-9.30, Thu-Fri L 12.30-2. Set menu from €32. Closed Sun-Mon (& Tue after bank hols). The Café at Delahunt: Open 8-12 & 2.30-3.30 for coffee & pastries. L 12-2.30.

DUNNE & CRESCENZI

14 & 16 SOUTH FREDERICK STREET DUBLIN 2   EAT

01 677 3815 | info@ dunneandcrescenzi.com

www.dunneandcrescenzi.com

A glass of wine, plate of antipasti and great coffee will transport you to Italy in this bustling and unpretentious spot where quality is a priority. Serving simple rustic food at reasonable prices, this is the original branch of Eileen Dunne and Stefano Crescenzi's hugely successful chain. Signature panini, authentic pasta dishes, Sicilian ice cream and wonderful desserts all add to the appeal, and a wine list with over 200 Italian labels includes really exciting choices by the glass. Expect to queue: this place has a loyal following.

Seats 60 (+20 outdoors). Open Mon-Sat 8-late, Sun 9.30-late; Casa (shop) closed Sun. B'fst to 12 (later Sat-Sun). Set L from €26. D à la carte. Set D available for groups (10+).CC. **Directions:** Off Nassau Street, between Kilkenny and Blarney stores. **Also at:** Blackrock (see entry); Sandymount. L'Officina at Dundrum; Kildare Village.

ELY WINEBAR

22 ELY PLACE DUBLIN 2   EAT | DRINK
01 676 8986 | elyplace@elywinebar.com
www.elywinebar.ie

Erik and Michelle Robson's original wine bar may have a younger sister in the IFSC, but the original Ely continues to appeal with its vast and dazzling wine selection and choice of dining options - from cosy cellar bar to private room, the comfortable décor and new menus ensure the perfect setting for all occasions. The exceptional wine list is backed up by other specialities including a list of premium beers, and appealing menus offer tasty, well-sourced food, including organic meat from the family farm in County Clare

Seats 90. Open Mon-Sat 12 noon-12.30am. Food served Mon-Fri 4-11, D Mon-Sat from 5. Children welcome before 7. Wine from €26. Georgian dining room available for private dining and wine tastings. Closed Sun, Christmas week, bank hols, Good Friday CC.
Directions: Off St Stephens Green, Baggot Street/Merrion Street junction.
Also at: IFSC.

ETTO

18 MERRION ROW DUBLIN 2   EAT I DRINK
01 678 8872 I info@etto.ie
www.etto.ie

Simon Barrett and Liz Matthews' pared-back little restaurant and wine bar serves rustic Italian fare with flair. Seemingly simple menus change daily, dazzling with seasonal ingredients and aiming to deliver maximum flavour with minimum interference. Dishes comprise a handful of choice ingredients married together for maximum flavour. Add in an interesting, well-priced wine list, with plenty of small producers, and palpable buzz and you'll see why the compact tables are all filled with chefs and restaurateurs on their days off.

Seats 24 (+ bar seating). Open Mon-Wed 12-9.30 (Thu & Fri to 10), Sat 12.30-10. Set L Mon-Fri 12-2.45 (Sat to 3), from €20. Pre-theatre Mon-Thu 5-6.30, from €24. A la carte D 5-9 Mon-Wed (to 10 Thu-Sat). Wine from €29. Closed Sun & Bank Hols. CC. **Directions:** Just off St Stephens Green on Merrion Row.

FALLON & BYRNE

11-17 EXCHEQUER STREET DUBLIN 2   EAT I DRINK I BUY
01 472 1000 I restaurant@fallonandbyrne.com
www.fallonandbyrne.com

Upstairs above Dublin's favourite food store, a bright and airy dining space serves classic French food with flair and panache. Simple menus feature authentic French cooking that's great tasting, good value and well presented. Professional staff and a lively buzz complete the picture, making it popular with groups. There's an atmospheric basement wine bar too, if you'd prefer a light bite surrounded by bottles of tempting wine.

Restaurant: **Seats 100**: L 12-3 daily; D Sun-Tue 5.30-9, Wed-Thu to 10, Fri & Sat to 11. **Food Hall & Deli:** Mon-Fri 8am-9pm, Sat 9-9, Sun & bank hol Mon 11-7. **Wine Cellar:** Mon-Wed 12-10, Thu to 11, Fri & Sat to 12am, Sun 11-9. Closed 25/26 Dec, Good Friday. CC. **Also at:** The People's Park, Dun Laoghaire.

THE FITZWILLIAM HOTEL

ST STEPHENS GREEN DUBLIN 2   STAY

01 478 7000 enq@fitzwilliamhoteldublin.com
www.fitzwilliamhoteldublin.com

Luxurious, discreet and contemporary, this intimate and stylish five-star is equally well suited to business or a shopping trip. A complete refurbishment has refreshed the hotel's sleek good looks with smart guestrooms, some overlooking St Stephen's Green. Breakfast, lunch and dinner are served daily in the attractive informal restaurant, Citron, and in the popular meeting place, Inn on the Green. And not only does the Fitzwilliam have a gym that's open around the clock and an in-house hair and beauty salon - but also Ireland's largest roof garden.

Rooms 138 (4 wheelchair friendly). Lift. B&B from about €110pps. Families welcome. Citron: set L Mon-Sat 12.30-2.30, about €20. D daily 5-30-10, à la carte. Set D Sun-Mon €25. Inn on the Green, food 12-10. A la carte. Open all year. CC. **Directions:** West side of St. Stephen's Green. **Also at:** Belfast.

THE GREENHOUSE

DAWSON ST. DUBLIN 2   EAT

01 676 7015 | info@thegreenhouserestaurant.ie
www.thegreenhouserestaurant.ie

Mickael Viljanen's cooking is in a league of its own and The GreenHouse delivers one of Ireland's finest culinary experiences. Everything from the intimate room to the warm staff enhance the special feeling you'll get when dining here on the extraordinary Finnish-Irish cooking. Together with restaurateur Eamonn O'Reilly, Viljanen promises an exceptional seasonal treat with lunch offering some of the best value in town. Stunning food will take your breath away, and even the most jaded diners never fail to be astounded by the level of creativity and brilliance poured into every dish.

⭐

Set L Tue-Sat 12-2, from about €40. D 6-9.30. 4/6 course Tasting menu Tue-Sat (€90/115). Surprise menu Fri & Sat. Wine from €41. Closed Sun & Mon. CC. **Directions:** At top of Dawson St.

L'ECRIVAIN

109A LOWER BAGGOT STREET DUBLIN 2
01 661 1919 I enquiries@lecrivain.com
www.lecrivain.com

EAT

One of Dublin's top restaurants, this destination dining room promises to please with its combination of Derry Clarke's cooking and Sallyanne's front of house hospitality. Classic French techniques meet the best of Irish produce in the kitchen to create a menu of imaginative and elegant dishes. The outstanding fine dining experience is complemented by a bright, stylish dining room and impressive wine list. The convivial vibe and sleek service have always been a trademark of L'Ecrivain, making it a destination for special occasions as well as an attractive option for a smart business lunch.

⭐

Seats 104 (+ 22 outdoors). Set L Fri 12.30 to 3.30, from €35. L Tasting menu €60. D Mon-Sat, 6.30-10. Seasonal 3 course D about €75. D Tasting Menu about €90. Wine from about €38. Closed Sun, bank hols, Christmas, New Year, Easter. CC.

LAS TAPAS DE LOLA

12 WEXFORD STREET DUBLIN 2   EAT
01 424 4100 | book@lastapasdelola.com
www.lastapasdelola.com

Re-live your holiday memories with a table at this buzzy tapas joint on Wexford Street. Raising the bar for Spanish food in Dublin, the stylish space offers a huge menu of over 50 flavoured-packed classics, from favourites like gambas al ajillo to the unexpected, maybe carrillada de cerdo, (marinated pigs' cheeks), all presented in authentic terracotta. The lively, colourful space extends to a little street-side terrace that's always first to fill. From the excellent sangria to piquant patatas bravas, this popular spot serves some of the best tapas this side of Barcelona.

Open: Mon-Thu 5-10.30, Fri & Sat 5-11, Sun 5-10. A la carte (group menu available). CC **Directions:** South-west of St Stephen's Green; Wexford Street is on the R114, parallel to Harcourt Street.

THE MERRION HOTEL

UPPER MERRION STREET DUBLIN 2

01 603 0600 | info@merrionhotel.com

www.merrionhotel.com

EAT | DRINK | STAY

Comprising four meticulously renovated Georgian townhouses, The Merrion is a luxurious retreat in the heart of Dublin. A warm Irish welcome, historic décor, plush bedrooms and classy service make it five-star all the way. Luxurious public areas, perfect for business meetings or the stunning **'Art Tea'**, are matched by beautifully furnished guest rooms and the sumptuous Tethra Spa. Dining options include Restaurant Patrick Guilbaud (see entry); The Garden Room, a lovely all-day restaurant overlooking the hotel's formal gardens; and the atmospheric vaulted Cellar Bar for informal meals. In a world of Identikit hotels with bland service, The Merrion feels incredibly special.

Rooms 142 (5 wheelchair friendly). Lift. B&B from abut €130pps. **The Garden Room:** 7.30-10. **Art Tea** 1.30 & 4.30 (must book). Cellar Bar L&D Mon-Sat 12-3 & 3-10, Sun Brunch 11.30-5. Open all year. CC. **Directions:** Opposite Government Buildings.

NUMBER 31

31 LEESON CLOSE LR LEESON STREET DUBLIN 2   STAY

01 676 5011 | info@number31.ie
www.number31.ie

Beloved by design buffs, Noel and Deirdre Comer's architectural gem marries cool guesthouse accommodation with a homely welcome and luxurious little extras. Formerly the home of leading architect, the late Sam Stephenson, the elegant bedrooms have exceptionally comfortable beds, and breakfasts, served at communal tables, are a treat. There's a lovely cosy feel and with its stay-in-all-day atmosphere, you might find it hard to leave.

Rooms 21 (all en-suite). Room rate from about €240; children welcome. Wifi. Secure parking. Open all year. CC.
Directions: From St. Stephen's Green, turn onto Lr Baggot Street, right onto Pembroke Street and left onto Lr Leeson Street.

ONE PICO RESTAURANT

5-6 MOLESWORTH PLACE SCHOOLHOUSE LANE DUBLIN 2   EAT

01 676 0300 | www.onepico.com

Quietly located in a laneway near St. Stephen's Green and very close to Leinster House (parliament buildings), Eamonn O'Reilly's stylish and con-sistently excellent One Pico is one of Dublin's most popular fine dining restaurants. The surroundings are elegant, as is the exceptionally good cooking. Sophisticated, technically demanding dishes, starring first class ingredients, are executed with con-fidence and flair. Service is profes-sional and friendly and a well-chosen wine list offers some 80 bottles. This is a fine restaurant and has earned its place among the city's best.

⭐

Seats 65. Open L Mon-Sat 12-2.45, Sun 1-4. Set L from €27. Pre-theatre 5.30-6.45 last orders, from about €29. D Mon-Sat 5.30-10, Sun 5-8. Set D from €49. Wine from €32. Closed bank hols, 24 Dec-5 Jan. CC. **Directions:** Off Kildare Street, beside multi-storey Dawson St carpark; 2 minute walk from St Stephens Green/Grafton Street.

OSTERIA LUCIO

THE MALTING TOWER GRAND CANAL QUAY DUBLIN 2   EAT | DRINK

01 6624 199 | info@osterialucio.com

www.osterialucio.com

Several cuts above your average pizza and pasta joint, real love has been put into the menu and cooking at Osteria Lucio. Co-owned by Ross Lewis of Chapter One, this buzzy restaurant offers up one of the most authentic Italian dining experiences in Dublin. Tucked beneath a railway bridge near the Grand Canal Theatre, this popular spot serves the finest Italian ingredients, authentic regional cooking and speciality wood-fired pizzas. The terrace is ideal for summer dining; the low-slung vaulted interior cosy for winter visits.

Seats 70 (+20 outdoors). L Mon–Fri 12-3, D Mon-Fri & Sun 5-10. Sat 5-10.30. Closed bank hol Mons, 23 Dec-5 Jan, Good Fri. CC. **Directions:** Just off Grand Canal Street beside the Treasury Holdings building.

PEARL BRASSERIE

20 MERRION STREET UPPER DUBLIN 2   EAT | DRINK
01 661 3572 | info@pearl-brasserie.com
www.pearl-brasserie.com

A few doors from The Merrion Hotel, and serving some of the best food in Dublin, Sebastien Masi and Kirsten Batt's chic basement brasserie deserves to be on everyone's speed dial. Luxurious, innovative and sophisticated, it's been serving consistently excellent food since opening in 2000. More fine dining than brasserie, the dazzling cooking and superb wine list ensure a meal here is always a treat. Exciting menus, fabulous flavour combinations and attentive service make this a gem of a restaurant in every way possible.

⭐

Seats 80. Set L Mon-Sat 12-2.30, from €25. D Mon-Sat 6-'late'. Early D Mon-Sat 6-6.45, from about €28. A la carte L&D available & vegetarian menu. Wines from €30. Children welcome; reservations recommended. Closed Sun, bank hol Mon, 25-26 Dec. CC. **Directions:** Opposite Government Buildings, near Merrion Hotel.

PICHET

14-15 TRINITY STREET DUBLIN 2

01 677 1060 | bookings@pichet.ie

www.pichet.ie

Offering French bistro classics with a modern edge, Stephen Gibson's delicious cooking is just one reason for Pichet's success. Add in prime ingredients, friendly service, a great wine list and central location and you've got a wonderful modern French restaurant with Irish heart and soul. The stylish, lively dining room and handsome cocktail bar make it a great choice for a late night.

Open daily L 12-3, early D 5-6.30, from €16. A la carte D Mon-Wed 5-9.30, Thu-Sat 5-10, Sun 3-9. CC. **Directions:** Half way up Trinity Street on right hand side (just off Dame Street).

PICKLE

43 CAMDEN STREET LOWER DUBLIN 2

01 555 7755 | info@picklerestaurant.com

picklerestaurant.com

From the colourful and chic décor to the original menu, Sunil Ghai is introducing Dubliners to the joys of North Indian cooking. The casual décor belies the serious pedigree in the kitchen. From guinea fowl masala to tiffin lunch boxes, Sunil's fine dining roots have seen this exciting cuisine finessed for a new audience. Casual dining at its best.

Open: L Tue-Fri 12-2.30, D Tue-Sat 5-10.30; Sun 3-10. Early D Tue-Fri 5-6, Sun 3-6. A la carte. CC. **Directions:** Southwest of St Stephen's Green area; near The Bleeding Horse pub (R114).

THE PIG'S EAR

4 NASSAU STREET DUBLIN 2   EAT
01 670 3865 | info@thepigsear.ie
www.thepigsear.ie

Anyone wondering whether Ireland has a culinary heritage should make a beeline for The Pig's Ear. Flying the flag for modern Irish cooking since 2008, chef-proprietor Stephen McAllister marries classic Irish tradition with the best in local ingredients. Diners will enjoy a menu packed with the finest Irish seasonal produce, from milk-fed lamb to Castletownbere crab and organic salmon to TJ Crowe's pork belly from Co Tipperary. Try to land a window table in the elegant dining rooms, to enjoy the lovely views of Trinity College's playing fields.

Seats 80, unsuitable for children. Open Mon-Sat L 12-2.45, D 5.30-10. Set L/early D from about €22. D à la carte; wine from about €20. Sister restaurant Mr Fox (see entry). Closed Sun & bank hols. CC. **Directions:** City centre overlooking Trinity College.

PIGLET

5 COWS LANE TEMPLE BAR DUBLIN 2   EAT
01 707 9786 | oink@pigletwinebar.ie
www.pigletwinebar.ie

Wine lovers should make a point of stopping by Piglet, an authentic wine bar on Cow's Lane, run by Italian wine importer, Enrico Fantasia, and front-of-house stalwart, Frenchman Thibaud Harang (ex-Pichet). Serving an excellent and affordable selection of mostly European, organic wines, there has been love poured into the food offering too, with imaginative tapas the real stars. Low-key, honest and accessible, this no-nonsense establishment is a gem and a welcome breath of fresh air in the capital.

Seats 25 (+ outdoor seating). Open daily 12-10 (Sun from 1) L Mon-Fri 12-3. Supper Mon-Fri 3 to close, Sat & Sun all day. CC.

RESTAURANT PATRICK GUILBAUD

21 UPPER MERRION STREET DUBLIN 2   EAT
01 676 4192 | restaurantpatrickguilbaud@eircom.net
www.restaurantpatrickguilbaud.net

Every capital city has its great restaurant and Guilbaud's is Dublin's gastronomic heaven. Elegant and luxurious, it is in a Georgian townhouse adjoining the Merrion Hotel. Head chef since opening in 1981, Guillaume Lebrun is renowned for exceptional modern classic cuisine, based on the best Irish produce in season. His wide-ranging menus include a wonderfully creative 8-course Dégustation Menu, with a shorter midweek alternative offered; by contrast, a daily table d'hote lunch menu has long offered the best value fine dining in Ireland. Each dish is a masterpiece of flavour and beautiful presentation matched by faultless service under the relaxed supervision of Restaurant Manager Stéphane Robin with Patrick Guilbaud often present to greet guests personally. Contemporary French cooking at its best.

★★

L Tue-Sat 12.30-2. (Sat from 1), D 7-10.
Closed Sun-Mon, bank hols, Christmas.CC.

ROSA MADRE

7 CROW ST TEMPLE BAR DUBLIN 2

01 5511 206 I lucademarzio@yahoo.it

www.rosamadre.ie

EAT

Temple Bar may be better known for its night life than the quality of its restaurants, but one establishment sits head and shoulders above all others. Luca De Marzio's spacious Rosa Madre could have been transplanted from Puglia or Tuscany, with its traditional Italian cooking, continental vibe and old school hospitality. From the glistening fresh fish counter inside the door to Luca's infectious hospitality, the welcome is warm and the food delicious. Fun, reliable and relaxed, this hidden gem of a restaurant in Temple Bar is ideal for any occasion.

L Mon-Sat 1-2.30, D Mon-Sun 5-10 (Thu-Sat to 11). A la carte. CC **Directions:** Off Dame Street, two blocks east of Olympia Theatre.

SABA

26 -28 CLARENDON STREET DUBLIN 2

01 679 2000 I feedback@sabadublin.com

www.sabadublin.com

EAT I LEARN

Since Paul Cadden's Saba burst onto Dublin's dining scene in 2006 it's been a go-to place for exciting Asian food. Offering delicious Thai and Vietnamese dishes, executed with flair and authenticity, a meal here will transport you to South East Asia. The menu is vast, packed with traditional dishes – including lesser-known ones – with their express lunch offering especially good value. Great cocktails and cool décor are part of the attraction with Saba delivering a reliable and lively dining experience.

Open daily noon-10.30 (Thu-Sat to 11). A la carte L 12-4. A la carte D from 4. Coeliac & vegetarian options available; food to go menu; wheelchair accessible; reservations recommended. Closed 25-26 Dec. CC. **Directions:** Parallel to top of Grafton Street, behind Westbury Hotel. **Also at:** 22 Upper Baggot Street, Dublin 4; several 'Saba to Go' locations in South Dublin.

THE SHELBOURNE HOTEL

27 ST STEPHEN'S GREEN DUBLIN 2

EAT I DRINK I STAY

01 663 4500 I rhi.dubbr.dts@renaissancehotels.com
www.theshelbourne.ie

Famed for its bars, afternoon tea and sense of old-world luxury, this impressive 19th century hotel is still the heart and soul of Georgian Dublin. A recent facelift has not compromised its iconic charm and, from uniformed doormen to sparkling chandeliers, the accommodation is equally luxurious, especially the rooms overlooking St Stephen's Green. The famous Horseshoe Bar and larger No. 27 Bar & Lounge are Dublin institutions, while dining can be enjoyed in the stylish Saddle Room or Lord Mayor's Lounge. The Spa at The Shelbourne is a sumptuous, high-spec pampering destination, and service throughout is exemplary.

Rooms 246 (7 wheelchair friendly). Room only rates from about €580. Saddle Room Restaurant: L daily 12-2 (Sun to 3.30). D daily 5.30-10. Wheelchair accessible; reservations recommended. Open all year. Bar food 11-9 daily CC. **Directions:** Landmark building on north side of St Stephen's Green.

SUESEY STREET

25 FITZWILLIAM PLACE DUBLIN 2

EAT I DRINK

01 669 4600 I info@sueseystreet.ie
www.sueseystreet.ie

The Kelly family's clubby basement hideaway with heated terrace offers cocktails and sharing platters at the low-lit bar as well as accomplished modern European cooking. Formerly Brasserie le Pont, the new incarnation is cool and casual while retaining touches of luxury. Smartly attired professional staff display impressive knowledge with the wine pairings particularly well-considered. The cooking is equally confident, with imaginative renderings of quality ingredients. Choose between a well-priced set menu or the full à la carte. A reliable spot for comfortable dining for business or family get-togethers, and an attractive hideout for a languid lunch or evening supper.

L Tue-Fri 12-2.30. Early D Tue-Thu 6-7.30 & Sat 6-6.45, from €25. D Tue-Sat 6-10, à la carte. CC. **Directions:** Fitzwilliam Place is on junction of Leeson Street and Adelaide Road.

TASTE AT RUSTIC BY DYLAN MCGRATH

17 SOUTH GREAT GEORGE'S STREET DUBLIN 2   EAT

01 526 7701 | info@tasteatrustic.com

www.tasteatrustic.com

Showcasing a creative menu influenced by Japan, Peru and Spain, Dylan McGrath's exciting venture, above Rustic Stone, harks back to his brilliance at his first restaurant, the star-spangled Mint. The fine dining frills are gone, but the exquisite food and magical flavour combinations remind us why he's one of Ireland's most thrilling chefs. Nab a comfy counter seat to watch the chefs in action or settle into a table. The third floor restaurant oozes New York luxe, with great staff, a lively buzz and some of the most creative food in town.

⭐

Seats 60, open Tue-Thu 5-10.30 (Fri & Sat to 11). Early 3 course D 5-6.30, about €39.50. Set menu from €45. Wine from €28. CC.

THE WESTBURY HOTEL & WILDE RESTAURANT

GRAFTON STREET DUBLIN 2   EAT | STAY

01 679 1122 | westbury@doylecollection.com

www.doylecollection.com/westbury

Possibly the most conveniently situated of all Dublin's luxury hotels, The Westbury Hotel is seconds from Grafton Street (and with underground parking). Unashamedly sumptuous, the hotel's public areas drip with chandeliers although the bedrooms are decidedly more contemporary. Fashionable for afternoon tea, the hotel is popular with business and corporate guests, but also makes a great base for a leisure break. Wilde, the beautiful

Art Deco-influenced restaurant, offers delicious all-day dining and great service while there's casual brasserie and bar fare at Balfe's.

Rooms 205 (3 wheelchair friendly). Lifts. Room rate from about €180. Wilde Restaurant: Mon-Sat 12.30 -11.30 (Last orders 9.30). Set L about €34. Set D from €35, also à la carte. House wine from €25. Balfes Bar & Brasserie: B'fst Mon-Fri 8-11.30; Brunch Sat-Sun 10-2.30, all day menu 5-close. The Gallery 12-10. Hotel open all year. CC.

WHITEFRIAR GRILL

16 AUNGIER STREET DUBLIN 2   EAT

01 475 9003 | info@whitefriargrill.ie

www.whitefriargrill.ie

You could almost miss Geoff Nordell's cosy restaurant on a dash up Aungier Street, but it's worth seeking out, especially for good steak or a relaxed weekend brunch. Chunky tables, chilled tunes, flickering nightlights, and a neat little bar all create a laidback vibe for the delightfully original menus. The cooking is precise, presentation pretty, portions generous and flavours superb, making this a great asset

to the area. Reasonably priced too, including the short but well considered wine list.

D daily from 5, a la carte, early D Mon-Wed all evening, Thu to 6.30, Fri & Sun to 6, from about €22. (No early D Sat). Brunch Sat, Sun & bank hols 10.30-4. Wine from €26. CC. **Directions:** Opposite Carmelite Church, 5 mins walk from St. Stephen's Green.

CLONTARF CASTLE HOTEL

CASTLE AVENUE CLONTARF DUBLIN 3

01 833 2321 I info@clontarfcastle.ie

www.clontarfcastle.ie

EAT I STAY

Located near the coast, this 17th century castle has been cleverly renovated to combine the charm of the old with the comfort of the new. It's welcoming, stylish and a short walk from the seafront. Popular with the business community, the luxurious, warmly decorated bedrooms and excellent staff ensure it's a comfortable spot for a leisure break too. The hotel has two bars – the chic Indigo Lounge and, for traditionalists, Knights Bar – and the striking Fahrenheit Grill majors in steaks and seafood.

Rooms 111 (2 wheelchair friendly). Lift. B&B from about €75pps. Fahrenheit Restaurant: D Sun-Thu 5-9.30 (Fri & Sat to 10). Sun all day set menu from €29. Early D Sun-Fri 5-7. Also à la carte. Bar food 10-9. Open all year. CC. **Directions.** From Howth Road turn onto Castle Avenue, continue to roundabout, take right into hotel.

DA MIMMO

148 NORTH STRAND ROAD DUBLIN 3

01 856 1714 I info@damimmo.ie

www.damimmo.ie

EAT

The family name Fuscardi is not unknown to many Dubliners who like their fish and chips but a whole new generation of Italian-Irish have now returned to their culinary roots and Tino Fuscardi's Da Mimmo is an example of this. Originally opened as a pizza restaurant with some fresh pasta dishes and a handful of deli items the tiny space's popularity required an inevitable expansion to a bigger, more stylish premises serving excellent freshly prepared antipasti, pasta, pizza and traditional Italian desserts. Take-away is also available.

Open daily 12-10pm. A la carte. Wine from about €23.

KINARA RESTAURANT

318 CLONTARF ROAD DUBLIN 3

01 833 6759 I info@kinara.ie

www.kinara.ie

EAT

Overlooking Bull Island and with sea views to enjoy with the delicious Pakistani and North Indian cuisine, there's little to fault at this smart and elegant Clontarf restaurant. Firmly established as the area's leading ethnic restaurant (and one of the best in Dublin), there's a declared commitment to local produce on the exciting menu and each dish is clearly described. The quality of cooking is exemplary and fine food is backed up by attentive, professional service and fair prices.

Seats 77. L Thu-Sun 12-4, set L about €17. Early D Chef Special Mon-Thu 5-8, about €22. Pre-theatre Fri & Sat from 4, last orders 6.30, from €24. D 5-11, a la carte. Closed 25-26 Dec, 1 Jan. CC. Also available at Kajjal, Malahide. **Directions:** 3km (1.5 m) north of city centre on coast road to Howth (opposite wooden bridge).

THE PIGEON HOUSE

11B VERNON AVENUE CLONTARF DUBLIN 3

01 805 7567 I clontarf@pigeonhouse.ie

www.pigeonhouse.ie

EAT I DRINK

Named after a much-loved Dublin feature at the decommissioned Poolbeg electricity station, chef patron Brian Walsh and business partner Paul Foley's Pigeon House has a subtle industrial theme. A handsome bar dominates the front of the restaurant, serving up cocktails, beers and a well chosen short wine list. Menus change often to reflect the seasons, offering smartly presented dishes packed with big flavours. There's nothing ordinary about Brian's confident, modern cooking and this family-friendly venue serves a satisfying meal every time. There's a good terrace for outdoor dining too.

Open: Bfst Mon-Fri 10-12; L Mon-Fri 12-4; Brunch Sat-Sun 10-4; D daily from 5.30. Neighbourhood menu from €22, Sun-Fri (times vary); also à la carte. Closed Christmas. CC. **Also at:** Old Delgany Inn, Co Wicklow. **Directions:** Off Clontarf Road, R807.

ARIEL HOUSE

50-54 LANSDOWNE ROAD BALLSBRIDGE DUBLIN 4   STAY
01 668 5512 | reservations@ariel-house.net
www.ariel-house.net

In the shadows of the Aviva stadium, this impressive family-run guesthouse offers luxurious accommodation, warmly professional service and immaculate housekeeping. The manager is Jennie McKeown (a daughter of the house), who is a professionally trained young hotelier - and it shows in every aspect of this well-run establishment and its engaging staff. Breakfast, served in an extended conservatory overlooking the garden, is especially lavish, catering for diverse appetites. Effectively a small hotel, Ariel House is a lovely place to stay, offering a very different experience to hotels nearby - and, not surprisingly it's a favourite port of call for many returning guests.

Rooms 37 (1 shower only). Children welcome. Free wifi. Room rate from about €99. Closed late Dec-early Jan. CC. **Directions:** On Lansdowne Road off Ballsbridge.

AVALON

89 MOREHAMPTON ROAD DONNYBROOK DUBLIN 4   EAT
01 614 4849 | info@avalonrestaurant.ie
www.avalonrestaurant.ie

Located above Donnybrook Fair, one of the city's smartest food stores, Avalon is in good company. Everything about this stylish restaurant exudes grown up comfort and ease – from the warm welcome of genial owner Sheerin Wilde, to the finely crafted food on the plate, including excellent beef and great Irish seafood. Avalon feels like a special occasion kind of place - a lucky one for locals and a destination worth travelling to, for something that little bit special.

Open: L Fri-Sun 12.30-3.30, set L from €22. Early D Tue-Wed all night, Thu-Sat 5.30-6.30, from €24. D Tue-Sun, 5.30-late. A la carte. Wine from €26. Closed Mon. CC.

DYLAN HOTEL DUBLIN

EASTMORELAND PLACE DUBLIN 4   EAT | STAY
01 660 3000 | justask@dylan.ie
www.dylan.ie

A haven of tranquility just yards from one of Dublin's busiest roads, this attractive boutique hotel offers edgy design wrapped up in a splendid Victorian building with luxurious, individually designed bedrooms fitted to a very high specification. Head chef Mark Bodie and the team have re-positioned the hotel's restaurant as a casual daytime dining room TAVERN, a stylish space that notches up the theatricality at night. Service is relaxed, professional and well-matched to the kitchen's confident handling of quality produce and grasp of classic culinary techniques.

Rooms 44. Room rate from about €200. TAVERN Restaurant: brunch Sat-Sun & bank hol Mon 11-4, L Mon-Fri 12-3, D Tue-Thu 6-10, Fri-Sat 6-10.30, Sun 6-9. A la carte; vegetarian menu. Afternoon Tea, €40. Bar food daily. Children welcome. Hotel closed 25-26 Dec. CC. **Directions:** Just off Upper Baggot Street before St. Marys Road.

FOREST AVENUE

8 SUSSEX TERRACE DUBLIN 4 EAT
01 667 8337 | sandy@forestavenuerestaurant.ie
www.forestavenuerestaurant.ie

Billed as a neighbourhood dining room, John and Sandy Wyer's hip restaurant is one of Dublin's hottest destinations. The Scandi ethos of pared back décor is matched by adventurous seasonal cooking that boasts clean, bold flavour combinations and striking presentation. There's nothing but an open pass separating diners from the kitchen, allowing guests enjoy the buzz of a creative team busy at work. There's a lively energy and relaxed charm here, ensuring guests enjoy dining at one of the busiest dining spots in town.

Seats 52. L Thu-Sat 12-2, D Wed-Sat 6-9.30. L from about €26, Tasting L €55. Wine from €32. Closed Sun-Tue, 2 wks Christmas. Full wheelchair access.
Also at: Forest & Marcy (wine bar), 126 Leeson St Upper, Dublin 4; 01 660 2480.
Directions: Between the Grand Canal and Clayton Hotel Burlington Road.

THE GREENERY

3 EIRPAGE HOUSE DONNYBROOK DUBLIN 4 EAT
01 219 5966 | info@thegreenery.ie
www.thegreenery.ie

With a cheery yellow awning and hedge-enclosed terrace tables, The Greenery Café-Restaurant has brought smart all-day casual dining to a tiny cul-de-sac just a few steps off the busy Donnybrook Road. Partners Joe Keegan and chef Albert Broderick aim for a friendly neighbourhood feel with tasty all-day crowd-pleasing food and some of the best coffee in town.

B'fst Mon-Fri 8.30-11.30, L Mon-Fri 12-4. Early D Sun-Thu 5-7, 2/3 courses €20/24. D Tue-Sun 5-9.45. Brunch Sat & Sun 9.30-4. CC. **Also at:** Coast Road, Malahide, Co Dublin (01 816 8576).
Directions: Opposite Bective Rugby Ground in Donnybrook, near town side of Donnybrook Bridge.

HERBERT PARK HOTEL

BALLSBRIDGE DUBLIN 4
01 667 2200 | reservations@herbertparkhotel.ie
www.herbertparkhotel.ie

STAY

With lovely views over leafy Herbert Park this large, privately-owned contemporary hotel is bright and comfortable - and overseen with quiet efficiency by long time General Manager, Ewan Plenderleith. Stylish public areas make a popular meeting place, with discreet waiting staff providing excellent light fare. The bright, modern style is repeated in the spacious bedrooms, and a good breakfast is served in the Pavilion Restaurant.

Rooms 153 (8 wheelchair friendly). Lift. B&B from €120pps. Pavilion Restaurant: Seats 200. Breakfast Mon-Fri 7-10 (Sat & Sun to 10.30, Sun from 8); L 12.30-2.30 from €25. D daily 5.30-9.30, à la carte. Terrace Lounge 8-10. Wine from about €30. Special Breaks from about €130 for two. No SC. Underground carpark; electric car charge point. Fitness room. Open all year. CC. **Directions:** In Ballsbridge, shortly before RDS heading out of city.

INTERCONTINENTAL DUBLIN HOTEL

SIMMONSCOURT ROAD DUBLIN 4   EAT | STAY
01 665 4000 | reservations@icdublin.com
www.intercontinentaldublin.ie

Set in gardens adjacent to the Royal Dublin Society's show grounds, this spacious five-star hotel offers opulent facilities and a warm welcome from hands-on General Manager Nicky Logue and his staff. Air-conditioned rooms appeal equally to leisure and business guests and, following re-styling of the main public areas, the feel is casual-sophisticated. Afternoon Tea is a speciality and, like the contemporary ICE Bar, it is popular with Dubliners; for a fine dining choice, Seasons Restaurant combines best local ingredients with classical French cooking. Outstanding conference and meeting facilities make this hotel an obvious choice for corporate events.

Rooms 197 (13 wheelchair friendly). Lift. Room rate from about €190. Seasons: B'fst daily. Sun Brunch, 1-3 about €39. D: Thu-Sat: 6.30-9.30. L&D available in The Reading Room & The Lobby Lounge. Spa. Open all year CC. **Directions:** Beside RDS at Merrion-Simmonscourt roads junction.

MULBERRY GARDEN

MULBERRY LANE DONNYBROOK DUBLIN 4   EAT
01 269 3300 | eat@mulberrygarden.ie
www.mulberrygarden.ie

Hidden down a mews lane behind a row of shops in Donnybrook, this stylish little gem opens just three nights a week offering nine dishes on its weekly-changing menu. Despite the limitations, food lovers flock to the contemporary restaurant with its intimate courtyard thanks to the imaginative cooking and excellent service. Seasonally-driven menus showcase Irish foods – a six-course tasting menu is available – and there's a large wine and cocktail list.

> **Seats 80**. D only, Thu-Sat, from 6 pm. Set 3-course dinner €49. Tasting menu €75. House wine €26. Extra opening L&D in Dec. (L about €40 when applicable). Heated outdoor terrace. CC. **Also at:** Brookwood, Lr Baggot Street, Dublin 2. **Directions:** Mulberry Lane is directly behind the Bang & Olufsen Store in Donnybrook

O'CONNELLS RESTAURANT

135 MOREHAMPTON ROAD DONNYBROOK DUBLIN 4   EAT | DRINK
01 269 6116 | info@oconnellsdonnybrook.com
www.oconnellsdonnybrook.com

Run by Tom O'Connell, a brother of Darina Allen and Rory O'Connell of Ballymaloe Cookery School, and his wife Annette, this casual brasserie's motto is to use only the very best Irish ingredients – local, artisan, free-range and organic where possible – all proudly credited, and cooked with great care. The menu sings of freshness and each dish is flavoursome and well conceived. Value for money has always been a key feature right down to the exceptionally informative wine list. A beacon of rural excellence in the heart of the city.

> **Seats 90**. D daily 5.30-9.30 (Mon from 5, Sun to 7.30). L Tue-Fri 12-3.30, Sat-Sun brunch and L 12.30-3.30. Children welcome. Wheelchair accessible. Wines from €26. Bar food also available. Closed Mon in Jan-Feb, Dec 25-26. **Directions:** On the N11 at the corner of Morehampton Road and Belmont Avenue.

WATERLOO HOUSE

8-10 WATERLOO ROAD BALLSBRIDGE DUBLIN 4   STAY
01 660 1888 | info@waterloohouse.ie
www.waterloohouse.ie

In Dublin's embassy belt, this pair of Georgian townhouses makes a luxurious and reasonably priced base in a quiet location, which is very convenient to the city centre and also Lansdowne Road, the RDS and some of the city's most famous restaurants. Equally attractive to the business or leisure traveller, excellent breakfasts are a high point of any stay.

Rooms 19 (1 wheelchair friendly). Lift. B&B from about €70pps. Children welcome. Conservatory & Garden. Free wifi. Wheelchair access. Own parking. Closed Christmas. CC. **Directions:** South on Stephens Green on Merrion Row for about 1.5km. First turn right after Baggot Street Bridge.

LA RESERVE

53 RANELAGH VILLAGE DUBLIN 6   EAT
01 496 8825 | info@lareserve.ie
www.lareserve.ie

La Reserve may be small but there's no limit to the capabilities of Burgundian chef-proprietor Jérome Fernandes, who champions the best of Gallic cooking. This chic and charming little French brasserie serves wonderful regional dishes – moules marinières, steak frites, tartines, galettes, coq au vin, boeuf bourguignon – all cooked with real flair. Service is great and lunchtime specials offer outstanding value. A little corner of France in Ranelagh.

Seats 24 (+6 outdoors). L Tue-Fri 12-4, D Tue-Sun 5-9.30p, Brunch Sat-Sun 11-4. Market Menu available at L & early D from about €20, otherwise à la carte. Closed Mon. CC. **Directions:** Centre of Ranelagh village

NIGHTMARKET

120 RANELAGH DUBLIN 6

EAT

01 538 5200 | contact@nightmarket.ie
www.nightmarket.ie

Restaurateur Conor Sexton and his partner Juturat Suwankeeree (aka R) have brought deeply-flavoured and intense regional Thai cooking to Ranelagh in their exciting restaurant, Nightmarket. Combining the best of Irish produce with traditional recipes learned from her grandmother, R's dishes sing with authentic Thai flavours – fiery chillies, fish sauce, lemongrass and fresh herbs – each fragrant with memories of her homeland. Lively and relaxed, Nightmarket is a firm favourite with local diners, and with a warm welcome, good wines and cocktails, and delicious dishes that transport the diner to Thailand with one mouthful, it's easy to see why.

Seats 55 (downstairs); 60 (upstairs). Open Wed-Fri 4-10 (Thu to 10.30, Fri to 11). Sat 12-11, Sun 12-10. A la carte. Closed Mon & Tue. CC.

CRAFT

208 HAROLD'S CROSS ROAD DUBLIN 6W   EAT
01 4978632 | info@craftrestaurant.ie
www.craftrestaurant.ie

Craft is chef Philip Yeung's first restaurant as owner, a chance for him to share and develop the skills that he learned in the kitchens of Bang and Town Bar & Grill. It's an intimate restaurant serving modern Irish food in a relaxed environment: exactly the kind of place that everyone would like to have in their own neighbourhood. Expect food with flair that's big on flavour, and low on pretension. Although billed as a neighbourhood restaurant, Philip is a talented chef and it was not long before his accomplished cooking began to draw in diners from further afield. Now the secret is well and truly out and reservations are strongly advised, especially at weekends.

Seats about 35. Open: L Fri 12-2.30, Brunch Sat 12-3, Sun 11-3, D Wed–Sat 5.30–9.30. Early D ("Neighbourhood") Wed-Sat 5.30-6.30, from about €22. Otherwise à la carte. CC. **Directions:** From city continue past Harolds Cross Park towards Terenure.

L MULLIGAN GROCER

18 STONEYBATTER DUBLIN 7   EAT | DRINK
01 670 9889 | table@lmulligangrocer.com
www.lmulligangrocer.com

An old Stoneybatter grocers shop that's been converted by owners Michael Fogarty, Colin Hession and Seáneen Sullivan into a quirky gastropub with lovely character. Over 150 whiskeys and a selection of Irish craft beers complement the artisan-inspired food, so even if you don't have so much as a bite to eat, a visit here would be well worth a small detour just to absorb the atmosphere and enjoy a drink. Friendly staff know their food and drink and this big-hearted place is hugely popular.

Open Mon-Fri 4, food from 5; Sat & Sun open 12.30, food all day; bank hols open 2, food 2.30-9. A la carte. **Directions:** Heart of Stoneybatter, around the corner from junction of Arbour Hill and Brunswick Street North

TWO BOYS BREW

375 NORTH CIRCULAR ROAD DUBLIN 7 — EAT
info@twoboysbrew.ie | www.twoboysbrew.ie

Kevin Roche and Taurean Coughlan have created a great little daytime café in Phibsborough that's bang on trend – and, as the name suggests, they take their coffee seriously here. Breakfast has a focus on oats, while the all-day brunch menu offers more substantial options like blueberry and ricotta hotcakes, The Boys' Smoky Beans or roasted mushrooms on sourdough with whipped feta. A soup and sandwich for lunch is unbeatable value, coming in at around €10, and to finish, you'd be hard pressed to pass up the baked treats displayed on the counter.

Seats 30-40. Open Mon, Wed-Fri, 7.30am-4pm; Sat-Sun 9am-4pm. CC.

BASTIBLE

111 SOUTH CIRCULAR ROAD DUBLIN 8 — EAT
01 473 7409 | hello@bastible.com
www.bastible.com

Chef-proprietor Barry Fitzgerald has serious form (St John's, Arbutus, The Harwood Arms, Etto) and it shows in deft handling of seasonal ingredients at his unmissable neighbourhood restaurant in Dublin 8. Bastible eschews unnecessary frills in the décor and short set menu as much as on the plate, relying on a cool palette to offset the pared-back cooking. Fitzgerald extracts big flavours from humble but judiciously sourced ingredients, with house-made dairy products a highlight alongside bold vegetarian explorations and hearty off-cuts. Some seats are reserved for walk-in customers, as long as you're happy to dine bar-side or at a communal table. And with food, wine and service as charming as this, who wouldn't be?

Seats 40. L Fri-12-2, Sat 12.30-2.30, Sun 12-3.45. D Wed-Fri 5.30-9.30 (Sat from 6.) Set L from €24, Sun L from €34. Set D from €32. **Directions:** At Leonard's Corner in Dublin 8.

THE CAKE CAFÉ

THE DAINTREE BUILDING PLEASANTS PLACE (BEHIND CAMDEN STREET) DUBLIN 8
01478 9394 | thecakecafe@gmail.com   EAT | BUY | LEARN | PRODUCER
www.thecakecafe.ie

A love of traditional food and recognition of the environmental impact of their business are the driving forces behind Michelle Darmody's paradise for cake lovers. Alongside an array of tempting baked delights you can stop by for a substantial lunch, or excellent breakfast. Everything here is made with love... and predominantly Irish ingredients. The colourful vintage-feel décor makes this a fun, relaxed spot for a refuel or catch-up with friends.

Seats 16 (+25 outdoors). Open Mon-Sat 8.30-6, (Sat from 9). Wheelchair accessible, children welcome, house wines about €19. Closed Sun, bank hols, 2-3 weeks at Christmas, 3 days at Easter. CC. **Also at:** Slice, a little Northside sister on Manor Street, Stoneybatter Dublin 7; 01 445 6100, www.asliceofcake.ie
Directions: Off top of Camden Street, R114.

THE FUMBALLY

FUMBALLY LANE DUBLIN 8   EAT | LEARN
01 529 8732 | thefumbally@gmail.com
www.thefumbally.ie

The Fumbally is as much a community as it is a café. Created by Luca D'Alfonso and Aisling Rogerson, good food, coffee and people are at the heart of its ethos. Simple organic food promoting provenance is key to its menus, with a focus on creating rustic, fresh, healthy and seasonal dishes for breakfast and lunch. The open-plan café space is a communal one, where tables are shared for meals, chats and meetings. It makes for a spirited, friendly atmosphere – often with a soundtrack of live music and an aroma of spices. Sharing the site is The Fumbally Stables , an atmospheric venue used for workshops and events, recipe development and more.

Seats about 50. Open Tue-Fri 8-5; Sat 10-5 (kitchen closes at 4); D Wed only, 7-9.30. No reservations. A la carte. Closed Sun & Mon. **Directions:** Near St Patrick's Cathedral.

PUPP

37 CLANBRASSIL STREET LOWER DUBLIN 8   EAT | BUY
01 445 4542 | info@pupp.ie
www.pupp.ie

Dublin's first dedicated dog-friendly cafe, opened by Ella Wallace and Paul Froggatt in early 2016 – offering treats for pooches, and Nick's coffee and simple food for their owners too – but, within just six months of opening, Pupp had expanded their seating capacity and their menu and started occasional evening pop-ups. To ensure harmony for all, a few simple health and safety ground rules apply: pets must be kept on leads, be housetrained and not annoy other customers. In a city with very few places where dog owners can bring their pets, Pupp is a real gem.

Seats about 25. Mon-Fri 10am-3.30pm, Sat-Sun, 10am-5pm. Dog boutique, online shop. CC. **Directions:** Between Portobello & Christchurch

THE WASHERWOMAN

60 GLASNEVIN HILL DUBLIN 9

01 837 9441 I info@thewsherwoman.ie

www.thewsherwoman.ie

EAT

From colourful brunch dishes, to a killer steak selection, Elaine Murphy (of The Winding Stair) has teamed up with chef Ian Connolly to create a stylish and vibrant destination in Glasnevin. Provenance is key – see the huge feature maps of Ireland on the walls, with supplier labels proudly pinned all over them – and each dish on the eclectic menus packs a big flavour punch. The stylish room, great staff and tasty food, including wonderful baking, make this family-friendly spot a sure-fire hit in the shadows of the Botanic Gardens.

> Breakfast Mon-Fri 9-12; L Mon-Fri 12-4. Coffee/snacks Mon-Fri 4-5, D Sun-Wed 5-9.15 (Thu-Sat to 10). Brunch Sat 12-4, Sun 11-4. A la carte. Meals available to take away. Some outdoor seating. CC.

ANANDA

2-4 SANDYFORD ROAD DUNDRUM TOWN CENTRE DUBLIN 14   EAT

01 296 0099 | info@anandarestaurant.ie

www.anandarestaurant.ie

A partnership between Asheesh Dewan, owner of the outstanding Jaipur restaurants, and Atul Kochhar, the first Indian chef to receive a Michelin star for his wonderful London restaurant Benares, Ananda is renowned for outstanding food and impeccable service. Cutting-edge Indian cuisine is bursting with flavour, now with Indian chef Sandeep Bhagat at the helm. There's a small selection of classic Indian dishes and a great vegetarian list, but it's the modern interpretations that are unique. Pure flavours, wonderfully presented dishes, smart service, beautiful setting and great value all set Ananda apart.

⭐

Seats 85. L Fri-Sat 12.30-2.30, Sun & bank hol Mon 1-2.45. D Mon-Sun 5.30-10.45 (Sun to 9.30). Early D Sun-Thu 5.30-7 (Fri & Sat to 6.30). Closed L Mon-Thu; 25-26 Dec. CC. **Also at:** Chakra by Jaipur, Greystones (see entry); Jaipur Dalkey, Co. Dublin; Jaipur Malahide, Co. Dublin.

FARMHILL CAFÉ AND RESTAURANT

9 FARMHILL ROAD GOATSTOWN DUBLIN 14

EAT

01 4413871 | info@farmhill.ie

www.farmhill.ie

Paul O'Connor and Keith Hallissey's bright and stylishly decorated Farmhill is a seven-day-a-week crowd-pleaser, which ticks all the boxes in terms of what's required in a successful neighbourhood restaurant. With Anita Thoma in the kitchen, visitors can expect a menu that features some of her Italian-influenced signature dishes, as well as the usual salads, steaks, pasta dishes and burgers. While good enough to be a destination in its own right, a well-priced wine list and dinner menu also make Farmhill a realistic alternative to cooking at home.

Seats about 45. Open Tue-Fri: B'fst from 9, L Tue & Wed 12-3, Thu & Fri to 4. Brunch Sat & Sun 10-4. D Thu-Sun from 5. A la carte. Market Menu May-Sep, 2 courses about €17, available all evening. Closed Mon. **Directions:** Larchfield Road end of Farmhill Road (near Lynams Fine Foods).

OVERENDS AT AIRFIELD

AIRFIELD HOUSE OVEREND WAY KILMACUD ROAD DUNDRUM DUBLIN 14

EAT | BUY | LEARN

01 969 6641 | overends@airfield.ie

www.airfield.ie/cafe

Using fresh local ingredients, cooked simply to produce great tasting seasonal dishes, Overends café takes its inspiration from the surrounding gardens and Airfield farm. The bright, modern glass building offers lovely baking too, and is especially popular with young families enjoying a day out at this special urban farm.

Open Mon-Fri 9-4, Sat, Sun & bank hol Mon to 5. Mon-Fri B'fst 9-12. L Mon-Fri 12-3.30 (Sat, Sun & bank hol Mon 12-4.30). Stables Café: daily 9.30-5. Visitor centre open daily, 9.30-5. CC. **Directions:** Near Dundrum Town Centre, off R826 (Kilmacud Road).

CHINA SICHUAN RESTAURANT

THE FORUM BALLYMOSS ROAD SANDYFORD INDUSTRIAL ESTATE DUBLIN 18   EAT

01 293 5100 | info@china-sichuan.ie

www.china-sichuan.ie

The modern interpretations of classic Sichuan cuisine offered by David Hui and his team are rightly renowned. A wide-ranging à la carte is complemented by value menus at lunchtime and in the evening. "Chef's Recommendations" highlight the kitchen's authentic Sichuan dishes based on centuries-old recipes, and well-versed servers explain dishes and their ingredients. Sunday lunches are especially popular with families.

Seats 90 (+ 20 outdoors). L Mon-Fri 12-3, from about €16 (excl bank hol). A la carte all day. Value menu Mon-Wed 5-9 (excl bank hols), Thu-Sun to 6.15, from about €23. D Mon-Sat 5-10, Sun 12-9. Closed L Sat, 25 Dec & Good Fri. CC. **Directions:** Opposite Stillorgan LUAS station.

HERON & GREY

19A MAIN STREET BLACKROCK CO DUBLIN

EAT

01 2123676 / 087 6083140 | heronandgrey@gmail.com

www.heronandgrey.com

Andrew Heron and Damien Grey opened their tiny restaurant in Blackrock Market in early 2016 and quickly garnered a host of fans. There's a no-choice tasting menu at dinner that's considered, inventive and modern, so every food lover in Dublin is keen to try it - but the challenge at this little place is getting a reservation, as its early fame has meant that a table here is something akin to gold dust. With only twenty two seats to fill, Heron and Grey run a tight ship, and do everything themselves with the help of just one other member of staff. Expect a menu that is hyper-seasonal, that changes each week, and with dishes that will never, say the owners, be repeated.

⭐

Seats 22. D Thu-Sat 2 sittings 7.30 & 8.30; Tasting Menu about €63. Closed Sun-Wed. CC. **Directions:** Centre of Blackrock, at Blackrock Market

DUNNE & CRESCENZI BLACKROCK

BLACKROCK SHOPPING CENTRE ROCK ROAD BLACKROCK CO DUBLIN   EAT
01 525 2012 | bookings@dunneandcrescenzigroup.ie
www.dunneandcrescenzi.com

Bywords for quality Italian food, Dunne & Crescenzi's winning formula brings delicious, no-nonsense Italian fare and wonderful wines to Blackrock. Fans of the original city centre venue will find a bigger, brighter version of the much-loved restaurant where antipasti, authentic pasta dishes, pizza and great coffee all feature alongside D&C's always excellent wine offering. The branch speciality, Spaghetti allo Scoglio – squid ink pasta with plump prawns, mussels and squid with cherry tomatoes – is really worth a detour.

Open daily 9am-6pm. A la carte. CC.
Directions: In Blackrock Shopping Centre; also with entrance from Rock Road.

DANIEL FINNEGAN

2 SORRENTO ROAD DALKEY CO DUBLIN

01 285 8505 I info@finnegans.ie

www.finnegans.ie

EAT I DRINK

A much-loved Dalkey institution for over 40 years, the cosy wood-panelled interior and traditional Irish 'snugs' are flooded by natural light. Great for pints and chat, and with an extensive whiskey selection, this celebrated family-run pub also specialises in good traditional fare (including fresh fish from the nearby harbour). A popular lunchtime spot with locals and visitors, the cosy interior is complemented by pavement seating on Sorrento Road that's especially in demand on sunny days.

Bar food daily 12.15-3.30. Breakfast on special occasions. Closed 25 Dec, Good Fri & New Year. CC. **Directions:** Near Dalkey DART station.

OUZOS

22 CASTLE ST DALKEY CO DUBLIN

01 285 1890 I dalkey@ouzos.ie

www.ouzos.ie

EAT

Flying the flag for Irish seafood, Padraic Hanley's buzzy neighbourhood restaurant serves up locally-caught fish and, as well as working closely with fishermen in other ports, their own fishing vessel is proudly named on the menu. Carnivores are well catered for too with a range of prime dry-aged steaks from Co Carlow, hand-cut to order in-house. Among its other attractions are cosy décor, a value wine list and an imaginative children's menu that makes it a popular choice for families. Warm hospitality and engaging service mean Ouzos enjoys a steady stream of happy customers - and they also own the smart contemporary Ouzos Bar & Grill, Main Street, Blackrock (01 210 1000).

Open daily noon-10 (Sun to 9). Set menu daily 4-7, from about €23. Closed 25-27 Dec, Good Fri. CC. **Directions:** Main Street Dalkey, 100m past the church.

CAVISTONS SEAFOOD RESTAURANT & FOOD EMPORIUM

59 GLASTHULE ROAD DUN LAOGHAIRE CO DUBLIN EAT I BUY
01 280 9245 I info@cavistons.com
www.cavistons.com

One of Dublin's top foodie destinations since opening in 1996, the well-known Caviston family are long-standing fishmongers-turned-restaurateurs. Their gourmet food store, one of Dublin's originals, complements the celebrated little seafood restaurant next door, where spanking-fresh seafood dishes delight food lovers across three packed lunch sittings and early weekend dinners. An interesting wine list works well with everything from their famous shrimp piri piri and garlic crab claws to chargrilled tuna loin and roast monkfish. Pricey, perhaps, but wonderful.

Seats 28. L (3 sittings) Tue-Sat: 12, 1.30 & 3. D (2 sittings) Thu-Sat, 6 & 8.30. Set 2 course early D 6-7, from €19, also à la carte. Wine from €26. Children welcome. Closed D Tue-Wed, all Sun, Mon & Christmas/New Year. Shop open Mon & Sat 8.30-6, Tue-Fri to 7. CC. **Directions:** 5 mins walk from Glasthule DART station.

RASAM

18-19 GLASTHULE ROAD DUN LAOGHAIRE CO DUBLIN   EAT

01 230 0600 | info@rasam.ie

www.rasam.ie

Book early to avoid disappointment, because Nisheeth Tak's stylish Indian restaurant in buzzy Glasthule has a devoted regular clientèle and is popular for family celebrations. Menus offer authentic dishes from several regions, including Kerala, Goa and Kashmir. The kitchen is mindful of modern dining preferences for lighter cuisine, and many special ingredients are used, including rare herbs and spices unique to Rasam, all ground freshly each day. Solicitous staff ensure a great Indian dining experience, and Rasam has earned its place at the top of the league.

Seats 85. D daily, 5.30-10 (Sun to 10.30). Early D daily except Sat (Mon-Thu 5.30-7, Fri 5.30-6.30, Sun 5-7), from about €24. D 2 sittings at weekends 5.30 & 8.30. Vegetarian & vegan dishes offered. Closed 25-26 Dec, Good Fri. CC. **Directions:** Above The Eagle pub.

ABBEY TAVERN

28 ABBEY STREET HOWTH CO DUBLIN
01 839 0307 | info@abbeytavern.ie
www.abbeytavern.ie

EAT | DRINK

Owned by Richard Tobin and Lorraine Gunne since 2014, this historic Howth stalwart is one of Ireland's most famous pubs. Partly dating back to the 15th century, it is immaculately maintained and retains authentic features including open turf fires, original stone walls, flagged floors and gaslights. Its long-running dinner-and-trad-music nights are popular with visitors, while pub grub and bistro fare with a focus on seasonal local ingredients are on offer in the bar. An atmospheric first floor dining room that was one of Dublin's longest-established restaurants (1950s) is a lovely space with open fires, currently used as a private venue. Although popular with tourists this is also a place where locals like to congregate, so the ambience is genuine.

Seats 70. Food served daily, 12.30-10pm. A la carte. Closed 25 Dec & Good Fri. CC. Directions: Howth village centre.

AQUA RESTAURANT

1 WEST PIER HOWTH CO DUBLIN
01 832 0690 | dine@aqua.ie
www.aqua.ie

EAT | DRINK

Sea views and modern cooking make this contemporary seafood restaurant a favourite. Formerly a yacht club, it has a cosy bar with a stove while floor-to-ceiling windows in the stylish dining room offer superb views - north across Howth Sound to Ireland's Eye and, to the west, some memorable sunsets. A la carte menus are influenced by fresh local seafood (and perhaps beef from nearby Lambay Island) and offer great choices. The restaurant's allotment supplies seasonal herbs and vegetables - and the value of the set menus ensure a loyal local clientèle.

Seats 110. L Tue-Sat 12.30-3.30, (Sun, bank hols 12-5), from about €25. Early D Tue-Fri 5.30-7.30 (excl bank hol Mon), Sat 5.30-6.30, from about €25. D Tue-Sat 5.30-10, Sun & bank hol Mon 6-8.30. Wine from €24. Closed Mon, 25-26 Dec. CC. **Directions:** End of West Pier

KING SITRIC FISH RESTAURANT & ACCOMMODATION

EAST PIER HOWTH CO DUBLIN   EAT | STAY
01 832 5235 | info@kingsitric.ie
www.kingsitric.ie

Established in 1971, Aidan and Joan MacManus's elegant sea-view restaurant with rooms is one of Dublin's original fine dining establishments. Aidan's famous commitment to the best of seasonal, local produce is seen on menus that offer outstanding, mainly seafood, dishes for every budget - treats matched by one of the country's finest wine lists. Their son Declan MacManus, and his wife Susan, are also closely involved with managing the business, which includes the affordable and hugely popular contemporary **East Café Bar**, on the ground floor, and the rooms, which have recently been refurbished in a smart nautical style.

Restaurant: Set D Wed-Sat from 6, from about €33. Set Sun L 1-5, from €28, also à la carte. Closed second half Jan. **East Café Bar** daily 10.30-10. **Rooms 8** (1 wheelchair friendly). B&B from €75pps. CC. **Directions:** Far end of seafront.

THE OAR HOUSE

8 WEST PIER HOWTH CO DUBLIN EAT
01 839 4562 | theoarhouserestauranthowth@gmail.com
www.oarhouse.ie

Relaxed and atmospheric, the nautically-themed Oar House is run by the Doran family, with chef John Aungier. Doran's fish shop is next door, and this lively spot does a brisk trade in deliciously fresh seafood, including some from their own trawler, the Celtic Fisher. Casual and accessible, this family favourite majors in a crowd-pleasing menu, including daily specials based on what's been landed that morning. Generous portions, caring service and good value ensure this affordable West Pier staple is popular year-round with locals and visitors alike - and outdoor tables are in high demand on sunny days.

Seats 50 (+20 outdoors). Open daily 12.30-late. Early D Mon-Fri 3-7 (excl bank hols), from about €20. Closed Good Fri, 25 Dec. **Also at:** Dorans at the Beachcomber, Raheny, Dublin 5 (01 833 7121) CC. **Directions:** Half way down the West pier.

FITZPATRICK CASTLE HOTEL DUBLIN

KILLINEY CO DUBLIN STAY
01 230 5400 | www.fitzpatrickcastle.com

Located in the fashionable suburb of Killiney, this imposing castellated mansion overlooking Dublin Bay dates back to 1741 and attracts a diverse clientèle, being a popular local meeting place and equally suited to business and leisure guests. Surrounded by landscaped gardens, it's an old-world hotel with modern facilities including spacious bedrooms, business and conference amenities and a fitness centre with swimming pool and spa.

Rooms 113 (1 wheelchair friendly). Lift. B&B from about €70pps. PJ's restaurant: Sun buffet L 12.30-3. Grill at the Castle: Mon-Fri 5.30-10, Sun 5-9.30, set menu & à la carte. Bar food daily 12-6, (Fri-Sat to 8). Closed 24-26 Dec. CC. **Directions:** On Killiney road.

BON APPETIT

9 ST JAMES TERRACE MALAHIDE CO DUBLIN   EAT

01 845 0314 I info@bonappetit.ie
www.bonappetit.ie

Housed in a handsome four-storey Georgian terrace near the marina, serial restaurateur Oliver Dunne's seaside restaurant offers broad menus that show his love of delicious food and exciting cooking. The casual décor belies the flair on display in the kitchen. No longer a fine dining temple, the elegant first floor is reserved for private functions, while the ground floor is home to a tapas bar and, in the basement, an informal restaurant serves everything from lunch and brunch to afternoon tea and dinner. A popular venue, offering excellent food – notably seafood -and value.

Open: Brunch Sat-Sun 11-3; L Fri-Sun 12-3. Afternoon Tea Fri-Sun, 12-3 (by reservation). D Tue-Thu, 6-9.30, Fri-Sat, 5-9.30, Sun 5-8. Early D (from €17). Midweek Menu Tue-Thu 7-9.30. Tapas menu Tue-Sun .Closed Mon, 1st week Jan, 1st two weeks Aug. CC. **Directions:** Centre of Malahide.

OLD STREET RESTAURANT

OLD STREET MALAHIDE CO DUBLIN   EAT

01 845 5614 I info@oldstreet.ie
www.oldstreet.ie

Local couple Mark and Adriana Fitzpatrick's beautifully reimagined cottages in Malahide village are now home to one of Dublin's most exciting restaurants. The super stylish interior blends old with a very new extension, creating a jaw-dropping dining space that's high on comfort. Imaginative menus feature exciting and delicious modern cooking by Fergus Caffrey, using the best seasonal Irish produce. A chic bar with extensive drinks menu is the perfect spot for pre-or-post-dinner drinks. Design aficionados will enjoy the beautiful décor and with brilliant service from manager Denise McBrien's team, dining at Old Street is a guaranteed treat.

⭐

Open L Wed-Sat, 12-3. Set L & early evening menu (5-6.30) from about €25. Also à la carte. D Wed-Sat 5-10. Closed Sun, Mon & Tue. **Directions:** West end of Malahide village - left up Old Street shortly before the railway bridge.

MICHAEL'S

57 DEERPARK ROAD MOUNT MERRION CO DUBLIN
01 278 0377 | info@michaels.ie
www.michaels.ie

EAT | BUY

Neighbourhood restaurant, Michael's of Mount Merrion, welcomed back Chef Gareth (Gaz) Smith and his wife Rita in 2016, this time as owners. Gaz's passion for good food, simply done and full of flavour is infectious, while the friendly and efficient staff ensure that a good time is had by all. Michael's has built a reputation for excellent responsibly-fished Irish seafood and dry-aged steaks (Wednesday is Steak Club, with excellent value on premium cuts), also traditional Italian dishes and a great wine offering. Provenance is prized here - as are children, who are made especially welcome by manager Talha and his front-of-house team.

Seats 24. Open Tue-Sat 11-10, L 12-3; early D Tue-Thu from about €22;'2-Course Tuesdays' D €20; Wed steak night from €23. A la carte all day. CC. **Directions:** Off Fosters Avenue on Deerpark Road just past Kiely's.

PORTMARNOCK HOTEL & GOLF LINKS

STRAND ROAD PORTMARNOCK CO DUBLIN
01 846 0611 | info@portmarnock.com
www.portmarnock.com

EAT | STAY

Originally home to the Jameson family of whiskey fame, this hotel is in a wonderful beach-side position, enjoyed to advantage from front bedrooms and the Seaview Lounge - an ideal meeting place for a drink or casual meal. A smart new entrance and major refurbishment have recently given the hotel a fresh contemporary feel, and there's also a beautiful Spa. Head Chef Tom Walsh and his team in the '1780' restaurant offer imaginative fine dining, and the characterful Jameson Bar - a popular meeting place in the old house - also offers informal fare.

Rooms 134. (Some wheelchair friendly). Lift. B&B from about €55pps. The '1780': D Sun-Thu 5.30-9pm, (Fri-Sat to 9.45). Set D, €42, (midweek €24), also à la carte. Reservations advised. Children welcome. Bar food daily. Open all year. CC. **Directions:** On the coast at Portmarnock.

CROWNE PLAZA DUBLIN AIRPORT HOTEL

NORTHWOOD PARK SANTRY DUBLIN   STAY

01 862 8888 | info@ crowneplazadublin.ie

www.cpireland.crowneplaza.com

Very attractively situated in a quiet and leafy off-road site, this impressive modern hotel is a sister property to Clontarf Castle Hotel (see entry). Located less than 3km from Dublin Airport and with a 24-hour shuttle service, it is a practical choice for international travellers - but, unlike most airport hotels, it is also a pleasant destination in itself, with a parkland setting and walking just outside the door. State-of-the-art conference facilities and meeting rooms make it a good choice for business meetings and corporate events, but private guests will be equally at home here.

Rooms 209 (some wheelchair accessible). B&B from about €84pps. Food available all day. Open all year, but accommodation only over Christmas (no restaurant). Wifi. Complimentary parking. CC. **Directions:** In Santry Demesne (off the old airport road and beside Morton Athletic Stadium).

OLIVE DELICATESSEN & CAFÉ

86A STRAND STREET SKERRIES CO DUBLIN   EAT | BUY | PRODUCER

01 849 0310 | info@olive.ie

www.olive.ie

Peter and Deirdre Dorrity's charming deli and café in the centre of Skerries has a wide pavement seating area – a pleasant place to enjoy a bite to eat while people-watching in fine weather – and an enclosed garden area at the back, with rugs to snuggle under if it gets chilly. Specialities include great coffee, trademark sandwiches, daily hot rolls made with local butcher's meats slow-cooked overnight, and tasty homemade deli food. A carefully selected range of artisan produce make this cosy café a firm favourite with food lovers.

Seats 30 (+30 outdoors). Café open daily 8.30-5.30 (Sun from 9). Deli open daily 9-6 (Sun 10-4). Toilets wheelchair accessible; children welcome. Closed Christmas. CC. **Directions:** Turn right at monument in town, on the right.

RED BANK HOUSE & RESTAURANT

5-7 CHURCH STREET SKERRIES CO DUBLIN

EAT | STAY

01 849 1005 | sales@redbank.ie

www.redbank.ie

This converted bank building with guest rooms promises a traditional fine dining experience focusing on Irish ingredients, old-style service and a good wine list. The well-known Euro-Toques chef-proprietor, Terry McCoy, is the culinary pioneer of the area and an avid supporter of local produce, with fresh seafood from Skerries harbour providing the backbone of his menu, supported by many other foods from the surrounding area. The dessert trolley is legendary, as is a great value traditional Sunday lunch.

Restaurant. **Seats 50**. D Mon-Sat 6.30-9.30, Sun 1-6. Set 3 course D €48. Early 2 course D Mon-Fri 6-8, Sat 6-7, Sun 1-7, €26. Also a la carte. **Rooms 18** (2 shower only, 1 wheelchair friendly, 4 pet friendly). Free wifi. Children welcome. B&B from about €35pps. CC. Closed 24–27 Dec. **Directions:** Centre of Skerries, opposite AIB Bank.

STOOP YOUR HEAD

HARBOUR ROAD SKERRIES CO DUBLIN

EAT | DRINK

01 849 2085 | www.stoopyourhead.ie

Serving up fresh, simple seafood at great prices the May family's lively harbour-side bar and restaurant majors in 'fresh, simple and wholesome' cooking to be enjoyed in relaxed surroundings overlooking the harbour. Regulars happily travel to tuck into more-ish specialities like Dublin Bay prawns (langoustines) in garlic butter or their famous fish pie - and, while seafood is the winner, non-fish eaters are well catered for at this cosy and buzzy spot. There's a short, well chosen wine list and, although reservations aren't taken, that's no hardship as you can pop into their pub, Joe May's, for a drink if you're waiting.

Seats 50 (+ 20 outdoors). Food served Mon-Thu 12-9.30 (Fri & Sat to 10). (Limited menu Mon-Fri 3-5.30). Sun & bank hols 12-30-8.30. A la carte. Closed 25 Dec & Good Fri. CC. **Directions:** On Skerries harbour front.

THE WHITE COTTAGES

BALBRIGGAN ROAD SKERRIES CO DUBLIN
01 849 2231 | joc11@indigo.ie
www.thewhitecottages.com

STAY

A stylish bed and breakfast on the Skerries shore, with unbroken sea views of the harbour and the Cooley and Mourne Mountains, this boutique hideaway is owned by Jackie and Joe O'Connor who offer guests the warmest hospitality. The four bedrooms are all charming and individual and the crisp décor is like a breath of fresh sea air. This unusual B&B serves up delicious breakfasts and even lobster lunches and afternoon tea by arrangement. Nearby Dublin seems a world away.

Rooms 4 (2 shower only). B&B from €50pps, single from €55. Open all year. **No CC. Directions:** On coast road to Balbriggan.

BEAUFIELD MEWS RESTAURANT & GARDENS

WOODLANDS AVENUE STILLORGAN CO DUBLIN   EAT
01 288 0375 | info@beaufieldmews.com
www.beaufieldmews.com

In sensitively modernised 18th century coach house and stables, Dublin city's oldest restaurant has been in the Cox family for over 50 years and is full of character. Upstairs the Loft Brasserie offers evening dining, while downstairs The Coachhouse is open for weekend lunches and groups. Surrounded by beautiful mature gardens it feels like a lovely country retreat; a summer Sunday lunch here is a special treat, with the outdoor patio wonderful for drinks.

Loft Brasserie **seats 70**. D Wed-Sun, from 6. Early D Fri-Sat 6-7 (all night Wed-Thu & Sun), from about €20; also à la carte. House wine from €23. Coachhouse Restaurant seats 130. Weekend L only: Sat-Sun from 12, 3 course L about €25. Children's Menu from €10 (up to age 12). Wheelchair accessible. Closed Mon-Tue, 24-26 Dec, Good Fri. CC. **Directions:** Off Stillorgan dual carriageway, N11.

ROGANSTOWN HOTEL & COUNTRY CLUB

THE NAUL ROAD SWORDS CO DUBLIN   EAT | STAY
01 843 3118 | info@roganstown.com
www.roganstown.com

A handsome country estate in north county Dublin, this privately owned golf hotel, with its Christy O'Connor Junior-designed course, offers much to non-golfing guests too. Good food, warm hospitality, comfortable modern rooms and a smart leisure centre make it a pleasant place to stay - a handy short-break destination and useful to consider as an alternative to standard airport hotels.

Rooms 52 (3 shower only, 3 wheelchair accessible). Lift. B&B from about €55pps. McLoughlin's Restaurant D daily 5.30-9 (Sun, public hols to 8), L Sun only 12.30-4, ('Family Lunch' from about €40). Set D from about €25, also à la carte. Bar food daily 12-9.30. Golf, leisure centre with pool, day spa, beauty salon. Helipad. Closed 24-26 Dec. CC. **Directions:** Take Ashbourne road from Swords village, take right turn for Naul, 500m on the left.

VISUAL Centre for Contemporary Art
& The George Bernard Shaw Theatre
Carlow

visualcarlow.ie
carlowtousism.com

COUNTY CARLOW

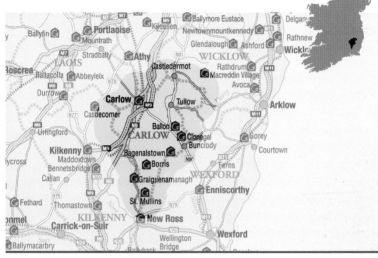

The character and charm of **County Carlow** (carlowtourism.com) is within easy reach of Dublin, and the metropolitan commuter spread is present, yet also kept at bay with a lively sense of place.

Although it is Ireland's second smallest county, it confidently incorporates such wonderful varieties of scenery that it has been memorably commented that the Creator was in fine form when He made Carlow. Whether you're following the **Carlow Garden Trail** (carlowgardentrail.com) lingering along the gentle meanderings of the River Barrow, or enjoying the upper valley of the River Slaney while savouring the soaring outlines of the Blackstairs Mountains as they sweep upwards to the 793m peak of Mount Leinster, this gallant little county will have you in thrall.

There's history a-plenty if you wish to seek it out. But for those who prefer to live in the present, the county town of Carlow itself fairly buzzes with student life and is home to the highly impressive **VISUAL Centre for Contemporary Art & The George Bernard Shaw Theatre** (visualcarlow.ie). As they say themselves, "VISUAL is constantly evolving ways to experience your world through the eyes of contemporary artists, both Irish and international. Families can enjoy a free place space to sit and make art with imaginative materials, themed on the current exhibition."

A more leisurely pace can be enjoyed at charming riverside villages such as Leighlinbridge and Bagenalstown. Leighlinbridge - pronounced "Lochlinbridge" – has for many years been Carlow's most community-conscious riverside village, the holder of a Tidy Towns Gold Medal and an Entente Florale winner.

At Bagenalstown - a proper miniature river port - the O'Hara family's Moneybeg **Carlow Brewing Company** (carlowbrewing.com) is a national pace-setter in craft brewing, with an astonishing variety of beers, stouts, ales and lagers, and a Visitor Centre, and, across the river at Royal Oak, the **Walsh Whiskey Distillery** (www.walshwhiskey.com) offers complementary products and another Visitor Centre. Both businesses have been instrumental in establishing Ireland's first degree course in brewing and distilling at IT Carlow, making it a centre of excellence in Ireland's independent drinks revival. And Carlow county really is serious craft brewing country - even the hidden hillside village of **Borris** (borrishouse.com; an enchantment in itself) is home to no less than ten micro-breweries.

KILGRANEY HOUSE

BORRIS ROAD BAGENALSTOWN CO CARLOW   EAT I STAY I LEARN
059 977 5283 I info@kilgraneyhouse.com
www.kilgraneyhouse.com

Monastic herb gardens and a productive kitchen garden provide an abundance of good things for delicious dinners at Bryan Leech and Martin Marley's stylish Georgian house near Altamont gardens. Set in wooded grounds and gardens on a lovely site overlooking the Barrow Valley, it is tranquil and restorative. Showcasing local and artisan produce, they offer a true taste of the area, both in the holistic overall experience and in Bryan's creative cooking.

> **Rooms 8** (3 shower only); Set D 8.15pm, open to non-residents (limited, must book). Open Fri, Sat & bank hol Sun, Mar-Sep incl. Weekend dinner packages only. Also self-catering cottages. AromaSpa. Herb gardens. Adults only. Helipad. CC. **Directions:** Just off the R705, halfway between Bagenalstown and Borris.

LORUM OLD RECTORY

KILGRANEY BAGENALSTOWN CO CARLOW   STAY
059 977 5282 I bobbie@lorum.com
www.lorum.com

Delicious home cooking using mainly organic and home-grown ingredients is just one reason to visit this mid-Victorian cut stone granite former rectory near Altamont gardens, which - thanks to Euro-Toques chef Bobbie Smith and her family - is now one of the county's most welcoming, elegant and comfortable places to stay. Everybody loves Bobbie's easy hospitality and the candlelit dinners and magnificent breakfasts served at the long mahogany table. A super place for a get-together or small conference (8), with so much to see and do nearby.

> **Rooms 4** (all shower only); B&B from about €80pps. Residents D by arrangement (8pm) about €45. Free wifi. Closed Dec/Jan incl. CC. **Directions:** Midway between Borris & Bagenalstown on the R705.

COOLANOWLE COUNTRY HOUSE

BALLICKMOYLER CARLOW CO CARLOW

059 862 5176 | info@coolanowle.com

www.coolanowle.com

STAY | BUY

Set on three acres of natural woodland with three lakes and lots for children to do, Bernadine and Jimmy Mulhall's organic farm is an ideal destination for family holidays, and for people of any age who enjoy rural life. They offer lovely homely B&B with an open fire to relax beside, home cooking featuring their own meats, fruit and vegetables, and self-catering accommodation too. There's a farm shop selling their organic meats (also available online and from farmers' markets), and they also host weddings and events and offer holistic treatments (nearby).

Rooms 8 (+ 2 in annexe, B&B or self-catering). B&B from €55. Residents organic L&D by arrangement (L from €12, D from €37.50, also a la carte). CC. Closed 24-28 Dec. **Directions:** Well signed off N80, between Carlow and Portlaoise.

CLASHGANNY HOUSE RESTAURANT

CLASHGANNY BORRIS CO CARLOW

059 977 1003 | clashgannyhouse@gmail.com

www.clashgannyhouse.com

EAT

Just a hundred yards from the famous Clashganny Lock, Robert and Karen White's impressive restaurant provides yet another reason to visit this beauty spot near the charming village of Borris. With its wonderful setting, Robert's excellent cooking and Karen's warmly professional supervision of the dining rooms, Clashganny House offers an accessible treat for discerning diners - and it has a well-earned place as a favourite dining destination, both for lucky locals and visitors to the area.

Seats 55. D Wed-Sat 6-9, from €34.95. L Sun only, 12.30-3, from €23.95. Wheelchair access. CC. **Directions:** R702 from Borris, then R729.

THE STEP HOUSE HOTEL

66 MAIN STREET BORRIS CO CARLOW
059 977 3209 I info@stephousehotel.ie
www.stephousehotel.ie

EAT I STAY

Redeveloped around a lovely old property - former dower house of the MacMurrough Kavanaghs (Borris House) and the pub next door (in the Coady family for 5 generations) - James and Cait Coady's stylish boutique hotel has made the pretty heritage village of Borris a destination for short breaks and weddings. Plush accommodation even includes a room with two bathrooms, one of them suitable for wheelchairs, and they have always had a reputation for good food. Head Chef Alan Foley's pride in the produce of the area is palpable and a meal here can be a special experience.

Rooms 20. B&B from about €80pps. Children welcome. Bar meals Wed-Sun, 12-9. Restaurant Sun L only, from €21. Wine from €21. Closed Mon & Tue (except bank hol Mon), 25 Dec, 3 wks Jan. Self-catering also available. CC. **Directions:** From main Carlow-Kilkenny road, take turning to Bagenalstown. 16km to Borris.

BARROWVILLE TOWNHOUSE

KILKENNY ROAD CARLOW CO CARLOW   STAY
059 914 3324 | barrowvilletownhouse@eircom.net
www.barrowville.com

Dermot and Anna Smyth's exceptionally comfortable and immaculately maintained period guesthouse is set serenely in lovely gardens, yet it's only a very short walk from the town centre. There's a pleasant and relaxing residents' drawing room with an open fire, grand piano and plenty to read - and very good breakfasts are served in a handsome conservatory (complete with a large vine) overlooking the riverside back garden.

Rooms 7 (2 shower only). B&B from about €40pps. Adults only. Garden; parking. Open all year. CC. **Directions:** South side of Carlow town on the N9.

LENNONS @ VISUAL

VISUAL CENTRE FOR CONTEMPORARY ART
OLD DUBLIN ROAD CARLOW CO CARLOW   EAT
059 917 9245 | eat@lennons.ie | www.lennons.ie

Visual is a stunning amenity in the heart of Carlow Town, its beautiful clean modern lines contrasting handsomely with the historic surroundings. And a fine setting for well known restaurateur Sinead Byrne and her son Ross's stylish venue, which - with a spacious sunny terrace and floor to ceiling windows - enjoys views of Carlow Cathedral and Carlow College across the grass. Local artists' paintings are displayed for sale and there's great pride of place - a perfect spot to enjoy simply prepared and extremely tasty food based on the best local and regional artisan produce. A super spot.

Seats 68. Open Mon-Sat 10.30-5, D Thu-Sat 6-9.30. Sun brunch 12-4. Early D all evening Thu, 6-7 Fri & Sat, from €22.50. Wine from €18.50. Children welcome. Wheelchair accessible. Closed bank hols, Good Fri, 25 Dec. CC. **Directions:** Centre of Carlow Town (Old Dublin Road).

MIMOSA WINE & TAPAS BAR

COLLEGE STREET CARLOW CO CARLOW   EAT | DRINK
059 917 0888 | info@mimosawinebar.com
www.mimosawinebar.com

In the centre of Carlow town, directly opposite the Cathedral, this stylish and sociable venue has everything that makes a good night out with friends. Like a little piece of Spain, the atmosphere is authentic with good music, wine racks around the bar and a hand-written blackboard tapas menu that delivers with well cooked food that's full of flavour.

D Wed-Sun from 5pm. Tapas portions about €6. Wine from €19. Children welcome. Closed Mon & Tue. CC. **Directions:** Centre of town, opposite the Cathedral.

HUNTINGTON CASTLE & GARDENS

CLONEGAL CO CARLOW   EAT | STAY | BUY
053 937 7160 | info@huntingtoncastle.com
www.huntingtoncastle.com

Ancient seat of the Esmonde family and now home to their descendants, Alex and Clare Durdin Robertson and their young family, the castle dates back to 1625 and is full of surprises - not least in the basement, where an exotic Temple to the Goddess Isis replaces the old dungeons - and, like all the very best castles, it even boasts a cast of resident ghosts. Add very special gardens, an adventure playground, gorgeous accommodation and a charming café (plus the wonderful Sha Roe Bistro at the end of the drive) and Huntington Castle adds up to a perfect destination.

Rooms 3, children welcome. B&B about €90pps incl guided tour of castle. Castle closed Nov-Mar. House and gardens open daily May-Sep; entry house & gardens €9, gardens only, €5; children €2.50 (incl adventure playground); no dogs. **Tearoom** and gift shop open daily Jun-Aug, weekends May and Sep. **Directions:** The castle gates are in the village of Clonegal.

SHA-ROE BISTRO

MAIN STREET CLONEGAL CO CARLOW

EAT

053 937 5636 | sha-roebistro@hotmail.com

www.sha-roe.ie

Just beside the driveway up to Huntington Castle in the charming riverside village of Clonegal, Henry and Stephanie Stone's restaurant is in a fine 18th century building. While small, it is beautifully appointed and atmospheric, with many quirky original features. A favourite destination for the many diners who appreciate Henry's outstanding, beautifully simple, seasonal cooking and Stephanie's caring service, it's friendly and professional, with welcoming fires for chilly days and a pretty courtyard for sunny ones. And the lovely grounds of Huntington Castle are perfect for a post-prandial stroll.

> **Seats 28**. D Thu-Sat, 7-9.30, à la carte; L Sun only, 12.30-2.30, about €34. Closed Sun D, Mon-Wed, all Jan. CC. **Directions:** On the borders of Wexford, Carlow and Wicklow - off N80 Enniscorthy-Carlow road.

MULLICHAIN CAFÉ

THE OLD GRAINSTORE ST MULLINS CO CARLOW   EAT | STAY
051 424 440 | info@oldgrainstorecottages.ie
www.oldgrainstorecottages.ie

"Great coffee, fantastic atmosphere and chat to beat the band" are the promises at the café in this fine restored grain house, where owners Martin and Emer O'Brien also offer "fresh scones with the morning coffee and a read of the paper, smoked salmon and a glass of wine for the lunch." All this and a good riverside walk in a beautiful and tranquil setting. What more could anyone ask for?

Open: Tue-Sun 11-6, closed Mon except bank hols (but closes the following Tue). Winter closure Nov-1st weekend Mar. Self-catering cottages (dogs welcome). **Directions:** On the quayside in St Mullins village.

MULVARRA HOUSE

ST MULLINS GRAIGUENAMANAGH CO CARLOW   STAY
051 424 936 | info@mulvarra.com
www.mulvarra.com

Hiberno-Dutch couple, Tim Dawson and Linda Huskes' friendly and well-maintained modern house is in a stunning location overlooking the River Barrow above the ancient and picturesque little harbour of St Mullins. And, although it may seem unremarkable from the road, this relaxing place is full of surprises - including some rooms with private balconies overlooking the river.

Rooms 5. B&B from €40pps. Children welcome. Licensed. Open all year. CC. **Directions:** Take R702 from Borris, turn right in Glynn; signposted from Glynn.

COUNTY CAVAN

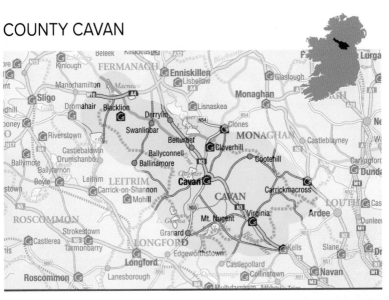

This is one of Ireland's most watery counties. It's classic drumlin territory, and the meandering waterways dictating the way of the roads means that much of Cavan www.thisiscavan.ie is hidden, and best discovered by the discerning visitor. It has quiet and utterly rural charm, seemingly remote yet not so very far from Belfast or Dublin - modern Cavan can surprise with its entrepreneurial flair.

Taking your time wandering through this green and silver land at the leisurely pace of the deservedly renowned Shannon-Erne Waterway www.waterwaysireland.org which has joined Ireland's two greatest lake and river systems, and you'll become aware of a place of rewardingly gentle pleasures. Yet you'll discover that it does have its own mountain, or at least it shares the 667 m peak of Cuilcagh with neighbouring Fermanagh.

No ordinary mountain, this - it has underground streams which eventually become the headwaters of the lordly River Shannon, while 47 kms to the southeast is the source of the River Erne near Bellanagh – it eventually flows northwest, so Ireland's greatest rivers are closely interwined, yet only connected by canal.

Cavan is much more extensive than is popularly imagined, for in the northeast it has Shercock with its own miniature lake district, while in its southeast it takes in all of Lough Ramor at the charming lakeside village of Virginia www.virginia.ie . It also has shores on Lough Sheelin, while in the far northwest its rugged scenery hints at rugged Donegal where it borders on Sligo and Fermanagh. And always throughout its drumlin heartlands you can find many little Cavan lakes that can be called your own for the day that's in it.

LOCAL ATTRACTIONS AND INFORMATION

>Bailieboro **Tourism Information** | 042 966 6666
>Ballyjamesduff **Cavan County Museum**
   049 854 4070
>Ballyjamesduff **International Pork Festival** (June)
   049 854 4242 / 087 632 0042
>Belturbet **Tourist Office** | 049 952 2044

>Cavan town **Cavan Crystal** | 049 433 1800
>**Cavan Arts Office** |
   www.cavanarts.ie | 049 437 8548
>Cavan town **Tourist Information**
   www.thisiscavan.ie | 049 4331942
>Cavan **Cavan Equestrian Centre** 049 433 2017

MACNEAN HOUSE & RESTAURANT

MAIN STREET BLACKLION CO CAVAN
071 985 3022 | info@macneanrestaurant.com
www.macneanrestaurant.com

EAT | STAY | LEARN

Weekends are booked out months ahead at this beacon of excellence, where celebrated chef Neven Maguire and his wife, Amelda, have transformed what was once a modest restaurant with rooms into a place of sumptuous comfort. It's a fine setting for exceptional cooking of the local foods that Neven has always championed with such passion. A meal here in this little border town - or a session in the adjacent Cookery School, where all classes are taken by Neven himself - is an experience to be treasured.

Seats 50. D Wed-Sat, two sittings 6 & 9.30; D Sun 7-8pm, L Sun only, two sittings 12.30 & 3.30, set 4 course Sun L €45; D Menu Prestige €85. Rooms 19. Rooms & suites €67-€111pps, courtyard house from about €55 pps. Restaurant closed Mon & Tue all year, house closed Jan 1-18. Cookery School. CC. **Directions:** On N17, main Belfast-Sligo road.

FARNHAM ESTATE SPA & GOLF RESORT

FARNHAM ESTATE CAVAN CO CAVAN
049 437 7700 | info@farnhamestate.com
www.farnhamestate.com

EAT | STAY

A winding driveway through a lush parkland golf course brings you to the dramatic entrance of this mainly modern hotel, where a giant glass atrium links the classical building dating from 1810 to the striking 21st century extension. Chef Gary Stinson offers good cooking in two bars, as well as the attractively situated smart-casual Botanica Restaurant, making Farnham Estate a pleasant place to break a journey.

A popular destination for golf and spa breaks, it has also earned a reputation for business and events.

Rooms 158. B&B from about €49.50pps. **Restaurant seats 180**. L daily 12.30-2.30, a la carte. D daily 6.30-9.30. Set D 2/3 course €37/45., also a la carte. Sun L €25 (children €12.) House wine €26.50. Open all year. CC. **Directions:** N3 to Cavan town; signed, on Killeshandra Road (3km).

OAK ROOM RESTAURANT

24 BRIDGE STREET CAVAN CO CAVAN
049 437 1414 | info@theoakroom.ie
www.theoakroom.ie

EAT

The Oak Room moved into spacious new premises in 2017, providing a smart setting for proprietor-chef Norbert Neylon's modern Irish cooking. Like several prominent Cavan chefs, he is a former Euro-Toques Young Chef of the Year and his background is in fine dining, but the focus at this popular town centre restaurant is on offering quality with value for money. The tasty cooking includes

'real food' options for children and there's a strong commitment to seasonal local produce. A very useful place to know about when visiting Cavan Town.

D Wed-Sat, 5.30-9.30, Sun 1-8. Early D (all evening Wed-Fri, Sat 5.30-6.30) from about €22, also à la carte. Wine from €21.50. Booking advised. Children welcome. Closed Mon & Tue, 24-26 Dec. CC. **Directions:** Town centre.

THE OLDE POST INN

CLOVERHILL CO CAVAN
047 55555 | info@theoldepostinn.com
www.theoldepostinn.com

EAT | STAY | LEARN

A cut stone building set in neatly landscaped gardens, Gearoid and Tara Lynch's restaurant served as a post office until the 1970s. Gearoid, a former Commissioner General of Euro-Toques Ireland, is a chef who is committed to supporting local producers and showing respect for regional and seasonal foods, so a meal at this atmospheric restaurant promises to be a true taste of Ireland. Tara manages front of house with quiet efficiency and, after dinner, residents' rooms are only yards from the fire in the cosy bar.

Seats 120. D Wed-Sat 6-9 (Fri & Sat to 9.30). Sun 5.30-8.30; L Sun only, 12.30-2.30, about €35. D from €45; Tasting Menu €82, also à la carte; Closed Mon & Tue. **Rooms 6** (2 shower only). B&B from about €65pps. Children welcome. Closed 24-27 Dec. CC.
Directions: 9km N of Cavan town: take N54 at Butlersbridge, 2.5km on right in Cloverhill village.

ST KYRANS COUNTRY HOUSE & RESTAURANT

DUBLIN ROAD VIRGINIA CO CAVAN   EAT I STAY
049 854 7087 I info@stkyrans.com
www.stkyrans.com

With views up Lough Ramor - where little fishing boats and wildlife activity around pretty wooded islets are a constant source of interest - Patrick and Helena Keenan's shoreside smart-casual restaurant with rooms enjoys a lovely location. With all this, and Chef Eddie Atwell working his magic in the kitchen, it's easy to see why this has become a destination restaurant, drawing diners from a wide area – and Eddie is also a keen kitchen gardener, which adds an extra dimension to any visit here.

Seats 45. L Wed-Sun 12.30-3.30; D Wed-Sat from 6pm (also Sun Easter-Sep); early D Wed-Fri 6-7pm, from €30, also à la carte. Afternoon Tea. **Rooms 8**. B&B from €50pps. CC. **Directions:** Signed on left when approaching Virginia from Dublin direction.

VIRGINIA PARK LODGE

VIRGINIA CO CAVAN

049 854 6100 | info@virginiaparklodge.com

www.virginiaparklodge.com

EAT | DRINK

Beautifully located overlooking Lough Ramor, this eighteenth century sporting lodge charmingly combines informality and grandeur. In 2013 a famous local man, the chef Richard Corrigan, bought the property and lost no time in renovating the house and establishing productive gardens, which now also supply his London restaurants in season. A desirable private venue for weddings, corporate events and sporting weekends, it also opens as a pop up (book online) and makes an elegant and atmospheric setting for Richard Corrigan's famously direct seasonal, ingredients-led cooking.

Rooms: about 50 (includes courtyard apartments & 'shepherds huts' in grounds). Available for weddings and events, exclusive hire; opens to the public for pop-up dinners, lunches and weekends. (Guide prices: DB&B from about €148pps; D €65; L €48) Cookery courses (12+) by arrangement. CC. **Directions:** Entrance off northern end of Virginia's main street (R194, Ballyjamesduff road.

COUNTY CLARE

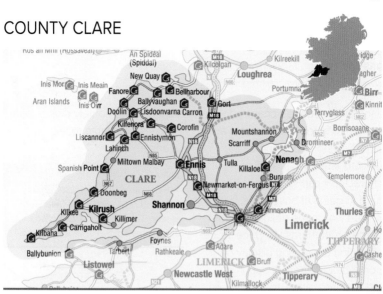

Clare www.clare.ie is impressive, a larger-than-life county which is bounded by the Wild Atlantic Way through Galway Bay to the north, on beside the Atlantic coast itself to the west and the outer part of the Shannon Estuary to the south, while to the east and southeast, Lough Derg and the River Shannon set the boundaries.

The Atlantic coasts include some of the WAW's most dramatic features in the astonishing and majestic Cliffs of Moher www.cliffsofmoher.ie Close under them in dangerous water is the majestic breaker known as Aileens, the surfer's Nirvana. Less challenging nearby, but still at the top of world standards, is one of Ireland's greatest surfing beaches at Lahinch, which is also a golfer's Nirvana, while close inland are hospitality hotspots like Lisdoonvarna and Ennistymon. As for that Galway Bay coastline, it is where The Burren www.burrennationalpark.ie , the fantastical North Clare moonscape of limestone which is home to so much unexpectedly exotic flora, comes plunging spectacularly towards the sea around the attractive village of Ballyvaughan.

In contrast to the spare beauty of The Burren and other rugged areas such as Loop Head which have to live in harmony with the nearby Atlantic, Clare is renowned for its comfortable hospitality and quality food. And you only have to move eastwards towards the convenient traffic-absorbing Atlantic Link Motorway to come on areas of sweet rural abundance. As for the Shannon Estuary, well, Ireland may have many estuaries, but needless to say the lordly Shannon has far and away the biggest estuary of all. It is the port of call for the largest freight ships visiting Ireland, and on its northern shore is Shannon Airport www.shannonairport.ie .

LOCAL ATTRACTIONS AND INFORMATION

>Ballyvaughan **Aillwee Cave** 065 7077036

>Bunratty **Bunratty Castle & Folk Park**
  www.shannonheritage.com | 061 360788

>**Cliffs of Moher** www.cliffsofmoher.ie
  Tourist Information 065 708 6141

>Ennis **Tourist Centre**
  www.visitennis.com | 065 6828366

>Killimer **Killimer-Tarbert Ferry**
  www.shannonferries.com | 065 53124

>Kilrush **Vandeleur Walled Garden**
  www.vandeleurwalledgarden.ie | 065 905 1760

>Shannon Airport **Tourist Information**
  www.shannonairport.ie | 061 471 664

AN FEAR GORTA (TEA & GARDEN ROOMS)

BALLYVAUGHAN CO CLARE   EAT

065 707 7157 | info@tearoomsballyvaughan.com
www.tearoomsballyvaughan.com

Jane O'Donoghue's charming harbourside tea room is set in an attractive stone building dating back to 1790, and it is full of character. It can sometimes be hard to get in at busy times, but a short wait in the delightful front garden is no hardship. Once inside you'll find a tempting display of home-baked fare laid out on an old cast-iron range, to be enjoyed in the pretty back garden, the sun lounge or the homely dining room - and also available to take away. Licensed.

Seats 40 (+ 15 outdoors). Open mid Apr-Oct, daily Jul & Aug 11am-5.30pm. Closed Nov-mid Apr; Tue & Wed early season; Tue in June. CC. **Directions:** On the harbour front.

BURREN FINE WINE & FOOD

CORKSCREW HILL ROAD BALLYVAUGHAN CO CLARE   EAT | BUY
065 707 7046 | info@burrenwine.ie
www.burrenwine.ie

Cathleen Connole's interesting seasonal restaurant is in an old coach house just off the Burren Waymarked Walk, and offers eco experiences (guided walks and cycles) as well as delicious local, home grown and home cooked food. Although primarily a charming spot for a daytime bite to eat (including traditional Afternoon Tea), they also offer packed lunches for walkers and sell gourmet hampers - and as for the wine, the house wine is the highly regarded additive-free Galway Bay Wine, produced in the Languedoc area of France by Cathleen's brother Noel O'Loughlen.

Seats 35 (+ 20 outdoors). Open daily May-Sep 11am-5pm. Closed Oct-Apr.
Directions: Corkscrew Hill road

GREGANS CASTLE HOTEL

BALLYVAUGHAN THE BURREN CO CLARE   EAT | STAY
065 707 7005 | stay@gregans.ie
www.gregans.ie

Simon and Freddie Haden's quietly luxurious and restorative country house hotel offers simple West of Ireland joys like warming turf fires and views across the Burren landscape - and it is one of Ireland's top food destinations. Gifted chef David Hurley cooks in a style that is 'modern European but distinctively Irish and unpretentious', and takes enormous pride in showcasing the wonderful foods of the locality in a memorable dining experience. When the restaurant is closed, a simpler but equally delicious fireside dinner is served in the atmospheric Corkscrew Bar.

⭐

Rooms 21. B&B from €245 per room. Pets permitted, children welcome (no concessions). Restaurant D from €75, Mon-Tue & Thu-Sat & bank hol Sun (6-9). Closed D Wed & D Sun, (except bank hol). Bar L daily 12-2.30, Afternoon Tea, 2.30-5. Reservations required. Hotel closed late Nov-mid Feb. CC. **Directions:** On N67, 5km south of Ballyvaughan.

O'LOCLAINN

BALLYVAUGHAN CO CLARE

065 707 7006 | www.discoverballyvaughan.com

DRINK

Aka O'Loclainn's Irish Whiskey Bar, Peter and Margaret O'Loghlen's little harbourside bar is the quintessential traditional Irish pub - and one that fans can sometimes be reluctant to want to share... It's very much an evening place and, in addition to the charm of its dimly characterful interior and friendly owners, the O'Loughlens' vast whiskey collection is a particular claim to fame. Just the place to drop into for a sampling session after dinner - and sometimes there is traditional Irish music too.

Open Mon-Sun, from 8pm-late (from 7pm in summer).

HAZEL MOUNTAIN CHOCOLATE

OUGHTMAMA BELLHARBOUR CO CLARE

065 707 8847 | info@hazelmountainchocolates.com

www.hazelmountainchocolates.com

EAT | BUY | PRODUCER

Although it is well signed near north Clare's famous Flaggy Shore, John and Kasha Connolly's charming little chocolate factory and café still comes as a surprise. Having trained with the Belgian chef and chocolatier Dirk Schonekeren, of Helena Chocolates in Castlebar, Kasha set up her little chocolate factory here in the cottage farmhouse that John inherited from his grandmother. Bean to bar stone-ground chocolate is the USP, producing both classic chocolates and unusual ones inspired by the landscape, such as wild berries, nuts and petals. The pretty café serves simple, quality homemade food, all gluten free.

Open 10-5 daily all year (L Tue-Sun, 12-3). Tour & Tasting 1pm (€15). Galway shop: 6 Middle Street, Mon-Sun 11-7.

THE LONG DOCK

WEST STREET CARRIGAHOLT CO CLARE
065 905 8106 | info@thelongdock.com
www.thelongdock.com

EAT | DRINK | BUY | PRODUCER

Tony and Imelda Lynch's classic 19th century pub has earned a well-deserved reputation for its friendly atmosphere and good food, especially local seafood. Well cooked and tasty, the menu features great seasonal local produce and there's nothing too fussy. Behind the pub you'll find a café, extra outdoor tables in a sheltered courtyard for sunny days, and a shop selling their own products - including the 'Famous Chowder' and an irresistible range of homemade ice creams - and those of other like-minded producers. A one off.

Seats 80 (+30 outdoors). Food daily in summer 11am-9pm, à la carte; Sun L about €20. Children welcome. Tourist Information; shop, café, ice-cream parlour. Closed Mon-Wed off-season (Nov-Mar), except Christmas. CC.
Directions: Signed from Kilkee (10 minutes).

BURREN PERFUMERY AND TEA ROOMS

CARRON CO CLARE   EAT | BUY

065 708 9102 | burrenperfumery@mac.com
www.burrenperfumery.com

When touring Clare you will be pleased to find this charming spot. Although small and simple, the rose-bedecked tea rooms at Sadie Chowen-Doyle's famous perfumery are pretty, with floral oilcloths, fresh flowers and mismatched crockery creating a happy riot of pastels. Blackboard menus proclaim the food philosophy: local and organic produce stars - and everything they do is simply delicious and made freshly on the premises.

Seats 20; open daily 11-4.15 (Sun to 5), Apr-Sep. (Perfumery open all year except Christmas.) CC. **Directions:** In the Burren, east of Gort - off R480 & N67.

FERGUS VIEW

KILNABOY COROFIN CO CLARE   STAY

065 683 7606 | deckell@indigo.ie
www.fergusview.com

Declan and Mary Kelleher's neat farmhouse and beautifully maintained gardens enjoy a lovely view of the Clare countryside and regular visitors will always notice the changes and improvements that are made each winter. While not large, the bedrooms and their en-suite shower rooms are immaculately presented and this makes an hospitable and inexpensive base for exploring this fascinating area - and Mary serves a very good breakfast too, showcasing local and home-grown foods.

Rooms 5 (1 shower only; 1 not en-suite, with private bathroom). B&B about €80 per room; closed mid Oct -Feb. Self-catering cottage available all year **No CC. Directions:** 3km north of Corofin, on Kilfenora Road (R476).

BALLINALACKEN CASTLE COUNTRY HOUSE & RESTAURANT

DOOLIN CO CLARE   EAT | STAY

065 707 4025 | ballinalackencastle@eircom.net
www.ballinalackencastle.com

Away from the bustle of Doolin and Lisdoonvarna, near Doolin Cave, and with wonderful views of the Atlantic and the West Coast, Declan and Cecilia O'Callaghan's unusual property is easily identified from afar by the 15th century castle standing on it - and it offers welcoming fires, comfortable sitting rooms for relaxing in, spacious rooms (many with sea views), and a proper bar as well good food in the restaurant. It's a popular evening destination for local diners who enjoy the classical cooking of local produce, notably fresh Atlantic seafood and Burren lamb, and the traditional dining room ambience.

Rooms 12 (1 shower only). B&B about €170 per room. Restaurant open to non-residents; D Wed-Mon, 6.45-8.45; à la carte (mains from €19.50). Establishment closed 1 Nov-mid Apr. CC. **Directions:** Coast road, R477. North of Doolin Village.

HOTEL DOOLIN

RIVERVALE DOOLIN CO CLARE
065 707 4111 | info@hoteldoolin.ie
www.hoteldoolin.ie

EAT | STAY | PRODUCER

Outstanding for its contemporary style - and a vibrant local food philosophy that has earned it a reputation beyond the county - this privately owned hotel offers something different, including smart accommodation and The Doolin Pantry speciality food & wine shop selling in-house products, plus other local and Irish speciality produce. Several appealing dining options are offered and local produce - including some from the hotel's own gardens - is the trademark, featuring strongly on all menus.

Rooms 17 (all shower only). B&B from about €35pps. Lift. Restaurants: Chervil (fine dining) D Wed-Sun, from 6.30pm, L Sun only 1-4. Stonewall Café & Pizzeria: café open 10-4 daily in summer, pizzeria 6-11, takeaway available; closed Nov-Mar; Fitzs Pub: carvery L and bar menu daily. Free wifi. Shops: Doolin Pantry & Shaggy Sheep (gifts), closed Nov-Mar. Hotel closed 3 days at Christmas. Centre of Doolin village.

STONE CUTTERS KITCHEN FAMILY RESTAURANT

LUOGH NORTH DOOLIN CO CLARE   EAT

065 707 5962 | stonecutterskitchen@eircom.net

www.stonecutterskitchen.com

Well-signed between Doolin and the Cliffs of Moher, Karen Courtney and Myles Duffy's family-friendly traditional thatched cottage has become a destination for many - with outdoor playground, indoor toys, quirky furnishings and Myles's good home cooking of the best local foods it's just what families want when they're out and about. You don't have to have children with you to enjoy a stop here, though - it's an attractive alternative to more famous destinations in the area, with appeal to all ages. A really useful place to know about when travelling in west Clare - and just beside the Clare Jam Company too.

Seats 50 (+24 outdoors). Open daily June-Aug 11-9.30, April & Oct 12.30-5; May & Sep 12-30-7. Children welcome. Wheelchair accessible. Closed Nov-Mar. CC. **Directions:** Opposite Doolin Pottery on the Doolin-Cliffs of Moher road (R478) 1.6km north of the cliffs.

MORRISSEY'S SEAFOOD BAR & GRILL

DOONBEG CO CLARE   EAT | DRINK

065 905 5304 | info@morrisseysdoonbeg.com
www.morrisseysdoonbeg.ie

This attractive family-owned bar/restaurant beside the River Cree in Doonbeg village is currently run by the energetic fourth generation owner Hugh McNally, who has skilfully extended and re-styled it in recent years, giving it a lovely riverside decking area and youthful appeal. Seafood is the speciality and everything is very fresh, with a good selection offered in season, and the cooking is consistently good - all that and very nice staff who are friendly and willing, no wonder it's always busy.

Seats 70 (+ 30 outdoors; private room, 30); toilets wheelchair accessible; children welcome before 10. D Wed-Sun 6-9.30 (Sun to 9), Sun L 12.15-2. A la carte; wine from about €20. Parking. Closed Mon-Tue, and early Jan-Mar. CC. **Directions:** In village, beside the bridge

TRUMP INTERNATIONAL HOTEL & GOLF LINKS

DOONBEG CO CLARE   EAT | STAY

065 905 5600 | doonbeg.reservations@trumphotels.com
www.trumphotels.com/ireland

Although Doonbeg Golf Club is a private club, both golf and accommodation are welcome to visitors when available. The Lodge has an Irish 'great house' feel with an American opulence - accommodation is not just very luxurious, but downright gorgeous. And the food is also very good - notably in the fine dining restaurant, overlooking the ocean, but also in the friendly bar where excellent Irish staff offset the strong branding somewhat.

Rooms 218. Room rate from €185. Ocean View Restaurant D daily 6-9.30, a la carte, mains from about €25. Trump's Bar & Restaurant food 12-9.30 daily. Wine from €28. Afternoon Tea, Mar-Oct. Self-catering cottages. CC. **Directions:** On N67, 16km north of Kilkee.

THE CLOISTER RESTAURANT & BAR

ABBEY STREET ENNIS CO CLARE

EAT

065 686 8198 | info@cloister.ie

www.cloister.ie

A popular dining destination within the atmospheric 13th century Ennis Friary cloistral buildings, Dermot Fetton's welcoming and relaxing bar and restaurant is known for good cooking and caring service. Head Chef Terry Connor values the quality ingredients of the locality and is not afraid of simplicity - they take pride in doing the simple things really well here, and he offers a tasty brasserie lunch menu as well as a dinner menu with a sense of occasion.

Drinks include craft cocktails and beers, as well as an excellent and accessibly priced wine list compiled by wine lover Dermot, with many by the glass.

Open Tue-Fri 12-3, Sat & Sun 12-9. Closed Mon. Set D from about €22. A la carte Tue-Sun 5.30- 9. Children's menu. Vegetarian Menu. Wine from €26. All cards except Diners.

OLD GROUND HOTEL

O'CONNELL STREET ENNIS CO CLARE

EAT | STAY

065 682 8127 | reservations@oldgroundhotel.ie

www.flynnhotels.com

The Flynn family's iconic ivy-clad hotel is a former manor house dating back to the 18th century and, set in its own gardens, it is an oasis of calm in the bustling centre of Ennis. It offers the quirky charm of the traditional Irish hotel, with comfortable and relaxing places to meet in the public seating areas and good food in the bar (Poet's Corner) and elegant old-world dining room (Brendan O'Regan Room Restaurant), and also in the atmospheric Town Hall Bistro next door, which is a destination in its own right.

Rooms 83 (8 shower only, 1 wheelchair friendly). Lift. B&B from €60pps. Restaurant seats 70: B'fst, L&D daily. Set L from €23, set D about €36, early D from €27. Also à la carte. Town Hall Bistro open from 10am daily, serving lunch, dinner and light food. Hotel closed 24 (5pm)-26 Dec (5pm). CC. **Directions:** Town centre.

BYRNES WINE DINE & STAY

MAIN STREET ENNISTYMON CO CLARE
065 707 1080 | byrnesennistymon@eircom.net
www.byrnes-ennistymon.ie

EAT | STAY

In a quirkily painted period house at the top of the main street in this old market town (near welcome new arrival, The Cheese Press www.facebook.com/pg/CheesePressEnnistymon), Richard and Mary Byrnes' stylish, high-ceilinged restaurant has views of Ennistymon's famous cascading river from the restaurant and an extensive outdoor dining area at the back. Their contemporary Irish cooking focuses on local seafood and meats, also interesting vegetarian options - all freshly cooked to order - and tasty light daytime food, with very good freshly ground coffee. Lovely service from friendly young staff and a lively, fun atmosphere.

Seats 85. Open daily mid-Feb-mid-Nov incl bank hols, 11am-9.30pm. A la carte. **Rooms: 6** (all with private bathrooms). B&B from €35pps, single from €50. CC Closed 3 days at Christmas. Phone to check opening times mid-Nov to mid-Feb. **Directions:** Town centre, on the main street.

VASCO

CRAGGAGH FANORE CO CLARE   EAT | BUY
065 707 6020 | karen@vasco.ie
www.vasco.ie

Situated in the heart of the Burren in 'Ireland's longest village', Karen and Ross Quinn's eye-catching business is an all-day café-restaurant and deli - and many other wonderful things besides. The much travelled multi-lingual pair offer eclectic menus, but their delicious food is firmly rooted in the foods of the area and they are keen supporters of local producers. Burren beef and lamb, and superb fish all feature - and tender goat meat from a local farm is a house speciality in season. Well worth a visit - and you can pick up a picnic from the adjacent deli too.

Open mid-Mar to mid-Sep. May-Aug, Tue–Sun 11.30-4.30 (Thu-Sun to 7.30), otherwise weekends only, 11.30-4.30. A la carte. Children welcome. Wheelchair accessible. Closed Mon (except bank hols) & mid Sep-mid Mar CC. **Directions:** On the coast road between Doolin and Ballyvaughan.

KILBAHA GALLERY & CRAFTS

LIGHTHOUSE ROAD KILBAHA CO CLARE   EAT | BUY | LEARN
065 905 8843 | kilbahagallery@gmail.com
www.kilbahagallery.com

Even if the stunningly beautiful Loop Head (and its lighthouse) weren't such a magnet, it would be worth heading to the peninsula just for the pleasure of a visit to Liz Greehy and Ailish Connolly's fascinating cottage galley and museum. Their shop stocks quality art, crafts and artisan food products, most of it local - and, behind it, the lovely little café is perfect for a comforting cuppa and one of the famously delicious cakes and goodies supplied by Pat and Imelda Bourke of The Pantry, in Kilkee.

Open daily Mar-Oct, 10-5; weekends only Oct-Christmas. Closed Jan-Feb, but open by appointment at any time. Wifi. Children welcome; wheelchair accessible (shop & café). Outdoor tables. Parking. CC.

BURREN GLAMPING AND FREE RANGE PORK

CAHIRMINNAUN KILFENORA CO CLARE   STAY | BUY | PRODUCER
086 881 5974 | burrenpork@gmail.com
www.burrenglamping.com

Already well known for their wonderful free range pork, Eva and Stephen Hegarty embarked on a new enterprise, Burren Glamping, in 2015 - and they now offer cosy accommodation in an imaginatively converted vintage horse truck on this small farm. Breakfast, available in Eva's kitchen, often features the pork produced by their happy, naturally fed Burren pigs - Saddlebacks and Saddleback/Tamworth cross - that Eva also sells at local markets and from the farm (by appointment). Quirky and simply gorgeous, Burren Glamping is a total one-off and has to be seen to be believed.

Sleeps up to 6. Open all year. **No credit cards** - pay by bank transfer, Paypal or cash.

LIR RESTAURANT & BAKERY

KILKEE GOLF CLUB EAST END KILKEE CO CLARE

EAT | BUY

065 908 3000 | kilkeegolfclub@eircom.net

This is no ordinary golf club - it has the best location in the area, for a start, and Deirdre Daly's restaurant / bakery is a stunner. Whether for a casual bite in the bar or something a bit more formal in the elegant restaurant, it's a wonderfully relaxing place and the views are stupendous. Local seafood naturally takes pride of place, and the cooking is outstanding; even the simplest dish - a fish hot pot or seafood linguini, perhaps -demonstrates finesse, and may also include less usual ingredients, such as delicious sweet-flavoured clams. A must-visit when in Kilkee.

Open Fri-Tue: Fri-Sat & Mon-Tue, 10-9, Sun 10-6. Closed Wed & Thu. A la carte. CC. **Also at:** Deirdre Daly's team also operates OPIA (www.facebook. com/Food-by-OPIA), the food side of the new House Limerick on Howleys Quay.

MURPHY BLACKS

THE SQUARE KILKEE CO CLARE   EAT
065 905 6854 | murphyblacks@hotmail.com
www.murphyblacks.ie

Cillian Murphy is an ex-fishing skipper who ensures the freshest fish possible - and the effort he puts into ensuring the best from suppliers shows, in succulent, well-flavoured food. He is in charge of front of house, and Mary is the chef - a winning combination that has earned Murphy Blacks a reputation well beyond the immediate area. And Cillian, a former Chairman of Loop Head Tourism, works tirelessly to get the word out about this wonderfully remote place, while also raising standards.

Seats 42 (+ 12 outdoors). Mid Jul-late Aug: D Tue-Sun; shoulder season: D Tue-Sat; Oct-Mar: weekends only. Call to check opening off season. CC. **Directions:** Centre of town.

THE PANTRY

O'CURRY STREET KILKEE CO CLARE   EAT | BUY | PRODUCER
065 905 6576 | info@thepantrykilkee.com
www.thepantrykilkee.com

Owned and operated by home economics teacher Imelda Bourke and her husband, Pat, baking starts at The Pantry at 5.30 each morning, and they produce the most amazing selection of breads, cakes and desserts. Later Imelda and her kitchen team create wonders for lunch... There is a marvellous and somewhat chaotic buzz here - and they also supply the café at the delightful Kilbaha Gallery & Crafts near Loop Head lighthouse.

Open daily 8-6.30 in season. Closed Oct-Easter. CC. Directions: Down O'Connell Street towards the bay, left into O'Curry Street just before the sea.

CHERRY TREE RESTAURANT

LAKESIDE BALLINA KILLALOE CO CLARE

EAT

061 375 688 | cherrytreerestaurant@gmail.com

www.cherrytreerestaurant.ie

The Cherry Tree enjoys a lovely waterside location and a reputation for consistently excellent contemporary cooking - and this imaginatively appointed restaurant has been the area's leading fine dining destination since it opened in 2000. Owner-chef Harry McKeogh's pleasing trademark is a direct cooking style, without too many cheffy twirls - allowing the great ingredients he sources with such care to take centre stage - and that, in addition to the beautiful setting and caring service, explains its enduring success.

Seats 60. D Tue-Sat (Thu-Sat in winter). Early D Tue-Sat 6-9pm, (Fri & Sat to 7.30pm.) Set 5 course D €35; also à la carte; wine from €21. Closed Mon, Tue (also Wed in winter), 24-26 Dec, last week Jan, 1st week Feb. CC. **Directions:** At Ballina side of bridge, turn down towards the Lakeside Hotel; just before the hotel, on the left.

CROTTY'S PUB

MARKET SQUARE KILRUSH CO CLARE

EAT | STAY

065 905 2470 | enquiries@crottyspubkilrush.com

www.crottyspubkilrush.com

Its corner location on the town square gives a clue to the historic importance of Rebecca Brew and Kevin Clancy's imposing 19th century pub with accommodation. It's a wonderful place, with all the features that make Victorian Irish pubs so special, and a first port of call for many visitors. Good wholesome food is important too at this hospitable place, ranging from light daytime bites to more substantial evening meals, and the spacious rooms are very comfortable too. True to its history, it's also a great music pub, with traditional musicians often featuring.

Rooms 5 (all en-suite), B&B from about €40pps. Food daily, à la carte (starters from €4.95, main courses from €11.95). CC. **Directions:** Centre of Kilrush. Parking on the square.

BARRTRA SEAFOOD RESTAURANT

LAHINCH CO CLARE   EAT

065 708 1280 | barrtra@hotmail.com
www.barrtra.com

Views of Liscannor Bay take centre stage from Paul and Theresa O'Brien's traditional, whitewashed cottage where, aside from the stunning location, local seafood is the star attraction - and also local Angus beef. Paul and Theresa's son, Ruben, is now Head Chef at this warmly charming restaurant and he continues the family tradition of putting quality and provenance first. An appealing à la carte is offered, but a highlight for many is Ruben's nightly Surprise Menu - choose from fish, meat or vegetarian - and carefully selected wines, all at customer-friendly prices.

Seats 40. Open from 5.30 (Sun from 12); L July & Aug only from 12.30. Fri-Sun (Mar & April, Oct – Dec); Wed Sun (May-Sep). Phone to check opening hours off season. Closed Jan-Feb. CC. **Directions:** Signed off N67, 6km south of Lahinch.

MOY HOUSE

LAHINCH CO CLARE   STAY
065 708 2800 | moyhouse@eircom.net
www.moyhouse.com

This stunning house just outside Lahinch is one of Ireland's most appealing (and luxurious) country houses and is run with warmth and efficiency. Like most of the gorgeous bedrooms, the large antique-furnished drawing room has wonderful sea views - a favourite spot to enjoy aperitifs from the honesty bar, or to relax in front of the fire with coffee and petits fours after dinner. And many come here especially for the food, notably chef Matthew Strefford's nightly tasting menu created around local seafood and produce from the 30-acre Moy House Farm, including chicken, duck and pork as well as organically grown seasonal fruit and vegetables. Delicious breakfasts too, of course.

Rooms 9 (3 shower only). Residents' D Tue-Sat; light supper Sun & Mon. Closed Nov-end Mar. CC. **Directions:** On the sea side of the Miltown Malbay road, outside Lahinch.

VAUGHAN LODGE & VL RESTAURANT

ENNISTYMON ROAD LAHINCH CO CLARE   EAT | STAY
065 708 1111 | info@vaughanlodge.ie
www.vaughanlodge.ie

Michael and Maria Vaughan's welcoming hotel - purpose-built to high specifications, mainly with the comfort of golfers in mind - offers peace and relaxation within easy walking distance of the town centre. There's a great sense of space in the clean-lined bedrooms and relaxing areas, including a clubby bar with leather easy chairs and sofas that golfers love - and a particular USP is the excellent VL Restaurant, where Head Chef, John Gilmartin cooks up a storm with local seafood (over half of the à la carte menu in summer) and interesting artisan foods from the area.

Rooms 20 (1 shower only); B&B from about €85pps. Lift. VL Restaurant seats 60. D Tue-Sun, set D from €42. Wine from €27. Closed Mon, Nov-Mar. CC. **Directions:** On N85 just at the edge of Lahinch on the left.

VAUGHANS ANCHOR INN

MAIN STREET LISCANNOR CO CLARE   EAT | DRINK
065 708 1548 | info@vaughans.ie
www.vaughans.ie

The Vaughan family's traditional bar has great character, with open fires and lots of memorabilia. Although famed for their seafood platters (and they are fantastic - and great value too), there's much more to the menu than that: Denis Vaughan is an exceptionally talented and creative chef and uses as much local produce as possible. And everything really is fresh - the menu may even be changed in mid-stream because there's something new coming up off the boats. Great cooking is matched by excellent service - and, while quality food can never be cheap, it's great value too.

Seats 106. Food 12-9.30 daily; wine from €18.95. Toilets wheelchair accessible; children welcome before 9.. Accommodation also offered. Closed 25 Dec. CC. **Directions:** 4km from Lahinch on Cliffs of Moher route.

THE ROADSIDE TAVERN

LISDOONVARNA CO CLARE   EAT | DRINK | PRODUCER
065 707 4084 | roadsidetavern@gmail.com
www.roadsidetavern.ie

Easily spotted by the mural on the gable wall, Peter Curtin's historic and hospitable hostelry oozes character and, famous for music for over a century, many legendary musicians have played here. More recent attractions are beers from their on-site microbrewery, the Burren Brewery, and the good food served at 'Kieran's Kitchen' where chef Kieran O'Halloran features smoked fish from the family's other equally famous business, the nearby Burren Smoke-house (burrensmokehouse.com) on his simply delicious menus. Next door, the latest enterprise, the multi-purpose venue, Burren Storehouse offers artisan pizzas and chargrills nightly in summer. All round it's the hub of activities in Lisdoonvarna.

Opening times are subject to change; L&D available daily in summer. Mar-Oct Mon-Fri 12-4, 6-9. Sat & Sun from 12. CC. **Directions:** Near town centre on Kincora Road /N67 to Ennistymon.

SHEEDYS COUNTRY HOUSE HOTEL & RESTAURANT

LISDOONVARNA CO CLARE   EAT | DRINK | STAY
065 707 4026 | info@sheedys.com
www.sheedys.com

John and Martina Sheedy run one of the west of Ireland's best-loved small hotels - it offers some of the most comfortable accommodation and the best food in the area, yet still has the warm ambience and friendly hands-on management which make a hotel special. John showcases local produce like Burren lamb and Atlantic seafood with style at every meal (and makes everything from scratch - breads, biscuits, jams, preserves, ice creams...). The same high standards apply at breakfast - and, while relaxed and informal, the sheer quality makes Sheedys an enduring destination for food lovers.

Rooms 11 (1 wheelchair friendly). B&B from about €63pps. Free wifi. Restaurant seats 22. D Mon-Sat 6.30-8.30, à la carte. Bar menu also offered. Hotel closed Oct-Easter. CC. **Directions:** 200m from town square on road to Sulphur Wells.

WILD HONEY INN

KINCORA ROAD LISDOONVARNA CO CLARE
065 707 4300 I info@wildhoneyinn.com
www.wildhoneyinn.com

EAT I DRINK I STAY

Aidan and Kate McGrath's Wild Honey is a true inn, offering rest, relaxation, refreshment and good company. Serving high quality food in a characterful pub setting, Aidan (our Chef of the Year 2012) describes his cooking as bistro style, 'informed by living on the rugged West coast of Ireland where there is an abundance of local produce from land and sea' - but, with its unique combination of finesse and simplicity, this is no ordinary bistro cooking. Lovely rooms too, reflecting the same understated philosophy.

Rooms 14 (10 shower only). B&B Mar-Oct from €60pps. Restricted hours Oct, Mar & Apr. Toilets wheelchair accessible. Meals: D Tue-Sat 6-9, also bank hol w/e Sun 6-9 (closed following Tue). D from €40. Booking essential for non-residents. CC. **Directions:** Ennistymon road from town; 300m on left.

THE OLD SCHOOL B&B

CROSS CARRIGAHOLT LOOP HEAD CO CLARE
086 154 9402 I theoldschoolcross@gmail.com
www.loophead.ie/placestostay

STAY

Although plain from the road, here's nothing ordinary about The Old School, which is full of character and has USPs a-plenty - but what makes it extra special is the hospitality. Ian and Teresa Glendinning really enjoy sharing their home - and the area around it - with their guests, and it shows. Breakfast is a treat (fresh line caught mackerel might be on the menu if you're lucky) and packed lunches can happily be made up by arrangement. A perfect place to be based while you explore this wonderful area.

Rooms 3 (2 double, 1 family, all en-suite shower, 1 wheelchair friendly). B&B from €35pps, family room sleeping 3/4 €90 (€80 for children under 5). Prices include teas, coffees and home baking. Free wifi. Bike storage. Garden. Pets (only in downstairs rooms and caged). Open all year. **No CC.**

LINNANES LOBSTER BAR

NEW QUAY CO CLARE

065 707 8120 I linnanelobster@gmail.com

www.linnanesbar.com

EAT I DRINK

Eileen and Vincent Graham's cottagey pub-restaurant on the edge of the Burren is right on the sea at New Quay, with wonderful views across Galway Bay and a traditional bar with an open fire for chilly days. There are other options, but local fish, especially shellfish, is the draw: try the impressive Seafood Platter, big enough to share between two and good value too.

Seats 80 (+36 outdoors). Food served from 12.30 daily in summer. Winter Mon-Thu bar open from 5, Fri-Sun from 12, (food from 12.30). A la carte. CC. Full wheelchair access. **Directions:** On the coast road, midway between Kinvara and Ballyvaughan

MOUNT VERNON

FLAGGY SHORE NEW QUAY CO CLARE
065 707 8126 | info@mountvernon.ie
www.mountvernon.ie

STAY

Set back from the shore with views to the cliffs of Aughinish, you enter another place at Mount Vernon, a magical and historic country house whose owner, Mark Helmore, seems to have a special empathy with it. Spacious, interesting bedrooms have views over the sea or the wonderfully tended gardens, which include sheltered walled gardens with seating and a meadow with a grass path leading down to the Flaggy Shore, of Seamus Heaney fame. There's a leisurely feel and an emphasis on organic and local foods, including Mark's own vegetables and foraged samphire and seabeet from the shoreline.

Rooms 5 (4 en-suite, 1 with private bathroom). B&B from €80pps, two night min stay. Residents D nightly, must book. Closed 1 Jan-1 Apr. Dogs allowed by prior arrangement. CC. **Directions:** Signed off N67, between Kinvara and Ballyvaughan.

THE RUSSELL GALLERY

NEW QUAY THE BURREN CO CLARE

065 707 8185 | info@russellgallery.net

www.russellgallery.net

EAT | BUY

It's well worth factoring in a call to Andy and Stefania Russell's impressive yet visitor-friendly gallery when exploring this beautiful coastline. It's a delightful place, with a focus on fine art but also plenty of interesting small items at accessible prices for the casual visitor to enjoy. And they have a stylish little wine bar/café area on the ground floor too, offering really tasty light food - hearty soups, good home baking - and interesting wines, served at glass-topped tables with prints (for sale) displayed under the glass. Some local and speciality foods for sale too.

Open all year: Thu-Tue 11-6 (Sun from 12). Closed Wed. Art classes (adult and children); online sales. Check website for off-season hours. CC.

CARRYGERRY COUNTRY HOUSE

NEWMARKET-ON-FERGUS CO CLARE
061 360 500 I info@carrygerryhouse.com
www.carrygerryhouse.com

EAT I STAY

It's only 10 minutes from Shannon airport, yet Niall and Gillian Ennis's lovely 18th century residence is a world away, in a beautiful rural setting and overlooking the Shannon and Fergus estuaries. The ambience is very pleasant, with spacious, comfortable reception rooms, open fires and an hospitable atmosphere, as well as a high standard of accommodation. Niall's menus in The Conservatory Restaurant showcase local ingredients - especially seasonal herbs and vegetables - and they produce a range of speciality food products that make perfect small gifts.

Rooms 11 (4 shower only). B&B from €65pps. Restaurant **seats 50**. D Tue-Sat 6.30-9.30. Set D about €29, also à la carte. Small weddings/events. House closed 23-27 Dec, midweek Jan. CC. **Directions:** Near Shannon airport, on the old Newmarket-on-Fergus road: from N18 take Exit 9 onto N19; next roundabout take 4th exit; next roundabout 2nd exit; straight for 3km. Right at T-junction; house 1km, on right.

DROMOLAND CASTLE HOTEL

NEWMARKET-ON-FERGUS CO CLARE   EAT I STAY
061 368 144 I sales@dromoland.ie
www.dromoland.ie

The ancestral home of the O'Briens, barons of Inchiquin and direct descendants of Brian Boru, High King of Ireland, this is one of the few Irish estates tracing its history back to Gaelic royal families. It is now one of Ireland's grandest hotels and, in the warm and watchful care of General Manager Mark Nolan and his team, one of the best-loved. Outstanding service - notably by **Earl of Thomond Restaurant** Manager Tony Frisby and staff - and Executive Head Chef David McCann's outstanding food invariably match the surroundings.

⭐

Rooms 98 (1 wheelchair friendly); rooms from about €250. **Restaurant:** D daily, 7-10, Set D about €75; also à la carte. The Gallery 11-11, incl Afternoon Tea; The Fig Tree Restaurant at Dromoland Golf and Country Club, 10-9. Hotel open all year. SC 16.5%. CC. **Directions:** 11km from Shannon. Take N18 to Dromoland interchange; exit & follow signage.

RED CLIFF LODGE

SPANISH POINT CO CLARE   EAT | STAY
065 708 5756 | info@redclifflodge.ie
www.redclifflodge.ie

One of the top destinations in West Clare, John O'Meara's attractive thatched restaurant with accommodation overlooks Spanish Point Beach and offers both delicious food and spacious, luxuriously appointed suites - with kitchenettes and their own front door. Although informality and pocket-friendly pricing is emphasised, it's an impressive set-up, and sumptuously decorated - and the food is excellent.

Restaurant seats up to 75. D daily in summer, L Sun only (call to check hours, especially off season). Small weddings (80). **Rooms 6** (3 shower only). B&B from €60pps off season (from €85pps high season). Children welcome. One suite pet friendly. CC. Closed Nov-Jan. **Directions:** Off N67, southwest of Miltown Malbay; on R482 coast road south of Spanish Point Golf Club.

Dunmanus Bay
Co. Cork

COUNTY CORK

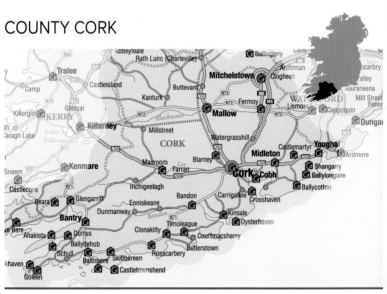

Cork is Ireland's largest county, and its individualistic people take pride in its variety, which ranges from the rich farmlands of the east to the handsome coastline of West Cork www.skibbereen.ie which is as much a state of mind as a place, where the light of the famous Fastnet Rock swings across tumbling ocean and spray-tossed headland.

In this extensive county, the towns and villages have their own distinctive character. In the west, their spirit is preserved in the vigour of the landscape. By contrast, East Cork's impressively prosperous farming country radiates towards the ancient estuary port of Youghal www.youghal.ie.

Multi-terraced and colourful Cobh www.visitcobh.com faces south over Cork Harbour, clearly asserting its own identity with a renewed sense of its remarkable maritime heritage being expressed in events such as a Sea Shanty Festival, while the town's direct link with the Titanic – Cobh was the ill-fated liner's last port of call – is also commemorated in many ways.

Different again in character is Kinsale www.kinsale.ie , a bustling sailing/fishing port which is home to many intriguing old buildings, yet is a place which is vibrantly modern in outlook, and has long been seen as Ireland's gourmet capital.

The county is a repository of the good things of life, a treasure chest of the finest farm produce, and the very best of seafood, brought to market by skilled specialists. As Ireland's most southerly county, it enjoys the mildest climate of all, and the well-lived life is seen at its most skilled in County Cork,

LOCAL ATTRACTIONS AND INFORMATION

>Bantry **Bantry House**
  www.bantryhouse.com | 027 50047
>Bantry **Murphy's International Mussel Fair** (May)
  C/O Westlodge Hotel 027 50360
>**Bantry Tourism Information**
  www.bantry.ie | 027 50229
>Blarney **Blarney Castle**

  www.blarneycastle.ie | 021 4385252
>**Carrigtwohill Fota Estate**
  (Wildlife Park, Arboretum) 021 481 2728
>Castletownbere **Mill Cove Gallery** (May to Sept.)
  027 70393
>Cobh **The Queenstown Story**
  www.cobhheritage.com | 021 4813591

>**Cork Airport** 021 4313131
>Glanmire **Dunkathel House** 021 482 1014
>Glengarriff **Garinish Island**
  www.glengarriff.ie | 027 63040
>Kinsale **Desmond Castle** 021 477 4855
>Kinsale **Tourism Information**
  www.kinsale.ie | 021 4772234
>Midleton **Jameson Heritage Centre**
  www.tours.jamesonwhiskey.com | 021 461 3594
>Millstreet **Country Park** 029 70810
>Mizen Head **Mizen Vision Signal Station**
  028 35115 I 35225

>Shanagarry **Ballymaloe Cookery School
  Gardens** www.cookingisfun.ie 021 4646785
>Schull **Ferries to Sherkin, Cape Clear and
  Fastnet** 028 28278
>Schull **Schull Planetarium** 028 28552
>Skibbereen **Tourism Information**
  www.skibbereen.ie | 028 21766
>**Slow Food Ireland** (c/o Glenilen Farm,
  Drimoleague) 028 31179 | 086 8141091

CORK CITY

It is Cork, of all Ireland's cities, which seems most warmly comfortable with itself, the heart of a land flowing in milk and honey. Cork is all about the good things in life. At its best, the southern capital has a Mediterranean atmosphere, and there's no doubting its Continental and cosmopolitan flavour, and Cork people's relaxed enjoyment of it all.

The central thoroughfare of St Patrick's Street is comfortably revitalised in a handsome and mainly pedestrianised style which is continued in the bustling urban network radiating from it, with streets which once were tidal rivers. The sense of the sea is never far away, and the potential of the city's old port area for sympathetic re-development is being actively progressed, while the vigour of business life is matched by a very active arts and entertainment scene, with a strong emphasis on music with the famous Cork Opera House www.corkoperahouse.ie

Cork's appreciation of natural produce, make it a favoured destination for connoisseurs. Trading in life's more agreeable commodities has always been what Cork and its legendary merchant princes are all about, and it continues to be unrivalled for the ready availability of superbly fresh produce, seen at its best in the famous English Market www.englishmarket.ie where Grand Parade meets Patrick Street.

The way in which sea and land intertwine throughout the sheltered natural harbour, and through the lively old city itself, has encouraged waterborne trade and a sea-minded outlook. Cork is at the heart of Ireland's most dynamically nautical area, a place world-renowned for its energetic interaction with the sea both for business or pleasure.

LOCAL ATTRACTIONS AND INFORMATION

>**Cork Airport**
  www.corkairport.com | 021 4313031
>**Cork Tourist Information**
  www.corkcity.ie | 021 425 5100
>**Guinness Cork Jazz Festival** (late October)
  www.guinnessjazzfestival.com | 021 421 5170
>**Cork International Film Festival** (October)
  www.corkfilmfest.org | 021 427 1711

>**English Market** (covered, with specialty food stalls),
  corner between Grand Parade & Patrick Street\
  www.englishmarket.ie | 021 4274407
>**Glucksman Gallery**, UCC
  www.glucksman.org | 021 490 1844
>**Good Food In Cork** (Consumer Group) –
  Cork Free Choice | 021 7330178
>**Railway Station** 021 450 4888

CAFÉ PARADISO

16 LANCASTER QUAY WESTERN ROAD CORK CO CORK   EAT

021 427 7939 | info@cafeparadiso.ie

www.cafeparadiso.ie

Since 1993, Denis Cotter's ground-breaking vegetarian restaurant has delighted diners with such exciting mainstream cooking that even the most committed of carnivores admit to relishing every mouthful, and it attracts devotees from all over Ireland - and beyond. Innovative, strongly seasonal menus are based on the best organic produce available, notably from Ultan Walsh of Gort-Na-Nain Farm near Nohoval. The cooking is never less than stunning and wines, carefully selected to complement the food, are all available in four sizes. Dennis Cotter's vision is shared in four beautiful, critically acclaimed cookbooks, available here and online.

⭐ **Seats 45** (+ 6 outdoors). Open Mon-Sat 5.30–10. Early D 5.30-6.30 Mon-Fri from about €23; Set D from about €33. B&B available as part of dinner package. Closed Sun, Christmas week. CC. **Directions:** On Western Road

CRAWFORD GALLERY CAFÉ

EMMET PLACE CORK CO CORK   EAT

021 427 4415 | crawfordcafe@gmail.com

www.crawfordartgallery.ie/dining.html

One of Cork city's favourite informal eating places since it was opened by the legendary Myrtle Allen of Ballymaloe House in 1986. This atmospheric café features artwork from the Crawford Collection and is currently run with style by Sineád Doran. The frequently-changed seasonal menus continue to reflect the Ballymaloe philosophy that food is precious and should be handled carefully, so freshly prepared dishes are made from natural local ingredients - and a meal here can be a real treat. Everything sings with flavour and the Crawford Gallery Café breakfast has become an institution in itself, especially on Saturday.

Seats 65. Open Mon-Sat, 8.30-4. A la carte. Closed Sun, bank hols, 10 days over Christmas. CC. **Directions:** City centre, next to Opera House.

FARMGATE CAFÉ

ENGLISH MARKET CORK CO CORK

021 427 8134 | farmgatecafe@yahoo.ie

www.farmgate.ie

EAT

A younger sister restaurant to the renowned Farmgate Country Store and Restaurant in Midleton, Kay Harte's Farmgate Café shares the same commitment to serving fresh, local food - and, as it is located in the gallery above the English Market where ingredients are purchased daily, it doesn't come much fresher or more local than this. Some dishes are unique - they make almost forgotten regional dishes using the food they buy in the market, and famous old Cork ones with a special market connection, like tripe & drisheen and corned beef & champ with green cabbage. A real education - and a delicious one too.

Seats 110. Meals Mon-Sat 8.30-5. B 8.30-11, L 12-3.30; wine from about €20. Closed Sun, bank hols, Dec 25-3 Jan. CC. **Directions:** English Market - off Oliver Plunkett Street and Grand Parade.

FLEMINGS RESTAURANT

SILVER GRANGE HOUSE TIVOLI CORK CO CORK

021 482 1621 | info@flemingsrestaurant.ie

www.flemingsrestaurant.ie

EAT | STAY

Overlooking the city at Tivoli, a large Georgian family house with a productive garden is home to Michael and Eileen Fleming's classical French restaurant with rooms. Michael is a pioneer of the Cork dining scene and Flemings is a model of timeless quality: his cooking is invariably excellent, presentation elegant, and the service both attentive and knowledgeable. A great antidote to the sameness of modern multicultural restaurants - a visit to a restaurant like this is a treat to treasure. Wine tastings and seasonal events are sometimes held here, also small weddings (90).

⭐

Seats 80 (+ 30 outdoors). L Tue-Sun, D Tue-Sat, 12.30-3; 6.30-10. Children welcome. Closed Sun D, Mon, 24-27 Dec. Accommodation: Four spacious en-suite rooms are comfortably furnished (B&B about €55pps). CC. **Directions:** Signed off main Cork-Dublin route, 4km from city centre.

HAYFIELD MANOR HOTEL

PERROTT AVENUE COLLEGE ROAD CORK CO CORK EAT | STAY
021 484 5900 | enquiries@hayfieldmanor.ie
www.hayfieldmanor.ie

Set in gardens near University College Cork, the city's premier hotel feels like a large period house and provides a remarkable level of privacy and seclusion, just a mile from the city centre. It also offers two destination dining choices: stylish bistro cooking in Perrotts Garden Bistro, which is popular with discerning Corkonians, or, for fine dining, the elegant evening restaurant Orchids, where 'Cork's Best Afternoon Tea' and a very good breakfast are served daily.

Rooms 88 (3 wheelchair friendly). B&B from about €99pps. Children welcome, pets by arrangement. Orchids: **Seats 90**. D Tue-Sat & bank hol Sun 7-9.30. Set D Thu-Sat, about €69, also à la carte. Aft Tea 1-2.30 (Fri-Sun 1& 3.30). Perrotts Garden Bistro: L&D daily 12.30-2.30 & 5.30-10.30. Bar food 11.30-5.30 daily. Spa, swimming pool. CC. **Directions:** Opposite University College Cork - signed off College Road.

HOTEL ISAACS & GREENES RESTAURANT

48 MACCURTAIN STREET CORK CO CORK EAT | STAY
021 450 0011 | cork@isaacs.ie
www.isaacscork.com

Opposite the Everyman Palace Theatre and approached through a cobbled courtyard, this attractive hotel offers comfortable spacious rooms (and some serviced apartments) at a fairly reasonable price. Some rooms at the back have a charming outlook onto a waterfall, which is floodlit at night. But its real USP is the destination Greenes Restaurant (www.greenesrestaurant.com), which has earned a national reputation and has a loyal following for the excellent ingredients-led cooking by well-known chef Bryan McCarthy, and friendly, professional staff. A newer wine/cocktail bar, Cask (www.caskcork.com), fronts onto MacCurtain Street.

⭐

Rooms 47 (4 shower only, 2 wheelchair friendly), B&B from €65pps. Greenes **Seats 100**: L Thu-Sun 12.15-2.15, (Wed to 2.30), from €22. D daily 5.30-9 (Thu-Sat to 9.30); early D 5.30-6.30 Thu-Sat (Sun-Wed to 7.30). Range of menus offered, also à la carte; barbecues in summer. Children welcome. Closed 24-27 Dec.

IDAHO.CAFÉ

19 CAROLINE STREET CORK CO CORK   EAT
021 427 6376 | www.idahocafe.ie

"Real food for real people" was the original motto of Richard and Mairead Jacob, whose small but perfectly formed café just behind BT has been providing a restorative treat in the city centre since 2001. The philosophy has been fine tuned down the years and, in a city of great food traditions but many faceless chain cafés, they not only source locally because it's best but 'because we believe in Ireland'. That aside, it's well worth the squeeze in this atmospheric spot for the simple but seriously delicious food (much of it home grown in season) great coffees, wholesome lunches and irresistible bakes - including a gorgeous coeliac friendly orange and almond cake that's been on the menu for ever. A one off.

Seats 30 (outdoors, 10). Open Tue-Sat, 8.30-5. Closed Sun, Mon, bank hols, 24-26 Dec. **No CC.**

IMPERIAL HOTEL

SOUTH MALL CORK CO CORK   EAT | STAY
021 427 4040 | info@imperialhotelcork.ie
www.flynnhotels.com

A Cork institution, this thriving hotel in the city's main commercial and banking centre dates back to 1813 and has a colourful history - Michael Collins spent his last night here, and that suite now bears his name. Recent renovations have brought new life to its fine old public areas - including the David Collins inspired bar, Seventy Six on the Mall, and stylish contemporary Pembroke Restaurant - and transformed the accommodation. And, for many, the Escape Spa is reason enough in itself to stay here.

Rooms 125 (12 shower only, 2 wheelchair friendly). Children welcome. Lift. Typical B&B €65pps. Pembroke Restaurant all meals daily. Lafayettes Brasserie: Mon-Fri 8-6 (Sat-Sun from 9.30). Destination spa. Closed bank hols. Hotel open all year. CC. **Directions:** City Centre

ISAACS RESTAURANT

48 MACCURTAIN STREET CORK CO CORK
021 450 3805 | Email: info@isaacsrestaurant.com
www.isaacsrestaurant.com

In 1992 Michael and Catherine Ryan, together with partner/head chef Canice Sharkey, opened this large, atmospheric modern restaurant in an 18th-century warehouse and it immediately struck a chord with people tired of having to choose between fine dining and fast food, a trend-setter in the modern Irish food movement. Ingredients are carefully sourced, the cooking is consistently accomplished and menus are freshened by occasional inspired introductions - and a visit here is always great fun.

Seats 120. L Mon-Sat 12.30-2.30, D daily 6-9.30 (Sun to 9) a la carte. Early D Wed-Sat 5.45-7, Mon & Tue to 9.30, 2/3 course €23/26. Wine from about €17. Children welcome. Closed L Sun, Christmas week, L Bank Holidays. CC.
Directions: 5 minutes from Patrick Street; opposite Gresham Metropole Hotel

JACQUES RESTAURANT

PHOENIX STREET CORK CO CORK   EAT
021 427 7387 | jacquesrestaurant@eircom.net
www.jacquesrestaurant.ie

An integral part of Cork life since 1982, sisters Eithne and Jacqueline Barry's delightful restaurant has changed with the years, evolving from quite a traditional place to a smart and - in recent years - much larger contemporary space. But the fundamentals of warm hospitality and great food never waiver and many would cite Jacques as their favourite Cork restaurant. Daytime is casual but evening menus recall the 'old' Jacques, showcasing carefully sourced (and sometimes unusual) ingredients from a network of suppliers built up over decades -which, in this creative kitchen, makes for magical meals.

⭐

Open Tue-Sat 10-9.30. L from 12 noon, à la carte; D, à la carte & Tapas Menu from 5.30. Early D from €24 (all night Tue-Thu, to 6.30 Fri- Sat), set D about €35. Children welcome. Closed Sun & Mon, 24-27 Dec. CC.

KINGSLEY HOTEL

CARRIGROHANE ROAD VICTORIA CROSS CORK CO CORK   EAT | STAY
021 480 0500 | info@thekingsley.ie
www.kingsley.ie

One of Cork's most attractively located hotels, this handsome riverside property is in the ownership of the Kang family of Beijing, who also own Fota Island Resort (www.fotaisland.ie). Just minutes from both Cork airport and the city centre, it has always been especially appealing to business visitors, and the comfortable, attractively situated public areas with river views (and very nice staff) make it a popular meeting place locally too. Spacious rooms include an impressive two-storey penthouse suite, and long stay apartments are available.

Rooms 131 (6 wheelchair friendly). Lift. Rooms from about €96. Restaurants: Springboard: D daily from 5, Sat-Sun from 12.30. Fairbanks: B'st daily, L Mon-Fri 12-5. The K Lounge 8-5. Afternoon Tea 12-5 (booking required). Bar food daily. Spa, swimming pool. Riverside walk. Open all year. CC. **Directions:** On main N25 Killarney road by Victoria Cross.

L'ATITUDE 51

1 UNION QUAY CORK CO CORK   EAT | DRINK
021 239 0219 | info@latitude51.ie
www.latitude51.ie

Billing itself as a wine café this quirky city centre riverside venue is part tapas bar, part wine bar with a distinctly continental flair. Open for quality coffee (Fermoy-roasted Badger & Dodo) and pastries in the morning, a short weekday lunch menu comprises imaginative soup, sandwiches on Arbutus bread and a daily hot dish. But the evening tapas menu is the real draw, with a selection of European and artisan ingredients served up as delicious taster plates.

Open Mon-Fri from 9.30, Sat from 4. L Mon-Fri 12.30-3. Evening menu daily 6-10, tapas, small and large plates.

LES GOURMANDISES RESTAURANT

17 COOK STREET CORK CO CORK   EAT

021 425 1959 | info@lesgourmandises.ie

www.lesgourmandises.ie

Just off South Mall, this little restaurant feels like an outpost of France - the menu at the neatly presented entrance will draw you in, and you'll be glad you noticed it. It's run by Patrick and Soizic Kiely - both formerly of Restaurant Patrick Guilbaud - but, although that says a lot about the key standards, there's nothing flash about the quiet style of this restaurant which offers stylish cooking with great flavour, based on the day's market and with local suppliers listed. It's understandably popular and reservations are strongly advised.

⭐

Seats 55. D Tue-Sat 6-9.30. Early D from about €27.50, available all evening Tue-Fri, Sat 6-7. Set D from about €40. Tapas Sharing Menus Tue-Fri. Also à la carte. House wine about €30. Children welcome before 7pm. Closed Sun & Mon. CC

MARKET LANE RESTAURANT & BAR

5 & 6 OLIVER PLUNKETT STREET CORK CO CORK   EAT | DRINK

021 427 4710 | info@marketlane.ie

www.marketlane.ie

Judy Howard, Tracy Corbett and Conrad Howard own this bustling two-storey restaurant and bar near the English Market. The flagship restaurant of a quality-led group (ORSO Kitchen Bar, Castle Café at Blackrock Castle and Elbow Lane, with Elbow Lane Brew & Smokehouse/ nanobrewery), it is a friendly and welcoming place with a lively atmosphere. They offer real value for money and ingredients come first, with fresh and flavoursome artisan produce from the English Market used - and, following investment in the Green Space organic hydroponics system producing food in the city centre, the already low food miles have been reduced even further.

Mon-Sat 12–9.30 (later Thu-Sat), Sun 1-9.30. A la carte. Early D about €25, Mon-Thu 5-7, Sun 1-7. Open most bank hols 1-9. Closed Good Fri, 25-26 Dec. CC. **Directions**: At Parnell Place end of Oliver Plunkett Street.

MARYBOROUGH HOTEL & SPA

MARYBOROUGH HILL DOUGLAS CORK CO CORK   EAT | STAY
021 436 5555 | info@maryborough.ie
www.maryborough.com

Quietly situated on the south of the city and very convenient to Cork airport and the Jack Lynch Tunnel, this very family-friendly privately owned hotel has a fine country house at its heart. A popular meeting place, with spacious public areas overlooking gardens and good food, it has well designed modern rooms and excellent leisure facilities. At Bellini's - a destination restaurant rather than hotel dining room - Chef Gemma Murphy has earned a local following for imaginative cooking and her thoughtfully planned menus offer an ambitious range of contemporary dishes that showcase local produce with style.

Rooms 93 (8 wheelchair friendly). Lift. B&B abut €75pps. Bellinis: L&D daily 12.30-2.30, 6.30-9.30. Set L about €30, D à la carte. Closed 24-26 Dec. CC. **Directions:** Adjacent to Douglas Golf Club; signed from roundabout where Rochestown Road meets Carrigaline Road.

MIYAZAKI

1A EVERGREEN STREET BALLYPHEHANE CORK CO CORK   EAT | BUY
021 431 2716 | miyazakicork@gmail.com
www.facebook.com/miyazakicork

Open since 2015, this tiny restaurant/takeaway on a busy city junction quickly established itself as a cult destination - and no wonder as Takashi Miyazaki's cooking is a revelation. The essential ingredient is Miyazaki's dashi broth, which brings the pleasant savoury 'fifth taste', Umami, to many of the dishes. Take your pick from the authentic flavours of Japan, from the Miyazaki treasure box. From Sushi Rolls to Bento boxes, from Noodle Dishes to Donburi specials and a whole lot more. A real Japanese jewel.

Open Tue-Sun, 1-4 & 5-9. Closed Mon. Multi-storey parking nearby. CC. **Directions:** City centre, south of English Market; junction of R608 and R8511. Look for large mural of geisha girl on exterior wall facing junction.

MONTENOTTE HOTEL

MIDDLE GLANMIRE ROAD MONTENOTTE CORK

021 453 0050 | info@themontenottehotel.com

www.themontenottehotel.com

STAY | EAT

Perched high over the city in a fashionable residential area, the Montenotte offers a pleasant alternative to city centre accommodation with good leisure facilities, smartly refurbished bedrooms, and an appealing dining set-up in the aptly named Panorama Bistro and Terrace, where all meals are served. Bistro menus have broad appeal (Beef Wellington is the house speciality) and give a nod to Cork's food traditions. All round a desirable destination - it was always a special location but, since recent investment, the standard now matches the view.

Rooms 108 (includes family rooms). Lift. B&B from about €65pps. Breakfast (non residents welcome) from 6.30am (w/e 7.30) brunch 10-12. L 12-3 (Sun L 2 sittings, 1 & 3), D 6-9.45; bar menu 3-9.45; Afternoon Tea 12-4 (reservations required). Leisure centre (swimming pool). Meeting rooms. Wi-Fi; free parking. No pets. CC.

English Market, Cork

GROWN BY
MR. RAY ANDERSON
ROSCARBERRY. CO.CORK

NASH 19 RESTAURANT

19 PRINCES STREET CORK CO CORK
021 427 0880 | info@nash19.com
www.nash19.com

EAT | BUY

Home from home for its many loyal customers since 1992, Claire Nash's bustling city centre restaurant is just a stone's throw from the English Market – the source of much of the local and indigenous produce they are known for, including vegetables, fresh sustainable catches and meats. A small but carefully chosen wine selection (mainly from small producers) changes regularly and all the very friendly staff are barista trained. 'Simple food cooked honestly' is their mantra, and it's a very child friendly place too, offering proper wholesome meals for little ones. In Claire Nash's own words 'We simply love our food! - and it shows.

Seats 110. Open Mon-Fri, 7.30-5 (Sat from 8.30). L menu 12.15-3.30. Shop open to 5.30. Children welcome. Closed, Sun, Dec 25-27, Jan 1&2, 3rd week Jan.

ON THE PIG'S BACK

UNIT 26 ST PATRICK'S WOOLLEN MILLS DOUGLAS CORK CO CORK   EAT | BUY

021 461 7832 | info@onthepigsback.ie

www.onthepigsback.ie

French woman Isabelle Sheridan's reputation in Cork was already established at her brilliant shop selling charcuterie, farmhouse cheeses and other gourmet products in the English Market, long before she opened up this branch of On the Pig's Back in Douglas. Here she has a lovely, lively deli and café, in a quirky room with a large tree as its centrepiece, where you may sit down and enjoy some great food when doing your shopping. As would be expected of Isabelle, it's all about the produce which, in both the café and the deli, features a wonderful selection from top local producers such as Kanturk's Jack McCarthy butchers, Arbutus Bread, Caherbeg Pork, G's Jams, and many more trusted names - and some carefully chosen French produce too, imported directly.

Seats 80. Open 7 days: Mon-Sat 9-3.30 (lunch 12-3); Sun Brunch 10-3.

RACHELS

28 WASHINGTON STREET CORK CO CORK
021 427 4189 | dine@rachels.ie
www.rachels.ie

EAT | DRINK

The popular Irish cook Rachel Allen - a graduate of, and teacher at, Ballymaloe Cookery School - owns this bright and contemporary restaurant and cocktail bar in the Courthouse Chambers in Cork city centre. It's a beautifully decorated and appointed venue, and Rachel Allen and chef Anne Zagar have worked together to design seasonal menus drawing on both classical and modern styles. Local food credentials are predictably strong here, including fresh fish straight from Ballycotton Bay and free range pork from Shanagarry. The end result is food that is fresh, delicious and nutritious - with warm and efficient service to match.

Seats 102. Open Mon-Sat from 12. L 12-12.30. D 5-11. Closed Sun. All cards.

THE RIVER LEE HOTEL

WESTERN ROAD CORK CO CORK   EAT | DRINK | STAY
021 425 2700 | cork@doylecollection.com
www.doylecollection.com

This modern Leeside property is one of Cork's most popular hotels, especially perhaps for business guests. Imaginatively designed to make the most of its riverside location, all the main public areas have balconies, including the aptly-named Weir Bistro where Head Chef Paul Lane and an enthusiastic team showcase local produce in classic modern cooking and serve it in a unique waterside setting. The uncluttered and very comfortable bedrooms are designed and finished to an unusually high specification, and leisure facilities are also excellent.

Rooms 182 (4 wheelchair friendly). Rooms from about €148. Lift. Weir Rooms (www.theweir.ie): From 6.30am daily, D 6-9.30. Set D from about €28.50, also à la carte; bar food daily. Leisure centre (swimming pool, gym, spa). Underground parking. Open all year. CC. **Directions:** On left, shortly before University College Cork. Watch closely for signs in one-way system

ARUNDELS BY THE PIER

KITCHEN COVE AHAKISTA CO CORK   EAT | DRINK

027 67033 | arundelsbythepier@gmail.com
www.arundelsbythepier.com

A welcome stopping place on the Sheep's Head Way, this delightful harbourside pub has been in the Arundel family for over 100 years and current owners, Shane and Fiona Arundel, have modernised without losing the spirit of the old bar. Managed with warmth by Liam and Eilis Hodnett, it's known for easy hospitality and the good food of the area - especially seafood - served in the bar, first floor restaurant and outdoors. French chef Dominique

Carucci, rustles up a wide range of tasty dishes - with some of the simplest, such as homemade Fish & Chips with mushy peas, topping the polls in the bar.

Open daily in summer, food served 12.30-8.30. Some outdoor tables in secure play area; children's menu. Bar open all year, food weekends only off season - advisable to check. CC. **Directions:** At Ahakista pier.

HERON GALLERY CAFÉ & GARDENS

AHAKISTA DURRUS CO CORK   EAT | BUY

027 67278 | annabellangrish@gmail.com
www.herongallery.ie

Artist Annabel Langrish's gallery and café is one of the most charming spots in this delightful corner. There's a collection of her current work, and accessibly priced gift items (many based on her paintings); also a lovely simple café which has seating outdoors in informal gardens which are open to visitors and supply much of the fresh organic produce used in the kitchen. To enjoy a slice of quiche and salad straight from the garden

here, or a gorgeous freshly-baked scone with home made jam and a cup of Fairtrade coffee - perhaps accompanied only by birdsong - is a very special treat.

Open Easter-end Aug, 10.30-5.30 daily. Mainly vegetarian. Picnics available to order. Supervised children & well-behaved dogs welcome in garden. Free wifi. **Directions:** Just outside Ahakista village, signed from the coast road after Arundel's pub.

DIVA BOUTIQUE BAKERY, CAFÉ & DELI

MAIN STREET BALLINSPITTLE CO CORK **EAT | BUY | PRODUCER**
021 477 8465 | diva.ballinspittle@gmail.com
www.divaboutiquebakery.com

Whatever the time, Ballinspittle is the perfect place for a journey break to visit Seattle native Shannen Keane's brilliant daytime bakery, café & deli. On one side of the main street you'll find the Diva bakery and food store and, across the road, the busy cafe, serving up breakfast, lunch and more besides. Expect the simple stuff, done really well: very special breads (many of them sourdough), terrific cakes, brilliant breakfasts (the German Breakfast, perhaps, or the Veggie Breakfast Wrap), superb sambos and wraps - and great local produce on sale too. Worth a detour.

> Open Tue-Sat: 9.30-5, Sun 11-5. CC. Directions: From Cork/Kinsale, follow signs from the Kinsale bridge on the R600 west.

GARRYVOE HOTEL

BALLYLONGANE GARRYVOE CO CORK **EAT | STAY**
021 464 6718 | Email: res@garryvoehotel.com
www.garryvoehotel.com

Across the road from the five-mile-long blue flag beach at Ballycotton Bay and with wonderful views of the Ballycotton lighthouse perched atop its tiny island, the Garryvoe is a magical family holiday destination and, with its generous rooms and wide range of amenities (including wheelchair accessibility in all areas), it has particular appeal for multi-generational groups. It's also a popular wedding and conference venue, making it an all year destination - and, like its more seasonal sister, the Bayview Hotel at Ballycotton (www.thebayviewhotel.com), it has a well-earned reputation for great food and friendly service. A good base for exploring the many attractions of East Cork.

> **Rooms 84** (4 wheelchair friendly). Room rate from about €75. Samphire Restaurant: D about €40 also à la carte. Health club (swimming pool). CC. **Directions:** Take Ladysbridge turning, R632, off main Cork-Youghal road in Castlemartyr.

PIER 26 RESTAURANT

THE PIER BALLYCOTTON CO CORK

EAT

021 2061449 | pier26restaurant@yahoo.com

www.facebook.com/pier26restaurant

A jaunty blackboard welcomes visitors to Ballycotton harbour into Colin Hennessy and Holly FitzGerald's appealing restaurant. It takes up a couple of rooms at The Inn by the Harbour pub and, while simple, is a very pleasant venue, with sea views on two sides which adds to the experience in fine weather. As to the food, it is a delight. Seafood is of course the speciality but Colin, who is the chef, aims equally to showcase 'the harvest of our local farms'. Simply and carefully cooked, every dish is appealingly presented without undue fuss, served with efficiency and charm - and tastes wonderful. No wonder this pleasing restaurant is so successful, it is well worth the journey.

Open: Wed-Thu, 530-9, Fri-Sat 5.30-9.30, Sun 12.30-7.30. (Times may vary seasonally) 2/3 course Early D from about €21, also à la carte. CC.

BUDDS

MAIN STREET BALLYDEHOB CO CORK

EAT | BUY

028 25842 | hi@budds.ie

www.budds.ie

Even before you've looked at a menu at Jamie and Emma Budd's lovely café-deli this place is working its magic - the counter displays all things delicious (huge chocolate chip cookies, delectable desserts), a chill cabinet is chock-a-block with super salads and craft beers, and shelves are crammed with carefully selected speciality foods and drinks. Great sandwiches, local food platters and hot dishes too, with carefully selected drinks to match. A great place to know about.

Seats 31 (+10 outside); open from 9 daily in summer. B'fst, L à la carte, set D about €40 from 6. Children's menu. Wheelchair accessible. Check opening off season. Closed Dec 25-26. CC. **Directions:** Street-side, midway through village.

LEVIS CORNER HOUSE

CORNER HOUSE MAIN STREET BALLYDEHOB CO CORK

DRINK

028 37118 I leviscornerhouse@gmail.com
www.leviscornerhouse.com

The Levis sisters, Julia and Nell, ran this 150-year-old bar and grocery for as long as anyone can remember and, after their deaths, it was taken over by their great-nephew, Joe O'Leary, who is a musician. Traditional music sessions have always been held here and Joe is a natural publican who values the tradition that goes with the pub. So the iconic shelves of groceries, the dressers and the sofas remain, but he has brought new life with his musical connections - and, while still a great traditional pub, this friendly place is now also one of West Cork's best small music venues. A true gem.

Opening times vary. Closed 25 Dec & Good Fri. **Directions:** Main street, opposite Budds.

MANNINGS EMPORIUM

BALLYLICKEY BANTRY CO CORK

BUY I EAT

027 50456 I lauracmanning@gmail.com
www.manningsemporium.ie

Once a classic country post office and shop, this famous roadside gourmet food store, deli and café is now an Aladdin's cave of good things - and not a place to pass by. A supporter of local West Cork artisan produce for many years, Val Manning is rightly credited for his important role in the Irish food revolution - and now his equally enthusiastic niece, Laura Manning, and her husband Andrew Heath, run this West Cork institution with the same dedication. West Cork cheeses in perfect condition are the crowning glory of their large and carefully selected stock in season and, while the delicious menus are wide ranging, many travel for the simple cheeseboards and charcuterie platters.

Open 8.30-6, Sat 9-9, Sun 9-5. Closed Mon-Tue off season. Themed food evenings in summer. Online shop (hampers). **Directions:** On N71 at Ballylickey.

SEAVIEW HOUSE HOTEL

BALLYLICKEY BANTRY CO CORK

027 50462 | info@seaviewhousehotel.com

www.seaviewhousehotel.com

EAT | STAY

Famous for many years for the exceptional hospitality extended by former owner Kathleen O'Sullivan, a genuine welcome and personal supervision remain the hallmarks of this restful country house hotel overlooking Bantry Bay. It is now owned by Miss O'Sullivan's nephew, Ronan, who is maintaining the much-loved traditional characteristics while also introducing subtle changes which will appeal to a new market seeking active holidays. Family antiques add warmth and character, and many rooms have sea views. Country house cooking is the style in the elegant restaurant where local produce, especially seafood, stars.

Rooms 25 (1 shower only, 2 wheelchair friendly). No lift. B&B from about €75pps. Restaurant **Seats 50**; children welcome. Toilets wheelchair accessible. D 7-10 daily, from about €30. Hotel closed mid Nov-mid Mar. CC. **Directions:** On N71 between Bantry and Glengarriff.

GLEBE HOUSE GARDENS

GLEBE GARDENS BALTIMORE CO CORK

028 20232 | info@glebegardens.com

www.glebegardens.com

EAT | BUY

Jean and Peter Perry's wonderful gardens just outside Baltimore attract a growing number of visitors each year and they have not only a delightful café for those in need of a restorative daytime bite, but a destination restaurant too. This wholesomely delicious food operation is run by the four Perry sisters, Tessa, Keziah, JoJo and Mia, but in summer 2017 they upped the ante by introducing celebrated Cork-born chef, Rob Krawczyk, to the team for an 8-week residency, adding an exciting dimension to the cooking and making this already excellent place one to watch.

Gardens and Café open Easter-Sep, Sat-Sun 10-5. Restaurant D Tue-Sat from 7pm in summer. Small shop; plants, preserves etc for sale. **No CC. Directions:** Off Skibbereen-Baltimore road: entrance directly opposite 'Baltimore' sign as you enter the village.

MEWS RESTAURANT

BALTIMORE CO CORK

028 20572 | mewswestcork@gmail.com

www.mewsrestaurant.ie

EAT

Down a laneway near the square, the Mews Restaurant is a distinctive low-beamed stone building, reminiscent of Brittany, with a sun room attached that floods the small restaurant with light. While perhaps an unlikely place to find an ambitious fine dining destination, that's just what this atmospheric place is. The team may vary each season, but their huge enthusiasm and love for what they do is unchanging. It's all about 'terroir' and, whether at one of the elegantly appointed tables or the convivial Chef's Table, it's a lovely place in which to enjoy outstanding local foods - and bound to be a memorable experience.

⭐

Open Mar-Sep. D from 6, about €45, (May, Wed-Sat; Jun-Aug, Tue-Sat; also bank hol Sundays); advisable to check opening, especially off season; reservations advised. Mention any dietary requirements when booking. CC. **Directions:** Village centre.

ROLF'S COUNTRY HOUSE & RESTAURANT

BALTIMORE HILL BALTIMORE CO CORK EAT | STAY
028 20289 | info@rolfscountryhouse.com
www.rolfscountryhouse.com

The Haffner family opened this delightful place in 1979 and the complex - a traditional farmhouse with fine old stone outbuildings - has been upgraded in recent years without loss of character. Quietly situated in lovely gardens, accommodation includes well-equipped self-catering cottages as well as B&B. Chef-owner Johannes Haffner uses home-grown, organic and local produce in both the daytime café (in summer) and evening restaurant and wine bar (all year). As well as local seafood, his menus offer more meats - and game, in season - than others in the area, perhaps also classics and retro dishes not seen elsewhere.

Rooms 10 (shower only), B&B from €40pps; children welcome, pets by arrangement. Meals, daily: B 8-11, L (summer) 12-2.30, D 6-9. Toilets wheelchair accessible. Closed 24-26 Dec. CC. *Self catering cottages. **Directions:** 10 minute walk up hill from village.

SLIPWAY

THE COVE BALTIMORE CO CORK   STAY
028 20134 | theslipway@hotmail.com
www.theslipway.com

Quietly located away from the bustle around the square, but within 10 minutes walk of several excellent restaurants, Wilmie Owen's unusual house is a little gem. The rooms (and shower rooms) are compact but there are uninterrupted views of the harbour and distant seascape from all the bedrooms, and some also have access to the pretty garden - and breakfast is served in a lovely first floor room overlooking the harbour.

Rooms 4 (all shower only); self-catering also available. Usually closed Nov-Mar, but phone to check, open over New Year. Not suitable for children; no pets. Prices vary. **No CC. Directions:** Through Baltimore village, to the Cove, 500 metres.

THE WATERFRONT

THE SQUARE BALTIMORE CO CORK   EAT | DRINK | STAY
028 20600 | info@waterfrontbaltimore.ie
www.waterfrontbaltimore.ie

This stylish hotel development, completed in 2008, is marked by the late Youen Jacob's commitment to quality - it doesn't merely fit into the square, it completes it. Now run by his son, Youen, and his wife Kate, it has generous big rooms (with lovely bathrooms), warmth and vibrancy. Some of the long-established Chez Youen dishes are still on the menu at the aptly-named first-floor Lookout Restaurant, and their continental-style café, the very popular La Jolie Brise Pizza & Grill, spills out cheerfully on to the square.

Rooms 13 (3 shower only). B&B from about €50pps. Bar meals 12.30-9 daily. Lookout Restaurant (with bar): open daily from 6.30 in season. Hotel open weekends only off season. Closed 24/25 Dec. CC. **Directions:** On the waterfront, overlooking the harbour.

THE POACHERS INN

CLONAKILTY ROAD BANDON CO CORK
023 884 1159 | poachersinn@gmail.com
www.poachersinnbandon.com

EAT | DRINK | LEARN

Seafood is the speciality at Barry and Catherine McLoughlin's smart blue and white painted bar and restaurant just outside Bandon. Fresh local produce is central to this kitchen and Barry's wonderfully flavourful dishes are based on freshest seafood from Castletownbere and other nearby ports; everything is cooked to order and service is excellent - the focus here is on pleasing the customer.

Restaurant: **Seats 50** (+ 10 outdoors). Open Mon-Thu 12-3 & 5.30-9, Fri & Sat from 12, Sun 12.30-7.30, bank hols 12-7.30. Set D Wed-Sat from 7, about €35. Early D to 9 Mon & Thu, (to 7 pm Wed-Sun), from about €24. Children welcome. D reservations required. Free wifi. Toilets wheelchair accessible. Cookery school. House closed 25 Dec. CC. **Directions:** On the main West Cork road heading out of Bandon, right hand side.

URRU CULINARY STORE

THE MILL MCSWINEY QUAY BANDON CO CORK
023 885 4731 | info@urru.ie
www.urru.ie

EAT | BUY

People come from afar to shop at Ruth Healy's stylish, modern culinary store on the river - and a stop en route to holiday in West Cork has become de rigeur. A kitchen shop, deli, foodstore and café, it has always offered a unique combination of quality products hand-picked because they're special - and great coffees and teas, to sip with your artisan snack. You can stock up on fresh produce too, including local honey, farm milk and garden flowers - and Ruth always has some interesting new foods to try, from innovative producers.

Seats 16. Open Mon-Sat 8-6. Wine from shop, €5 corkage. Closed Sun (also Mon Sep-Oct & Feb-Mar), bank hols, 25-28 Dec. CC. **Directions:** Entering Bandon from Cork, turn right at Methodist church, then immediate left. River on right, shop on left at end of quay.

BANTRY HOUSE & GARDEN

BANTRY HOUSE & GARDEN BANTRY CO CORK EAT | STAY | BUY
027 50047 | info@bantryhouse.com
www.bantryhouse.com

Whether as a destination stay in their beautiful rooms, or for refreshment when visiting the house and garden at the Shelswell-White family's 18th century mansion overlooking Bantry Bay, (both open to the public), a visit to their Tearoom is highly recommended. Once you have seen the mouth-watering food laid out for display, you will be very glad you chose to come here - and the elegant surroundings and wooded walks are wonderful.

Afternoon Tea (pre-booked) is also available, in The Library.

House and Garden open mid Apr-end Oct, 10-5 (Jun-Aug 7 days, off season Tue-Sun). B&B from about €85pps.
Tearoom: times as House & Garden. Pre-concert D, before events at the house. Set L for groups of up to 35 (pre-booked). Children welcome. Wheelchair access to public areas & toilets. CC. **Directions:** Main car park located off N71 entering Bantry town.

FISH KITCHEN

NEW STREET BANTRY CO CORK EAT
027 56651 | thefishkitchen@gmail.com
www.thefishkitchen.ie

This agreeable little restaurant is above the Central Fish Market - and the location is no coincidence, as Colman Keohane and Anne Marie Murphy, owners of the fish shop and restaurant respectively, are siblings. Much of the simply cooked fish and seafood comes from Bantry Bay, and the real story at the Fish Kitchen is told on the blackboard daily specials list - which is where you'll also find out about the craft beers offered to complement the wine list. 'Freshness, simplicity, quality' are the buzz words here and that's what keeps their happy customers coming back.

Seats 28. Open Tue-Sat L 12-3pm D 5.30-9pm. Closed Sun & Mon. Open all year. CC. **Directions:** Town centre – above the Central Fish Market.

ORGANICO CAFE SHOP BAKERY

2 GLENGARRIFF ROAD BANTRY CO CORK EAT | BUY
027 51391 | info@organico.ie
www.organico.ie

Sisters Hannah and Rachel Dare run this highly popular bakery, food shop and vegetarian café near the centre of town. Spelt loaves are a particular speciality at the bakery, which produces an irresistible range of breads, cakes and pizza, and many others are also offered at the café, where Rachel, a Ballymaloe-trained cook, is the force behind menus that inspire a dedicated following.

Seats 50. Open Mon-Sat, 9.30-5.30. L 12-3.30. Closed Sun, bank hols, 24 Dec -mid Jan. CC. **Directions:** On road from Main Square to Glengarriff, 3 minutes walk from tourist office.

THE SNUG

THE QUAY BANTRY CO CORK

027 50057 | www.thesnug.ie

EAT | DRINK

Maurice and Colette O'Donovan's well-named bar in Bantry is a cosy and welcoming place, bustling with life and ideal for a wholesome bite at moderate prices - a real unpretentious Irish pub and all the better for that. Maurice is the chef and he takes pride in using local produce and giving value for money; his menus feature a wide range of favourites - including Bantry Bay mussels, of course. The Snug is one of West Cork's most likeable and consistent pubs and its popularity is well deserved - the wholesome fare and ambience, together with good value and good company, keeps 'em coming back for more.

Food served Mon-Sat 10-9.30 (off season to 9), Sun 12.30-9.30 (off season to 9). Closed 25 Dec. CC. **Directions:** Beside Garda Station, on the quay as you enter Bantry.

THE STUFFED OLIVE

2A BRIDGE STREET BANTRY CO CORK

027 55883 | thestuffedolive@gmail

www.facebook.com/pg/TheStuffedOlive

EAT | BUY

Welcoming aromas of coffee and the sight of happy customers tucking in at the appealing pavement tables introduce passers-by to a cornucopia of fine fare at The Stuffed Olive: excellent coffee by Cork Coffee Roasters, delicious freshly baked cakes and desserts, filled homemade baps and salads from the blackboard menu (also soup, homemade pies and individual quiches, falafels and quinoa burgers). Run by Patricia Messom along with her daughters Sarah and Grace O'Shea, this delightful little shop and deli is proud to fly the flag for local producers and it's crammed with specialist foods and wines. Great food to go, as well as on-site treats.

Open Mon-Sat 8.30am-6pm. Closed Sun. Open all year. Catering offered. Wifi. **No CC. Directions:** Town centre, opposite SuperValu.

RHONWEN'S EYERIES BISTRO

EYERIES BEARA CO CORK

027 74884 | rhonwen@eyeriesbistro.ie
www.eyeriesbistro.ie

Run by chef Rhonwen Lewis, her parents Caroline and Tony Lowes, and three of her siblings, this appealing family-run restaurant and gallery in picturesque Eyeries is a real find for travellers, offering good home cooking, local art works and a deliciously affordable menu (including for children), with options for vegetarians, vegans, and gluten-free diets. The sunny back garden is a pleasant spot to relax on a warm afternoon and, regardless of the weather or season, Rhonwen's Eyeries Bistro will be a very good place to be - you'll be glad you found it. 'Be welcome and eat well!' is Rhonwen's motto, and she means it.

Open Tue-Thu 1-8.30, Fri-Sun 12.30-8.30 in summer. Closed Mon. A la carte. Phone call advised to check hours, especially off season. **No CC. Also at:** Rhonwens Beara Bistro, Main Street, Castletownbere; www.facebook.com/ RhonwensBearaBistro.

BLAIRS INN

CLOGHROE BLARNEY CO CORK
021 438 1470 | blairsinn@gmail.com
www.blairsinn.ie

EAT | DRINK

In a quiet, wooded setting near Blarney, this pretty riverside pub is run by John and Anne Blair and their sons Duncan and Richie, a warmly hospitable family who take real pride in welcoming visitors. Duncan, who trained at Ballymaloe, works alongside a long-established kitchen team - and they are well known for the quality of the food. Skilfully cooked meals feature plenty of Cork and Kerry produce, notably local Angus beef and seafood, in wholesome dishes, and an impressive range of craft beers and ciders is offered.

Seats 45 (restaurant/bar) & 100 in garden. Bar menu 12.30-9.30 daily. Restaurant L & D à la carte; wine from about €23. Closed 25 Dec & Good Fri. CC. **Directions:** 5 minutes from Blarney village, on the R579.

THE SQUARE TABLE

5 THE SQUARE BLARNEY CO CORK   EAT
021 438 2825 | info@thesquaretable.ie
wwwthesquaretable.ie

Now an established dining destination, Martina and Tricia Cronin are serving up really good things here in the heart of Blarney. The experienced sisters offer Irish cuisine, with a hint of French, based on the best of seasonal local produce. Martina is the chef (ex Chapter One and The Residence) while Tricia works front of house, and what you get when spending an evening at The Square Table is effectively fine dining in an informal setting. Expect both classic and innovative cooking, some local specialities - maybe spiced beef, for example - outstanding poultry and seafood, and lovely service. A little gem.

Open Wed-Sat 6- 10. Early D Wed-Thu 6-9, Fri-Sat 6-7 (from about €25), also a la carte. L Sun only, 12.30-4.30 from about €20. House wine about €23. Closed Mon & Tue; early Jan to Feb. CC.

CASTLEMARTYR RESORT

CASTLEMARTYR CO CORK   EAT | STAY
021 421 9000 | reception@castlemartyrresort.ie
www.castlemartyrresort.ie

Built around a 17th century manor house and the ruins of an adjacent castle that belonged to the Knights Templar, this impressive property dates back to 1210 and its sheer spaciousness is the trump card for many guests. The low-impact modern design entails some very long corridors but the huge rooms are predictably luxurious, likewise amenities that include a destination leisure centre and spa. Dining options range from fine dining to casual, and there's no shortage of fine local ingredients for Executive Chef Kevin Burke to call on.

Rooms 103 (8 wheelchair friendly). Room rate from about €120. Lift. Children welcome. Pets permitted (charge). Leisure centre, swimming pool; spa. Self-catering available. Restaurants: Bell Tower (fine dining, D daily, L Sun), Franchini's (Italian, D daily) Knight's Bar (informal, à la carte daily). Helipad. Open all year. CC. **Directions:** On N25 between Midleton and Youghal.

BEARA COAST HOTEL

CAMETRINGANE POINT CASTLETOWNBERE CO CORK
027 71446 | reception@bearacoast.com
www.bearacoast.com

STAY I EAT

In 2015 hoteliers Mark Golden and Mark Johnston purchased the old hotel overlooking Castletownbere harbour - and, determined to provide a year round amenity, began a new chapter for the town. Now, the bedrooms in this friendly hotel have all been stylishly refurbished and Mark Johnston and his kitchen team provide varied bar food every day as well as fine dining at weekends. The conference and banqueting facilities are popular all year for weddings and other events. This busy, big-hearted hotel is a huge asset to the area, and it is good to see it thriving.

Rooms 16 (1 suite, 1 junior suite, 1 family room). Rooms from about €150. The Coastal Re staurant: D Fri-Sun from 6pm. L Sun only, 12.30-4pm, about €25. Arches Bar: food daily, 12.30-9. *Call to check hours and prices advised, especially off season. CC.

MACCARTHY'S

THE SQUARE CASTLETOWNBERE CO CORK   EAT I DRINK

027 70014 I amac08@gmail.com
www.maccarthysbar.com

Dating back to the 1870s, Adrienne MacCarthy's famous old pub and grocery store really is the genuine article and the family history is both intriguing and inspiring (just ask about her father's Japanese sword - or buy the book behind the bar). Atmosphere and live traditional music are the most obvious attractions of this terrific place, but the grocery is real and provisions the local fishing boats. You can also get a very good, simple bite to eat here - a superb freshly-made crab sandwich perhaps, bulging with spanking fresh crabmeat, and a big pot of tea - for amazingly little. One to savour.

Food available Mon-Sat, 10.30am-6pm. Closed 25 Dec. **No CC.. Directions:** In town square.

THE CASTLE

THE CASTLE CASTLETOWNSHEND CO CORK

EAT | STAY

028 36100 | bookings@castle-townshend.com

www.castle-townshend.com

The Townshend family's fascinating and beautifully located property opened for guests as a boutique B&B in 2016, offering a unique opportunity to stay in one of Ireland's most interesting historic houses. Much of the original furniture, portraits and oak panelling still remain, so its character is intact, and the guest rooms are elegant and very comfortably furnished, with individually styled en-suite bathrooms. Since the opening of the café and terrace, you can drop in for a coffee or a light meal - and, in autumn and early winter, it is popular on Sundays when a proper Sunday roast lunch is offered.

Rooms 11 (1 single; all en-suite with bath and/or shower). B&B from about €90 per room. Café daily Jul-Aug, 12-5, off season weekends and bank hols 12-5. Closed 25-26 Dec, all Jan-Feb. Holiday cottages also available. **Directions:** On waterfront in village.

MARY ANN'S BAR & RESTAURANT

CASTLETOWNSHEND SKIBBEREEN CO CORK
028 36146 I maryanns@eircom.net I
www.facebook.com/Mary-Anns-Pub-and-Restaurant-

EAT I DRINK

Dating back to 1846, this famous pub has been in the energetic and hospitable ownership of Fergus and Patricia O'Mahony since 1988; they have loved it and maintained it well - and have built up a great reputation for food in both the bar and the restaurant. Seafood is the star, of course, with house specialities including a magnificent Platter of Castlehaven Bay Shellfish and Seafood and their lovely home-baked brown bread.

Restaurant **Seats 30** (100 outside). Open 11-11; L12-2.30 & D 6-9 daily in summer. A la carte. Wine from about €18.95. Closed Mon Nov-Mar, 25 Dec & 3 weeks Jan. CC. **Directions:** 8km from Skibbereen, on lower main street.

DUNMORE HOUSE HOTEL

MUCKROSS CLONAKILTY CO CORK

023 883 3352 | enq@dunmorehousehotel.ie

www.dunmorehousehotel.ie

STAY

The magnificent coastal location of the O'Donovan family's immaculately maintained hotel has been used to advantage to provide sea views for all rooms and to allow guests access to their own stretch of foreshore. Hands-on owner-management, appealing public areas, well-appointed bedrooms (many with superb views) - and, most of all, the professional, friendly staff make this an exceptionally pleasing hotel, and it's a wonderful venue for weddings and other occasions. A great base for exploring West Cork, and with a 9-hole golf course too.

Rooms 30 (6 shower only). B&B from €85pps. Wheelchair accessible. Children welcome. Dog friendly. Restaurant: B'fst, L & D. Sun L 1-3, from €35. D daily, 7-9pm from €45, also à la carte. Bar food 12-9 daily. Equestrian breaks & stabling. Closed 25 & 26 Dec; early Jan-early Mar. CC. **Directions:** 4 km from Clonakilty town, signed.

THE EMMET HOTEL

2 EMMET SQUARE CLONAKILTY CO CORK
023 883 3394 I info@emmethotel.com
www.emmethotel.com

EAT I DRINK I STAY

Owned by the O'Keeffe family since 1998, 'The Emmet' is run by chef Marie O'Keeffe (famed for great 'real food'), her son Robert and his wife Rebecca, a terrific team who have reinvented this historic premises to create a boutique hotel of character. The rooms have all been stylishly upgraded (details include Lavazza coffee machines) and there's loads of old world atmosphere, especially The Front Bar, where excellent local food is served all day. All round a great place to visit, with a sense of hands-on family care, tasty food and a lovely buzz.

Rooms 20. B&B room rate from about €80. Wifi. Breakfast 8-11 daily, brunch Sat-Sun 11-4; bar food 12–10. Children's menu, vegetarian menu; Afternoon Tea. Live music (Front Bar, Sun night). Parking, bike storage. **Directions:** In the centre of Clonakilty.

FARM RESTAURANT

30 ASHE STREET CLONAKILTY CO CORK
023 883 4355 I moo@farmrestaurant.ie
www.farmrestaurant.ie

EAT I DRINK

Originally built in 1772 as part of an adjoining brewery, Jason and Aoife Smith's smartly presented restaurant and wine bar in the heart of Clonakilty town has lost none of its character and charm. Original features, some quirky decor details and interesting music create an atmospheric setting for excellent cooking that showcases the area's best seasonal produce in a pleasingly informal style.

Seats 50. D Wed-Sat 5.30-9.30; L Sun only 12.30-3.30, D Sun 6-8. Closed Mon & Tue. CC. **Directions:** Town centre, on main street.

HARTS COFFEE SHOP

8 ASHE STREET CLONAKILTY CO CORK   EAT
023 883 5583 | hartscoffeeshop@gmail.com | |
www.hartscafeclonakilty.com

For over a decade, good home cooking has been the attraction at Aileen Hart and Tony O'Mahoney's friendly coffee shop, and the consistently high standard they have maintained over that time has regulars making a beeline for this welcoming spot as soon as they hit town. A nifty little menu offers all kinds of deliciously healthy meals, ranging from breakfast and lunch specials (if you're lucky the special might be Ummera smoked chicken Caesar) to gorgeous cakes and home-baked scones just like your granny used to make, served with cream...

Seats 30; Open Mon-Sat, 10-5.30. Closed Sun, 3 weeks Christmas. **No CC.** **Directions:** Clonakilty town centre.

INCHYDONEY ISLAND LODGE & SPA

INCHYDONEY ISLAND CLONAKILTY CO CORK   EAT | STAY
023 883 3143 | reservations@inchydoneyisland.com
www.inchydoneyisland.com

One of Ireland's first seawater spa destinations, this famous hotel enjoys views over Inchydoney's two 'Blue Flag' beaches - which bring crowds to the area in summer, making an off-season visit an attractive option. Special breaks are a major attraction - fishing, equestrian, golf, therapies and, more recently, kayaking - and the hotel has introduced some imaginative initiatives for families. Several dining options are offered, with Chef Adam Medcalf's Gulfstream Menu showcasing West Cork food nightly in the smart first floor restaurant.

Rooms 67 (2 wheelchair friendly). Lift. B&B from €75pps. Children welcome. Gulfstream Restaurant seats 70 (+30 outdoors); D daily 6.30-9.45; set D about €60, also à la carte; L Sun only. Informal / bar meals 12-9 daily. Spa (seawater swimming pool). Conferences/ meetings. Closed Christmas. CC. **Directions:** N71 from Cork to Clonakilty, then causeway to Inchydoney.

THE PUFFIN CAFÉ

LONG STRAND CASTLEFREKE CLONAKILTY CO CORK · · · · · · · · · · · EAT

023 883 1697 | puffin.Long.Strand@gmail.com

www.thepuffincafe.com

In a stunning location on the edge of the Atlantic at the aptly named Long Beach, Spencer and Kate Treacy's quirky café provides a highly unusual experience. Offering stone baked pizza, Italian ice-cream and wine, a relaxed atmosphere and a unique location, the aim of The Puffin Cafe is to be an amenity, to bring people together with food, art and music. A place to smile, relax and watch the waves roll in.

Seats about 40 (+ample outside seating). Seasonal: open Jun-Aug: Mon, Thu & Fri 12-4, Sat 10-10, Sun 11-8. Self-catering accommodation available nearby. **No CC. Directions:** Between Clonakilty and Rosscarberry, on the coast - R598 via Castlefreke to Long Beach.

DEASY'S HARBOUR BAR & SEAFOOD RESTAURANT

RING VILLAGE CLONAKILTY CO CORK · · · · · · · · · · · EAT | DRINK

023 883 5741 | www.facebook.com/Deasys-Restaurant

Just across the road from the water in the pretty village of Ring, this traditional pub has a decking area and large windows with views of Clonakilty Bay and the boats moored nearby. Renowned for its atmosphere and chef Caitlin Ruth's great seafood cooking, this has become a popular spot so book well ahead, especially in high season. Friendly staff are always good humoured and helpful, even under pressure.

Seats 50. D Wed-Sat 6-9.30; 'light L' Sat, 12.30-3; L Sun 1-3. Closed D Sun; Mon, Tue and 24-26 Dec. CC. **Directions:** At Ring, 2km outside Clonakilty.

FOTA ISLAND RESORT

FOTA ISLAND COBH CO CORK
021 488 3700 | reservations@fotaisland.ie
www.fotaisland.ie

EAT | STAY

Owned since 2013 by the Kang family of Xiu Lan Hotels, who also own the Kingsley Hotel in Cork city, this beautifully located Resort is one of Ireland's most desirable destinations. Luxurious accommodation includes a high proportion of suites, many enjoying panoramic views over woodlands or golf course. The three championship golf courses and Fota Spa are big attractions among the resort's many activities and families are well catered for, with a dedicated kids programme in school holidays. Serving local food has always been a focus here, and the offering is wide ranging.

Rooms 131 (7 wheelchair friendly). Lift. Room rate about €165; families welcome. Golf. Spa, leisure centre (swimming pool). Fota Restaurant: Seats 120. D daily 6-9.30; Bar food daily 12-8. Helipad. Hotel closes 3pm Dec 24, reopens 1pm 26 Dec. CC.
Directions: N25 east from Cork 8 km, then left and follow signs for Fota Island.

KNOCKEVEN HOUSE

RUSHBROOKE COBH CO CORK
021 481 1778 | info@knockevenhouse.com
www.knockevenhouse.com

STAY

John and Pam Mulhaire's large and peacefully situated 1840s house is an exceptionally comfortable place to stay, offering guests the best of every world: lavish decor and facilities worthy of a top-class hotel, along with great hospitality, and reasonable prices. And Pam is a natural hostess who enjoys treating her guests to delicious breakfasts, and snacks at any time.

Rooms 4 (superior doubles, shower only), B&B about €60pp. Families welcome. Closed 20-26 Dec. CC.
Directions: Signed, on the outskirts of Cobh.

THE CROOKHAVEN INN

CROOKHAVEN SKIBBEREEN CO CORK
028 35309 | crookhaveninn@eircom.net
www.thecrookhaveninn.com

EAT | DRINK

Emma and Freddy Olsson run
this popular pub-cum-restaurant
and chef Freddy is serious
about his food. The evening
menu of a couple of soups and
about a dozen main courses is
supplemented by daily blackboard
specials, emphasising the ready
availability of locally caught fish
and seafood. Great for daytime too
- for flavoursome fare and great
atmosphere, it is worth seeking
out, particularly in summer.

Open daily in summer, 12.30-9pm. A la
carte. Wine from about €21. Children
welcome. Closed Oct-Easter. CC.
Directions: Mizen Peninsula.

CRONIN'S PUB

CROSSHAVEN CO CORK
021 483 1829 | info@croninspub.com
www.croninspub.com

EAT | DRINK

In the family since 1970, the Cronin's harbour front pub has oodles of character; with its walls and high shelves crammed with maritime memorabilia, it's an unofficial exhibition of local history. They've always had a reputation for good food, especially seafood, and Ballymaloe-trained chef Denis Cronin and sister Joeleen (front of house) are doing a great job with both the bar food and the Mad Fish Restaurant; there's bias towards local seafood (don't miss the Mad Fish Soup) but also a balanced choice, including Tom Durcan steaks. Genuine hospitality, the best local ingredients (suppliers credited) and consistently good, unfussy cooking make this a go-to destination.

Restaurant **Seats 35**. D only, Thu-Sat 6-9 (reservations advised); Bar L daily (Mon-Sat 12-3, Sun 12.30-4); children's menu. Restaurant closed Sun-Wed & Jan. CC. **Directions:** Straight into village, at harbour car park.

BLAIRSCOVE HOUSE & RESTAURANT

DURRUS BANTRY CO CORK

027 61127 I mail@blairscove.ie

www.blairscove.ie

EAT I STAY

In a stunning waterside location at the head of Dunmanus Bay, Philippe and Sabine De Mey's beautiful Georgian property is a very special place to eat – and to stay. Together with their daughter Ann, her husband Chris Woodward and Sabine's brother Ronald Klotzer, who is head chef, the De Meys offer the wonderful food and service that this atmospheric restaurant is famous for: the renowned buffet starter display; the superb meat and fish dishes simply cooked on the wood-fired grill; delectable dessert display... Stylish accommodation options for B&B or self-catering range from a modern apartment to a cottage at Dunmanus Pier.

⭐

Rooms 4 (2 shower only). B&B from about €75pps. Children welcome. Events 80/100. Restaurant; D Tue-Sat, 6.30-9.30, about €60. Closed Sun (except bank hol weekends), Mon. House closed early Nov-mid Mar. CC. **Directions:** 3km outside Durrus on Crookhaven Road.

CARBERY COTTAGE GUEST LODGE

DURRUS BANTRY CO CORK

STAY

027 61368 I Carberycottage@gmail.com
www.carbery-cottage-guest-lodge.net

With well-maintained gardens, plenty of parking and beautiful views, Mike Hegarty and Julia Bird's purpose-built B&B and adjoining self-catering cottage makes a great first impression - and their hospitality extends to your four-legged friends too. "Our house is your house, Relax and Enjoy" proclaims the message on their website - and they really mean it. It's a lovely, comfortable place to stay (the spacious, simply furnished bedrooms and bathrooms have all been upgraded recently) and everything about the house and the way it is run is guest focused. It's a real can-do place and would make a wonderfully relaxed holiday base, and with very good food too.

Rooms 3 (1 wheelchair friendly). B&B about €45pps. Family suite. Dogs welcome. Residents D Mon-Sat, 6-7.30; also Lite Bites; à la carte (must pre-book meals). Open all year. CC. **Directions:** Between Durrus and Ahakista.

GALLAN MOR

KEALTIES DURRUS BANTRY CO CORK

027 62732 | hello@gallanmor.com

www.gallanmor.com

STAY

Noel and Lorna Bourke relocated here from London to start a new business and their Boutique Bed & Breakfast, Gallán Mor (the mighty standing stone), is perched high on a hill with stunning views over Dunmanus Bay. No expense has been spared and rooms with smart en-suites and walk-in showers also boast wifi and satellite television - although many guests will be happy to leave television and laptops switched off.

Rooms 4 (all with underfloor heating and power showers). B&B from about €55pps, min 2 night stay; not suitable for children. Hot tub. Self-catering cottage also available (sleeps 6, families welcome). No pets. **Directions:** 5.5km from Durrus on the Ahakista road.

BALLYVOLANE HOUSE

CASTLELYONS FERMOY CO CORK   STAY
025 36349 | info@ballyvolanehouse.ie
www.ballyvolanehouse.ie

Justin and Jenny Green are the current custodians of this gracious mansion. Surrounded by its own farmland and magnificent wooded grounds, it has wonderful gardens (cared for by Justin's father, Jeremy), a trout lake and salmon beats on the River Blackwater. Justin and Jenny are an extremely hospitable couple, committed to continuing the standards of hospitality, comfort and food and drink (including their own gin, Bertha's Revenge www.ballyvolanespirits.ie) for which this lovely house is renowned. Families are welcome and it's an atmospheric wedding venue.

Rooms 6 (1 shower only). B&B from about €135pps; children welcome; free wifi; dogs permitted (in bedrooms). D daily 8pm, by reservation (non residents welcome); D about €60. Glamping. Meetings/events. French spoken. Closed 23 Dec-1 Jan. CC.
Directions: Off N8 (Dublin-Cork); Midleton road south of Rathcormac; follow house signs on to R628

ECCLES HOTEL

GLENGARIFF HARBOUR GLENGARRIFF CO CORK   STAY

027 63003 | info@eccleshotel.com
www.eccleshotel.com

Famous for its mild Gulf Stream climate Glengariff has been a popular tourist destination since Victorian times. The rather grand-looking Eccles Hotel (1745) came into the ownership of Ray Byrne and Eoin Doyle (of Wineport Lodge, Co Westmeath, and BrookLodge Hotel, Co Wicklow) in 2016, and it is a fascinating work in progress - while maybe not yet as luxurious as expected in a hotel of this style and vintage, renovations are under way and many original features are being revealed. It's a good stop-off - the open fire burning in the large reception area is welcoming on chilly days.

Rooms 64 (14 shower only, 1 wheelchair friendly). B&B from €50pps. Lift. Bar food 12-9 daily. Restaurant D daily 6-9, L Sun 12-4. Accommodation mainly closed mid-Nov-late Apr (details from hotel); bar food Nov-Feb, Fri-Sun only from 1pm. **Directions:** Coast road, 17km from Bantry. CC.

FORTVIEW HOUSE

GURTYOWEN TOORMORE GOLEEN CO CORK   STAY

028 35324 | fortviewhousegoleen@eircom.net
www.fortviewhousegoleen.com

Violet and Richard Connell's remarkable roadside farmhouse in the hills behind Goleen is immaculate and full of charm. They have been welcoming guests since 1993 and have thought of every comfort, including a cosy sitting room with comfy sofas and armchairs, the makings of a cup of tea or coffee, television and lots of books to browse. Bedrooms beautifully furnished with antique beds have all sorts of thoughtful little details to surprise and delight, and Violet's idea of a 'standard Irish breakfast' - showcasing local produce - has to be seen to be believed.

Rooms 3 (1 single). B&B about €50. Unsuitable for children. No pets. Self-catering cottages also available. Closed Oct-Apr. **No CC. Directions:** Between Schull and Goleen, 2km from Toormore on main Durrus-Bantry road (R591).

THE HERON'S COVE

THE HARBOUR GOLEEN CO CORK

028 35225 | info@heroncove.ie

www.heronscove.com

EAT | STAY

Quietly situated overlooking Goleen harbour, Sue Hill's atmospheric restaurant with rooms has been a magnet for seafood lovers since 1985. Superb ingredients, pleasing cooking, and friendly, attentive local staff make for a very enjoyable meal, and it's a lovely place to stay too - the rooms, which have been revamped recently, all have views over the tidal harbour. While specialising in fish and seafood (including crab and lobster in summer), local meats are also excellent and there's something for everyone.

Restaurant: D from 7 daily Jun-Sep; off season Sat only, from 7 (call to check). Set D about €30, also à la carte. **Rooms 5** (4 shower only), DB&B about €70pps. Wifi. Rooms open all year except Christmas, booking advisable (essential Sep-May). Closed Christmas & New Year. Bike store. CC. **Directions:** Take to the harbour in Goleen; 100m from village.

GOUGANE BARRA HOTEL

GOUGANE BARRA MACROOM CO CORK
026 47069 | gouganebarrahotel@eircom.net
www.gouganebarrahotel.com

EAT | DRINK | STAY

In one of Ireland's most peaceful and beautiful locations, Neil and Katy Lucey's delightfully old-fashioned family-run hotel overlooks Gougane Barra Lake, famous for its monastic settlements. It's a popular base for walking holidays, and bike hire, fishing and rowing (for residents) are all available too, but it's the warmth and hospitality of the Luceys and their staff that makes it special. Whether to stay or drop in for a meal in the bar or restaurant, it's a lovely place to visit - and Katy's excellent ingredients-led cooking (including a good breakfast) is worth travelling for.

Rooms 26 (11 shower only, 1 wheelchair friendly); children welcome; B&B from about €60pps. No pets. Meals: L&D daily, 12.30-2.30 (Sun 1-2.30) and 6-8.30 (Sun to 8), set menus & à la carte. Closed end Oct-early Apr. CC. **Directions:** In Gougane Barra National Forest.

BASTION

MAIN STREET KINSALE CO CORK

021 470 9696 | helenbastion@hotmail.com

www.bastionkinsale.com

EAT

Prosecco on tap is one of the more unusual features of this relaxed venue where Helen Noonan and Paul McDonald offer an outstanding food experience, even for this foodiest of towns. Chef Paul brings experience in top kitchens to their venture here and, not only is his cooking innovative and the presentation excellent, but his menus - styled 'international' - showcase local produce creatively and proudly credit suppliers. Tasting Menus actively encourage diners to be adventurous, as does the wine list, with many by the glass. Attention to detail, delicious food and excellent service from friendly and helpful staff make Bastion special.

⭐

Seats 45. Open Wed-Sun (summer open Mon). D 5-10. Set early D from €45. Tasting €65 (Vegetarian €50), booking advised, also à la carte. Closed last week Nov, all Feb. CC. **Directions:** Junction of Market Street and Main Street.

THE BLACK PIG WINEBAR & CAFÉ

66 LOWER O'CONNELL STREET KINSALE CO CORK

021 477 4101 | theblackpigwinebar@gmail.com

www.facebook.com/pg/theblackpigwinebar

EAT | DRINK

Formerly of Ely Wine Bar (Ely Place, Dublin), Siobhan Waldron and Gavin Ryan's superb wine and artisan 'tapas' bar has hit all the right notes in Kinsale from the day of opening in 2013. It's simple, but that is part of the rustic charm; the buzz is good, there's a glowing stove in winter and outdoor seating in the cobbled back garden for fine weather. The magnificent wine list includes a wide selection of organic, biodynamic and natural wines (over 100 available by the glass) to partner the boards, slates and platters of delicious artisan foods, and there's also limited hot food offered. Very agreeable.

Opening hours vary seasonally. Usually open daily in summer, 5.30-12. Booking recommended. Off season may be weekends only - a phone call is advised.

BLINDGATE HOUSE

BLINDGATE KINSALE CO CORK

021 477 7858 I info@blindgatehouse.com

www.blindgatehouse.com

STAY

Set quietly in its own gardens high up over the town, yet within a short (if rather steep) walk of its restaurants and bars, Maeve Coakley's purpose-built guesthouse is perfect for travellers who like to be away from the crowds - and with spacious rooms, uncluttered lines and a generally modern, bright and airy atmosphere it is very much its own place. There's a peaceful residents' sitting room to retreat to and bedrooms are thoughtfully furnished with elegant simplicity and good bathrooms - and Maeve is an engaging host, known for her tasty breakfasts.

Rooms 11 (2 wheelchair friendly). B&B from about €50pps. Children over 7 welcome. Free parking. Closed end Oct-mid Mar. CC. **Directions:** From The Pantry, take left up the hill, keeping left after St Multose Church. Blindgate House is after St Joseph's Primary School, on the left.

THE BLUE HAVEN HOTEL

3/4 PEARSE STREET KINSALE CO CORK
021 477 2209 | info@bluehavenkinsale.com
www.bluehavenkinsale.com

EAT | DRINK | STAY

This famous old hotel is attractively presented and hands-on proprietor Ciaran Fitzgerald ensures that frequent refurbishment (and reinvention) keeps it smart and appealing. Due to the nature of the building, public areas and rooms are quite compact, but space is well used and extra accommodation is offered nearby at The Old Bank House (see entry), which is in common ownership. Several dining options include The Fish Market, which showcases a wide range of local fish and seafood, and bars featuring craft beers and live music as well as food.

Rooms 17 (4 shower only) B&B from €100pps. Children welcome. Seafood café seats 65. Open daily 8-6 (summer to 10), à la carte. Food daily from 7.30am. Afternoon Tea from €19.50. Open all year. CC. **Directions:** Centre of town.

FINN'S TABLE

6 MAIN STREET KINSALE CO CORK   EA
021 470 9636 | info@finnstable.com
www.finnstable.com

When John and Julie Finn relocated from Timoleague to open Finn's Table in 2013, it moved effortlessly into the top rank of a very competitive class, with many fans following them to Kinsale. Inviting from the street and gorgeously comfortable inside, the welcome and the chat are delightful - and John's cooking is a class act. Valued local suppliers are of course a central feature of his menus, including the Finn family themselves, who are butchers in Mitchelstown and supply the beef and lamb. Lip-smackingly good food, together with a sense of personal care and value, makes for a lot of returning customers at this excellent little restaurant.

D only, from 5.30, a la carte. Open Thu-Sat Jan-Mar & Dec; Mon & Tue, Thu-Sat April & May; Thu-Tue June- Oct. Closed Nov. **Directions:** Centre of Kinsale

FISHY FISHY

CROWLEY'S QUAY KINSALE CO CORK   EA
021 470 0415 | fishyfishycafe@eircom.net
www.fishyfishy.ie

Martin and Marie Shanahan's almost-harbourside restaurant began nearby as a small daytime café with a fish counter. Today Martin is a household name and this stylish two-storey restaurant with continental-style dining terrace is Ireland's most famous seafood restaurant, attracting visitors from all over the world who are determined to fit a visit into their Irish itinerary. Their reputation is based on offering the freshest of local fish - handpicked by Martin, who takes pride in knowing who has caught it that morning - and the cooking is unfussy and known for clear, direct flavours that never fail to please. Although big, by West Cork standards, it's invariably full to capacity at peak times and booking is strongly recommended.

⭐

Seats 130 (+ 30 outdoors); open daily in season, 12-9; check hours off season. Closed 24-26 Dec, 10-24 Jan. CC.

THE OLD BANK HOUSE

1 PEARSE STREET KINSALE CO CORK
021 477 4075 | info@oldbankhousekinsale.com
www.oldbankhousekinsale.com

EAT | STAY | BUY | PRODUCER

A sister property to the Blue Haven Hotel, this fine boutique guesthouse is very golf friendly, with a lift and very comfortable, spacious bedrooms and lovely bathrooms. Cookies on arrival, King Koil pocket sprung beds, pillow menus, and Nespresso machines in each room are among the details that make guests feel pampered here, and there are plenty more. On the ground floor, there's a Gourmet Food Store and **Café @ The Old Bank House** offering casual daytime food, including breakfast - and treats from the in-house bakery, served all day.

Rooms 17. B&B from about €50 (low season). Children welcome. Lift. Free wifi. **Café** daily. Closed 25 Dec. CC. **Directions:** In the heart of Kinsale, next to the Post Office.

PERRYVILLE HOUSE

LONG QUAY KINSALE CO CORK   STAY

021 477 2731 I sales@perryvillehouse.com

www.perryvillehouse.com

More country house than townhouse, Andrew and Laura Corcoran's harbour-front home is the prettiest in Kinsale and it has been renovated imaginatively and furnished with style. The whole building is immaculately maintained inside and out, and not only provides excellent, spacious accommodation in generous and extremely comfortable rooms (with luxurious bathrooms), but also plenty of relaxing space including a handsome bar and garden room. Light meals can be served here and it is a great additional amenity for residents. And, reflecting the Corcorans' Slow Food philosophy, the good things offered at breakfast include Andrew's own honey as well as home-baked breads, West Cork cheeses and yogurt and much else beside. Simply gorgeous.

Rooms 22. B&B from about €85pps. House closed 1 Nov–end Mar. Not suitable children under 13. CC. **Directions:** Town centre.

TODDIES AT THE BULMAN

SUMMERCOVE KINSALE CO CORK
021 477 7769 I toddies@eircom.net
www.toddies.ie

EAT I DRINK

Pearse and Mary O'Sullivan's very popular restaurant is located at the famous Bulman bar and named after Pearse's grandfather, the legendary notelier Toddy O'Sullivan, who was synonymous with the Gresham in the golden years. Looking over to Kinsale, The Bulman has a uniquely sunny western aspect and it's popular for its interesting, good value bar food - and cosy open fires in winter. Fittingly for a pub, the style is informal but Pearse's classical training underpins the cooking and, upstairs, Toddies restaurant offers smart-casual dining and seasonally-led menus that showcase local and artisan produce in stylish contemporary dishes cooked with verve.

Restaurant: **seats 54**; D Tue-Sat 6.30-9. Bar L daily 12.30-5. D Tue-Sat 6.30-9. A la carte. Daily specials. Children welcome. Bar & toilets wheelchair accessible. CC. **Directions:** Beside Charles Fort, near Kinsale.

THE CASTLE HOTEL & LEISURE CENTRE

MAIN STREET MACROOM CO CORK
026 41074 I reservations@castlehotel.ie
www.castlehotel.ie

STAY

The hub of local activities, this friendly and well-managed hotel has been in the caring ownership of the Buckley family since 1952. The personal touch is seen everywhere, including some quirky artwork, and, while ideally located for touring the scenic south-west, this immaculately maintained and very comfortable hotel is equally attractive to business guests. It's great for families - extensive leisure facilities include a fine swimming pool with separate children's pool - there's a choice of dining options, and special breaks are offered, including golf specials (tee times reserved at Macroom's 18-hole course). Every town should have a hotel like this.

Rooms 60. B&B from about €48pps. Families welcome, pets permitted (charge). Wifi. Meals: 'B's' Restaurant 12-3 & 6-8.45; 'Next Door Café' 9.30-5.30; bar food 12-9.30. Closed 24-28 Dec. Carpark. CC. **Directions:** On N22, midway between Cork & Killarney.

GRANVILLE'S BAR & RESTAURANT

CASTLE STREET MACROOM CO CORK   EAT | DRINK
026 20191 | info@granvilles.ie
www.granvillesbarandrestaurant.com

The oldest licensed premises in Macroom, Paul and Leonie Granville renovated this handsome stone building from derelict in 2007 and it's now a comfortable, welcoming place where you can come to dine, or to just have a quiet pint, a glass of wine or one of their speciality beers and read the newspaper. It has earned a reputation for wholesome fare based on fresh produce from local suppliers, notably great steaks and seafood, with menus changing through the day and plenty of choices for children too. A great place to know about when travelling this family-friendly restaurant gives good value and the well trained staff are exceptionally efficient and accommodating.

Seats 76. Open Tue-Sun, from 12 noon-9.30 (to 9 Sun). Closed 25 Dec. CC.
Directions: On the hill just off the town square on main Cork-Killarney road, N22.

TOONS BRIDGE DAIRY & THE REAL OLIVE CO

OLD CREAMERY TOONS BRIDGE MACROOM CO CORK   EAT | BUY
087 345 7790 | toonsbridgedairyfrontofhouse@gmail.com   PRODUCER
www.therealoliveco.com / www.toonsbridgedairy.com

You can buy Toby Simmonds's cheeses and his familiar Real Olive Co imports - olives, cured meats, speciality cheeses - here in the little shop, and eat them in the lovely conservatory café, which is run by Toby's wife Jenny-Rose Clarke. Deliciously simple dishes use other local artisan foods as well as their own dairy products, which star in delicious mozzarella salad, ricotta cake, ice cream and the Toons Bridge cheese board. Also authentic Neapolitan pizzas, made with their own freshly made mozzarella and cooked in an impressive outdoor pizza oven. Organic wine to accompany, also craft beer and cider.

Shop & Café open Fri & Sat 12.30–4 & 6–9, Sun 12.30–6. Outdoor tables in summer. Online shop. **Directions:** Heading west into Macroom on N22 take the Inchageelagh road, R584.

LONGUEVILLE HOUSE

MALLOW CO CORK
022 47156 | info@longuevillehouse.ie
www.longuevillehouse.ie

EAT | STAY | BUY | PRODUCER

Well located for exploring an exceptionally rewarding area including Cork city, the O'Callaghan family's beautiful yet relaxed 18th century house is a luxurious and interesting place to stay. The river, farm and garden supply virtually all the fresh produce for chef-proprietor William O'Callaghan's kitchen and their artisan products, including Longueville House Cider and Irish Apple Brandy. Country pursuits, including falconry, are available or you can just visit the walled garden (a productive working garden rather than a showpiece), pigs and orchards. Dining here is special - and their breakfasts are a particular treat.

Rooms 20 (2 shower only). B&B from about €80pps. **Presidents Restaurant** D Wed-Sun, from €55 (& light à la carte 6.30-8) Sun L 1-2.30, from €29. Light meals Wed-Sat 12.30-5.30. House closed Mon, Tue & 2 weeks Feb. CC. **Directions:** N72 Cork-Killarney, signed 5km west of Mallow.

FERRIT & LEE

DISTILLERY WALK MIDLETON CO CORK
021 463 5235 | info@ferritandlee.ie
www.ferritandlee.ie

EAT

Attractively situated near the gates of the Old Midleton Distillery, opposite the river and a small park, this smart modern restaurant is known for excellent modern Irish cooking, and good service. Formerly the popular Raymond's Restaurant, it was taken over by Pat Ferriter and former head chef Stephen Lee in 2017 and retains a loyal local following. The new owners wasted no time in putting their own stamp on it however. By doing what Raymond's had always been committed to in relation to showcasing local foods and supporting producers in a more energetic and engaging way, Ferrit & Lee quickly proved a great asset to the town. Very convenient for visitors to the distillery.

Seats 55; L & D Tue-Sat 12-3 (Fri-Sat to 4) & 5-9.30 (Tue-Wed 5.30-9); all day Sun 12-9. Closed Mon, bank hols, 25 Dec-1 Jan. CC.

FARMGATE

THE COOLBAWN MIDLETON CO CORK
021 463 2771 | farmgate@ireland.com
www.farmgate.ie

EAT | BUY

Older sister of Farmgate Café at the English Market in Cork (see entry), Marog O'Brien's unique shop and restaurant has been drawing people to Midleton in growing numbers since 1985 and - with a wonderful display of local produce, speciality foods and in-house baking leading through into the simple but evocatively decorated restaurant - it has lost none of its allure. An iconic business, and central to Midleton's development as a food destination.

Seats 100 (outdoors, 30). Store & bakery open Tue-Sat 9-6. Restaurant Tue-Sat, 9-5. L 12-3.30. Light supper Thu-Sat 5.30-7, D Thu-Sat 6.30-9.30. Closed Sun, Mon, Christmas/New Year. CC. **Directions:** Town centre near Jameson Heritage Centre.

SAGE RESTAURANT

THE COURTYARD 8 MAIN STREET MIDLETON CO CORK

EAT

021 463 9682 I info@sagerestaurant.ie
www.sagerestaurant.ie

Local produce is at the heart of Chef Kevin Aherne's impressive courtyard venue. The philosophy goes way beyond crediting producers and suppliers, they are central to everything and Kevin draws them right into the structure through his famous 12 Mile Menus. The intensely seasonal nature of the available ingredients inspires constant change and creativity in daily menus, resulting in beautiful, appetising - and unusual - dishes. In addition to the lovely refurbished Sage restaurant, there's an all-day café-restaurant, The Greenroom, and a covered outdoor area, The Courtyard, available as a venue (50). Quite the place to meet and eat.

⭐

Sage: Tue-Sat early D 5.30-6.30, D 7.30-9 (to 9.30 Fri & Sat). Sun 4.30-8.30. L Sat & Sun 12-3 (Sun 3.30). Greenroom: Tue-Fri 9-9, Sat 9-10, Sun 11-10. Closed Mon. CC. **Directions:** Gated archway 100m on left after main Midleton roundabout.

BALLYMALOE HOUSE

SHANAGARRY MIDLETON CO CORK

021 465 2531 | res@ballymaloe.ie

www.ballymaloe.ie

EAT | STAY

The legendary Myrtle Allen and her late husband, Ivan, opened The Yeats Room restaurant at Ballymaloe in 1964, beginning the story of Ireland's most famous country house. Today, its intensely restorative atmosphere and simplicity remain remarkable - and there are few greater pleasures than a wholesome Ballymaloe dinner followed by a good night's sleep in one of their thoughtfully-furnished country bedrooms. And the house is the centre of a unique range of family enterprises including the excellent Ballymaloe Shop Café, famous for its delicious light lunches and cakes.

Rooms 29 (2 wheelchair friendly), B&B from about €100pps. No lift. Restaurant: L&D daily, 1-2, 7.30-9.30 (Sun 7.30-8.30, buffet only). Ballymaloe Shop & Café, 10-5 daily. Also Ballymaloe Cookery School & other businesses. Closed Christmas, 4 weeks Jan-Feb. CC.
Directions: From N25, follow signs to Ballycotton; 3km beyond Cloyne.

STEPHEN PEARCE POTTERY

SHANAGARRY MIDLETON CO CORK   EAT | BUY
021 4646 807 | info@stephenpearce.com
www.stephenpearce.com

The Stephen Pearce pottery is well worth building into any itinerary when visiting East Cork - it is a delightful place, the pottery is superb and there are always bargains to be found among the seconds. The charming café has also earned a following for tasty daytime fare including great brunch and lunch dishes, well chosen drinks including a short wine list - and delicious home baking. A lovely rustic spot to enjoy the simple goodness of the area's artisan foods, and with seating outside for fine weather.

Open: Showroom Mon-Fri 10-5, Sat 10-6, Sun & bank hols 11.30-6. Café: Open daily Jun-Aug 10-5, off season closed Tue & Wed. Brunch 10-12.30, light lunch until 4; home bakes & coffee all day. **Directions:** Centre of Shanagarry

---

BALLINWILLIN HOUSE

MITCHELSTOWN CO CORK   STAY | BUY | PRODUCER
025 84979 | ballinwillinhouse@gmail.com
www.ballinwillinhouse.com

At the end of a suburban cul-de-sac, Pat and Miriam Mulcahy's farm is famous for the tender Ballinwillin venison and free range wild boar that features on leading hotel menus. Deer graze peacefully beside the 18th century house, and accommodation is offered in the main house and a courtyard with some modern conversions. Their tasty produce - venison or wild boar sausage, fresh eggs, rashers and black and white puddings from their free range pigs - stars in excellent breakfasts and at dinner. And the couple also own a vineyard in Hungary - their characterful old stone wine cellar reveals more surprises...

Rooms 4 (all shower only). B&B about €45pps. Residents D about €25. Children welcome. Free wifi. CC. **Directions:** From Firgrove Hotel roundabout, first exit left, to Mitchelstown; next left into cul-de-sac before Maxol garage; large white gates at end.

WALTON COURT

OYSTERHAVEN CO CORK

EAT | BUY | STAY

021 477 0878 | enquiry@waltoncourt.com
www.waltoncourt.com

Scenically situated overlooking Oysterhaven Bay, near Kinsale, Paul and Janis Rafferty's lovely old house is a listed building dating back to 1645. Following years of restoration, it is home to various activities and events – and the atmospheric Courtyard Café, serving tasty lunches based mainly on their own organic seasonal produce, a great range of home baking, locally roasted coffee, homemade cordials and pressed juices. It has become a treat destination for local aficionados - and is a boon for guests staying in the excellent accommodation on site, or holidaying in the area.

Seats 25 (+40 outdoors) Tue-Sun 10-5 (L Menu 12.30-4), closed Mon. Closed Nov- Easter. Check for seasonal changes. **Accommodation:** 12 self-catering cottages, houses & 1 apartment; swimming pool, honesty bar. CC (min spend €10). **Directions:** 9km east of Kinsale; R600 to Belgooly, signs to Oysterhaven.

O'CALLAGHAN-WALSHE

THE SQUARE ROSSCARBERY CO CORK   EAT
023 884 8125 | fun.fish@hotmail.com
www.ocallaghanwalshe.com

Well off the busy main West Cork road, this unique seafood restaurant on the square of the picturesque old village of Rosscarbery has a previous commercial history that's almost tangible. Its unique atmosphere is well-matched by proprietor-host Sean Kearney's larger-than-life personality and the simplicity of Martina O'Donovan's cooking is a joy - everything is super fresh and the superb West Cork Seafood Platter is a particular treat. A West Cork institution since 1991.

Seats 40 (+ pavement tables). D Tue-Sun, early D about €27, also à la carte. May open for lunch Jul-Aug. Closed Mon, open weekends only in winter (a phone call to check is advised). CC. **Directions:** Main square in Rosscarbery village.

PILGRIMS

THE SQUARE ROSSCARBERY CO CORK   EAT
023 883 1796 | contact.pilgrims@gmail.com
www.pilgrims.ie

Opened in 2015 by a talented duo, Sarah Jane Pearce and chef Mark Jennings, this flower-bedecked restaurant is much more than just a pretty face. Inside, it is simple and rustic and Mark cooks some of the region's most exciting food, with short daily menus created around whatever is best in local seasonal ingredients. While not a vegetarian restaurant (local fish and meats are excellent), Mark has worked with Denis Cotter of Cork's Café Paradiso and there's a strong focus on vegetables and foraged foods, so vegetarians will be very happy here. Attractively presented without being over-worked, everything is delicious, including unusual sides and desserts. Good short wine and drinks list too, and super service.

⭐

Seats 35. Open: D Wed-Sat 6-10, L Sun only, 1-4. A la carte. Reservations advised. Closed mid-Jan to mid-Mar. CC. **Directions:** Off N71, Rosscarbery village centre.

GOOD THINGS @ DILLON'S CORNER

68 BRIDGE STREET SKIBBEREEN CO CORK   EAT | LEARN
028 51948 | bookings@thegoodthingscafe.com
www.thegoodthingscafe.com

Since first opening the original Good Things in Durrus, in 2003, Carmel Somers - chef, teacher and author - has done more than any other chef in the region to promote local produce, and her menus at this stylish and atmospheric café and restaurant reflect this. Simplicity and fresh flavours are the essence of the cooking style and the local producers who are hailed as heroes include many famous names. Seasonality is a byword: roasted summer vegetables, sea beet, lightly boiled, Kilcrohane new potatoes, the tartness of gooseberries with mackerel and the same fruit in a memorable dessert... Even the most demanding will know they are in safe hands here.

⭐

Open: Tue-Sat. B'fst Tue-Sat 9-12, L 12.30-4; D Thu-Sat 6-9. Closed Sun (except some bank hol w/ends) & Mon, and D Tue- Wed. Cookery School. CC.
Directions: Town centre

ISLAND COTTAGE

HEIR ISLAND SKIBBEREEN AREA CO CORK
028 38102 | info@islandcottage.com
www.islandcottage.com

EAT | LEARN

John Desmond and Ellmary Fenton describe their restaurant as unusual, in a unique and beautiful setting. This is an understatement; it is extraordinary by any standards. Chef/artist John Desmond's single-handed cooking of the freshest ingredients is that of a consummate professional and, while some may find the rules – advance booking only with deposit, no credit cards, no-choice menu, dos and don'ts – a bit off-putting, most are won over by the singular dining experience, unchanging and successful since 1990.

⭐

Seats 24 (max table 10; may share table). Open 15 June-15 Sep, Wed-Sat in Jul & Aug. D from €40, 7.45-11.45 ; one sitting. 'Late Lunch' Sat & Sun, Apr-Jun from €20. Closed D Sun (except for private groups) Mon-Tue, and mid Sep-mid May (phone to check off season opening). **No CC.** *Off season cookery courses available. Gallery. **Directions:** Ferry from Cunnamore pier.

WEST CORK HOTEL

ILEN STREET SKIBBEREEN CO CORK
028 21277 | info@westcorkhotel.com
www.westcorkhotel.com

STAY

'Three star hotel, five star hospitality' just about sums up Tim and Marion Looney's welcoming hotel, on the western side of Skibbereen town. Old-fashioned in the best possible way, it's at the heart of everything that goes on in the area and the spacious public areas enjoy a pleasant riverside view beside the bridge. With comfortable accommodation, friendly and helpful staff giving the hotel a homely feeling, and food with a strongly local flavour, it would make an interesting base for exploring this beautiful area.

Rooms 34 (2 family, 10 shower only). B&B about €75pps. Lift. Dog kennels (charge). Garden. Parking. CC. **Directions:** Follow signs N71 to Bantry through Skibbereen.

DILLON'S

MILL STREET TIMOLEAGUE CO CORK   EAT
023 886 9609 | info@dillonsrestaurant.ie
www.dillonsrestaurant.ie

Well-known West Cork chef Richard Milnes runs this little restaurant with his partner Antje Gessche in what was once a traditional grocery shop, and they retained the original name. His short menus are packed with quality, reflecting the superb local produce available from both land and sea - and, while thinking very local in terms of main ingredients, influences that come from far and wide ensure plenty of variety.

The cooking is exquisite and this, plus great service from Antje and her staff, is a sure-fire recipe for success. A little gem.

Seats 24 (groups 34) (+16 outdoors); open Fri–Tue 6-9. Closed Wed & Thu. A la carte. Set menu available for groups. Wines from €25. CC. *Ring to check opening times off season. **Directions:** On main street of village.

MONK'S LANE

15 MILL STREET TIMOLEAGUE CO CORK

EAT | DRINK

023 884 6348 | info@monkslane.ie

www.monkslane.ie

Timoleague is blessed with a choice of good eating places and, alongside the historic abbey and behind a traditional frontage painted in their trademark blue, Michelle O'Mahony and Gavin Moore's welcoming restaurant is atmospheric with ecclesiastical echoes to the furnishings, and an attractive beer garden at the back. Focused on local foods and craft drinks, the bar is open all day and it's a great place to know about when travelling in West Cork as you can just drop in for coffee and cake (apricot and raspberry cake, perhaps, with fruit, ice-cream and cream on the side...), afternoon tea, or something more substantial.

Open Wed-Sat, L 12.30-3, D 6-9.30. Sun 1-7. A la carte. Set menu for groups 20+. Bar open all day. Closed Mon & Tue, 2 weeks Jan. A la carte. Outdoor area. CC. **Directions:** Village centre

AHERNE'S SEAFOOD RESTAURANT & ACCOMMODATION

163 NORTH MAIN STREET YOUGHAL CO CORK

EAT | DRINK | STAY

024 92424 | ahernes@eircom.net
www.ahernes.com

The historic walled town of Youghal has connections with Sir Walter Raleigh and, to many, it's also synonymous with Aherne's. While John FitzGibbon supervises the front of house in this third generation business, his brother David reigns over the busy kitchen, and their wives Katie and Gaye ensure warm hands-on service. Local seafood stars and it's worth planning a journey around a bar meal at Aherne's - or dine in the restaurant and have a restful night in their spacious, comfortable accommodation, followed by an excellent breakfast.

Rooms 13 (1 wheelchair friendly, some SC). B&B from about €55; children welcome. Free wifi. Restaurant: D 6-9, from about €30, also à la carte. Bar food daily, 12-9.30. Toilets wheelchair accessible. Closed 23-26 Dec. CC. **Directions:** on N25, main Cork-Waterford route.

COUNTY DONEGAL

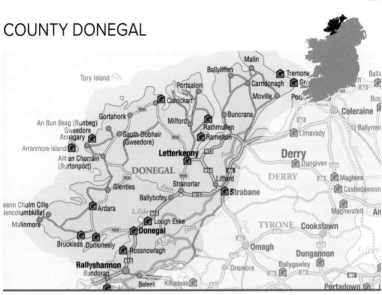

Donegal www.donegal.ie is landscape on an epic scale, one of the defining counties on the Wild Atlantic Way. It's a world apart with Glenveagh National Park www.glenveaghnationalpark.ie in the northern part of the county serving as the focal point of a programme for the re-introduction of the golden eagle to Ireland.

For many folk, particularly those from Northern Ireland, Donegal is the holiday county par excellence. But in recent years there has been growth of modern industries and the re-structuring of the fishing, particularly at the developing harbour of Killybegs www.killybegs.ie , home port for the largest fishing vessels. This Donegal entrepreneurial spirit has led to a more balanced economy, with the pace being set by the county town of Letterkenny, where the population has increased by 50% since 1991. More recently, Letterkenny has become home to an impressive Arts Centre, a masterpiece of modern architecture, while the An Grianan Theatre www.angrianan.com thrives.

But Donegal county is still a place of nature on the grand scale, where the landscape is challenged by the winds and weather of the Atlantic Ocean if given the slightest chance. Yet at communities like Bundoran and Rossnowlagh, where splendid beaches face straight into the Atlantic, enthusiastic surfers have demonstrated that even the most demanding weather can have its sporting uses.

For most folk, however, it is the contrast between raw nature and homely comfort which is central to Donegal's enduring attraction. For here, in some of Ireland's most rugged territory, you will find many sheltered and hospitable places whose amenities are emphasised by the challenging nature of their broader environment. And needless to say, that environment is simply startlingly beautiful as well.

LOCAL ATTRACTIONS AND INFORMATION

>**Arranmore Ferry Burtonport-Arranmore**
 www.arranmoreferry.com | 074 9520532
>Bundoran **Tourism Information** 071 984 1350
>Glencolumbcille **Folk Museum** 074 973 0017

>**Glenveagh National Park** (Castle, gardens, parkland) 074 9137090
>**Tory Island Ferry**
 074 953 1320 | 953 1340 | 913 5061

DANNY MINNIE'S RESTAURANT

ANNAGRY CO DONEGAL   EAT | STAY

074 954 8201 | info@dannyminnies.ie
www.dannyminnies.ie

The O'Donnell family has run Danny Minnie's since 1962, and there's nothing about the exterior as seen from the road to prepare first-time visitors for the atmosphere of this remarkable restaurant. Brian O'Donnell's cooking (strong on local meats as well as seafood) matches the surroundings well: fine, with imaginative saucing, but not a bit pretentious. They also have accommodation and, like the restaurant, the spacious rooms are full of character with antiques, including brass and four poster beds, adding charm.

Seats 80. D Mon-Sat 6.30-9.30pm. Set D about €42; also à la carte (summer only). L Sun 1-4pm Jul & Aug. D Oct- May, Thu-Sat only. **Rooms: 5** (all shower only). B&B about €50pps. Children welcome. Wheelchair access to bar and part of the restaurant. Closed 2nd week Jan- mid Feb. CC. **Directions:** R259 off N56 - follow Airport signs.

NANCY'S BAR

FRONT STREET ARDARA CO DONEGAL   EAT | DRINK

074 954 1187 | nancysbarardara@gmail.com

Now in its seventh generation, the McHugh family's famous pub is a cosy, welcoming place. Although the legendary Charlie and Ann may have officially handed over the reins to their son, Conor, and daughter Jenny McHugh, they're still very much in situ and it's a real family affair. Everybody loves the higgledy-piggledy rooms and the wholesome home-made food, especially seafood, that - along with a good pint and live music - is now a big part of its charm. Probably most famous for oysters and a terrific seafood chowder, they keep things simple and local at Nancy's - and offer a good range of craft beers and ciders too. Magic.

Bar food all year, 12-9 daily, except Dec 24 & 26. Children welcome before 9pm. Wheelchair access. Free wifi. Reservations for groups only. Closed 25 Dec. CC. **Directions:** Ardara village centre.

WOODHILL HOUSE

WOOD ROAD ARDARA CO DONEGAL

074 954 1112 | yates@iol.ie

www.woodhillhouse.com

STAY | EAT

Scenically located on the edge of picturesque Ardara village, overlooking the Donegal Highlands, this interesting and hospitable big house was once the home of Ireland's last commercial whaling family. Following years of restoration work by the current owner, John Yates, and his late wife, Nancy, it is now run by John and his son James, and has a lovely atmosphere. Rooms are in the main house and in converted outbuildings, where some have balconies overlooking the lovely walled gardens. The restaurant is popular locally, so booking is recommended, and there's a proper bar - where you may find some unusual guest beers on offer.

Rooms 14 (6 shower-only, 1 wheelchair friendly); B&B from about €55pps. Restaurant: D 6.30-10pm daily, Set D about €43; bar open normal hours Children welcome; pets permitted in some areas. Closed Christmas; check opening off season.

MULDOWNEYS B&B

ARRANMORE ISLAND CO DONEGAL

087 908 1277 | nmuldowneyie@yahoo.co.uk

www.muldowneysbb.com

STAY | LEARN

Just a scenic 20 minute ferry crossing from Burtonport on the mainland (itself just 15 minutes from the Regional Airport, Carrickfinn) Arranmore (Arainn Mhor) is a lesser known gem on the Wild Atlantic Way - which, alone, would make it a destination of choice for many. Jim and Noreen Muldowney offer excellent accommodation and Jim's boat trips are so professional - how often do you get a chance to catch your own fish, and eat it at the end of the trip? Walkers will love it too - visitor information and walking map provided. A lovely place to visit all year round - another reminder that Donegal just has to be discovered.

Rooms 4, all en-suite; double B&B about €75. D by arrangement. 2 night offers, Mar-Sep. Free WiFi. Open all year. All year ferry from Burtonport. CC.

THE OLDE GLEN BAR

GLEN CARRIGART CO DONEGAL
074 915 5130 | oldeglenbar@gmail.com
www.facebook.com/pg/Theoldeglentearoom

EAT | DRINK

Just the sort of old pub advertising people dream about, this charming bar looks as it must have done a hundred, maybe two hundred years ago. Low ceilings, ancient weathered bar and furniture, fires in winter - and a great reputation for good food in the restaurant at the back, plus craic and music in the bar. The seafood and steaks, especially, are the stuff of legend and there's a newer daytime alternative, The Olde Glen Tea Room, next door - another delightful place, serving good food and full of fun.

Restaurant D 6-9pm: Wed-Mon Jul & Aug, Wed–Sun Jun & Sep, weekends only Oct-Mar, closed second half Jan. Bar all year: Jul-Aug daily from noon, otherwise Mon-Fri from 3pm; Sat & Sun from noon. Olde Glen Tea Room: 11am-5pm, closed Mon-Tue. CC. **Directions:** 5 minutes south of Carrigart.

ARD NA BREÁTHA

DRUMROOSKE MIDDLE DONEGAL CO DONEGAL
074 972 2288 | www.ardnabreatha.com
info@ardnabreatha.com

STAY

Theresa and Albert Morrow's welcoming guesthouse is tucked into a quiet corner of their busy working farm and has a pleasant view of the countryside beyond. It is, as they say in their brochure, 'a place worth finding', and was one of the first in Ireland to receive the EU flower award for Eco tourism. The rooms are simple but very comfortable, with a nice country feel, and this is one of the most appealing places to stay in the Donegal area. The restaurant no longer operates, but the town's restaurants are only a short walk away — and there is a comfy bar/seating area to return to. And you can be sure of a very good breakfast each morning.

Rooms 6. B&B from about €38pps. CC. Closed 1 Nov-14 Feb. **Directions:** 1.5km from Donegal town, on the Lough Eske road.

AROMA

THE CRAFT VILLAGE DONEGAL CO DONEGAL   EAT
074 972 3222 | tomandarturo@yahoo.com

Just outside Donegal Town, the Craft Village is an interesting place to browse, with plenty of parking - and Tom Dooley's smart little café and 'mini-bakery', which has won a lot of friends for its warm and friendly atmosphere and excellent freshly cooked food that offers much more than would be expected of a coffee shop. Ingredients are impeccably sourced and everything both looks and tastes delicious. The home bakes, espe-cially, are worth travelling for and, for many regular visitors, a coffee and cake here is de rigeur on any trip to Donegal. And, although the café is small, there's a large out-door eating area for fine weather.

Seats 30 (outdoors, 16); Open Mon-Sat, 9.30am-5.30pm. Closed Sun, 25-26 Dec, 1 Jan. (Call to check hours off season.) CC. **Directions:** 1.6km outside town on old Ballyshannon road.

THE BLUEBERRY TEA ROOM

CASTLE STREET THE DIAMOND DONEGAL CO DONEGAL   EAT
074 972 2933 | birchill88@hotmail.com
www.facebook.com/pg/The-Blueberry-Tearooms

Going strong since 1993 and just as good as ever, Brian Gallagher's popular, moderately priced café and restaurant looks cosy and appealing with its traditional small-paned windows, window boxes and welcoming menus at the door to draw you in - and once inside this friendly little place, you will be hooked by the sight and aromas of the wholesome home cooking that is their stock in trade. The home-made desserts come in for special praise, also the wide range of home-baked cakes, cookies and biscuits to eat in or take away - all cannily displayed on the way in, so you can't miss them; not too many people leave without having the dessert they didn't mean to order.

Seats 60; open all day Mon-Sat from 9am. Closed Sun. No credit cards. **Directions:** Just off the diamond on Castle Street.

THE OLDE CASTLE BAR & RESTAURANT

DONEGAL CO DONEGAL   EAT | DRINK

074 972 1262 | info@oldecastlebar.com
www.oldecastlebar.com

In an atmospheric restored stone building overlooking the ruins of O'Donnell Castle in Donegal town, The Olde Castle may seem a little touristy at first, but the O'Toole family offer real Irish hospitality at their traditional bar and restaurant - and the food is good. Local seafood is the main speciality, especially in summer, and daily lunch specials include excellent traditional dishes such as a hearty bowl of traditional Irish Lamb Stew.

It is just the kind of place visitors will enjoy finding, and has earned its place as a favourite destination for local diners too.

Seats 70. Bar meals Mon-Sat, 12-9 (L Menu 12-5, D5-9). Restaurant open for D daily in summer, 6-9.15pm; D weekends in winter. CC. **Directions:** Centre of Donegal, opposite Donegal Castle.

THE MILL RESTAURANT & ACCOMMODATION

FIGART DUNFANAGHY LETTERKENNY CO DONEGAL

EAT | STAY

074 913 6985 | info@themillrestaurant.com

www.themillrestaurant.com

Beautifully located on the shore of the New Lake, which is a special area of conservation, the mill was the home of Susan Alcorn's grandfather and, as they are a family of accomplished painters, the walls are hung with wonderful watercolours. Susan and her husband Derek, who is the chef, have earned a dedicated following here, for the superb location, warm welcome and assured local ingredients-led cooking - and they also offer great value. Delightful accommodation includes a romantic 4-poster room, the Studio, added in 2016, and you can be sure of a delicious breakfast. A magic place.

Open; D high season Tue-Sun 7-9pm. Closed Mon Jul-Aug & extra nights other months. **Rooms 7** (2 shower only). B&B from about €50pps, (The Studio, €75pps). Children welcome. Free wifi. Closed mid Dec-mid Mar. CC **Directions:** N56 1km outside Dunfanaghy on Falcarragh road.

CASTLE MURRAY HOUSE

ST. JOHN'S POINT DUNKINEELY CO DONEGAL

074 973 7022 I info@castlemurray.com

www.castlemurray.com

Most of the stylish bedrooms at Marguerite Howley and Peter Lawler's beautifully located clifftop property have wonderful sea and coastal views. It has a well deserved reputation as a relaxing hideaway, and, although the once-famous restaurant no longer operates, a delicious breakfast - and dinner for residents on some evenings - is served there, in the seaward corner of the hotel overlooking the sea and the ruined castle after which the house is named. A very special place - and pet friendly too.

Rooms 10 (4 shower only, 2 pet friendly). B&B about €150 per room. Dining room Seats 20. Residents' D Fri & Sat, enquire about other evenings; set menu (changes daily). Bar; house wine €25. Closed Dec-Feb.CC. **Directions:** N56, 8km from Killybegs; first left outside Dunkineely village.

STAY

KEALYS SEAFOOD BAR

THE HARBOUR GREENCASTLE CO DONEGAL

EAT

074 938 1010 | kealysseafoodbar@yahoo.ie
www.kealysseafoodbar.ie

The summer ferry between the fishing port of Greencastle and Magilligan Point in Northern Ireland brings many new visitors to an area that used to seem quite remote - and those in the know plan their journeys around a meal at Kealys. It's a low-key little place where simplicity has always been valued and, even if it's just to pop in for a daytime bowl of Tricia Kealy's Greencastle chowder and some home-baked brown bread, don't miss the opportunity of a visit to Kealys.

Seats 65 (+20 outdoors). Bar food all day Wed-Sun; restaurant L & D Wed-Sun 12.30-4pm & 5-9.30pm. D à la carte; wine from €24. Toilets wheelchair accessible; children welcome to 9pm. Closed Mon-Tue, 2 weeks Nov, 25 Dec, Good Fri. CC.
Directions: On the harbour at Greencastle.

KITTY KELLYS

LARGY KILLYBEGS CO DONEGAL   EAT

074 973 1925 | reservationsatkittykellys@gmail.com
www.kittykellys.com

Heading out west on the scenic road towards Glencolumbkille, you can't miss this smartly presented former farmhouse, now a destination restaurant run by well known French chef Remy Dupuy and his wife Donna. Whether for a lunchtime bite in summer or an evening meal in the (surprising) restaurant, Remy's take on local produce is always a treat. Killybegs seafood tops the list and fans will be delighted to find an old favourite taking pride of place among the starters - Prawn & Monkfish in Garlic Butter, which has been Remy's best selling dish for over 20 years.

Open all year, daily July & Aug, light L 12.30-3.30, D 6.30-9. Autumn/winter Wed-Sun D 6.30-9pm Sun to 8pm, Sun L 1pm-3.30. Closed last 2 wks Nov & 2 wks Jan. Wheelchair accessible. CC. **Directions:** On R263 Killybegs-Glencolumbkille road, west of Killybegs.

THE FLEET INN

21 BRIDGE STREET CASHELCUMMIN KILLYBEGS CO DONEGAL

EAT | DRINK

074 973 1518 | killybegsaccomodation@gmail.com

www.fleetinnkillybegs.com

Fresh fish of all varieties is on the daily menu in this charming traditional Irish pub and restaurant near the harbour. With owner-chef Colin Bradley at the helm, delights such as The Fleet Inn seafood hors d'oeuvre with oysters, garlic mussels, smoked salmon, prawns, crab meat and claw are sure to impress. Although pride of place goes to expertly prepared fish, main courses also offer a wider choice, with honey roast Silver Hill duck and prime Hereford sirloin steak especially popular - and classic desserts are hard to resist. A great seafood destination in Killybegs and deservedly popular - reservations are advised.

Restaurant Thu-Mon 6pm-9pm. Bar food Mon-Sun 5pm-9pm. Live music Sun. Free wifi. Accommodation also offered. CC.

BROWNS ON THE GREEN

BARNHILL GOLF COURSE ROAD LETTERKENNY CO DONEGAL

EAT | DRINK

074 912 4771 | eat@brownsrestaurant.com

www.brownsrestaurant.com

A lovely place with all the Browns of Derry hallmarks of outstanding cooking and classy surroundings, this stylishly renovated bar and restaurant are on the first floor at Letterkenny Golf Club, overlooking the course - and perhaps a glimpse of Lough Swilly, if you are lucky with your table. 'Fine dining, great wines and excellent service at affordable prices' is the promise and, with Ian Orr, famed executive head chef of the Browns Group, overseeing a talented kitchen team, the bar is set high - but they are well able for it. A great dining destination - and not just for special occasions.

L Thu-Sun 12.30-3 (Sun to 3.30), D Wed-Sun, 5.30-9. Early D about €25 (Wed-Thu & Sun to 9pm, Sat to 7.30), also à la carte. Closed Mon-Tue. CC. **Directions:** Ramelton road from Letterkenny, signed on right.

CASTLE GROVE COUNTRY HOUSE HOTEL

LETTERKENNY CO DONEGAL   EAT | STAY

074 915 1118 | reservations@castlegrove.com

www.castlegrove.com

Parkland designed by "Capability" Brown in the mid-18th century creates a wonderful setting for Raymond and Mary Sweeney's beautiful period house overlooking Lough Swilly. A lovely house with gracious reception rooms and spacious, comfortably appointed bedrooms, it has always had a name for promoting the good food of the area and produce from their own gardens. Daughters Karoline and Irene are now on the management team and, while that won't deprive guests of the company of Mary Sweeney, with her keen interest and exhaustive local knowledge, it brings a youthful new dimension to the business.

Rooms 15 (12 separate bath & shower; 2 shower only) B&B from about €45pps. Children welcome. Restaurant: D 6-9pm daily in summer (5 days off season), from about €35; L Sun, from about €25, reservations advised. Afternoon tea; bar menu. Closed Christmas. CC. **Directions:** Off R245, Letterkenny-Ramelton road.

THE COUNTER

CANAL ROAD LETTERKENNY CO DONEGAL
074 912 0075 | info@thecounterdeli.com
www.thecounterdeli.com

EAT | BUY

Belying its unpromising location in an industrial retail park, Richard Finney's wine shop, coffee bar and deli is a gem to seek out. From the sharp black and white exterior to the cool interior, it's all about presenting the produce to best advantage. The food is healthy, tasty and modern (Badger & Dodo coffee, Scarpello sourdough...) with a simple and delicious menu for both breakfast and lunch. It's also a brilliant place to shop for gifts. Personal shoppers have great choices and there's an imaginative range of hampers on-line, including many wine treats (and - a nice touch - local Kinnegar beer), and lots more, including personalised wedding hampers. Allow time to browse when visiting this place.

Seats 30. Mon-Sat 8.30am-6pm (Fri-Sat to 7pm). Breakfast 8.30am-12 noon, L 12-3pm. Deli 9.30am-6pm. CC. **Directions:** In Letterkenny Retail Park, near Dunnes and M&S.

LEMON TREE RESTAURANT

UNIT 32-34 COURTYARD SHOPPING CENTRE
LOWER MAIN STREET LETTERKENNY CO DONEGAL EAT I DRINK
074 912 5788 I lemontreerestaurant@hotmail.com I www.thelemontreerestaurant.com

Having moved around the corner to spacious new premises (with parking) at the Courtyard Shopping Centre, after nearly twenty years on Lower Main Street, it's a case of "Same staff, same food, just new location" at the Molloy family's popular restaurant - much to the relief of their many fans. Inside, the smartly understated decor and open kitchen remain familiar features and you can still watch the three brothers - Thomas, Gary and Euro-Toques chef, Christopher Molloy - at work preparing and serving excellent modern meals that proudly showcase the local Donegal produce they hold in such high esteem.

Seats 60. D daily, 5-9.30pm (Fri-Sat to 10pm), L Sun only 1-2.30pm. Closed 3 days at Christmas. CC. **Directions:** Centre of town.

THE YELLOW PEPPER RESTAURANT

36 LOWER MAIN STREET LETTERKENNY CO DONEGAL EAT
074 912 4133 I ypepper@indigo.ie
www.yellowpepperrestaurant.com

Located in the former McIntyre Hog and March shirt factory, dating back to the 19th century, this historic building was restored by the current owners Carol Meenan and Kieran Davis in the early '90s. Since then these 'real food' pioneers, have done what they do best, providing consistently good fresh food and friendly service during the day and evening, seven days a week. Long before it became de rigeur, they promoted fresh, local food and credited their valued sources - including their own organic garden. There are no gimmicks at this caring and family friendly restaurant and it's a good place to know about.

Open Mon-Sun, 12-10pm. CC. Centrally located on the main street.

HARVEY'S POINT

LOUGH ESKE DONEGAL CO DONEGAL

074 972 2208 | stay@harveyspoint.com

www.harveyspoint.com

EAT | STAY

The Gysling family opened this stunningly located hotel on the shores of Lough Eske in 1989, and it's now run by Marc Gysling and his wife Deirdre McGlone. Aside from the setting, it has many claims to fame including the increasingly luxurious accommodation, the special activity breaks offered throughout the year - and, its greatest USP, the engaging friendliness and helpfulness of the owners and staff. Good food has always

been a key feature too - choose between excellent lake view fine dining or informal waterside meals at Harvey's Bar & Terrace.

Rooms 64 (14 wheelchair friendly; some pet-friendly). Lift. B&B from about €89pps. Conferences/events. Restaurant: D daily 6.30-9pm. Set D from €55; Set L €35; Sun L from €30 (children €15). Bar menu daily, 12.30-9. NB: opening hours/days vary off-season. Open Christmas. CC. **Directions:** 6km from Donegal Town on N15 /N56.

FREWIN

RECTORY ROAD RAMELTON CO DONEGAL   STAY

074 915 1246 | frewin.ramelton@gmail.com

www.frewinhouse.com

Thomas and Regina Coyle restored this large Victorian house with the greatest attention to period detail -Thomas specialises in restoring old buildings and is a collector by nature, so much of his collection finds a place in this interesting house. It's a lovely relaxed place set in mature gardens, and the rooms have individual style and old-fashioned charm. Thomas and Regina are great hosts - and, while evening meals are not normally offered (the pretty riverside town of Ramelton is just a short walk), you'll get a delicious breakfast, including freshly baked breads warm from the oven, served at a long table where guests can chat about their experiences and plan the day ahead.

> **Rooms 3** deluxe (2 shower only), B&B tom about €75pps. Wifi. Not suitable for children under 8. Closed Dec, Jan. CC. **Directions:** 12km from Letterkenny (on R245).

BELLE'S KITCHEN / SALT N BATTER

PIER ROAD RATHMULLAN CO DONEGAL   EAT

074 915 8800 | saltnbatter@fastmail.fm

Just a short hop up Pier Road from the harbour, Ronnie and Caroline Blake's neatly presented pair of businesses cater well to the informal dining needs of Rathmullan. Salt'n'Batter knows how to do the simple things really well - gleamingly fresh, succulent fish and perfect chips - while the posher half next door is Belle's Kitchen, a nice buzzy little smart-casual spot to enjoy a bite of something wholesome and homemade. Thanks to their consistent quality both have always been very popular - and, since Belle's Kitchen got a stylish modern makeover recently, it's been busier than ever.

> Open Tue-Sun 10am-9pm (times vary seasonally, probably closed Mon-Tue in winter). CC.

RATHMULLAN HOUSE

RATHMULLAN CO DONEGAL   EAT | STAY
074 915 8188 | info@rathmullanhouse.com
www.rathmullanhouse.com

Run with warmth and enthusiasm by Mark and Mary Wheeler, this gracious nineteenth century house just outside Rathmullan village has been in their family for over 50 years. It is fairly grand yet, set in lovely gardens on the shores of Lough Swilly, it has a laid-back holiday charm. Very comfortable accommodation includes ten especially appealing newer rooms and good food has always been a big attraction: the modern Irish cooking is based on the very best of local and artisan foods, including produce from their own restored walled garden. Excellent breakfasts too.

Rooms 32 (22 separate bath & shower, 4 wheelchair friendly, 1 pet friendly), B&B from €90pps. Cook & Gardener: D daily from 6.15pm. Informal meals Batt's Bar, 12-4.30pm, and the Tap Room. Closed midweek Nov-Dec, Feb-Mar, all Jan. CC. **Directions:** From Letterkenny, far side of Rathmullan village.

SAND HOUSE HOTEL

ROSSNOWLAGH CO DONEGAL   EAT I STAY
(071) 985 1777 I info@sandhouse.ie
www.sandhouse.ie

Perched on the edge of a stunning sandy beach two miles long, this famous hotel is now owned by its former General Manager, Paul Diver, who - in a legendary purchase that is recorded in framed documents along the walls beside the bar - secured its long term future and kept the long time staff together as a team. Unrivalled sea views and easy access to the beach are the big attractions, but this immaculately maintained hotel also offers extremely comfortable accommodation, wholesome food, a friendly bar and a spa.

Rooms 50. B&B from about €70pps. D daily 6.30-8.30pm (semi à la carte, mains about €20), L Sun only, 1-2pm about €25. Closed Dec & Jan. CC. **Directions:** Coast road from Ballyshannon to Donegal Town.

TREAN HOUSE

TREMONE LECAMY INISHOWEN CO DONEGAL   STAY
074 936 7121 I treanhouse@gmail.com
www.treanhouse.com

Way out on the Inishowen peninsula, Joyce and Mervyn Norris's immaculately presented farmhouse is tucked into a sheltered corner in stone-walled countryside beside the sea. Surrounded by a large garden with mature trees and welcoming flowers, it is a substantial house and offers a comfortable base for a relaxing away-from-it-all holi-day in a homely atmosphere. Just the place for anyone who wants to experience the real Ireland.

Rooms 4 (3 shower only). B&B about €40pps. Children welcome. Free wifi. Closed Dec-Apr. CC. **Directions:** From Moville follow R238 5km, turn right & follow house signs.

Galway Oyster Farmers
Kelly Brothers
Co. Galway

galwaygastronomy.ie

COUNTY GALWAY

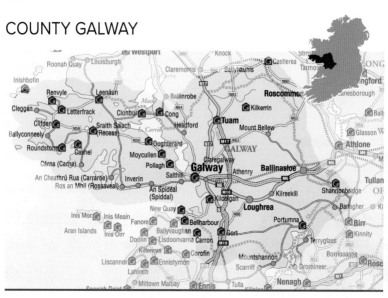

Bounded by the Atlantic Ocean on one side and the Shannon and Lough Derg on the other, County Galway would be hard to beat for the spectacular variety and charm of its many scenic routes. But it is also a cultural gem with much to offer in the way of offbeat expeditions and experiences, in addition to the dramatic visual attractions of Ireland's **Wild Atlantic Way. The Aran Islands** (www.aranislands.ie) for instance, are very accessible and can be visited by air as well as by sea. Then too, there are many coastal boat trips, including an informative seaborne tour from **Killary Harbour** on the county's northwest coast, Ireland's only genuine fjord, while Lough Corrib can also be enjoyed on a Lake Cruise.

Ashore, sport - and notably equestrian activity - is a vital part of the culture; the **Galway Races** (www.galwayraces.com) at the end of July, for example, have developed into a six day meeting which is firmly established as Ireland's premier summer horse racing event, while the **Ballinasloe International Horse Fair** in the autumn is simply unique. It dates back more than 280 years.

This has to be Ireland's most generous county, for in effect you get two counties for the price of one. They're neatly divided by the handsome sweep of island-studded **Lough Corrib**, with the big country of many mountains to the west, and rolling farmland to the east as far as the River Shannon and Lough Derg. As a bonus, where the Corrib tumbles into Galway Bay, we find one of Ireland's - indeed, one of Europe's - most vibrant urban centres.

Galway city - known for its atmosphere, cobbled streets, medieval walls, history, character, music and great food - is a bustling port which cheerfully sees itself as being linked to Spain and the 'New' world beyond the Atlantic. It is Ireland's only bi-lingual city, for Galway - with An Gaeltacht and the Irish speaking community in the west of the County in magical Connemara, 'the Land of the Sea' - carries the traditions, heritage and culture of the Irish language. Yet it continues to look outwards too, as the City of the Tribes and the West of Ireland have been designated **European Region of Gastronomy** (www.galwaygastronomy.ie) from 2018.

The designation celebrates the area's rich landscape, food heritage, innovative and creative people, and multi-cultural communities. The festivities from 2018 onwards will in turn generate strong roots for a developing strategy around food in the West, gaining momentum for the **Capital of Culture Celebration in 2020**.

Quality food plays a central role in the lives of Galway people, from farmer and fisherman to chef, restaurateur and consumer. The city and county produce enough to feed over 1.5 million people, the produce of more than 12,000 farms, 689km of coastline, 52 Islands and over 350 restaurants - including some with prestigious international recognition. And all that in the midst of some of the most wonderful scenery to be found in Ireland.

LOCAL ATTRACTIONS AND INFORMATION

>Tourism Information: www.visitgalway.ie

Galway City Tourist Office (All Year) 091 537700

Aran Tourist Office (All Year) 099 61263

Oranmore Tourist Office (All Year) 091 790811

Oughterard Tourist Office (All Year) 091 552808

Portumna Tourist Office
www.portumna.net/tourism/touristoffice.html

Gort Burren Lowlands Visitor Information Point
086 1300303

>**Galway Races** (late July/early August, Sept & Oct)
www.galwayraces.com | 091 753870

>**The Galway Food Festival** (Easter)
www.galwayfoodfestival.com

>**Galway Food Tours**
www.galwayfoodtours.com | 086 733 2885

>**Clarenbridge Oyster Festival**
(late September/early October)
www.clarenbridge.com | 091 796342 / 089 490 6779

>**Galway International Oyster & Seafood Festival** (September)
www.galwayoysterfestival.com | 091 394637

>**Bia Lover Food Festival**, Athenry
www.bialover.ie

>**Loughrea Medieval Festival**
www.loughreamedievalfestival.com

Connemara landscape near Lough Inagh

ANIAR RESTAURANT

53 DOMINICK STREET GALWAY CO GALWAY

EAT | LEARN

091 535 947 | food@aniarrestaurant.ie
www.aniarrestaurant.ie

Owned by leading restaurateurs JP McMahon and Drigin Gaffey, Aniar – meaning 'from the west' - has been the most talked about restaurant in Galway since opening in 2011. The name refers to the stated focus on seasonality, local suppliers, foraged foods and sustainably caught fish. JP regularly instructs small, hands-on classes in the Boutique Cookery School held in the restaurant kitchen. A sister restaurant, Tartare, is directly across the road, by day serving a menu of sourdough sandwiches and coffee, by night the focus is on biodynamic wines with plates of oysters, pickled fish, artisan boards and the classic dish it is named for, beef tartare. Great for a seasonal nibble and a tipple.

⭐

Seats 30. Open Wed-Thu 6-9.30, Fri-Sat from 5.30, Sat L 12-2. D from about €55. Wine from about €34. Boutique Cookery School. Closed Sun-Tue. CC

ARD BIA AT NIMMO'S

SPANISH ARCH GALWAY CO GALWAY

EAT | DRINK

091 539 897 | reservations@ardbia.com
www.ardbia.com

A wonderful stone-built medieval customs house overlooking the Claddagh Basin is home to Ard Bia (literally 'High Food'), plus a constantly changing exhibition of modern art. Proprietor Aoibheann MacNamara's enthusiasm, energy and commitment to quality are evident throughout. A shelved area offers an eclectic mix of their own craft, produce, ceramics and tweed for sale. Menus read lip-smackingly well, everything is cooked in-house and striving to provide food that is 'Great for Galway', local suppliers are the stars of every delicious meal served here. Great value for the quality, and lovely friendly service too.

Seats 100 (+ 10 outdoors); open Mon-Fri B'fast 10-12 L 12-3.30. Sat & Sun Brunch 10-3, L 12-3. D Daily 6-9. A la carte. Closed 25-26 Dec. CC. **Directions:** Harbour front, beside the Spanish Arch and Galway City Museum.

ASIAN TEA HOUSE RESTAURANT

15 MARY STREET GALWAY CITY CO GALWAY   EAT
091 563 749 | info@asianteahouse.ie
www.asianteahouse.ie

Terry Commons and Alan Wong's relaxed restaurant is loosely based on the ancient Chinese Tea House concept (a café centered around tea drinking); it offers something different in Galway city, and is good value. Quite lengthy menus representative of Malay, Vietnam, Thai, Japan and China, feature a large range of dishes, which are all MSG free and based mainly on locally sourced ingredients - and all dishes are cooked to order. Next door is the Buddha Bar with its Asian inspired interior, specialising in well priced cocktails and serving a condensed version of the main menu from the shared kitchen. Its success is well deserved.

Seats 46. D daily, 5-10.30, à la carte. Buddha Bar, open Wed-Mon from 5pm (Mon, Wed, Thu to 11.30, Fr-Sat to12.30, Sun to 11pm) CC. **Directions:** Galway City Centre, north-west of Eyre Square.

CAVA BODEGA

1 MIDDLE STREET MEWS MIDDLE STREET GALWAY CO GALWAY   EAT
091 539 884 | food@cavarestaurant.ie
www.cavarestaurant.ie

This inconspicuous premises on Middle Street is the second home for JP McMahon and Drigín Gaffey's Cava Bodega, a welcome reincarnation of the popular Cava. At street level, there's a tall bar and a small dining space with a mix of seating and downstairs in the cosy bodega, everything from bread to ice-cream is produced in the open kitchen. The menu is easily navigated, divided into vegetable, fish and meat sections, nibbles and desserts. All meats are Irish, free-range, local, or wild - and, reflecting their 'nose to tail' policy, there are plenty of slow cooked and offal dishes. Cava offers the best of Irish and Spanish produce, a happy balance between food cultures.

Seats 60. Open daily: Mon-Wed 5pm-10, Thu 5-10.30; Fri 4-11, Sat 12-11; Sun 12-9.30. Reservations recommended; children welcome. Tapas from about €5.50. CC. **Directions:** West End Galway city centre

CORRIB HOUSE TEA ROOMS & GUEST ACCOMMODATION

NO. 3. WATERSIDE WOODQUAY GALWAY CITY CO GALWAY   EAT | STAY

091 446 753 | info@corribhouse.com

www.corribhouse.com

Victoria and David Bohan's handsome waterside Georgian house was built in the early 1800s and sensitively restored before opening as Tea Rooms and Guest Accommodation in 2011. Four of the five spacious, stylishly furnished guest rooms have river views, while the fifth overlooks an attractive courtyard, used for al fresco lunches in summer. Excellent breakfast and brunch menus are offered (also available to non-residents) and pride in provenance is seen in the supplier list. A visit to this delightful spot is sure to be enjoyable.

Tea Rooms: **seats 42** (+15 outside), open daily 9.30- 5, brunch all day Sat & Sun. Closed Mon Nov-Feb. Unlicensed. Full wheelchair access. **Rooms 5**. B&B room rate from about €100, 15% discount for single occupancy. House closed Dec & Jan. CC. **Directions:** Centre of Galway, next to the Courthouse and Town Hall Theatre.

DELA

51 LOWER DOMINICK STREET GALWAY CO GALWAY   EAT
091 449252 | letseat@dela.ie
www.dela.ie

Owned and run by local couple Joe and Margaret Bohan and famed for great brunches, Dela ('Share' in Swedish) has become one of Galway's best loved restaurants. The Bohans are very hands on - Margaret at front of house and Joe at the farm that supplies his kitchen team with vegetables, herbs, salads and gorgeous edible flowers from spring onwards. In a pretty Scandi-inspired rustic setting, they offer brilliant brunches and, in the evening, sharing plates and classic bistro dishes; excellent wine and craft drinks list to match. A great reason to make the journey across the river.

Seats about 60. Mon 11.30-3, Tue-Sat 11.30-3 & 6-10, Sun 10-4. A la carte. CC

THE DOUGH BROS

CATHEDRAL BUILDINGS MIDDLE STREET GALWAY CO GALWAY   EAT
087 176 1662 | thedoughbros@hotmail.com
www.thedoughbros.ie

A famous Galway partnership, The Dough Bros are artisan pizza makers who insist on nothing but the best. Having built a cult following from their pizza truck at Moycullen market (still used for events and festivals), brothers Eugene and Ronan Greaney, together with their childhood friend and chef, Laurence Enright, opened what has become a much loved casual dining venue right at the heart of Galway city. semi-permanent pop-up in Abbeygate Street giving that entire area a new identity and a lease of life. Neapolitan pizza is their speciality and, with respect for ingredients and immense pride in their product, The Dough Bros provide elevated street food with no compromise on quality. Locally inspired relaxed dining.

Seats 70.Open Sun-Mon 12-9 (Tue-Sat to 10pm). CC. **Directions:** City centre.

THE G HOTEL & SPA

WELLPARK GALWAY CITY CO GALWAY
091 865 200 | reservetheg@theg.ie
www.theg.ie

EAT | STAY

One of the finest hotels in the West - and certainly the most original - the G is renowned for its interior by the London-based Galwegian milliner, Philip Treacy, who was given free rein to indulge his quirky creativity. Public areas are arresting but suites and guestrooms are much quieter in tone, making for a restful stay. A popular wedding and 'treats' venue, there's a strong emphasis on food at the G (including a pretty Afternoon Tea) and it's a fun place that brings a smile to people's faces.

Rooms 101. Children welcome. Spa. B&B from about €70pps. Restaurant: L & D daily, 12-3pm & 6-10pm. Midweek early D from about €30; also à la carte. Sun L from about €25. Closed 24-26 Dec. CC. **Directions:** East Galway City on the old Dublin Road, 5 minute drive from Eyre Square.

GLENLO ABBEY HOTEL & PULLMAN RESTAURANT

BUSHYPARK GALWAY CO GALWAY   EAT | STAY

091 526 666 | reception@glenloabbey.ie
www.glenloabbeyhotel.ie

Glenlo Abbey offers something different from other luxury hotels and, despite major refurbishment, it has not lost its pleasingly old world feel - and its Pullman Restaurant, in four 'Orient Express' railway carriages, is perhaps the country's most novel dinner venue. An atmospheric setting for Head Chef Alan McArdle's excellent modern classical cooking - showcasing local (and Irish) ingredients - it is recommended as much for its unique, special occasion experience as for the fare - it's great fun and a visit is always enjoyable.

Rooms 50 (1 wheelchair friendly). Lift. Rooms from about €160. **Pullman Restaurant:** D daily in season from 6.30pm (Nov-Apr, Fri & Sat only). D from about €57. River Room Restaurant: B'fast daily, D some nights (details from hotel). Bar food daily 12-9. Open all year. Helipad. CC. **Directions:** N59 Galway-Clifden 4km from city.

GOYA'S BAKERY

2/3 KIRWANS LANE GALWAY CO GALWAY   EAT | BUY | PRODUCER

091 567010 | info@goyas.ie

www.goyas.ie

If only for a cup of cappuccino or hot chocolate and a wedge of chocolate cake, or a slice of quiche, a restorative visit to Emer Murray's delightful contemporary café, bakery and deli is a must on any visit to Galway. While best known for their tempting range of pastrics and treats they also have an equally appealing deli and savoury takeaway. There's something very promising about the cardboard cake boxes stacked up in preparation, the staff are super, there's a great buzz and the food is simply terrific. Also specialises in wedding and special occasion cakes and seasonal baking.

Seats 56 (+ 20 outdoors). Open all day Mon-Sat (Mon-Fri 9.30-6, Sat 9-6). Wheelchair accessible. Licensed. Wi-Fi. CC. **Directions:** Laneway off lower end of Quay Street.

THE HERON'S REST B&B

LONGWALK SPANISH ARCH GALWAY CITY CO GALWAY   STAY

091 539 574 | theheronsrest@gmail.com
www.theheronsrest.com

The location of Sorcha Molloy's delightful B&B must be the best in Galway - in the centre of the city just seaward of Spanish Arch with everything within easy walking distance, yet quietly situated with views across the river and out to sea. And it is a charming house, with lots of TLC lavished on the sweet waterside rooms, and a lot of care in everything Sorcha does - including a typically generous and unusual breakfast menu showcasing local and other Irish artisan foods. Magic.

Rooms 3 (also 3 for self-catering); B&B from about €65pps. Gourmet B'fast: Mar–Oct; Continental B'fast: Nov-Feb. Unsuitable for children under 3. Free wifi. No evening meals; afternoon tea & gourmet picnic baskets available on request. Off street parking (complimentary). Closed Jan. CC.
Directions: On the Longwalk near the Spanish Arch.

HOOKED

65 HENRY STREET GALWAY CO GALWAY   EAT
091 581752 | hookedonhenryst@gmail.com
www.hookedonhenryst.com

A combination of restaurant, café and chipper, this small family-run business sits in a row of terraced houses west of the river - next to its older sister, Ali's Fish Shop, which supplies ultra fresh local fish daily. Run by Ali's daughter, Nuisin Jalilvand, its cool, urban identity is very much in tune with the West end vibe and it has earned a reputation for serving the best fish and chips in the city. However, the menu doesn't stop there, with everything from seafood tagliatelle to crab cakes and chowders on offer. Hooked is funky and fun, serving fabulous fish - a real treat for seafood lovers with none of the fuss.

> Open: Mon & Tue 5-10, Wed -Sun 1-10. A la carte. CC. **Directions:** Western side of the river, across the upper (more northerly) New Road bridge; next to Ali's Fish Shop.

HOTEL MEYRICK

EYRE SQUARE GALWAY CO GALWAY   EAT | STAY
091 564 041 | reshn@hotelmeyrick.ie
www.hotelmeyrick.ie

Formerly the Great Southern, this historic railway hotel was built in 1845 and has always had a special place in the hearts of Galway people. Recent additions have given it a fresh and vibrant new feel, but the older guestrooms still hint at the grandeur and elegance of its 19th century heyday. The Meyrick has earned a reputation for good food, notably at the atmospheric basement restaurant, Number 15 on the Square (fine dining); Afternoon Tea in The Parlour lounge is popular too, also the pleasant Gaslight Bar & Brasserie for informal meals and cocktails. This piece of Galway history succeeds also in making itself relevant for today's guests while retaining its vintage appeal.

> **Rooms 97.** B&B from about €60pps. Number 15 in the Square, D daily 6.30-9.39. Closed 23-27 Dec. CC. **Directions:** In heart of the city overlooking Eyre Square.

L VICOLO RESTAURANT & BACARO

THE BRIDGEMILLS O'BRIEN'S BRIDGE GALWAY CO GALWAY   EAT | DRINK

091 530 515 | bookings@ilvicolo.ie

www.ilvicolo.ie

Just a short stroll over O'Brien's Bridge, Gerry McMahon's atmospheric restaurant at Bridge Mills reflects his devotion to Italian food and wine. The River Corrib runs underneath the main room, where the original mill wheel is a focal point, and the wine bar is flanked by two handsome stone dining rooms. A pleasant buzz, downtempo jazz, a stunning riverside terrace and keen, mostly Italian, staff create a relaxed atmosphere in which to enjoy authentic north Italian cooking. And - just as in a traditional Venetian bacaro - you can sip a glass from the all-Italian wine list wine at the bar, with some spunciotti (Venetian 'tapas').

Seats 50. Open D Tue-Thu 5-10 (Fri to 11). Sat & Sun L 12-4 & D 5-11 (Sun to 10) Closed Mon. CC. **Directions:** Over O'Brien's Bridge, a couple of minutes' walk from Shop Street .

JOHN KEOGH'S - THE LOCK KEEPER

22-24 UPPER DOMINICK STREET GALWAY CO GALWAY **EAT | DRINK**
091 449 431 | info@johnkeoghs.ie
www.johnkeoghs.ie

Matt Hall's atmospheric gastropub is named after a former lock keeper on the 19th century Eglinton Canal. Although only built in 2016, John Keogh's - The Lock Keeper feels at home in Galway's oldest neighbourhood, among the restaurants, music venues and cafés. It stocks plenty of craft beers, dozens of whiskeys and gins alongside the usual products and good food too. Chef Joe Flaherty is from Renvyle in Connemara and the cooking at this fine pub shows his passion for taste and quality. A pub for people who love pubs.

Food served Mon-Fri 5pm-9pm, Sat-Sun 1pm-9pm. A la carte. CC. **Directions:** West of main bridge in Galway city.

KAI RESTAURANT

SEA ROAD GALWAY CITY CO GALWAY   EAT
091 526 003 | kaicaferestaurant@gmail.com
www.kaicaferestaurant.com

A must-visit for food lovers visiting the West, Kai has earned a top place in the Irish food scene. Run by chef Jess Murphy, a New Zealander, with her Irish husband David front-of-house, Kai ('food') is a rustic restaurant where intensely seasonal menus change daily and throughout the day. While informal, Jess Murphy is a serious chef and her punchy, flavourful cooking is testament to an original talent. The short ethically-sourced dinner menu features the best local produce, with carefully selected wines to accompany, and queues regularly form for lunch and the famous Sunday brunch. Good value for the quality of the food and its popularity is well deserved.

⭐

Open Mon 9.30m-3pm, Tue-Fri 9.30am-9.30pm, Sat 10.30am-9.30pm, Sun Brunch 12-3pm; à la carte. Closed D Sun-Mon, bank hols. CC. **Directions:** Westside - Sea Road runs between Father Griffin Avenue and Upper Dominick Street.

LOAM

GEATA NA CATHRACH FAIRGREEN GALWAY CO GALWAY   EAT | DRINK
091 569727 | info@loamgalway.com
www.loamgalway.com

In a stretch of industrial-looking glass buildings near the Radisson, chef Enda McEvoy's modern, casual and fine dining hybrid has an inviting wine bar, and a serious dining area set up to face the show in an open kitchen. Whether you choose the Simplicity Menu (a snip) or the exciting tasting menu, it will be meticulously seasonal - inspired by ingredients like native oysters, Connemara lamb and foraged foods such as dillisk - with an astonishing array of textures and flavours on the (beautiful) plate. Enda McEvoy has captured a little bit of the magic of the west of Ireland here - and there's more than a touch of alchemy in this kitchen.

⭐

Open Tue-Sat: Wine Bar 5pm-midnight, Restaurant D only, 6-11pm. Bar menu. Simplicity Menu midweek, from €40. Tasting Menu from €75. Closed Sun-Mon. **Directions:** Just off Eyre Square

McCAMBRIDGES

38-39 SHOP STREET GALWAY CITY CO GALWAY   EAT | BUY

091 562 259 | retail@mccambridges.com
www.mccambridges.com

Established in 1925 and now run by siblings Eoin, Natalie and Norma McCambridge , who take pride in continuing the family tradition, this Galway gem offers an ever-changing range of carefully selected food and wines from Ireland and abroad, including artisan jams, preserves, chutneys, Irish cheeses, speciality meats, ice creams - and irresistible Irish and continental chocolates. Upstairs at McCambridges is a casual - but quality-conscious - restaurant that uses only Irish meats and poultry and asserts its support for local and artisan producers. It's a very popular spot so you may have to queue, but the cooking should be worth the wait. A great feature of the vibrant Galway dining scene.

Open Mon-Sat 8.30-5.30 (Thu-Sat to 9pm), Sun 10.30-6 (Brunch 10.30-4.30). Closed Sun in Jan. CC **Directions:** City centre - on main shopping street

NOX HOTEL

LIOSBAN ROAD OFF HEADFORD ROAD GALWAY CO GALWAY   STAY

091 735 555 | sleep@noxhotel.ie
www.noxhotelgalway.ie

With quirkily decorated public areas in vibrant tones of turquoise, orange and metallics, this youthful budget hotel is a lively spot and has filled a niche, becoming a popular meeting place for a casual bite to eat or a drink in the busy open plan bar, where craft beers and cocktails are the thing. Guest rooms are quieter in tone and quite minimalist - and, while there's an emphasis on leisure travel, including families, at weekends, business travellers will be glad to find a good work station with a data port as well as high speed wifi, flatscreen TV, individual thermostat control - and free parking.

Rooms 102, room rate from about €80. Families welcome. Wifi. Fork Restaurant: B'fast Mon-Fri 7-10.30, Sat-Sun 8-11, L daily 12.30-5, D daily 6-9pm. Children's menu. Free parking. **Directions:** Off Headford Road roundabout (N6/N84)

OSCARS SEAFOOD BISTRO

DOMINICK STREET GALWAY CO GALWAY

091 582 180 | oscarsbistro@gmail.com

www.oscarsbistro.ie

EAT

Together with his wife, Sinead Hughes, chef Michael O'Meara runs this Galway favourite, just a couple of minutes' walk across the bridge in the city's lively Westside area. Showcasing the finest of local seafood, Michael O'Meara's bustling restaurant offers some of the best fish cooking in the country - and some of the most interesting thinking about fish and the environment too, as shared in his remarkable book Sea Gastronomy, Fish & Shellfish of the North Atlantic (www.artisanhouse.ie).

Carefully sourced seasonal dishes also include several interesting meat choices and his kitchen wizardry garners praise from locals and tourists alike. Charming service too, making a meal here a thoroughly enjoyable experience.

Seats 45. Open Mon-Sat from 6pm. Closed Sun & bank hol Mon. A la carte. Early D Mon-Thu 6-6.30. CC. **Directions:** 2 minutes across bridge from Jurys.

PAPA RICH STREET FOOD KITCHEN

3 DALYS PLACE GALWAY CO GALWAY   EAT | LEARN
091 450147 | paparichstreetfoodkitchen@gmail.com
www.paparichkitchen.com

In the constantly evolving world of 'street food' themed restaurants in Galway, Papa Rich is one of the younger kids on the block, having only been welcoming the crowds since late December 2015. Yet, thanks to their talent in creating Asian street food inspired dishes from family recipes at affordable prices, husband and wife team Kevin Tan and Rebecca Tan Lee's place quickly became a firm favourite on Galway's casual dining scene. And such is the demand for Kevin's cuisine that there are now three to choose from since Papa Rich Bistro opened at Born in Newtownsmith (Galway city) and Papa Rich Express, a thriving takeaway on the Headford Road.

Seats about 40. Open daily 12.30-10.30pm. Weekend reservations advised. **Directions:** In Woodquay, above Bar an Chaladh and just across from McSwiggans

PARK HOUSE HOTEL

FORSTER ST. EYRE SQUARE GALWAY CO GALWAY   STAY | EAT
091 564 924 | parkhousehotel@eircom.net
www.parkhousehotel.ie

If you want a thoroughly Irish welcome in the heart of Galway, you could not do better than stay at this cosy and central hotel. Guest rooms are spacious, thoughtfully furnished and well-equipped for business travellers, the food is good and private parking for residents is a real plus. Park House Hotel has the individuality that comes with owner-management and provides an exceptionally friendly and comfortable haven from the bustle of Galway, which seems to be constantly in celebration.

Rooms 84. (1 shower only, 4 wheelchair friendly). Lift. Children welcome. All day room service. Park Room Restaurant seats 70. L & D Mon-Sun 12-3 & 6-10pm, set menus and à la carte; bar food daily 12-9.30. Full wheelchair access. Closed 23-26 Dec (incl). CC. **Directions:** Adjacent to Eyre Square, near bus and train station.

LE PETIT POIS RESTAURANT & WINE BAR

VICTORIA PLACE GALWAY CO GALWAY   EAT | DRINK | LEARN
091 330880 | info@lepetitpois.ie
www.lepetitpois.ie

Through a picturesque stone archway just off Eyre Square, a once-neglected space has become a culinary oasis - and the laneway has been transformed into a heated wine garden, with twinkling fairy lights and brightly upholstered stools. Owned by Gallic husband and wife team, Philippe and Michèle Renaut - Michèle creates delicious traditional French dishes whilst husband Philippe advises you on the perfect wines to accompany them - this friendly little two storey restaurant is now the place to enjoy French cuisine, French cheese and French wines. One of the city's most popular restaurants - and a real treat for Francophiles.

Seats 30 (+12 outdoors). Open Tue-Fri 6-10pm, (to 11pm Sat, 5-10pm Sun). Discovery menu from €40. Also a la carte. Closed Mon; early Jan. Outdoor seating (heated). CC. **Directions:** Just off Eyre Square (Meyrick Hotel end)

RADISSON BLU HOTEL & SPA AND RAW - SUSHI IN THE SKY

LOUGH ATALIA ROAD GALWAY CO GALWAY   EAT | STAY
091 538300 | sales.galway@radissonsas.com | www.radissonhotelgalway.com

Attractively situated overlooking Lough Atalia, this pleasing contemporary hotel is more central than its scenic location suggests, as it's very close to the shops and restaurants around Eyre Square. It's known for good business and conference facilities and the destination spa, Spirit One - but a less likely USP is that the dining options include a rooftop Japanese restaurant, RAW, where the renowned chef Hisashi Kumagai (Kuma) delights diners with Japanese Sushi, showcasing the best of Galway's fresh raw seafood, fastidiously selected and artfully arranged. Guided by the very helpful, informed waiting staff, a meal in RAW is an adventure.

Rooms 261, B&B from €95pps. RAW: D only, Tue-Sat 6-10. Marinas Grill: seats 220; L Mon-Sat & D daily. Bar food daily. CC. **Directions:** Signed off shore road (Lough Atalia); 3 minutes' walk from bus & train station. CC.

SHERIDANS CHEESEMONGERS AND WINE BAR

14-16 CHURCHYARD STREET GALWAY CITY CO GALWAY   EAT | BUY

091 564 829 | galway@sheridanscheesemongers.com
www.sheridanscheesemongers.com

Synonymous with good cheese in Ireland, brothers Seamus and Kevin Sheridan started the business that is now a household name by selling cheese at Galway farmers' market many moons ago. Stocks reflect the seasons and are mainly Irish, but equally carefully sourced European foods are also stocked. Above the shop, a rustic wine bar overlooks St. Nicholas's Church square. A visit here is a convivial affair. Aromas from the deli below accompany you up the stairs, and knowledgeable staff assist your choice of wines from the rustic, blue tiled bar, to be enjoyed with wonderful cheese and charcuterie boards selected from below. A seat by the window overlooking the Saturday market is always a pleasure.

Wine Bar: Tue-Fri 2-9 Sat to 8. (Shop open Mon-Fri 9-6, Sat 9.30-6; Sun 1-6 in summer). CC.

THE KING'S HEAD

15 HIGH STREET GALWAY CITY CO GALWAY   EAT | DRINK

091 566 630 | info@thekingshead.ie
www.thekingshead.ie

This atmospheric casual dining destination benefits greatly from the personal touch from its caring owners, the Grealish family. A piece of Galway's medieval architectural history, The King's Head could be seen as the original super-pub - at over eight hundred years old, this popular three storey bar caters to a broad audience to fill its seats and does so with style. It serves fresh wholesome food - and speciality drinks, including their own Kings Head 'Blood Red Ale' (from local craft brewers, Galway Hooker), every day - and there's free live music every night, big screen sports, and lunch-time comedy too.

Seats 200 (+30 outside; private room 80). Food served Mon-Sat 10.30am-10pm; Sun from 11.30. Children welcome. Wheelchair access from Middle Street; wheelchair friendly toilets. CC. **Directions:** Top of High Street.

TIGH NEACHTAIN

17 CROSS STREET GALWAY CO GALWAY
091 568 820 | info@tighneachtain.com
www.tighneachtain.com

DRINK

If you have to choose one traditional Galway pub to visit, it would have to be Tigh Neachtain (Naughton's). One of the city's oldest pubs, Neachtain's has long been at the centre of the city's arts and music communities and it has great charm, an open fire, a friendly atmosphere, impromptu music sessions - and their own seasonal craft beer. The restaurant upstairs is operated independently but supplies some casual food (oysters, chowder) and a seat by the fire or in the snug on a chilly day is as sought after as a chair in the seating area outdoors in summer, the traditional vantage point for people watching on Galway's main thoroughfare. An essential place to know about in Galway, and full of character.

Seats 45 (outdoors, 20). D daily 6-10, L Fri-Sun 12-3. Closed 25 Dec & Good Fri.

WA CAFÉ

13 NEW DOCK STREET GALWAY CO GALWAY
091 895850 | info@wacafe.net
www.wacafe.net

EAT | BUY
LEARN | PRODUCER

Yoshimi Hayakawa had done her sushi training in Tokyo before coming to Ireland, where she began by serving traditional sushi in Galway's Saturday market, later opening Wa Café. This taste of Japanese life is now a firm fixture on Galway's dining scene, a cosy little spot where there's a good choice for vegetarians as well as the best that Gannet Fishmongers has on offer - and everything on the short menu is authentically Japanese, from sushi rolls, miso soup, bento boxes to green teas. They're still at Galway Market every Saturday and Yoshimi also runs sushi workshops teaching traditional sushi making methods.

Open Mon-Thu 5-9.30pm, Fri-Sat, 12-9.30pm, Sun 12-9pm. CC. **Directions:** Almost dockside, near Galway City Museum.

O'GRADY'S ON THE PIER

SEA POINT BARNA CO GALWAY

091 592 223 | ogradysonthepier@hotmail.com

www.ogradysonthepier.com

EAT

In a stunning harbourside position, Michael O'Grady's charming restaurant is a favourite destination for seafood lovers. The best dishes are the simplest and, although the ubiquitous tiger prawn may make a surprising appearance, the wide range of fish and seafood is mainly fresh local produce, delivered daily: Cleggan crab, Rossaveal clams, Galway oysters (in season), Galway Bay lobster, local mussels, Aran salmon, locally caught mackerel, and sea fish landed at nearby Rossaveal. Well worth a visit.

Seats 85 (outdoors 25). A la carte L daily 12.30-3. Set Sun L from €27.95. D from 6pm. Closed 24-26 Dec (reopens D 27 Dec). CC. **Also at:** Kirwans Lane, a sister restaurant in Galway City, also has a strong focus on seafood. **Directions:** 7km west of Galway city on the Spiddal Road.

THE TWELVE HOTEL

BARNA VILLAGE GALWAY CITY CO GALWAY
091 597 000 I enquire@thetwelvehotel.ie
www.thetwelvehotel.ie

EAT I DRINK I STAY
BUY I PRODUCER

Fergus O'Halloran's unique hotel has achieved national recognition thanks to hands-on management and marketing by an inspired proprietor. It sings of quality and innovation at every level, from romantic rooms and **Upstairs at West**'s exceptional fine wining-and-dining experience, to quality casual food. Pizza in the busy child-friendly Pins Bar Bakery Bistro - and sales in the Pizza Dozzina artisanal shop next door - there is huge focus on the best local and artisan foods and craft beers. A great destination for wine-lovers aswell.

⭐

Rooms 47 (4 shower only, 3 wheelchair friendly). Lift. Rooms from about €100. Children welcome. **Upstairs at West:** D Wed-Sun 6-10pm (from 2pm Sun); D from about €33; Tasting Menu €65 (add 4 glasses wine for €30). L Sun only, 12-5.30, à la carte. Pins Bakery Bistro open all day. Music (weekends). CC. **Directions:** At crossroads in Barna village.

INIS MEÁIN RESTAURANT & SUITES

INIS MEAIN ARAN ISLANDS CO GALWAY   EAT | STAY
086 826 6026 | post@inismeain.com
www.inismeain.com

This wonderful place on the most tranquil and least visited of the Aran Islands group has earned an international reputation as one of Ireland's most desirable destinations. Chef Ruairí de Blacam, a native of Inis Meain, and his wife, Marie-Therese, offer a unique experience, serving beautifully simple seasonal food in a modern restaurant with a panoramic view of the island. Suites are designed to help guests discover the peace and quiet of the island, with fishing rods, bicycles and books instead of TV or a spa. Simply magic.

⭐ **Restaurant Seats 16**. Island D 4 course (no-choice) 7.30 for 8pm, suite guests Mon-Sat, non-residents Wed-Sat. Rooms 4 & 1 suite apartment; min 2 night stay. Accommodation from €480. Closed Sun & Oct-Mar. CC. **Directions:** After passing only pub on your right, take next right, then take first left.

TEACH AN TAE TEA ROOMS & CAFÉ

INIS OIRR ARAN ISLANDS CO GALWAY   EAT | BUY
099 75092 | teachantae@gmail.com
www.teachantae.com

Michael and Alissa O'Donoghue understand the value of doing homely things well, and the menu at their charming tea rooms is very simple. Their hens provide beautiful, fresh eggs for the baking, and the organic garden - replenished each year with sand and seaweed from the shore - is the source of vegetables and salads. Everything is made from scratch and they sell homemade preserves and locally made crafts.

Seats 30. Open 10.30am-4.30pm daily, May- Sep. Children welcome. Free wifi. **No CC. Directions:** In the centre of the island; about 100m from the beach.

TEACH NAN PHAIDAI

KILMURVEY INIS MOR ARAN ISLANDS CO GALWAY   EAT
099 20975 | nanphaidi@eircom.net

Catherine Concannon's pretty thatched cottage is just the kind of place that visitors to Ireland dream of finding - and it's no dream, but a delightful daytime restaurant, where an open turf fire is lit on cold days. Delicious homemade food is listed on a large blackboard, while an array of wonderful cakes and buns and Fair Trade coffees take over the counter... Catherine's daughter, Orla, and her husband Gabriel (a former fisherman), have a goat farm on the island and produce the acclaimed Aran Goat's Cheese, so that is sure to be on the menu.

Seats 45 (+ 20 outdoors). Open 10am-5pm daily (earlier closing in winter months). Closed 1 week over Christmas. Children welcome. CC. **Directions:** In Kilmurvey Craft village

TIG CONGAILE

MOORE VILLAGE INIS MEAIN ARAN ISLANDS CO GALWAY   EAT | STAY
099 73085 | bbinismeain@gmail.com
www.inismeainbb.com

Sitting outside on a fine day, the peace and the view make Vilma and Padric Conneely's restaurant and accommodation the best spot on the island. Vilma has always loved using organic and sea vegetables - long before it became popular - and her wonderful Sea Vegetable Soup is a speciality known well beyond the islands. Dinner here is really good and, even though less publicised than some of the restaurants on the islands, Vilma's cooking is on a par with the best.

> B&B from €45pps, single from €55. **Seats 45**; D 7-9pm; à la carte, reservations required. Children welcome. Toilets wheelchair accessible. Licensed (wines from about €6 per glass). Open Easter-Oct. CC. **Directions:** Thirty minutes' walk from the pier.

CONNEMARA SANDS HOTEL

BALLYCONNEELY MANNIN BAY BALLYCONNEELY CO GALWAY   EAT | STAY
095 23030 | reservation@connemarasands-hotel.com
www.connemarasands-hotel.com

Right on the beautiful white coral strand at Mannin Bay, near Clifden, this four star boutique hotel is blessed with a dream location. Its unusual, colourful style is striking, and the comfortable accommodation is simple and restful. There has always been a focus on good local food here and, in 2017, the bar was raised with the arrival of renowned Executive Head Chef Stefan Matz and Head Chef Sinead Quinn who are responsible for the food in both the theatrical fine dining experience, **Erriseask Restaurant** at Connemara Sands Hotel and the casual Sands Bar.

> Rooms 18 (some shower only). B&B from €50pps. Voya Seaweed Spa. Free wifi. Self-catering available. **Erriseask Restaurant:** D Fri & Sat, 7-10pm from first week June, 6 nights in high season. Sands Bar: open daily. Hotel closed in winter. CC. **Directions:** Signed off Ballyconneely-Roundstone road.

CASHEL HOUSE HOTEL

CASHEL CONNEMARA CO GALWAY

095 31001 | res@cashel-house-hotel.com
www.cashel-house-hotel.com

EAT | STAY

While some might say it is old-fashioned - and it is far from being a fashion-led destination - relaxed hospitality combined with professionalism have earned an international reputation for the McEvilly family's long-established hotel. Cosy and restoring, its many high points include the very comfortable accommodation; open fires and comfy places to unwind; mainly classic cooking of local foods (including a great breakfast) and, especially,

Kay McEvilly's warm hospitality. The gardens are open to the public - you can even admire the view from President de Gaulle's favourite seat, when he stayed in 1969.

Rooms 29. B&B from about €75pps. Pet friendly; children welcome. D daily 7-9 from, about €32; L Sun 12.30-2.30. Set D. Bar L à la carte; Afternoon Tea 2.30-5pm. Small weddings. Gardening courses Closed Jan-mid Feb. CC. **Directions:** Off N59; 1.5km west of Recess signed left.

ARDAGH HOTEL & RESTAURANT

BALLYCONNEELY ROAD CLIFDEN CO GALWAY

EAT | STAY

095 21384 | ardaghhotel@eircom.net
www.ardaghhotel.com

You could easily miss this modest-looking hotel outside Clifden, which would be a pity. Beautifully located overlooking Ardbear Bay, it is run by Stéphane and Monique Bauvet and known for quiet hospitality, low-key comfort and Monique's excellent cooking. The interior has style, in a relaxed homely way: turf fires, comfortable armchairs, earthy colours, and a plant-filled conservatory area upstairs are all gently pleasing to the eye. The rooms are very comfortable and the long-established restaurant - a light-filled room on the first floor, with wonderful sea and mountain views - is a seafood-lovers destination, with warmly efficient staff ensuring an enjoyable evening. Lunch is also available in the atmospheric bar, or on the terrace, in summer.

Rooms 17. Restaurant: D 7.15-9.30pm daily. Daytime bar menu. WiFi. Shuttle bus to Clifden. Closed Nov-Mar. CC. **Directions:** 3 km outside Clifden on Ballyconneely Road.

DOLPHIN BEACH COUNTRY HOUSE

LOWER SKY ROAD CLIFDEN CO GALWAY

EAT | STAY

095 21204 | stay@dolphinbeachhouse.com
www.dolphinbeachhouse.com

Legendary for its magical location and the Foyle family's hospitality, this beachside house is set in 14 acres of wilderness, 'with the Atlantic at the bottom of the garden' (safe swimming too). Bedrooms, all with magnificent views, combine comfort and originality (notably Billy Foyle's unusual woodwork), and you can snuggle up beside an open fire after dining in a wonderful sun room overlooking the beach. Now run by sisters Clodagh and Sinead, many regulars would say this is their favourite place in the world - and it is easy to see why.

Rooms 9 (5 shower only). B&B double €100-145. Not suitable for children under 12. Not wheelchair accessible. D 7-8pm, from €40; (booking essential, residents only). Closed end Oct-early Apr. **Directions:** Left off Sky Road, about 5km (3 miles) from Clifden.

FOYLES HOTEL

MAIN STREET CLIFDEN CO GALWAY

095 21801 | info@foyleshotel.com

www.foyleshotel.com

EAT | STAY

Eddie Foyle's handsome 19th century hotel in Clifden town centre has played a central role in the hospitality of the area for many a year. Comfortably old-fashioned, with good beds and modern bathrooms, it is in a wonderful time warp - and its Victorian origins are seen in pleasingly wide corridors, to accommodate ladies in the hooped dresses of the era... The hotel's Marconi Restaurant specialises in seafood and, combining quality and atmosphere with good value, it is one of the most popular in the town.

Rooms 25. B&B from about €50pps, short breaks offered. Restaurant open 6-9pm daily. Hotel closed Christmas & Jan. CC. **Directions:** Centre of Clifden.

GUYS BAR AND SNUG

MAIN STREET CLIFDEN CO GALWAY

095 21130 | info@guysbarclifden.com

www.guysbarclifden.com

EAT | DRINK

Dating back to the early 19th century, when it was a traditional pub-grocery, Clancy's, Shane O'Grady's excellent pub has adapted well, combining the best of old and new to make a very agreeable casual dining destination, known for its warmth and good food. While there's an emphasis on seafood (house Seafood Chowder and Guys Seafood Platter among the favourites), menus offer something for everyone and there's a good choice for vegetarians and for children (including a free baby bowl). There is also a gourmet pizza menu, available to take away.

Open Mon-Thu, 10.30am-11.30pm, Fri & Sat 10.30-12.30am, Sun 12.30pm-11.30pm. No reservations. CC.

MALLMORE COUNTRY HOUSE

BALLYCONNEELY ROAD CLIFDEN CO GALWAY   STAY

095 21460 | info@mallmore.com
www.mallmore.com

Offering a truly rural away-from-it all experience near Clifden, Alan and Kathleen Hardman's restored Georgian home is set in 35 acres of gardens and woodland grounds; Connemara ponies are bred here, and old woodland has been retained so the grounds are teeming with wildlife. Warm and welcoming, with a turf fire in the lovely drawing room and individually decorated rooms, it is a special, peaceful place to stay.

Rooms 6 (all shower only). B&B from about €45pps. Closed 1 Nov-Easter. **NO CC. Directions:** 1.5 km from Clifden; signed off Ballyconneely road.

MITCHELL'S RESTAURANT

MARKET STREET CLIFDEN CONNEMARA CO GALWAY   EAT

095 21867 | mitchellsclifden@gmail.com
www.mitchellsrestaurantclifden.com

JJ & Kay Mitchell's attractive and well-managed restaurant offers efficient, welcoming service and consistently pleasing, stylishly simple "good home cooking" all day, every day throughout the season. The emphasis is on local fish from sustainable sources, but there's a fair choice for non-fish eaters, especially on the all-day menu which offers a wide range of lightish fare.

Seats 75; open daily, 12-10, early D in Jul-Aug to 6.45pm, from about €24.95. Set D about €27.50; also à la carte. Wine from about €18.50. Closed Nov-Feb. CC. **Directions:** Across the road from SuperValu supermarket.

THE QUAY HOUSE

BEACH ROAD CLIFDEN CO GALWAY
095 21369 | res@thequayhouse.com
www.thequayhouse.com

STAY

The Quay House is the oldest building in Clifden and was built around 1820. Since 1993 it has been relishing its most enjoyable phase, in the incomparable hands of long-time hoteliers, Paddy and Julia Foyle. It's a fine house, with spacious rooms, including a stylishly homely drawing room with an open fire and exceptionally comfortable accommodation in wittily decorated and sumptuously furnished rooms. Breakfast is a treat to relish and Paddy and Julia are con-

summate hosts, making a stay here a luxuriously enriching experience. Irish hospitality at its best.

Rooms 15 (2 shower only, 1 wheelchair friendly). B&B double from about €155. Children welcome. Closed Oct-end Mar. CC. **Also at: Blue Quay Rooms** (www.bluequayrooms.com) nearby; quirkily stylish budget accommodation from about €70 for two. **Directions:** 2 minutes from town centre, overlooking Clifden harbour - follow signs to the Beach Road.

SEA MIST HOUSE

CLIFDEN CONNEMARA CO GALWAY

095 21441 | sgriffin@eircom.net

www.seamisthouse.com

Offering comfortable accommodation in lovely bright rooms, Sheila Griffin's attractive house is just off the square in Clifden town. It was built in 1825 and, while recent renovations have added modern comforts, it was not at the expense of character and - although there is a pleasantly contemporary tone to the furnishing style - the ambience of the old house has been retained. There's a large conservatory overlooking the lovely cottage garden, which produces some of the delicious things appearing at breakfast, and guests are welcome to relax here and enjoy the garden.

Rooms 4 (all shower only). B&B from €45pps. Wifi. Closed Nov-Mar. CC. **Directions:** Left at square, down on right.

BALLYKINE HOUSE

CLONBUR AN FHAIRCE CO GALWAY

094 954 6150 | ballykine@eircom.net

www.bedandbreakfastcong.com

Very comfortable accommodation and Ann Lambe's warm hospitality make this an appealing base for a peaceful holiday. With a library room, pool table, drying room for anglers and walkers, and a comfy sitting room and conservatory for lounging and chatting, it's a sociable house. The guest rooms include a suite and all of the bedrooms have lake and mountain views - and so does a patio/barbecue area which is a very pleasant spot on fine evenings - when guests also like to walk to a local pub or restaurant and get a lift back later. A lovely place to stay.

Rooms 4 (1 suite, all shower only). B&B from €40pps. Closed mid Oct- early Apr. **No CC. Directions:** Between Cong and Clonbur on the R345.

JOHN J. BURKE & SONS

MOUNT GABLE HOUSE CLONBUR CO GALWAY

EAT | DRINK

094 9546175 | tibhurca@eircom.net
www.burkes-clonbur.com

Everybody loves Burkes pub in Clonbur - this characterful fourth generation family-run pub is one of this attractive village's greatest assets, well known for atmosphere, music and homely food. It's a friendly, welcoming place no matter when you might drop in, and very much the heart of the community and sporting activities.

Seats 140 (outdoors 20); Food served from 10am daily. Closed 24-26 Dec, possibly Good Fri; open weekends only Oct-Mar. CC. **Directions:** 5 km from Cong (R345).

THE GALLERY CAFÉ

MARKET SQUARE GORT CO GALWAY

EAT

091 630 630 | galcafe@gmail.com
www.thegallerycafegort.com

Gorgeous Gort is what they call the town these days and it is well worth leaving the M18 for a bite at Sarah Harty's famously funky all day café and gallery. With a constantly changing exhibition of Irish art, regular music and readings, it's the cultural hub of the community - and you'll find that the food is all about Gort and the locality too, albeit with some exotic influences in the cooking style. Whether for a Badger & Dodo coffee and one of their gorgeous home bakes and or a full meal, it's a great place to eat and chill out - well worth a detour.

Open Wed & Thu 11-9, Fri & Sat to 10, Sun 11-7. Closed Mon & Tue. L & D a la carte. **Directions:** On the market square in Gort, beside Sullivans Hotel.

DOONMORE HOTEL

INISHBOFIN ISLAND CO GALWAY   EAT | STAY

095 45804 / 14 | info@doonmorehotel.com

www.doonmorehotel.com

Locally known simply as 'Murray's' after the family who have run it for three generations, this much-loved family-friendly hotel overlooks the sea and sand dunes of Inishbofin. With geraniums along the front lounge, it looks more like a traditional guesthouse than an hotel, and offers good home cooking and old fashioned comfort. Whether you're into diving, bird watching, walking, painting, or just an old-fashioned bucket and spade holiday, it's a great base for a relaxing break on this delightfully away-from-it-all island. Simply special.

Rooms 20; B&B about €50-€60pps. Children welcome. Toilets wheelchair accessible. Free wifi. Restaurant & bar open daily 12-9 (L & D) for residents & non-residents. House closed Oct-Mar. Helipad. CC. **Directions:** 10 minute walk from harbour.

MORAN'S OYSTER COTTAGE

THE WEIR KILCOLGAN CO GALWAY   EAT | DRINK

091 796 113 | info@moranstheweir.com

www.moransoystercottage.com

As pretty as a picture, with a well-kept thatched roof and a lovely waterside location, people from throughout the country beat a path to Morans at every available opportunity. Famed for wonderful local seafood, they specialise in native oysters from their own oyster beds (in season from September to April), and always have farmed Gigas oysters on the menu. But there's more to Morans than oysters; they offer a balanced menu all year round - and just something very simple, like a bowl of chowder and some freshly baked bread, is always a pleasure in this atmospheric place - enjoyed outside in summer or beside a cosy fire in winter.

Seats 120 (outdoors 60). Food served Mon-Thu 12-9.30, Fri & Sat 12-10, Sun 12-9.30. Closed 24-26 Dec, Good Fri. CC. **Directions:** Off the Galway-Limerick road (N18), signed between Clarenbridge and Kilcolgan.

COYNES BAR & BISTRO (TIGH CHADHAIN)

KILKIERAN CONNEMARA CO GALWAY   EAT | DRINK
095 33409 | coynesbar@gmail.com
www.facebook.com/CoynesBarWildAtlanticWay

Friendly donkeys amble over to the wall as you park at Michael and Annemarie Coyne's neatly presented pub overlooking Kilkerrin Bay - a typical welcome to the Connemara Gaeltacht and this real old-fashioned Irish pub. A proper informal dining experience is offered, with accessibly priced bi-lingual menus catering for all tastes and everything cooked to order. The house speciality is a delicious seafood chowder: thick and plentiful with good chunks of fresh local fish and, served with a homemade brown scone, it's a meal in itself. Coynes is the real deal.

Seats 56 (bar 44, Bistro 12 +24 outside). Bistro open May-Sep 12-8.30, off season 10-5. Bar open Mon-Thu 10.30am-11.30pm, Fri & Sat 10.30am-12.30am, Sun 12.30pm-11.00pm. Free wifi. Music.
Directions: South Connemara, on the coast road R340.

DELPHI LODGE

LEENANE CO GALWAY STAY
095 42222 | info@delphilodge.ie
www.delphilodge.ie

Owned by the enthusiastic and hospitable Michael Wade, this beautifully located 19th century sporting lodge is large and impressive in a relaxed, understated way. The accommodation is excellent and Delphi Lodge has always been known for having a good table - dinner, enjoyed communally around the big dining table, is a convivial affair. Although most famous for salmon and trout fishing, it is also an ideal holiday hideaway for those who simply seek a quiet rural retreat - indeed, Prince Charles famously found it the perfect destination for a painting holiday.

> **Rooms 13** (all executive standard). B&B from about €135pps, Residents D 8pm from €60; L Sun only 1-2pm from €20, must be pre-booked. Children welcome. B&B only mid Oct-early Mar. Open all year to private groups of 18+. Helipad. CC. **Directions:** 13km northwest of Leenane on the Louisburgh road.

KYLEMORE ABBEY, MITCHELL'S CAFÉ & GARDEN TEA HOUSE

KYLEMORE LETTERFRACK CO GALWAY EAT | BUY | PRODUCER
095 52001 | info@kylemoreabbey.ie | www.kylemoreabbey.ie

Providing you are tolerant of tour buses and high season crowds, this scenically located Abbey offers a surprising range of things to see, do, buy - and eat. An informative blackboard at the main restaurant, Mitchell's Café, conveys a sense of place and Chef John O'Toole does a good job, producing wholesome and tasty locally-sourced food for the large numbers of hungry visitors who visit the Abbey. As well as featuring in their three quality-conscious food outlets, all specialising in traditional home cooked food and baking, produce from the farm and Victorian Walled Garden is used in the many jams and preserves made by the Benedictine community.

> **Seats 200** (outdoors, 60). Mitchell's Café: 9.30-5pm, daily. Closed Christmas week. The Garden Tea House: Mar-Nov, 10.30-5; entry fee applies. Coffee Shop: summer, 11-5. CC. **Directions:** N59 from Galway, 3km from Letterfrack

ROSLEAGUE MANOR HOTEL

LETTERFRACK CO GALWAY   EAT | STAY

95 41101 | info@rosleague.com

www.rosleague.com

A member of the legendary Connemara hospitality family, the Foyles of Clifden, the energetic young owner-manager, Mark Foyle, is gradually working his way through a major renovation programme at this lovely, graciously proportioned, pink-washed Regency house. It looks out over Ballinakill Bay through gardens planted with rare shrubs and plants and, although the area also offers plenty of active pursuits, there is a deep sense of peace at Rosleague and it's hard to imagine any better place to recharge the soul. Interestingly furnished in an upbeat traditional style, accommodation is luxurious and it also offers relaxed fine dining with specialities including local Leenane lamb and Killary lobster.

> **Rooms 21**. B&B from €75pps; children welcome. Restaurant: D 7-9 daily, 2/3 courses €36/50; non-residents welcome by reservation. Weddings. Closed Nov-Mar. CC. **Directions:** On N59 main road, 11km (7 miles) north-west of Clifden.

TASTE MATTERS

MILLENNIUM HOUSE WESTBRIDGE LOUGHREA CO GALWAY   EAT

091 880 010 | info@tastematters.ie

www.tastematters.ie

Housed in a large commercial building on the edge of town, this is a no-frills operation yet it has a certain style and a quality feel to it, and interesting paintings by local artists on the walls. The stated aim of serving 'honest, fresh tasty food in a friendly casual environment' is refreshing and, under the direction of Slovakian chef Michal and his front of house partner Jirka from the Czech Republic, they combine to make this a cheerful and hospitable restaurant with friendly, welcoming staff, good ingredients-led food with a real sense of place, and a small but excellent drinks list.

> Open Tue-Fri, 5-9pm; Sat-Sun,1-9pm (hours may vary off season). L & Early D from about €22, also à la carte. Wines (all organic/biodynamic) from about €23. CC. **Directions:** 5km off the M6 motorway, exit for Loughrea.

WHITE GABLES RESTAURANT

MOYCULLEN VILLAGE MOYCULLEN CO GALWAY

EA

091 555 744 I info@whitegables.com

www.whitegables.com

Kevin and Ann Dunne have run this atmospheric cottagey restaurant since 1991, and it remains one of the area's most consistently popular dining destinations. Kevin's cooking is refreshingly traditional and features local meats including Connemara lamb and excellent beef, both from the famous butchers McGeoughs of Oughterard, alongside seafood - and the trademark duckling à l'orange. Next door to their atmospheric restaurant, the lovely deli/bakery, gift shop and café 'Enjoy' and 'More... from White Gables' offer irresistible artisan products, home-cooked seasonal foods, breads and cakes as well as a coffee shop. It's all so charmingly presented that it would be hard to pass through Moycullen without stopping to have a peep.

Seats 45. Wed-Sun 6.30-10.30; L Sun 23.30-3. 'Enjoy More' Tue-Sat 10-6 (+Sun to 4) 'Enjoy' (shop) Tue-Sat 10-7, Sun to 5. CC. **Directions:** Centre of Moycullen village.

CURRAREVAGH HOUSE

GLANN ROAD OUGHTERARD CO GALWAY   EAT | STAY
091 552 312 | mail@currarevagh.com
www.currarevagh.com

Tranquillity, trout and tea in the drawing room - these are the things that draw guests back to Henry and Lucy Hodgson's gracious, but not luxurious, early Victorian manor overlooking Lough Corrib. Offering old-fashioned service and hospitality, it's more like a private house party than an hotel and country pursuits, especially fishing, are the ruling passion. Lucy, a Prue Leith trained cook, showcases fresh local produce in season, maintaining the Currarevagh motto 'keep it simple, unfussy and ultimately delicious'.

Rooms 11 (2 shower only). B&B + Afternoon Tea from €75pps. Children welcome. Set D from €50, at 8pm, non-residents welcome by reservation. Closed Nov-Feb (house available for private hire in winter). CC. **Directions:** Take N59 to Oughterard. Turn right in village square and follow Glann Road for 6.5km.

BRIGIT'S GARDEN & CAFÉ

POLLAGH ROSCAHILL CO GALWAY

091 550 905 I info@brigitsgarden.ie

www.brigitsgarden.ie

EAT

Well-signed off the main Galway-Clifden road, these beautiful themed gardens near Oughterard have long been a favourite destination for families, school outings and everyone who finds a unique mix of history, legend and delightful garden design appealing. A walk through the gardens is a journey through the year, each garden representing one of the Celtic festivals - Samhain, Imbolc, Bealtaine and Lughnasa - a seasonal cycle that mirrors the cycle of life from conception to old age and death. Overlooking the gardens, the bright and airy café has a local following for simple wholesome, food that is full of flavour.

Seats 40 (+30 outdoors). Open April-Sep, 10.30am-5pm daily, weekends Oct-Mar. Toilets, Visitor Centre and most of gardens wheelchair accessible; children welcome. Playground. Closed 25 Dec & Jan. CC. **Directions:** Just off the N59 between Moycullen and Oughterard

LA BOUCHE

PATRICK STREET PORTUMNA CO GALWAY   EAT

090 974 1780 | laboucheportumna@gmail.com
www.labouche.ie

Diners looking for something out of the ordinary to eat come from a wide area to enjoy the pleasing combination of French cooking and Irish hospitality that husband and wife team David and Siobhan Avrillier-Grange offer here. Lying behind a smart marble frontage, their attractive two-storey restaurant is bright and uncluttered, with a pleasant decked area that can be used for drinks (or occasional eating out) in fine weather. The simplicity of the interior is an effective foil for the carefully sourced and attractively presented food, all made from scratch. A very useful place to know about if you're visiting the area - and it gives value too.

Open L Fri-Sun 1.30-4, D Wed-Sat 5.30-10, Sun 5.30-7. Children welcome. Closed Mon. (Hours may vary off season) **Directions:** Town centre, a couple of doors from the Post Office, opposite credit union.

BALLYNAHINCH CASTLE HOTEL

RECESS CO GALWAY

EAT | DRINK | STAY

095 31006 | info@ballynahinch-castle.com
www.ballynahinch-castle.com

Renowned as a fishing hotel, this wonderful place is much loved for its beautiful setting, high standards and atmosphere. Despite the impressive scale, hands-on General Manager Patrick O'Flaherty and his outstanding staff make sure the atmosphere is relaxed, and the comfort and friendliness combined with huge open fires, excellent local food and a little quirkiness (plus an invigorating mixture of residents and locals in the bar at night), keeps bringing people back. Recent renovations include redesigning the Walled Garden - well worth a look - and great breakfasts include their own rare breed pork products. Simply magic.

Rooms 48 (1 shower only). B&B from about €110pps. Lift. Free wifi. Owenmore Restaurant D daily 6.30-9 (Set D from €65), wine from €30. Bar meals 12.30-9 daily. Open for Christmas. CC. **Directions:** N59 from Galway - Clifden; left after Recess (Roundstone road), 6 km.

LOUGH INAGH LODGE

RECESS CONNEMARA CO GALWAY

095 34706 | inagh@iol.ie

www.loughinaghlodgehotel.ie

EAT | STAY

Maire O'Connor's former sporting lodge on the shores of Lough Inagh makes an exceptionally comfortable small hotel, with a country house atmosphere. While it has special appeal to sportsmen, it makes a good base for touring Connemara - or for a bite in the appealing bar, where there's a welcoming fire. Bedrooms, which include one recently added room and several with four-posters, are unusually spacious, with views of lake and countryside. Off-season breaks offer especially good value and its genuine pet-friendliness make it very attractive for people travelling with a dog.

Rooms 13. B&B from about €175. Free wifi. Pet friendly. Finisglen Restaurant: Seats 36. D daily 6.45-9pm (reservations required), Set D from €44. Bar meals daily, à la carte. Closed mid Dec-mid Mar. CC. **Directions:** N59 from Galway, take right N344 after Recess; 5km on right.

RENVYLE HOUSE HOTEL

RENVYLE CO GALWAY   EAT | DRINK | STAY
095 46100 | info@renvyle.com
www.renvyle.com

In one of the country's most appealingly remote and beautiful areas, the Coyle family's house has a romantic and fascinating history, having been home to people as diverse as a Gaelic chieftain and Oliver St John Gogarty. Its setting and quirky charm is unrivalled in Ireland and, with outstanding hospitality and food from legendary General Manager Ronnie Counihan and head chef Tim O'Sullivan respectively, it's no wonder that this unique hotel has developed a cult following. A wonderfully away-from-it-all place to stay - and a great place to plan a break when touring the area, too.

Rooms 68 (1 wheelchair friendly). B&B from €45pp. Roisin Dubh Restaurant D 7-9 daily. Bar meals 12-8 daily (excl 25 Dec & when private functions are on). Families welcome; pet-friendly. Closed 1-23 Dec & 1 Jan-14 Feb. Helipad. CC. **Directions:** 18km north of Clifden.

PADDY COYNES PUB

TULLYCROSS RENVYLE C GALWAY   DRINK
095 43499 | 1811@paddycoynespub.com
www.paddycoynespub.com

A Connemara institution, Gerry Coyne's lovely big-hearted pub dates back to 1811 and, judging by the memorabilia on display in the bar, it might still be familiar to customers from that time. It's a true traditional pub, with cosy snugs, a welcoming open fire, very friendly staff - and great seasonal local food (some of it from their own garden). Seafood stars, especially in summer, and it's the centre of activities at the Connemara Mussel Festival (May bank holiday weekend annually), so big, fat local mussels are a particular favourite, here, with lovely brown bread to mop up the juices. Plenty of other flavoursome traditional dishes too... and music, craic and one-off events all year. A terrific place altogether, and not to be missed.

Seats 50. Food daily, 12 noon-9pm. CC. **Directions:** On the Connemara Loop road, centre of Tullycross village

O'DOWDS SEAFOOD BAR & RESTAURANT

ROUNDSTONE CO GALWAY   EAT | DRINK
095 35809 | info@odowdsseafoodbar.com
www.odowdsseafoodbar.com

The O'Dowd family has been welcoming visitors to this much-loved pub for longer than most people care to remember. Overlooking the harbour, it remains one of those simple places, with the comfort of an open fire and a good pint, where people congregate in total relaxation - spilling out to sit on the low stone wall in the busy summer months. A reasonably priced bar menu majors in seafood or, for more formal meals, the restaurant next door does the honours. Special diets are catered for and there are good traditional dishes, some with interesting variations. The seafood chowder is ace.

Restaurant seats 36 (+6 outdoors). Meals 12-10 daily (to 9.30 in pub); reservations required in restaurant. Value dining daily 12-7, also à la carte. Closed 25 Dec. CC. **Directions:** On harbour front in Roundstone village.

THE ANGLERS RETURN

TOOMBEOLA ROUNDSTONE CONNEMARA CO GALWAY   STAY

095 31091 I info@anglersreturn.com
www.anglersreturn.com

Built as a sporting lodge in the eighteenth century, Lynn Hill's charming and unusual house on the Ballynahinch River near Roundstone offers comfort, peace and tranquillity. Fishing is an option, also walking, golf and horse-riding, but it would be perfect for a painting holiday in this stunningly beautiful area, or for garden lovers. In tune with its special away-from-it-all ambience, there is no television; instead there are views of the river and garden, lots of books to read - and the opportunity to slow down. Best of all, there is Lynn herself: an original.

Rooms 5 (3 with shared bathrooms). B&B from €58pps. Not suitable for children; no pets. Small groups welcome, kitchen available. Fishing (pre-book ghillie). Closed Dec-Feb. **No CC. Directions:** N59 from Galway; left onto R341 Roundstone road for 6.5km; house is on the left, after Ballynahinch Castle.

BROWNES

MARKET SQUARE TUAM CO GALWAY

093 60700 | info@brownestuam.ie

www.brownestuam.ie

EAT | DRINK

After spending some time honing their hospitality skills in Dublin, husband and wife team Stevie Lane and Amanda Fahy returned to their hometown to breathe new life into Brownes - the very place where they first met. Having lovingly restored this landmark pub, they reopened it as a restaurant and bar. The small front room, The Grocery Bar, welcomes arriving diners with a cheery fire and Guinness on tap (a nod to the past), as well craft beers.

In the dining room, the focus is on Stevie's contemporary cooking - everything is made freshly in-house and designed to showcase the quality of his ingredients. With good service to match the food, Brownes makes a pleasing dining destination.

Open Wed-Thu L 12-2.30, D5.30-10; Fri-Sat L 12-2.30, D 5.30-midnight; Sun, D only 6-11pm. Closed Mon-Tue. CC. **Directions:** Town centre.

Geokaun Mountain
Valentia
Co. Kerry

COUNTY KERRY

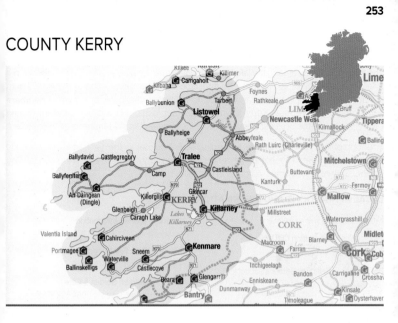

It's something special, being Kerry. This magnificent county in the far southwest has Ireland's highest and most varied mountains, and certain favoured areas also have our longest-lived citizens. Its county town **Tralee** (www.tralee.ie) is world famous for the global celebration of Irish culture that's been running for almost 60 years, The Rose of Tralee (www.roseoftralee.ie) - while the north Kerry town of **Listowel** (www.listowel.ie) is equally renowned for creativity (notably its most famous writer, John B Keane), its Writers' Week, (www.writersweek.ie) Ireland's longest running Food Fair (www.listowelfoodfair.ie) - and horse racing. And it's a region which has long been a global pioneer in the hospitality business - in 2004, the scenically-blessed town of **Killarney** (www.killarney.ie) celebrated 250 years in the forefront of Irish tourism.

So visitors inevitably arrive with high expectations. But Kerry can confidently face the challenge. This magnificent county really is the Kingdom of Kerry. Everything is king size. Not only has Kerry mountains galore - more than anywhere else in Ireland - but there's a rare quality to Carrantuohill, the highest of all.

By international standards, this loftiest peak of MacGillicuddy's Reeks (try pronouncing it "mackil-cuddy") may not seem particularly notable at just 1038 m. But when you sense its mysterious heights in the clouds above a countryside of astonishing beauty, its relative elevation is definitely world league. And all Kerry's mountains sweep oceanwards towards a handsome coastline which rings the changes between sheltered inlets and storm tossed offshore islands. Visually, Kerry has everything.

But these days, spectacular scenery isn't enough on its own. Like other leading visitor destinations, Kerry is well aware of the need to provide accessible entertainment, activities and an increasing choice of places with cultural and historical interest. Here too, the Kingdom can oblige. And it can also oblige those with sporting interests – the place is sports mad. As for history, the oldest fossil footprints in the Northern Hemisphere are in Kerry, and they're about 350 million years old. You'll find them way down west, on **Valentia Island** (www.valentiaisland.ie) and they're reckoned one of the seven wonders of Ireland.

The town of Killarney among the lakes and mountains has long been a magnet for visitors, but Killarney is determined to reinvent itself from time to time, while retaining all that is best from the past. And across the purple mountains from Killarney, the lovely little town of **Kenmare** (www.kenmare.ie) in South Kerry is both a gourmet focus, and another excellent touring centre. As one of the prettiest places in Ireland, Kenmare puts the emphasis on civic pride.

In geographical contrast, **Dingle** (www.dingle-peninsula.ie) in the far northwest is a salty seaport at the heart of a magnificent peninsula, a magically independent fishing and farming community which welcomes visitors with experienced skill.

LOCAL ATTRACTIONS AND INFORMATION

>Activities in **Kerry** www.gokerry.ie

>Ballybunion - **Ballybunion Cliff Walk**
www.ecotrekballybunion.com

>Caherciveen - **Kells Bay Gardens** (subtropical)
www.kellsbay.ie

>Castleisland - **Crag Cave**
www.cragcave.com | 066 714 1244

>Dingle - **Ocean World**
www.dingle-oceanworld.ie | 066 915 2111

>Dunquin - **Great Blasket Centre**
www.blasket.ie | 066 915 6444 / 915 6371

>Farranfore - **Kerry International Airport**
www.kerryairport.ie | 066 976 4644

>Killarney - **Muckross House, Gardens & Traditional Farm** www.muckross-house.ie | 064 31440

>Killarney - **Tourism Information**
www.killarney.ie | 064 663 1633

>Killorglin - **Puck Fair** (ancient festival, mid-August)
www.puckfair.ie | 066 976 2366

>Lauragh - **Derreen Garden & Café**
www.derreengarden.com | 064 668 3588

>Listowel - **Listowel Heritage Trail**
www.discoverireland.ie/Activities-Adventure/
listowel-self-guided-historic-town-walk/85649

>Tralee - **Kerry County Museum**
www.kerrymuseum.ie | 066 712 7777

>Tralee - **Siamsa Tire Arts Centre**
www.siamsatire.com | 066 712 3055

>Valentia Island - **The Skellig Experience**
www.skelligexoerience.com | 066 947 6306

>**Waterville** www.visitwaterville.ie

River Laune at the Dunloe Estate

CILL RIALAIG CAFÉ

CILL RIALAIG ARTS CENTRE DUN GEAGAN BALLINSKELLIGS CO KERRY   EAT | BUY
066 947 9277 | theorigingallery@gmail.com
www.cillrialaigartscentre.org

One of Ireland's most interesting visitor destinations, offering exhibitions, workshops and events all year, the Cill Rialaig Arts Centre is also a great place to shop, whether for serious artwork or for unusual gift items. And the inner man is well looked after here too, at the Cill Rialaig Café, which has a well earned reputation for the quality daytime food served in summer, and occasional evening buffets at exhibition openings.

Excellent homemade pizzas are baked in the outdoor pizza oven beside the front door, and they do nice light lunchtime fare, coffee, tea and cakes.

Open: Off-season (Oct to mid-May) Thu-Sun, 11 to 5; summer season (mid-May-Sep), open daily 11-6. Centre open Sun-Tue 10-5, Wed-Fri 12-8, Sun 12-9. CC. **Directions:** On the R566 Ballinskelligs road, via the N70 Ring of Kerry Road 14.5km from Caherciveen or 11km from Waterville.

KILCOOLY'S COUNTRY HOUSE

MAIN STREET BALLYBUNION CO KERRY   EAT | DRINK | STAY
068 27112 | john@golfballybunion.com
www.golfballybunion.com

Formerly known as Iragh Tí Connor ("the inheritance of O'Connor"), John and Joan O'Connor's fine establishment dates back to the 19th century and now has a quality country house feeling, with exceptionally large, comfortable bedrooms. Open fires, an interesting whiskey collection and a handsome traditional dining room add to the charm, while the old bar and lounge areas (wih street entrance) now have a modern bistro vibe. A good base for exploring the

area - golfers need no introduction to Ballybunion, of course, but there are many other reasons to visit, including the classic family holiday (beautiful sandy beaches), fishing, horse riding - and walking the recently opened Ballybunion Cliff Path.

Rooms 17.Children welcome. Food Mon-Fri 5.30-9, Sat & Sun from 1pm. Closed Nov, Dec & Jan. CC. **Directions:** Top of main street, opposite statue of Bill Clinton.

TEACH DE BROC & STROLLERS BISTRO

LINKS ROAD BALLYBUNION CO KERRY   EAT | STAY
068 27581 | info@ballybuniongolf.com
www.ballybuniongolf.com

You don't have to play golf to appreciate this outstanding guesthouse, but it certainly must help as it is almost within the boundaries of the famed Ballybunion links. Aoife and Seamus Brock offer great hospitality, an extremely high standard of comfort - and good food. What was initially a service for overnight has become Strollers Bistro, a popular dining destination which - with a pianist playing a baby grand in the fine lounge / bar area - can have quite a lively ambience.

Rooms 14 (2 shower only, 1 wheelchair friendly). Free wifi. Strollers Bistro open D Mon-Sat from 6 in summer. Lounge menu Sun 4-8. Open L 25 Dec, 1-4. Open Dec 26-Jan 6 accommodation only. Strollers Bistro open for groups in Dec. House closed Jan 7-April 7. CC. **Directions:** Directly opposite entrance to Ballybunion Golf Club.

O'NEILLS - THE POINT BAR

THE POINT BAR RENARD POINT CAHIRCIVEEN CO KERRY · EAT | DRINK
066 947 2165 | info@oneillsthepoint.ie
www.oneillsthepoint.ie

In the same family for 150 years, Michael and Bridie O'Neill's pub is scenically located beside the Valentia Island car ferry and is renowned for its seafood. It's immaculately clean, full of character and has a great friendly atmosphere - and the secret of its success is simple food based on top quality ingredients. Famous for crab and lobster in summer - there's nothing to beat their locally caught crab mixed with mayonnaise served on Irish soda bread - and hot specialities like the Monkfish 'Point Special' - a casserole of monkfish served on diced potato with garlic, olive oil, some chilies and a sprinkle of fresh parsley. Simply special.

⭐ Food available daily Apr-Oct; L 12-3, D 6-9.30. Hours vary out of season. Children welcome. Fully wheelchair accessible. **No CC. Directions:** Overlooking pier where Valentia Island ferry runs.

PETIT DÉLICE

MAIN STREET CAHERCIVEEN CO KERRY · EAT
087 990 3572
www.facebook.com/pg/Petitdelicekerry

Proper French patisserie and all day lunches are the treats to be found at David Aranda's delightful little bakery and café in the centre of Caherciveen. Since opening in 2013 it has become a key destination for returning visitors keen to stock up with their delicious breads, savouries, cakes and pastries - or to squeeze into the tiny seating area for a coffee and something moreish. It wasn't long before Petit Délice Killarney (064 662 6723) followed. At the end of High Street, this big sister to the Caherciveen original is where the baking is now done for both, and there's a delightful eating area to relax in.

Open (Caherciveen & Killarney) Mon-Sat 8am-6pm. CC in Killarney, Caherciveen cash only. Closed Jan.

QUINLAN & COOKE BOUTIQUE TOWNHOUSE & QCs SEAFOOD RESTAURANT

3 MAIN STREET CAHIRCIVEEN CO KERRY

EAT | DRINK | STAY

066 947 2244 | info@qcbar.com
www.qcbar.com

With its welcoming fire, striking modern zinc-topped bar, and nautical antiques and pictures, Kate and Andrew Cooke's atmospheric bar and restaurant with rooms abounds with character. Ultra fresh local fish and seafood supplied by the family company, Quinlan's Kerry Fish at Renard's Point, QC's Seafood Restaurant has made it a favourite Kerry destination for many years, and it is now equally sought out for its splendidly spacious and quirkily stylish townhouse accommodation. The comfort and enjoyment of guests come first here, making it a very special place.

Rooms 10 (1 ground floor). B&B from about €50pps. Children welcome. Free wifi. Residents' parking. Food daily, Apr-Oct: L 12-3pm (bar only Sun), D from 5.30pm. Nov-Mar: D Fri-Sun from 5.30pm (phone to check). Early D about €21; also à la carte. Closed 25 Dec, early Jan-mid Feb. CC.
Directions: Centre of Caherciveen.

CAIFÉ NA CAOLOIGE @ LOUIS MULCAHY POTTERY

CLOGHER BALLYFERRITER DINGLE CO KERRY   EAT

066 915 6229 | caife@louismulcahy.com
www.louismulcahy.com

'A slice of West Kerry' is the promise at the Louis Mulcahy café, and - with Dingle crabmeat, Dingle Peninsula cheese, and local spiced beef all favourites on the menu, amongst a host of other delicious foods from the area and the wider region - that's just what you'll get. So, after you've done the tour of the pottery, had a good browse or even tried your hand at being a potter, make a point of heading to the café.

What you'll find here is certain to exceed all expectations, and well worth a special visit. Everything is homemade and delicious and the Mulcahy's support for their area, and for artisan producers and suppliers throughout Ireland, is clear to see on the menu, where the provenance of all food is listed.

Seats 30. Open 10-5pm daily. CC. **Directions:** 16km west of Dingle on the gorgeous Slea Head Drive.

CASTLEWOOD HOUSE

THE WOOD DINGLE CO KERRY   STAY

066 915 2788 | info@castlewooddingle.com
www.castlewooddingle.com

Just five minutes' walk west of Dingle Town, this luxurious purpose-built guesthouse is a younger sister of Heatons House and, although they are independent businesses, the gardens are linked and it's a close family unit. It's run by Brian and Helen Heaton - who have both worked in some of Ireland's finest hotels, and for whom nothing is too much trouble to ensure that their guests enjoy the very best of Irish hospitality. Attention to detail is seen in everything they

do, from the outstanding in-room facilities provided to the delicious breakfasts freshly cooked to order from a wide-ranging menu and served in the seaview dining room.

Rooms 12 (1 wheelchair friendly). Children welcome. Free wifi. B&B from about €85pps. Lift. Closed Dec-mid Feb (open few days over New Year). CC. **Directions:** Take Milltown road from Dingle, 500m from town centre on the right.

THE CHART HOUSE

THE MALL DINGLE CO KERRY EAT

066 915 2255 | jim@thecharthousedingle.com
www.thecharthousedingle.com

Jim McCarthy's attractive stone-built restaurant has been one of Dingle's favourite dining destinations since opening in 1997. Jim, ever the perfect host, ensures that everyone is well looked after and generally having a good time, while head chef Noel Enright's menus are steadfastly based on the best of local foods - always kept simple to allow the special qualities of ingredients to take centre stage. And that - despite the ever-growing number of interesting new eating places in Dingle - is the secret of this atmospheric restaurant's enduring success.

Seats 45. D daily in summer (May-Oct), early D 6-7, about €33, also à la carte. Restricted opening off season. Wines from about €26. Closed early Jan-mid Feb. CC. **Directions:** Left at the roundabout as you enter the town.

GLOBAL VILLAGE

UPPER MAIN STREET DINGLE CO KERRY EAT

066 915 2325 | martinbealin@hotmail.com
www.globalvillagedingle.com

There's an air of quiet confidence about Martin Bealin and Nuala Cassidy's long-established restaurant and Martin's cooking is sure-handed, exceptionally creative and consistently well-judged. There's an understandable emphasis on local seafood (and it's good to see the humble mackerel given equal billing alongside prime fish and shellfish), and meats including Kerry lamb but, unusually, vegetables are also accorded exceptional respect here. Everything – the local provenance and seasonality, the cooking, the balance of flavours, the pride in service - works together to make a memorable experience. One not to be missed.

Open daily Mar-Oct, from 5pm. Early D 5-6, from about €26, also à la carte. Open w/ends only Nov & Dec. Closed Christmas, open Dec 28–early Jan, then closed until early Mar. CC. **Directions:** Dingle town centre - top of Main Street on right, opposite turning to Green Street.

GREENMOUNT HOUSE

UPPER JOHN STREET DINGLE CO KERRY   STAY
066 915 1414 | info@greenmounthouse.ie
www.greenmounthouse.ie

Just five minutes walk from the centre of Dingle, John and Mary Curran have run one of Ireland's finest guesthouses since the mid-'70s. They've also played a major part in establishing the town's reputation for quality accommodation - and now, with son and daughter, Gary and Maria, in the business too, the warmth, professionalism, meticulous housekeeping and terrific breakfasts are better than ever. Exceptionally comfortable and quietly located, with spacious rooms, private parking, sitting rooms with open fires - and wonderful views across Dingle Bay to the mountains beyond - it's a great place to stay.

Rooms 14 (3 shower only, 1 wheelchair friendly). B&B from about €45pps. Children welcome, free wifi; no pets. Afternoon Snacks menu 2.30-5.30. Honour Bar. Garden hot tub (April–Oct). Parking. SC discretionary. Closed 20-27 Dec. **Directions:** Turn right and right again on entering Dingle

---

THE HALF DOOR

JOHN STREET DINGLE CO KERRY   EAT
066 915 1600 | halfdoor@iol.ie
www.halfdoor.ie

A long-established dining destination in the centre of Dingle, Denis and Teresa O'Connor established The Half Door in 1991 and this cottagey fine dining restaurant is one of the prettiest and consistently excellent in the town. It's well-known for great seafood and now, with the next generation also playing their part, chef Teresa continues to delight diners with the excellent cooking and depth of flavour in specialities including the house chowder and a wonderful seafood platter, available hot or cold. Engaged, professional service too, matching the high quality of food in this atmospheric restaurant.

Seats 50. D Mon-Sat, 5-10. Early D 6-6.30 only; later, à la carte. Closed Sun; Christmas. CC. **Directions:** On entering Dingle, turn right onto The Mall at roundabout, then right onto John Street

HEATONS HOUSE

THE WOOD DINGLE CO KERRY   EAT | STAY
066 915 2288 | heatons@iol.ie
www.heatonsdingle.com

Established by Cameron and Nuala Heaton in 1997 and now run by their son, David, this fine purpose-built guesthouse is set in well-maintained gardens just across the road from the water and, although convenient to Dingle town, it's beyond the hustle and bustle of the busy streets. A spacious foyer-lounge area offers comfort for relaxation, as do the regularly refurbished bedrooms, which includes junior suites and superior rooms. And not only is good food at the heart of the Heaton family philosophy but David is a chef, so you may expect great breakfasts too.

Rooms 16 (1 wheelchair friendly). B&B from about €45. Closed 4-27 Dec, Jan 2-Feb 4. CC. **Directions:** 600 metres beyond marina, at front of town

IDÁS

JOHN STREET DINGLE CO KERRY   EAT
066 915 0885 | info@idasdingle.com
www.idasdingle.com

A self-taught chef who trained as an artist, Kevin Murphy has established a reputation as Dingle's most innovative young chef and he has introduced the town to a unique, deeply local and seasonal, style of cooking that has French influences at its heart but never stands still. Local meats and seafoods star, with seaweed and other foraged foods playing great supporting roles in memorable, artfully presented dishes.

Open Wed-Sun, 6-10pm. Feb Mar, Nov weekends only. Shoulder season Thu-Sun. Tasting Menu only 5 course about €50; 5 course vegetarian about €40. Daily wine-pairing options; house wine €25, glass €6.75. Full wheelchair access. Reservations advised. Call to check hours off season. CC. **Directions:** Town centre.

LORD BAKER'S RESTAURANT & BAR

DINGLE CO KERRY   EAT I DRINK
066 915 1277 I info@lordbakers.ie
www.lordbakers.ie

Dating back to 1890, John Moriarty's excellent bar and restaurant is believed to be the oldest pub in Dingle and is full of character. Local seafood stars and, as well as more formal restaurant seating, tables are set up in front of an open fire in the front bar, a cosy spot to enjoy speciality dishes such as a very good chowder with freshly- baked brown soda bread. Now also with his son Jonathan working alongside him, John is the consummate host, caring and watchful; no detail escapes his notice, ensuring that every guest in Dingle's largest restaurant will leave contented - and well-informed too, as he is a mine of local information.

Seats 120. Open D 6-9.30 Fri-Wed, closed Thu. House closed 24-26 Dec. CC. **Directions:** Town centre.

MURPHYS ICE CREAM & CAFÉ

STRAND STREET DINGLE CO KERRY
066 915 2644 | dingle@murphysicecream.ie
www.murphysicecream.ie

Many would make the trek to Dingle solely for the pleasure of tucking into one of the treats on offer at Kieran and Séan Murphy's cheerful blue and white fronted café down near the harbour. They've made ice cream here with fresh Kerry milk and cream since 2000 and, although the café offers only coffees and ice cream, the range - which is all homemade using natural ingredients and includes unusual flavours such as sea salt (made themselves from sea water) and Dingle Gin - is growing all the time.

Seats 25 (+ 8 outdoors). Open daily 11-6. **No CC. Directions:** In town centre. **Also at:** The Pier, Dingle; Main Street, Killarney; High Street, Galway; Rose Inn Street, Kilkenny; Wicklow Street, Dublin.

OUT OF THE BLUE

WATERSIDE DINGLE CO KERRY   EAT

066 915 0811 | bookings@outoftheblue.ie
www.outoftheblue.ie

You can't miss Tim Mason's bright blue seafood-only restaurant on the Dingle harbour front - and it's an absolute delight. Everything depends on the fresh fish supply from the boats that day and if there's no fresh fish, they don't open (their motto is "No chips. Nothing frozen. Everything fresh or alive"). The ambience is rustic but they take their food seriously; the daily-changing menu is on a blackboard and, while prime fish and shellfish command a predictable premium, less used fish are good value. Just the kind of place that visitors dream of finding - and it is not unusual to hear a different language spoken at every table.

Seats 35 (outdoors, 30). D daily from 5pm, L Sun & bank hol w/e 12.30-3pm. Special Fish Deal Mon-Fri 5-6.30.Closed Nov-mid Mar. CC. **Directions:** Opposite the pier on Dingle harbour.

PAX HOUSE

UPPER JOHN STREET DINGLE CO KERRY   STA

066 915 1518 I info@pax-house.com

www.pax-house.com

Just outside Dingle, John O'Farrell's modern house enjoys what may well be the finest view in the area, and it is also one of the most comfortable and relaxing places to stay. The recently re-styled main living area is designed around the views and absolutely gorgeous, while the thoughtfully furnished bedrooms have every amenity; two suites have their own terraces - and so does the stylish lounge. Eggs for breakfast are supplied by free-range chickens that strut around the garden.

Rooms 12 (8 shower only, 4 separate bath and shower, 6 ground floor, all no-smoking); B&B from about €75 per room. Children welcome. Pets permitted. Free wifi in lounge area. Wine licence. Garden, walking. Closed Jan, Feb. CC.
Directions: Turn off at sign on N86.

GORMAN'S CLIFFTOP HOUSE & RESTAURANT

GLAISE BHEAG BALLYDAVID DINGLE PENINSULA CO KERRY   EAT I STAY

066 915 5162 I info@gormans-clifftophouse.com

www.gormans-clifftophouse.com

Beautifully situated near Smerwick Harbour on the Slea Head scenic drive and Dingle Way walking route, Sheelagh and Vincent Gorman's guesthouse is, as they say themselves "just a great place to relax and unwind". Laid-back and welcoming with open fires, very comfortable rooms, great views - and a lovely restaurant where Vincent's good cooking introduces guests to the life of the area through the local foods.

Rooms 8 (1 shower only, 1 wheelchair friendly). B&B from about €75 pps. Children welcome. **Restaurant seats 35**. Set 3 course D Mon-Sat by reservation at 6.30, about €37.50. House open mid-March-mid-Oct, or by prior arrangement; closed 1 Jan-10 Feb. CC. **Directions:** 12.5km from roundabout west of Dingle Town - sign posted An Fheothanach. Keep left at V.

THE BOATHOUSE WINEBAR & BISTRO

DROMQUINNA MANOR KENMARE CO KERRY   EAT I DRINK

064 664 2889 I admin@dromquinnamanor.com

www.dromquinnamanor.com

An atmospheric 19th century boathouse overlooking the harbour at John "At Your Service" Brennan's Dromquinna Manor makes a great restaurant for holidaymakers and wedding guests "glamping" in the grounds - and it's a favourite destination for locals, as well as visitors to Kenmare. Chef Benny Scannell's refreshingly short menus deliver on stylish deliciousness and, with well trained and welcoming staff to match, it's hard to imagine a more appealing setting for a relaxing bite - especially when the weather favours al fresco dining on the terrace. It's magic in sunshine and can be romantic at night, as the light fades on the mountains across the bay... A very special place.

Seats 70 (+ 40 outdoors). Open daily in summer, 12.30-9. A la carte. Evening reservations advised, especially at weekends. CC. **Directions:** At Dromquinna Manor, 5km west of Kenmare on the N70.

BROOK LANE HOTEL

KENMARE CO KERRY

EAT | STAY

064 664 2077 | info@brooklanehotel.com

www.brooklanehotel.com

Una and Dermot Brennan's smart boutique hotel on the edge of the town is sleek and modern, offering all the flair and comfort of a custom-built hotel yet with the service and intimacy of the very best kind of B&B. It has also earned its place as one of the town's most popular smart-casual food destinations - Una and Dermot champion local produce at every opportunity and even produce their own Saddleback pork, which features on menus here and at their excellent and atmospheric No. 35 Restaurant (www.no35kenmare.com), on Main Street.

Rooms 21 (2 family rooms, 1 wheelchair friendly). Lift. B&B from about €60pps. Free wifi. Casey's Bar & Bistro: meals 12.30-9.30 daily; live music (check details). Closed 24-26 Dec. CC.
Directions: Just outside Kenmare on the Ring of Kerry Road (take the turn off for Sneem).

JAM

6 HENRY ST KENMARE CO KERRY

EAT | BUY

064 664 1591 | info@jam.ie

www.jam.ie

Eat in or take away, James Mulchrone's delightful bakery and café is the original of a small group of 'Jams' in Kerry and Cork. From small beginnings in 2001, he has built their reputation on the fact that everything is homemade using the best of local produce and, with fair prices and friendly service, it's a winning combination. The stated aim is "to provide fresh, quality, imaginative food at affordable prices in nice surroundings"; this they do very well, both here and at their branches in Killarney and Cork, which are supplied by their Kenmare bakery. A great spot to stock up on goodies - and perfect for picnics.

Seats 55. Open Mon-Sat 8am-5.30pm. Closed Sun (except high season), 4 days Christmas. CC. **Directions:** Lower Henry Street on the left. **Also at:** Old Market Lane Killarney; Hanley's of Cork.

LIME TREE RESTAURANT

SHELBURNE STREET KENMARE CO KERRY   EAT
064 664 1225 | limetree@limetreerestaurant.com
www.limetreerestaurant.com

In a beautifully atmospheric building dating back to 1832, The Lime Tree Restaurant has been delighting visitors to Kenmare for over 30 years - and 2013 marked a new era as the original chef, Michael Casey, returned to his favourite restaurant as proprietor-chef. Now working with his wife Gillian, who is also a chef, he is once more making the best of the stunning local produce from the nearby ocean and from the rivers and lands of Kerry and West Cork at Kenmare's landmark restaurant. There's a real sense of place to Mike's classically-based cooking and this, plus excellent service, makes for a memorable experience - and, not surprisingly, the Lime Tree remains one of the town's most popular dining destinations.

Open April–Oct 6.30-9.30pm. A la carte; wine from about €25. **Directions:** Top of town, next to Park Hotel

MULCAHY'S RESTAURANT

MAIN STREET KENMARE CO KERRY   EAT | DRINK
064 664 2383 | info@mulcahyskenmare.ie
www.mulcahyskenmare.ie

Bruce and Laura Mulcahy have been setting the bar in this foodiest of foodie towns since 1995, when they opened a small but stylish contemporary restaurant around the corner in Henry Street - and got a name for an edgily creative combination of classic and modern influences in Bruce's uniquely big-flavoured cooking. Now happily relocated to much bigger premises on Main Street, they're thriving on the opportunities it offers. Wild, free range, seasonal and local produce remain the foundation of Bruce's exciting cooking and the informal style and engaging service are as good as ever. One to try.

D daily, 5.30-10pm (longer hours in summer); à la carte. Wheelchair Accessible. Children welcome. Free wifi. Full Bar. Weddings/events (100). Closed 23-26 Dec and one week in autumn/winter. CC. **Directions:** Top of Main Street.

MUXNAW LODGE

CASTLETOWNBERE ROAD KENMARE CO KERRY STAY

064 664 1252 I muxnaw@eircom.net

www.muxnawlodge.eu

Set in lovely gardens, Hannah Boland's wonderfully cosy and homely house was built in 1801 and enjoys beautiful views across Kenmare Bay. Constant improvement is the name of the game here and Hannah has transformed all of the rooms and bathrooms in recent years, without changing the warm and tranquil character of this pleasant house in any way - and it remains very much a home where you can relax. Just across the bridge from Kenmare, it has all the advantages of a quiet location, yet it is also within easy walking distance of the town's bars and restaurants in fine weather.

Rooms 5 (all en-suite & no-smoking). B&B about €45 pps. Not suitable for children. Garden. Tennis court. Private parking. Closed 24-25 Dec. **No CC.** **Directions:** 2 minutes drive from Kenmare Town (Bantry road, first right past the double-arched bridge towards).

PACKIE'S

HENRY STREET KENMARE CO KERRY EAT

064 664 1508 I eat@packies.com

www.kenmare.com/packies

In a town blessed with an exceptional choice of wonderful eating places, the Foley family's buzzy little restaurant in Kenmare has long been a favourite for returning visitors. Established by Maura Foley (of Shelburne Lodge), in 1991, in her Uncle Packie's old shop, this small restaurant became one of the pioneering businesses that made a reputation for Kenmare as a food destination. Thriving today, it's oozing with atmosphere and the founding principles still apply - "honest, clean cooking with genuinely friendly service" is the stated promise and an underlying discipline of professionalism from proprietor-chef Martin Hallissey and his team ensures that it is delivered every time. Informal and relaxed with 'honest, clean cooking' and genuinely friendly service, it remains a Kenmare classic.

Seats 35. D Tue-Sat 5.30-10. Closed Mon. CC. **Directions:** Town centre.

PARK HOTEL KENMARE

KENMARE CO KERRY

064 664 1200 I info@parkkenmare.com

www.parkkenmare.com

EAT I STAY

A magnificent waterside location and mountain views belie the convenience of the Park Hotel Kenmare, right at the heart of this Heritage Town. Its fame dates back to Victorian times and, in the ownership of Francis "At Your Service" Brennan since 1985, it is a benchmark for exceptional standards of service, comfort and cuisine. A stay here is always a treat - luxury and hospitality are the bywords - also outstanding food, overseen by talented Head Chef, James Coffey.

⭐

Rooms 46. Room rate from about €190 (value off-season breaks). Wifi. Restaurant: D 7-9 daily, about €70 (closed D Sun off season). The Terrace: D nightly 6.30-9 (à la carte bistro menu). Wines from about €35. Afternoon Tea and short lounge menu also available, 11-6pm. Hotel open early March-late Nov, and Christmas/New Year 23 Dec-3 Jan. CC. **Directions:** Top of town.

SEA SHORE FARM GUEST HOUSE

TUBRID KENMARE CO KERRY   STAY

064 664 1270 | seashoreguesthouse@gmail.com
www.seashorekenmare.com

Everybody loves Owen and Mary Patricia O'Sullivans' farm guest-house, for its lovely rural location, simple charm, and the exceptional friendliness and hospitality of the hosts, who like nothing better than sharing local knowledge with their guests. It is very beautifully situated overlooking the Beara peninsula, with walks down to the shore yet, despite the peace and privacy, it's also convenient to Kenmare town. Spacious, comfortably furnished bedrooms have the considerate small touches that make all the difference to the comfort of a stay - and breakfast is a feast. Old-fashioned Irish hospitality at its best.

Rooms 6 (2 with Jacuzzi bath, 3 shower only, 1 wheelchair friendly); B&B from about €50pps. Children welcome; no pets. Wifi. Parking. Wheelchair access. Closed 1 Oct-April. CC. **Directions:** 1 mile from Kenmare off Ring of Kerry N70 Kenmare/Sneem road; signposted at junction with N71.

SHEEN FALLS LODGE

KENMARE CO KERRY   EAT | STAY

064 664 1600 | info@sheenfallslodge.ie
www.sheenfallslodge.ie

Set in a 300-acre estate across the river from Kenmare town, this gently contemporary hotel has welcoming fires burning in the handsome foyer and in a lounge bar which - like the highly-regarded Falls restaurant - overlooks the tumbling waterfall. Accommodation is predictably luxurious, in a modern style, and Tony Schwarz - known for his commitment to promoting quality local produce - is Executive Chef, which bodes well for both resident and visiting diners; the cooking principles are classic, but menus are light and modern, with due attention to the wide dietary requirements of today's diners.

⭐

Rooms 66 (12 suites, 1 wheelchair friendly). Lift. B&B from about €185 (max 2 guests). Children welcome. The Falls Restaurant: D daily 7-9.30, from €49. Helipad. Spa. Hotel closed Jan, midweek Feb/Dec. CC. **Directions:** Take N71 Kenmare (Glengariff road); turn left at sign.

SHELBURNE LODGE

CORK ROAD KENMARE CO KERRY   STAY
064 664 1013 | shelburnekenmare@eircom.net
www.shelburnelodge.com

The oldest house in Kenmare, Tom and Maura Foley's house is a fine stone building with lovely gardens, and it has great style and attention to detail. Elegant and extremely comfortable, with an inviting log fire and interesting books to read, the feeling is of being a guest in a private country house. Their superb breakfasts are legendary and at night guests are directed to the family's restaurant, **Packie's**. Another classic Kenmare destination, **The Purple Heather**, on Henry Street, is run by Maura's sister, Grainne O'Connell; open since 1964, this daytime restaurant/bar was among the first to establish a reputation for good food in Kenmare, and well worth a visit.

Rooms 10 (3 shower only). B&B from about €60pps. Children welcome. Free wifi. CC. Closed Dec-Feb CC. **Directions:** 500 metres from town centre, on the Cork road R569.

THE MEWS

HENRY COURT HENRY STREET KENMARE CO KERRY   EAT
064 664 2829 | info@themewskenmare.com
www.themewskenmare.com

A respected team in Kerry hospitality, Gary Fitzgerald and Maria O'Sullivan have made their mark at a number of top destinations. Now, their own lovely restaurant offers the best from their culinary journey: the warmest of welcomes from Maria and the best of carefully sourced ingredients transformed into wonderful dishes by Gary. Friendly, well trained staff have time for a chat, and a well selected wine offering is a good match for the menu. Good value for the quality too - The Mews is proving very popular in a town exceptionally well served with interesting dining choices.

Seats about 60. D Tue-Sat from 6 (Sat from 5.30). Closed Sun & Mon. Early D to 7pm, from €32, also à la carte. Children welcome at first sitting. CC. **Directions:** Kenmare town centre, just off Henry Street.

THE STRAWBERRY FIELD

MOLL'S GAP BLACKWATER KILLARNEY CO KERRY   EAT
064 668 2977 | info@strawberryfield-ireland.com
www.strawberryfield-ireland.com

High up in hills, on the lovely road between Moll's Gap and Sneem, Peter and Margaret Kerssens specialise in making pancakes. "The biggest little treat in Kerry" is the promise and it is a really useful place to know about when touring the area, especially as it's open all year. In fine weather the views from the terrace are stupendous, and there's a characterful restaurant with a cosy stove - either way, the original and varied pancahes are a treat. Savoury choices include Garlic Cheese with leeks, walnuts and Ballymaloe relish, for example, and on the sweet side you might fancy apple, cinnamon and walnuts. A one-off.

Open 11am-6 pm, daily April–Sep and holidays. Sat/Sun Oct–Mar. (Call ahead to check opening times off season). Ample parking; children's playground. CC. **Directions:** Near Moll's Gap (Sneem Road, R568).

AGHADOE HEIGHTS HOTEL & SPA

LAKES OF KILLARNEY KILLARNEY CO KERRY EAT | STAY
064 663 1766 | info@aghadoeheights.com
www.aghadoeheights.com

This stylish contemporary property enjoys stunning views of Killarney's famous lakes and the mountains beyond, and also overlooks the town's two 18-hole championship golf courses. It is one of the country's most luxurious hotels and, with its magical setting, a destination spa and welcoming staff, it is a very special place. Good food has always been a feature of the hotel and the view from the restaurant, lounge and bar is wonderful.

Rooms 74 (1 wheelchair friendly). Lift. B&B from about €70 pps. **Restaurant seats 110** (+40 outdoors); D daily, 6.30-9.30. Set D about €55, also à la carte. Reservations accepted; children under 8 welcome before 7pm. Informal menus offered in The Heights Lounge and The Terrace Bar & Patio (11-9.30 daily). Afternoon Tea, The Heights Lounge 12-7.30 daily. Open all year.CC. **Directions:** 3.2km north of Killarney; signposted off N22.

ARBUTUS HOTEL

COLLEGE STREET KILLARNEY CO KERRY STAY
064 663 1037 | stay@arbutuskillarney.com
www.arbutuskillarney.com

In the Buckley family since 1926, this warm and welcoming hotel now has almost the feeling of a large, well-run and very comfortable family home, with an emphasis on genuine hospitality and good cooking – the things that make guests feel at home, like fresh home baking and a great breakfast. Since the present owner, Sean Buckley, took over in 1986, renovations have included replacement of the antiques that were discarded when the previous generation modernised the hotel in the 1960s. There's a library and a cosy drawing room for guests' use - and fun too, as the adjacent Buckley's Bar is one of Killarney's best pubs, renowned for traditional music sessions and craic.

Rooms 35. Lift. B&B from about €70pps. Free wifi. CC. **Directions:** Town centre; within walking distance of railway station.

CAHERNANE HOUSE HOTEL

MUCKROSS ROAD KILLARNEY CO KERRY
064 663 1895 I info@premgroup.com
www.cahernane.com

EAT I STAY

This historic hotel is in a lovely quiet location, convenient to Killarney town, yet - thanks to a long tree-lined avenue and parkland, which stretches down towards the water - it has a charmingly other-worldly atmosphere. In new ownership since 2016, a programme of refurbishment is bringing this lovely property back to its best; bedrooms in the main house have been beautifully restored, for example, also some of the main reception rooms including the classically elegant Herbert Room Restaurant, which is known for good cooking of local foods.

Rooms 38 (20 with separate bath & shower). B&B from about €80pps. (NB: bedrooms include some in a modern wing). Restaurant: D 6-9pm daily; set D about €50, also à la carte. Closed Christmas, all Jan and midweek Nov, Dec, Feb. **Directions:** Outskirts of Killarney, off the N71 near Muckross Park.

CELTIC WHISKEY BAR & LARDER

93 NEW STREET KILLARNEY CO KERRY
064 6635700 I info@celticwhiskeybar.com
www.celticwhiskeybar.com

DRINK I EAT

A sister to Ally Alpine's renowned Dublin business, The Celtic Whiskey Shop - and the only one of its type outside the capital - the Celtic Whiskey Bar & Larder opened in March 2016 and not only brought something new to Killarney but instantly became a must-see attraction in Ireland's longest-established tourist region. Very handily located, right at the centre of town, it's in a fascinating old building, and, whether or not you're into whiskey, the Irish Whiskey Experience (master classes) offers plenty to please the inquiring mind - and some wholesome artisan food and traditional dishes too.

Seats 60. Open Mon-Thu, noon-11.30pm; Fri-Sat, noon-12.30am; Sun 12.30-11pm. Food served: Mon-Sat 12-9.45; Sun 12.30-9.45. All day menu & daily specials (families welcome). Closed 25 Dec & Good Fri. CC. **Directions:** One minute's walk from Killarney tourist infor-mation office.

THE DUNLOE

BEAUFORT KILLARNEY CO KERRY   STAY
064 664 4111 | reservations@thedunloe.com
www.thedunloe.com

Famed for its spectacular views of
the Gap of Dunloe this luxurious
riverside sister hotel to the Europe
Hotel & Resort, Fossa and Ard na
Sidhe Country House, Caragh Lake
(see entries), is set in a 64-acre
estate, complete with ruined Norman
castle and Haflinger ponies. With
its generous scale and exemplary standards of maintenance and
housekeeping, it has much in common with The Europe and, following
recent renovations, the public areas
are also a match for its big sister. Perhaps surprisingly, it's a good choice
for families - and also the family pet.

Rooms 102. B&B from €240 per room.
Children welcome; pets permitted (charge).
Breakfast 7am-10.30am. D 7pm-9.30pm.
Leisure centre (25m pool), gym, therapies.
Horse riding, fishing, boating. Destination
gardens. Children's playground. Open
May-Oct (Oct weekends only, Thu-Sat).
Closed end Oct-Easter. CC. **Directions:** Off
main Ring of Kerry road.

THE EUROPE

FOSSA KILLARNEY CO KERRY

064 667 1300 | reservations@theeurope.com

www.theeurope.com

EAT | STAY

Open since 1965, this impressive hotel may be over fifty years old, but its spacious style, quality furnishings, beautiful views and lakeside balconies are timeless qualities and it has continued to outshine many a new top level hotel - notably since the gorgeous ESPA was added, along with a state-of-the-art conference and events centre and an impressive general refurb. Both restaurants are popular dining destinations and, like all public areas, share the stunning views.

Rooms 187 (2 wheelchair friendly, 11 shower only). Lift. B&B from €120pps. Children welcome. Free wifi. Panorama Restaurant: B'fast daily 7-10.30am, D Mon-Sat 7-9.30pm, à la carte; closed D Sun & other days off season. Children's menu. Brasserie Bar & Restaurant, with terrace (open daily, 11am-11pm). Spa Café 12-5pm. Hotel closed mid-Dec-mid-Feb. Open Thu-Sat Feb-April. CC. **Directions:** On main Ring of Kerry road, N72.

GABY'S SEAFOOD RESTAURANT

27 HIGH STREET KILLARNEY CO KERRY

EAT

064 663 2519 | info@gabys.ie

www.gabys.ie

One of Ireland's longest established seafood restaurants and a great classic kitchen, Gaby's was established by the parents of the current proprietor-chef, Gert Maes, in the 1970s when they moved their deli from Dingle to Killarney and added a restaurant. The business philosophy has always been about quality, freshness and high standards - and it has earned Gert much well deserved acclaim since he took over in 1988. There are some concessions to non-fish eaters but the real experience here is the great seafood dishes like Lobster 'Gaby' (a secret recipe) and the Kerry Shellfish Platter. Menus at this atmospheric restaurant are offered in several languages and, although expensive, it is special.

Seats 75. D Mon-Sat 6-10pm, reservations advised. A la carte. Closed Sun. Off season weekends only (call to check). CC. **Directions:** On the main street.

KATHLEENS COUNTRY HOUSE

MADAMS HEIGHT TRALEE ROAD KILLARNEY CO KERRY

STAY

064 663 2810 | info@kathleens.net

www.kathleens.net

If you like staying in a quietly situated owner-run establishment of character rather than an hotel, Kathleen O'Regan Sheppard's long-established four star guesthouse just outside Killarney could be the place for you. Set back from the road in well kept gardens, the house is meticulously maintained and Kathleen - who has been welcoming guests here since 1980 - enjoys engaging with guests and helping to ensure that everyone gets the most out of their stay in Killarney. It's just at the beginning of the Ring of Kerry route, convenient for a wide range of outdoor pursuits - and serves an excellent breakfast.

Rooms 17 (3 shower only, 1 wheelchair accessible). B&B about €45 to €70pps. Closed early Oct - Easter. CC. **Directions:** 1.6km north of Killarney Town (straight up from High Street); off N22 Tralee road, on the left.

Killarney Royal

GREAT SOUTHERN KILLARNEY

TOWN CENTRE EAST AVENUE ROAD KILLARNEY CO KERRY   STAY
064 663 8000 | res@themalton.com
www.themalton.com

Formerly The Malton, Killarney's most famous hotel has reverted to the name that most people always called it, becoming the Great Southern Killarney once again. Now in the Scally family's hotel group - prestigious sister properties are the **Killarney Royal** (www.killarneyroyal.ie) and Cork City's premier hotel, **Hayfield Manor** (www.hayfieldmanor.ie) - the recent modern makeover has been reversed in many areas, restoring this classic railway hotel to something much nearer to its Victorian self. The ivy-clad facade and welcoming open fire in the pillared foyer still convey a sense of occasion, and the six acres of gardens surrounding the hotel provide a lovely setting for the gracious old building. A comfortable and historic place to stay.

Rooms 172; room rate from about €115, Conferences/events. Leisure Centre (15m pool). Open all year. CC. **Directions:** In the heart of Killarney town beside Railway Station.

KILLARNEY LODGE

COUNTESS ROAD KILLARNEY CO KERRY **STAY**
064 663 6499 | stay@killarneylodge.ie
www.killarneylodge.ie

Set in private walled gardens just a couple of minutes walk from the town centre, this is one of the most conveniently located places to stay in Killarney. Run with warm professionalism by a member of one of the area's most respected hotelier families, Catherine Treacy, it is also one of the best. It's a fine, very comfortable purpose-built guesthouse: the large rooms have all the amenities expected of an hotel, plus the care that only hands-on owner management can give - and a good Irish breakfast, including home-baked breads and scones. All that, and private parking too.

Rooms 16 (1 shower only). B&B from €55pps. Children welcome. Room service all day. Free wifi. Closed 1 Nov-1 Mar. CC. **Directions:** Off Muckross Road, 2 minutes' walk from town centre.

THE KILLEEN HOUSE HOTEL & ROZZERS RESTAURANT

AGHADOE KILLARNEY CO KERRY

EAT | STAY

064 663 1711 | charming@indigo.ie

www.killeenhousehotel.com

Just 10 minutes from Killarney (5 from Killeen and Mahony's Point golf courses), this pretty 19th century rectory is now Michael and Geraldine Rosney's "charming little hotel". A home from home for leisure and business travellers, it's very friendly and informal - unique features include a pubby little bar, where guests' golf balls are accepted as tender, and 'Rozzers' restaurant, which is very popular locally as well as with residents.

Head chef Paul O'Gorman has overseen the kitchen since 1997, a rarity which speaks for itself - and, as elsewhere in this unusual hotel, the owners' hospitality is outstanding.

Rooms 23. B&B from €70pps. Rozzers Restaurant: Seats 50. D daily 6.30-9.30pm; D from about €37. Non-residents welcome. Closed Nov 1-Mar 31. CC. **Directions:** 6.5km from Killarney town centre - just off Dingle Road

THE LAKE HOTEL KILLARNEY

MUCKROSS ROAD KILLARNEY CO KERRY

064 663 1035 | info@lakehotel.com
www.lakehotelkillarney.ie

STAY

Adjacent to the National Park and Muckross House, on a prime lakeshore site with mountain views, the Huggard family's historic hotel lays fair claim to 'the most beautiful location in Ireland' - and Tony, Colman, Niall and Joe Huggard do everything possible to ensure that the visitor's experience matches up to the scenery. The hotel marked its century in 2012 and today it offers a unique blend of old style and modern comforts, together with great family pride.

Rooms 131 (3 wheelchair friendly, 70 bath & separate shower); B&B from about €70. Children welcome. Free wifi. Spa (treatments). Castlelough Restaurant D 6- 9pm, from €43, also à la carte; casual food 12–9.30). Huggard Craft beer available. Classic Afternoon Tea daily in the Piano Lounge. Closed Dec & Jan. CC. **Directions:** 2 km from Killarney town centre, on the Muckross Road.

LOCH LEIN COUNTRY HOUSE HOTEL

GOLF COURSE ROAD FOSSA KILLARNEY CO KERRY EAT | STAY
064 6631260 | stay@lochlein.com
www.lochlein.com

Offering seclusion, lake and mountain views, good food and good value, Annette and Paul Corridan's comfortably appointed small hotel is one to seek out. The spacious rooms are thoughtfully furnished with attention to detail, and there are plenty of quiet lounging areas to relax in. This is one of the most comfortable places to stay in the area and makes a great base for an active holiday - and with a fine restaurant, too, so you don't have to go out again after a long day out and about. You'll be glad you found it.

Rooms 23. B&B from about €75pps. D Mon-Sat, from about €40. Restaurant closed D Sun; hotel closed mid-Oct to mid-Apr. CC. **Directions:** From Killarney, take N72 (Killorglin) for 4km; through Fossa village, then left after Macken Wool Store. Hotel is 100m on right.

MUCKROSS PARK HOTEL & SPA

MUCKROSS KILLARNEY CO KERRY   EAT | DRINK | STAY
064 662 3400 | info@muckrosspark.com
www.muckrosspark.com

Located within the Killarney National Park, handy to all the championship golf courses in the area, and ideally situated for exploring south Kerry, this luxurious hotel makes an ideal base on the edge of Killarney town. The interior mood ranges from romantic to smart contemporary, with warmly Irish service and fine food to match.

Rooms 70. B&B from about €75pps. Children welcome. Free wifi. Spa. Yew Tree Restaurant D from 6.30 daily (by reservation); Monks Lounge, daily from 11am, light L from 12.30pm; Afternoon Tea. The Jarvey's Rest traditional pub (pub grub, entertainment) daily from 12.30 in summer. CC. **Directions:** 4km from Killarney, on main Kenmare/Ring of Kerry road, almost opposite entrance to Muckross House.

THE ROSS

TOWN CENTRE KILLARNEY CO KERRY   EAT | DRINK | STAY
064 663 1855 | hello@theross.ie
www.theross.ie

Once the grand old lady of Killarney's impressive hotel collection, the Treacy family's much loved property was given a complete revamp a while ago and lovers of contemporary style will now adore this impressively funky boutique hotel - and the theatrical Cellar One restaurant provides a stunning setting for great cooking. The accommodation is quieter in tone, and exceptionally comfortable. Across the road, the traditional looking Killarney Park Hotel (killarneyparkhotel.ie) is actually a much younger sister property; built in the 1990s, it includes a destination spa among the amenities and shares with The Ross a reputation for good food.

⭐
Rooms 29 (1 wheelchair friendly). Lift. B&B from about €80pps. Children welcome. Cellar One: D daily, set menu & a la carte. Bar food daily, 12.30-8.30pm. Free wifi. Hotel closed 24-27 Dec. CC. **Directions:** Town centre. Also at Killarney Park Hotel.

TREYVAUD'S RESTAURANT

62 HIGH STREET KILLARNEY CO KERRY   EAT
064 663 3062 | info@treyvaudsrestaurant.com
www.treyvaudsrestaurant.com

A favourite in the town since 2003, brothers Paul and Mark Treyvaud's attractive and friendly restaurant has a well-deserved following. Carefully planned menus offer an appealing combination of well-made popular dishes (Treyvaud's fishcakes), traditional Irish favourites (a great version of bacon and cabbage) and continental influences (venison pie, perhaps) – and they're famous for their special Wild Game Night in November. Consistently good cooking of fresh and local foods, moderate pricing, long opening hours and well-trained staff with a clear desire to send customers away happy with their meal have proved a winning formula.

Seats 80. L Tue-Sun, 12-5; D daily 5-10pm (to 10.30 Fri/Sat). L & D à la carte (early D 5-7pm); Gourmet D €75, Sun L about €23. Children welcome before 8pm; bookings advised. Closed Mon-Tue off season (Nov-Feb). CC. **Directions:** Middle of main street, on the left.

ARD NA SIDHE COUNTRY HOUSE

CARAGH LAKE KILLORGLIN CO KERRY EAT | STAY
066 976 9105 | reservations@ardnasidhe.com
www.ardnasidhe.com

In a beautiful mountain setting overlooking Caragh Lake, this charming revivalist Elizabethan style country house hotel is one of the most impressive Arts and Crafts houses in Ireland. In 2010 a major restoration of the entire building was undertaken, including the commission of new Arts and Crafts style furniture in both the common areas and the bedrooms, and the result is an architectural jewel of national significance.

Set in woodland and delightful gardens (which are a destination in themselves), this romantic sister hotel to The Europe Hotel & Resort and The Dunloe (see entries), makes a peaceful retreat.

Rooms 18. B&B from about €90pps. Free wifi. Fairyhill Restaurant seats 45, D Tue-Sun, 7.8.30. Hotel closed mid Oct-May. CC. **Directions:** Off N70 Ring of Kerry road, signed 5 km west of Killorglin.

CARRIG COUNTRY HOUSE & RESTAURANT

CARAGH LAKE KILLORGLIN CO KERRY   EAT | STAY
066 976 9100 | info@carrighouse.com
www.carrighouse.com

Set in fine gardens with lake and mountain views, Frank and Mary Slattery's Victorian country house was originally a hunting lodge - and it's a very attractive property with a relaxed atmosphere, charming sitting rooms where you can enjoy a drink beside the fire, and spacious bedrooms furnished with antiques. A 'proper country house', Carrig is a quietly luxurious and serene place to stay - a perfect escape from the modern world, and with excellent food served in the lovely lakeside dining room.

Rooms 17. B&B from about €75pps. Children over 8 welcome. Lakeside Restaurant D daily May-Sep from 6.30; off season, restaurant open Wed, Fri & Sat. A la carte. Non-residents welcome (booking essential). House closed Nov-Feb. CC. **Directions:** left after 4km on Killorglin/Glenbeigh Road N70 (Ring of Kerry); sharp right at Caragh Lake School (2.5km), 1km on left.

JACK'S COASTGUARD RESTAURANT

WATERS EDGE CROMANE KILLORGLIN CO KERRY EAT | DRINK
066 976 9102 | info@jackscromane.com
www.jackscromane.com

Beautifully situated, just a stone's throw from the sea at Cromane, where the famous mussels are landed, this handsome stone building sends out all the right signals - as does the restaurant, which is fresh and original. Owned by Brian and Grainne Keary, and with Brian's brother Jonathan doing an excellent job in the kitchen, this is a great place to drink in the view while enjoying the best of fresh produce that includes the meats of the area - Kerry lamb and beef, speciality foods such as Annascaul puddings - and, most notably, fish and seafood. Bookings advised.

Seats 130. D Mon & Wed-Sun, 6-9pm; Sun L 1-3.30pm; Bar Menu L Mon & Wed-Sat, 1-3pm; children welcome before 10pm (high chair); toilets wheelchair accessible. Closed Tue; open bank hols. Hours vary off season. CC. **Directions:** Waterside in Cromane.

ALLO'S RESTAURANT, BAR & BISTRO

41/43 CHURCH STREET LISTOWEL CO KERRY   EAT | DRINK | STAY
068 22880 | allosbarbistro@gmail.com
www.allosbarbistro-townhouse.com

Helen Mullane and Armel Whyte's traditional-feeling café-bar is the type of contemporary, self-confident Irish eating house that visitors hope for but do not always find in every provincial town. Armel and his team source great raw materials and cook them with flair, while Helen is an impressive hostess. Even a quick bar lunch can be memorable. And there's more to Allo's - upstairs they have some absolutely beautiful accommodation, available on a room-only basis; stylishly furnished with antiques and lovely bathrooms, it is well worth investigating.

Seats 50 (outdoors, 20). Open Tue-Fri 12-6.45, Fri & Sat to 9. Closed Sun & Mon, 25 Dec. Rooms 3 (POA). CC. **Directions:** Coming into Listowel on the N69, located half way down Church Street on the right hand side (almost opposite Garda Station).

THE MOORINGS & THE BRIDGE BAR

PORTMAGEE CO KERRY   EAT | DRINK | STAY

066 947 7108 | enquiries@moorings.ie
www.moorings.ie

An institution in South Kerry long before Star Wars came to town, Gerard and Patricia Kennedy's quayside bar and restaurant is a true inn, offering refreshment, rest and good company, and it's full of character. Their Skelligs Package at the homely guesthouse is a winner (the island boats operate just beyond the front door), and the restaurant is famous for local seafood like pan-fried Valentia scallops, Cromane mussels and the Hot Seafood Platter. Or you can just call into the bar, for a bowl of chowder or the catch of the day - and, with open fires, and music at night, it's an atmospheric spot.

Restaurant: D Tue-Sun (reservations required). Bar food 12-8.30pm. **Rooms 16**. B&B from €45pps. Cois Cuain Gift Shop Closed 25-26 Dec. CC. **Directions:** Off N70 Caherciveen-Waterville; 5km after Caherciveen turn right onto R565 for Portmagee; premises in village, facing bridge.

THE PARKNASILLA RESORT & SPA

PARKNASILLA SNEEM CO KERRY   EAT | STAY

064 667 5600 | info@parknasillahotel.ie
www.parknasillahotel.ie

Set in 500 acres of sub-tropical parkland, overlooking Kenmare Bay, this classic Victorian hotel is blessed with one of the most beautiful locations in Ireland; having opened under new ownership in 2013, with many key staff retained, an ongoing refurbishment programme continues. Open fires and comfy lounging furniture sum up the indoor mood, while the hotel and estate offer a very wide range of activities. Rooms vary greatly in size, outlook and type, offering both traditional and contemporary styles, and some - like the formal dining room - have sea and mountain views.

Rooms 85. B&B from €70pps; children welcome. Restaurant: D daily, from 7pm, à la carte; children's tea 5-5.30pm. Bar food daily 12-8.30. Spa; swimming pool. Self-catering available, Open weekends only mid Nov-mid Dec; closed early Jan-early Mar. CC. **Directions:** 25km west of Kenmare, on Ring of Kerry.

BALLYGARRY HOUSE HOTEL & SPA

LEEBROOK TRALEE CO KERRY   EAT | STAY

066 712 3322 | info@ballygarryhouse.com
www.ballygarryhouse.com

Now in the third generation of ownership by the McGillicuddy family, this is an appealing hotel, with exceptionally friendly and helpful staff, and it is moderately priced for the high standard of accommodation, food and service offered. The hotel is held in affection locally and many features of the original 18th century Ballygarry House, and the traditions of hospitality that were established in the early days, have been maintained. Good food has always been a feature here, and the modern classical cooking style has broad appeal.

Rooms 64 (1 master suite, 12 junior). B&B from about €70pps. Restaurant: D daily 6.30-9.30. Set D and à la carte. L Sun only. Bar meals 12.30-9.30pm daily. Children welcome. Spa, treatments; banqueting, events. Closed 24 & 25 Dec. CC. **Directions:** 1.5km from Tralee, on the N21 Killarney road.

BARROW HOUSE

BARROW WEST ARDFERT TRALEE CO KERRY   STAY

089 2463 342 | info@barrowhouse.ie
www.barrowhouse.ie

With a private jetty and beach, the focus at this serene eighteenth century property is on the tidal bay, and it has wonderful views across water to the Slieve Mish Mountains and Dingle peninsula. Owner Daragh McDonogh returned from London in 2016 to breathe new life into this lovely place, and - thanks to her eye for colour and original artwork by both Irish and international artists - it is now luxurious yet with a simple sophistication that is alluring. A very special place.

Rooms 8 (6 shower only, 2 separate bath & shower). B&B from about €130 per room. Not suitable for children under 12, or for wheelchairs. Dogs permitted in Coach House (sleeps 4; pets €10 per night). Open all year. CC. **Directions:** Follow directions for Tralee Golf Course; Barrow House is signed.

SPA SEAFOODS DELI & CAFÉ

THE SPA TRALEE CO KERRY
066 713 6901 | spa_seafoods@iolfree.ie
www.spaseafoods.com

EAT | BUY | PRODUCER

Going strong in the quality fish processing business since 1996, the Walsh family have not only a fishmongers shop and a smart delicatessen here - but, above it, a lovely modern seafood café with views across the bay. Very simple in décor and ambience, the café has earned a following for its good food, value and friendly staff. Except for a few token vegetarian and meat dishes, the menu is designed to showcase the fresh seasonal fish and shellfish that is so good in this region, with local lobster, crab and Glenbeigh oysters and mussels likely to be among the treats in season.

Seats 47 (+ 12 outdoors). D Tue-Sat 6-9. L Fri –Sun 12.30-5.30. A la carte. Children welcome. Closed Mon, also other days off season (call ahead to check). CC.
Directions: 6km west of Tralee on the Fenit road.

BUTLER ARMS HOTEL

WATERVILLE CO KERRY
066 947 4144 | reservations@butlerarms.com
www.butlerarms.com

EAT | STAY

The Huggard family celebrated a century in the hotel business in 2012, and this fine hotel which dominates the seafront at Waterville has attracted a starry clientèle over the years - it is one of several to have strong links with Charlie Chaplin, for example - and many other celebrities have been photographed here. Like others that have been owner-run for several generations, this comfortable and well-presented hotel has established a special reputation for its homely atmosphere and good service - and good food too, in both bar and restaurant.

Rooms 36. B&B from about €55pps. Charlie's Restaurant Seats 70; D 6-9.30 daily. Fishermans Bar food daily, 12-3 & 6-9pm. Hotel closed late Oct-end Mar, except for special bookings. CC.
Directions: on Ring of Kerry road.

COUNTY KILDARE

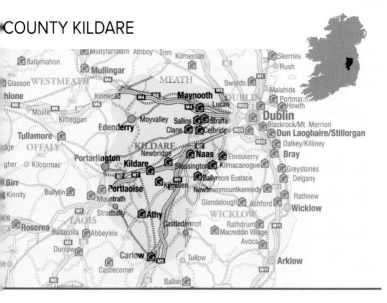

As would be expected of an area which includes the famed racecourses of The Curragh www.curragh.ie, Punchestown www.punchestown.com and Naas www.naasracecourse.com among its many amenities, Kildare www.kildare.ie is the horse county par excellence. The horse is so central and natural a part of Irish life that you'll find significant stud farms in a surprisingly large number of counties. But it is in Kildare that they reach their greatest concentration in the ultimate equine county. Thus it's ironic that, a mere 400 million years ago, Kildare was just a salty ocean where the only creatures remotely equine were the extremely primitive ancestors of sea horses.

But things have been looking up for the horse in County Kildare ever since, and today the lush pastures of the gently sloping Liffey and Barrow valleys provide ideal country for nurturing and training champions. Apart from many famous private farms, the Irish National Stud www.irishnationalstud.ie in Kildare town just beyond the splendid gallops of The Curragh is open for visitors, and it also includes a remarkable Japanese garden, reckoned the best Japanese rock garden in Europe, as well as the Museum of the Horse.

The development of Ireland's motorway network has been particularly beneficial to Kildare, as it has lightened the traffic load through the county's towns. In fact, with its proximity to Dublin, getting off the main roads is what enjoyment of life in Kildare is all about. It's surprisingly easy to get away from the traffic, and you'll quickly find areas of rural enchantment and unexpected swathes of relatively untamed nature.

LOCAL ATTRACTIONS AND INFORMATION

>Celbridge **Castletown House**
www.castletown.ie | 01 628 8252

>Curragh **The Curragh Racecourse**
www.curragh.ie | 045 441 205

>Kilcock **Larchill Arcadian Gardens** (follies) 01 628 7354

>Kildare (Tully) **Irish National Stud**
www.irishnationalstud.ie | 045 521617

>Straffan **Steam Museum**
www.steam-museum.com | 01 6273155

BURTOWN HOUSE, GARDENS AND GREEN BARN

BURTOWN LITTLE BALLYTORE ATHY CO KILDARE   EAT | BUY | PRODUCER

059 862 3865 | info@burtownhouse.ie
www.burtownhouse.ie

A visit to the Fennell family's early Georgian property is one of the most rewarding days out to be found anywhere in Ireland; the beautiful gardens, woodland and artworks feed the soul - and, although the transition from the previous small café may sometimes put pressure on service, **The Green Barn** (restaurant, exhibition space, artisan foods and retail) continues to offer very seasonal food (much of it home produced), alongside favourites like sour-dough pizzas and Burtown organic beef burgers.

The Green Barn: Wed-Thu 11-5.30, Fri-Sat to 8.30 (D 6.30-8.30), Sun & bank hol Mon 11-6. A la carte. Reservations advised. Farm produce for sale; books, artwork, gifts. Self-catering (3 rooms; family friendly; pet friendly; POA) Private venue (50). House/garden tours by arrangement. Property closed Oct-Feb (re-opens for snowdrop season). CC. **Directions:** M9 motorway, exit 3 to Athy; 2nd left.

THE BALLYMORE INN

BALLYMORE EUSTACE CO KILDARE

045 864 585 I theballymoreinn@eircom.net

www.ballymoreinn.com

EAT I DRINK I BUY

A benchmark destination for the quality of its food, ambience and service for over 20 years, the O'Sullivan family's stylish pub-restaurant was the ultimate Irish gastro-pub long before the much-misused term was familiar here. Nobody understands the importance of careful sourcing better than Georgina O'Sullivan, and their policy of using only the very best ingredients (including home-grown produce), careful cooking, and providing a relaxed ambience has proved a winning formula. There is always fresh fish from Duncannon, and the famous speciality pizzas - and many travel especially for their 28-day dry-aged steaks - chargrilled sirloin or fillet, perhaps, or a juicy steak sandwich or a salad. Super service too - and a small artisan shop.

Food daily, 12.30-9.30; L 12.30-3, D 6-9. Set menus & à a la carte. Children welcome. Reservations advised for Café Bar. Closed 25 Dec. CC. **Directions:** Centre of Ballymore Eustace.

CANTEEN CELBRIDGE

4 MAIN STREET CELBRIDGE CO. KILDARE   EAT

01 627 4967 | themarketcanteen@gmail.com

www.canteencelbridge.com

Canteen epitomises all that is good about the food renaissance in Ireland. James Sheridan and Soizic Humbert started out in a modest little space in Blackrock Market, drawing gourmands from all over the city to eat Sheridan's sophisticated and full-flavoured modern local ingredients-led European cooking. Now located in smart premises in Celbridge with a larger kitchen, they have been able to expand their menu and seat more diners, which is very good news for the neighbourhood - and for the growing numbers of fans who are travelling specially for the pleasure of a meal here. A relaxed ambience and accessible yet interesting menu make for a happy eating experience - well worth a detour.

⭐

Seats about 40. D Wed-Sat 5.30-9.30 (early D Tue-Thu 5.30-6.45), 2 sittings nightly. Vegetarian menu on request. L Sat 12-2.15. Closed Sun-Mon. CC.

CLIFF AT LYONS & THE ORANGERY RESTAURANT

THE VILLAGE AT LYONS CELBRIDGE CO KILDARE   EAT | STAY | BUY | LEARN

01 630 3500 | info@cliffatlyons.ie

www.cliffatlyons.ie

A sister property to the famed Cliff House Hotel, Co Waterford, and Cliff Townhouse, Dublin, this historic estate is beautifully situated alongside the Grand Canal and is a fascinating destination for a special occasion, or simply a day out. Accommodation (rooms and cottages) is luxurious in a very special way, and Chef Nathan Dimond's seasonal, botanically-themed cooking makes for memorable meals at the lovely **Orangery** fine dining restaurant. Afternoon Tea and Sun-

day Lunch are also particular treats, and the family-friendly Trellis café offers informal all-day fare.

⭐

Orangery Restaurant: D Tue-Sat 5.30-9.30 (early D Tue-Thu 5.30-7), from about €50. Trellis 11-10pm daily (set D from €38); Afternoon Tea; Sunday Lunch (some weekends). Reservations advised for all. **Rooms 40**. B&B from €170 per room. Weddings/ events; Chefs Academy. Establishment closed 25-26 Dec, Good Fri. Helipad. CC. **Directions:** Left for Ardclough just before bridge in Celbridge village, follow signs.

ZEST CAFÉ & RESTAURANT

UNIT 6/7 CLANE SHOPPING CENTRE CLANE CO KILDARE   EAT

045 893 222 I info@zestcafeandrestaurant.ie
www.zestcafeandrestaurant.ie

It's unlikely to be spotted by casual visitors to Clane town, but this hidden gem is well worth seeking out. Since opening in 2003, owner Mark Condron, head chef Alan Lee and their talented young team have built up a loyal local following at this appealing restaurant – and their reputation for excellence has also made it a hot destination for discerning diners in the wider area, including those visiting the county's many attractions. The secret of Zest's success is offering consistent quality and great value over a great range of options – a very customer-friendly policy, which is most noticeable at dinner.

Seats 55. Open Mon-Sat, 8.30-10; Sun 12.30-9. B'fst 8.30-12, L 12-4.30, D 4.30-10 (all day Sun). Brunch Sun 12.30-4. CC. **Also at:** Jolly Café & Restaurant, Naas (www.jolly.ie). **Directions:** Off Main Street - turn at AIB, left hand side.

MARTINSTOWN HOUSE

CURRAGH CO KILDARE   STAY

045 441 269 I info@martinstownhouse.com
www.martinstownhouse.com

Edward and Roisin Booth's delightful 200-year-old 'Strawberry Hill' gothic house is set in 170 acres of beautifully wooded land close to Ireland's premier flat racing course, The Curragh. They call it 'a sort of hybrid between a luxury hotel and a private home', which gives fair idea of the unique combination of charm and attention to detail to expect. The lovely walled kitchen garden provides seasonal ingredients for the table: fine food, comfort and the warmth of welcome will ensure an enjoyable stay.

Rooms 9. B&B from €110pps. Not suitable for children under 12. Residents D 7-9pm, about €55 (by arrangement - book the previous day). Weddings. Closed Christmas. CC. **Directions:** Kilcullen exit off M9 then N78 towards Athy. Sign at 1st crossroads.

RATHSALLAGH HOUSE

DUNLAVIN CO KILDARE   EAT | STAY
045 403 112 | info@rathsallagh.com
www.rathsallagh.com

The O'Flynn family's large, rambling country house on the Wicklow-Kildare border is just an hour from Dublin, but it could be in a different world. Insistent that it is 'not an hotel', it has a classic country house atmosphere - but it's very professionally run and has all of the expected amenities. Rooms range from spacious ones with great views in the old house to cottagey rooms in the stable yard, all very comfortable. Good food is central to Rathsallagh - starting with seasonal produce from the farm and beautiful walled garden, you will eat well here.

Rooms 35. B&B from €95pps. Restaurant: D daily 7-9.30 (to 9 Sun), à la carte. L Sun only 1-2.30 about €39. Non-residents welcome for D. Not suitable for children under 6. Reservations required. Food at Rathsallagh Golf Club 9-9 daily (to 7pm in winter). Open all year. CC. **Directions:** Signed from Dunlavin.

FALLONS OF KILCULLEN

MAIN STREET KILCULLEN CO KILDARE   EAT | DRINK
045 481 063 | info@fallonb.ie
www.fallonb.ie

A smartly understated exterior leads into the beguiling interior of this atmospheric restaurant and buzzy bar which offers food with a sense of place and personality. Owned by Brian Fallon (of Fallon & Byrne, Dublin), menus read temptingly - and not only because the dishes themselves sound so delicious although they certainly do — but also because of the quality of their ingredients, and this is matched by commitment and talent in the kitchen. Friendly service too, and (as befits this sporting area) the portions are generous.

Seats 65; food served Tue-Sun 12.30-9pm (Fri-Sat to 10pm). Closed Mon. 25 & 26 Dec, Good Fri. CC. **Directions:** Centre of village.

HARTES BAR & GRILL

MARKET SQUARE KILDARE CO KILDARE

045 533 557 | info@hartesbar.ie

www.hartesbar.ie

EAT | DRINK | LEARN

Behind brothers-in-law Paul Lenehan and Ronan Kinsella's traditional flower-decked pub frontage lies a very modern hybrid, combining the qualities of the classic Irish bar with something altogether different - and it's all to do with good food. While many come for the fun of cooking their own 'steak on a stone', it would be a pity to miss Barry Liscombe's excellent cooking: every delicious-sounding dish shows real interest and care.

This is a great dining destination and the commitment to support Irish producers is commendable - and there is a cookery school here too, aiming "to inspire you to throw out every old rule... and let your taste, smell and touch rule all."

Open Tue-Thu 12-9, Fri & Sat 12-9.45, Sun 12.30-8.30. (Kitchen closes Tue-Sat 3.45-5pm). Cookery school. CC. **Directions:** Town centre.

CARTON HOUSE HOTEL

MAYNOOTH CO KILDARE

01 505 2000 | reservations@cartonhouse.com

www.cartonhouse.com

EAT | STAY

Once the residence of the Dukes of Leinster, Carton House is an imposing mansion set in one of Ireland's finest country estates – and home to two championship golf courses - and it is worth a visit if only to see the property. While the luxurious accommodation is contemporary, prices are reasonable for a hotel of this style and the public areas lend themselves to entertainment on a grand scale. The Linden Tree restaurant (fine dining) takes full advantage of the magnificent setting.

Rooms 165. B&B from about €60pps. Children welcome. Room service. Restaurant: D Sun-Fri 7-9.30, Sat from 6.30; D from about €40. Kitchen Bar: food served 9am-9pm (Afternoon Tea daily, 1-4pm). Weddings; conferences. Leisure centre & spa (18m pool). CC. **Directions:** Close to Maynooth and signed from the town.

VIE DE CHATEAUX

THE HARBOUR NAAS CO KILDARE   EAT | BUY
045 888 478 | reservations@viedechateaux.ie
www.viedechateaux.ie

Tucked away off the beaten track, many visitors to Naas will miss this harbourside French restaurant but it is well worth seeking out. It has struck a chord with local diners for its fine dining quality and practical customer-friendly attitude, especially for time-pressed lunchtime diners. Platters of charcuterie, soups and tartines, terrific lunch platters (starter & main course on one plate), cheerful bistro classics like moules frites and an à la carte menu make for a lively range of choices and the chic ambience is special. Good choice of mainly French wines by the glass.

Open: L Wed-Fri 12-2.30; D Mon-Sat 6-10; Sun 1-9pm. Early D (Mon-Fri) & Sun L from about €22; also Bis-tro D & à la carte. CC. **Directions:** Beside the canal harbour. **Also at:** VDC@Home (food to go) Castle Building, Friary Road, Naas [(045) 889200; vdchome.ie].

CAFÉ CARLETON

NEWBRIDGE SILVERWARE VISITOR CENTRE
ATHGARVAN ROAD NEWBRIDGE CO KILDARE   EAT | BUY
045 488 439 | silverrestaurant@newbridgesilverware.ie
www.newbridgesilverware.com

Tropical leaf prints and sky blue car-ousel stripes give a fresh new look to Newbridge Silver's popular restau-rant, now re-christened Café Carleton after the American designer responsi-ble for the design. Ballymaloe-trained Natalie Collins' food is vibrant as ever, with fresh soups, salads, main cours-es and baked goods made in-house with best quality ingredients. The day begins with healthy breakfasts, and many options offered throughout the day are vegan and gluten-free. A very reasonably priced afternoon tea is served on elegant rose patterned Newbridge porcelain - with perhaps the extra sparkle of prosecco.

Open Mon-Sat 9am-5pm. Sun & Public Hols from 10. L 11.45am-3.30pm, Afternoon Tea 3-4.45pm, from €12.50 (booking advised). Children welcome. Fully wheelchair accessible. Self-pour wines by the glass, €5.50; craft beers available. Parking. Closed 3 days Christmas, 1 Jan. CC. **Directions:** At Newbridge Silverware (well signed).

TWO COOKS RESTAURANT & WINE BAR

5 CANAL VIEW SALLINS CO KILDARE
045 853 768 | nicola@twocooks.ie
www.twocooks.ie

EAT | DRINK

Scenically located overlooking the boats moored in the canal at Sallins, Josef and Nicola Zammit's terrific little restaurant and wine bar offers an exceptional 'fine dining without the fuss' experience - and outstanding value for money. Constantly evolving menus - including a mid-week dinner that's a snip yet makes no compromise on quality - revolve around seasonal produce, especially vegetables; there is great finesse, depth of flavour and textural interest in Josef's cooking, and attention to detail in the kitchen is matched by warm and informative service. Downstairs, the rustic wine bar offers a casual alternative with a tapas style blackboard menu.

⭐

Open Wed-Sat 6.30-9.30, Sun 12.30-4.30. Tasting Menu €49 (with matching wines, €85), set D from about €30 (vegetarian available), also à la carte. Families welcome. CC. **Directions:** Harbourside -Naas side of the bridge in Sallins village.

BARBERSTOWN CASTLE

STRAFFAN CO KILDARE

EAT | STAY

01 628 8157 | info@barberstowncastle.ie
www.barberstowncastle.ie

Located just 25 minutes from Dublin, this 13th century castle has been occupied for over 400 years and a wing added by current owner Kenneth Healy is in keeping with its style. Several romantic suites are in the ancient Castle Keep, but most rooms are more recent; some have four-posters and all are decorated to reflect the historic nature of the Castle. An elegant bar, two drawing rooms and big log fires are among the comforts of this historic destination, which also offers atmospheric fine dining and an events venue of character.

Rooms 55 (1 shower only, 3 wheelchair friendly). Lift. B&B from €75pps. D Sun-Thu 6-8, Fri-Sat, 7.30-9.30; about €50, also à la carte. Bar 10am-4pm daily. Weddings. Closed 24-26 Dec, Jan and Feb. CC.
Directions: West M4-Straffan exit at Maynooth - follow signs for Naas/Clane.

THE K CLUB

STRAFFAN CO KILDARE

EAT | STAY

01 601 7200 | sales@kclub.ie
www.kclub.ie

Its origins date back to the 6th century but it was the Barton wine family who established the tone of the elegant Straffan House in the 19th century. Set in lush countryside, and overlooking formal gardens and two championship golf courses, this opulent riverside hotel boasts sumptuous furnishings and original artwork including a Jack B.Yeats collection. The resort offers every amenity and several dining experiences: The Byerley Turk, fine dining (signature wine list), showcases local and estate-grown seasonal produce - Legends Restaurant (Arnold Palmer clubhouse) offers classic international cuisine, and K Thai (Smurfit Clubhouse) contributes Asian flavours.

> **Rooms 140**, from about €280. Families welcome. Byerley Turk 7-9.15pm daily; Legends, 7am-9.30pm daily; K Thai, 5-10pm Wed-Sun. Afternoon Tea, 2.30pm & 4.15pm. K Spa; 16.5m pool. Wide range of activities. CC. **Directions:** 29km southwest of Dublin airport and city (M50 - N4).

Kilkenny Castle
Co. Kilkenny

visitkilkenny.ie

COUNTY KILKENNY

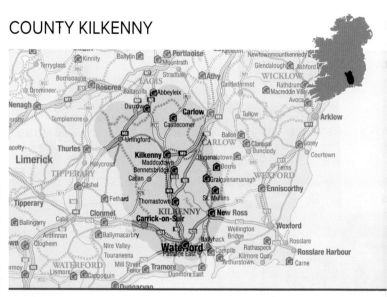

County Kilkenny is a land of beautiful valleys where elegant rivers weave their way through a rich countryside spiced by handsome hills. It is a city and county that is steeped in a rich and well-preserved history, a love of festivals and entertainment and a pride in the quality of their hospitality and the warmth of the welcome.

Kilkenny (www.visitkilkenny.ie) is proudly positioned as the **Medieval Capital of Ireland's Ancient East** and its array of historic buildings is unrivalled. Yet by today's standards of huge populations, it's very compact - making a perfect setting for hosting its many famous **festivals** (visitkilkenny.ie/calendar/festivals) including, The Cat Laughs and Kilkenomics, The Kilkenny Arts Festival, Subtitle Film Festival, The Craft Beer Festival, Savour (food and drink), and many more. And, thanks to its superb food producers and restaurants - showcased through the **#tastekilkenny** brand - Kilkenny's national and international reputation as a food destination is growing apace.

Of the iconic city attractions **Kilkenny Castle** (www.kilkennycastle.ie) and the **Medieval Mile Museum** (www.medievalmilemuseum.ie) stand out, but there are many rural treats (visitkilkenny. ie/places_to_visit) in this beautiful county too, including **Kells Priory** south of the city, **Woodstock Gardens** at Inistioge, and **Arboretum and Castlecomer Discovery Park** to name but a few.

Only an hour's drive from Dublin city, Kilkenny is an ideal escape, offering great food and accommodation, unrivalled festival atmosphere, beautiful scenery and a unique range of activities. There's everything from boutiques and jewellers to browse in the city, to riverside walks and cycles – and even Ireland's longest over water zipline, at **Castlecomer Discovery Park** (www.discoverypark.ie). That just has to be a must on any adventurous visitor's itinerary, when exploring what Ireland's Ancient East has to offer.

LOCAL ATTRACTIONS AND INFORMATION

>Gowran - **Gowran Park Racecourse**
www.gowranpark.ie | 056 772 6225

>Graiguenamanagh - **Cushendale Woollen Mills**
www.cushendale.ie | 059 972 4118

>Kilkenny - **Rothe House** (16c house, exhibitions)
www.rothehouse.com | 056 7722893

>Thomastown - **Jerpoint Abbey**
www.visitkilkenny.ie/jerpoint_abbey | 056 7724623

NICHOLAS MOSSE IRISH COUNTRY SHOP & CAFÉ

THE MILL BENNETTSBRIDGE CO KILKENNY   EAT
056 772 7505 | eshop@nicholasmosse.com
www.nicholasmosse.com

Two floors of pottery, including a large seconds area where good bargains are to be found, constitute one excellent reason to visit this venue in a lovely rural setting on the banks of the River Nore. Another is the food offering in the café, featuring appealing savoury dishes and good home baking. Well worth a visit.

Shop hours: Mon-Sat 10-6, Sun 1.30-5. **Café seats 35**. Mon-Sat 11-5, Sun 1.30-4. Children welcome. Toilets wheelchair accessible. Closed 25-27 Dec & 1 Jan. CC. **Directions:** J9 off M9; on R700, 7km south of Kilkenny - turn off just before bridge in Bennettsbridge.

WANDESFORDE HOUSE

DUBLIN ROAD CASTLECOMER CO KILKENNY   STAY
056 444 2441 | anna@wandesfordehouse.com
www.wandesfordehouse.com

Anyone looking for somewhere hospitable and relaxing to stay in the rural South-East should consider Wandesforde House - Michael and Anna McDonald extend a warm welcome to their charming early 18th century home and are always happy to share their local knowledge. Only 20 minutes from Kilkenny, it was built as a school by the Duchess of Ormonde in 1824, and now makes a delightful country house B&B, with old family furniture and comfortable beds in the individually furnished bedrooms - and a very good breakfast.

Rooms 5 (all shower only). B&B about €40pps. Reduced prices if staying more than 1 night. Complimentary tea, coffee, hot chocolate and snacks. Kitchen available for guests. Closed Nov-Apr. **No CC. Directions:** From Castlecomer - N78 Athy direction, 5km on the right.

WATERSIDE GUESTHOUSE

THE QUAY GRAIGUENAMANAGH CO KILKENNY
059 972 4246 | info@watersideguesthouse.com
www.watersideguesthouse.com

EAT | STAY

In the heart of medieval Graiguena-managh, an attractive 19th century stone warehouse on the River Barrow quayside makes an interesting setting for Brian and Brigid Roberts' well-run guesthouse and restaurant. Although some (and their en-suite shower rooms) are 'neat', the rooms - which all have views of the river and the beauti-ful old bridge, plus the soothing sound of water at night - are comfortable and full of character. Brigid offers varied menus and good home cooking in very pleasant waterside surroundings - and there are café tables out on the quay in summer. Walking, cycling, fishing and boating bring active holi-daymakers here - also bikes for hire (collection/delivery service).

Rooms 10 (all shower only, some family), B&B from about €45pps. Restaurant: D weekends & some other nights in summer; daytime café daily in summer. Establishment closed Nov-Jan. CC.
Directions: Centre of Graiguenamanagh.

ANOCHT RESTAURANT KILKENNY

KILKENNY DESIGN CENTRE CASTLE YARD KILKENNY CO KILKENNY   EAT
056 77 22118 | info@kilkennydesign.com
www.kilkennydesign.com/anocht-restaurant

Situated in what was once the stables and dairy of Kilkenny Castle, the famous **Kilkenny Design** craft shop is also known for tasty fare - especially at the evening restaurant, Anocht. Often described as the surprise highlight of a visit to the region, and in a uniquely atmospheric setting, Chef Rory Nolan's delicious dinners are inspired by seasonal local and Irish produce, with suppliers of foods like superb beef (from local butcher Paddy White), fresh fish from Duncannon and maybe Kerry mountain lamb in season, proudly credited on menus. Also a carefully curated wine list, and local craft brews to enjoy.

Anocht: D Thu-Sat 6-9.30pm; early D from about €23; also à la carte. Food Hall 8-6 daily; Café 10-6 daily. Children welcome; toilets wheelchair accessible. Lift. Wifi. Closed Sun, and bank hols off-season (Jan-Mar). CC. **Directions:** Opposite Kilkenny Castle.

A SLICE OF HEAVEN

5-6 REGENCY COURT FRIARY STREET CO KILKENNY   BUY | LEARN | PRODUCER
087 953 3870 | mary@asliceofheaven.ie
www.asliceofheaven.ie

Renowned baker Mary McEvoy has a national following for her gorgeous creations, which are astonishingly detailed and exquisitely presented in decorative boxes. She pays great attention to the ingredients, which are all natural and local if at all possible, and the inviting coffee shop serves Java coffee and a selection of her cakes, desserts and baked goods, including wonderful macaroons, pear and almond tart, mini and full sized cup cakes with the most imaginative toppings, home made brown breads and much more. Next door to the bakery and café, Mary and her chef husband, Neil, offer a wide range of courses at the Kilkenny Cookery School (kilkenny-cookeryschool.com)

Hours: Cafe & shop open Mon-Sat 9.30am-5.30pm, also Sun in summer.

BUTLER HOUSE

16 PATRICK STREET KILKENNY CO KILKENNY   STAY | EAT
056 776 5707 | res@butler.ie
www.butler.ie

This elegant Georgian townhouse – the original Dower House of Kilkenny Castle - was restored (by Kilkenny Design) with interesting results in the 1970s, in a style combining contemporary design and period architecture. Unusually spacious bedrooms and generous (recently refurbished) bathrooms are a happy outcome of this redesign. Breakfast is served in the Kilkenny Design Centre across the gardens, but daytime food is available here at the elegantly appointed Butler House Tea Room & Pantry which offers all day dining in lovely surroundings.

Rooms 13 (1 shower only). B&B €100pps, sc discretionary. Children welcome. Tea Room & Pantry: daily 10am-7pm; L from 12 noon, Afternoon Tea from 2.30. Closed 24-29 Dec. CC. **Directions:** City centre, close to Kilkenny Castle.

CAKEFACE

6 IRISHTOWN GARDENS KILKENNY CO KILKENNY   EAT | BUY | PRODUCER

086 601 7045 | us@cakefacepastry.com

www.cakefacepastry.com

Although it's on a quiet street and a little out of the way, what a great destination Laura and Rory Gannon's patisserie and café has turned out to be. The wittily named cakes and pastries (aka "Quirky and Unusual Desserts"), are simply stellar. Anything but classical, each has its own name and personality, including favourites such as The Passionate Tart, The Zesty Nutcracker and FIGure it Out. And, while simple, the savoury food - including deeply flavoured soups, and sandwiches made with gorgeous breads from carefully selected craft bakeries - is delicious. Superb coffee too - the best in Kilkenny they claim, and they could be right. Small but mighty, Cakeface is a little treasure.

Seats about 25. Free wifi. Open Mon-Sat, 10-6pm, Sun 10-4pm. CC. **Directions:** Irishtown, near St Canice's Cathedral.

CAMPAGNE

THE ARCHES 5 GASHOUSE LANE KILKENNY CO KILKENNY

056 777 2858 | info@campagne.ie

www.campagne.ie

The benchmark for fine dining in Kilkenny for a decade, this well-named French-inspired restaurant is run by chef Garrett Byrne and his wife, restaurant manager Brid Hannon. Central to the décor, a set of colourful contemporary paintings vividly depicting rural life, by celebrated Kilkenny artist Catherine Barron, illustrates their passionately held food philosophy of involving local food producers. From the superb service to the rustically-inspired cooking, understated finesse is the hallmark of Campagne; the meticulously-selected ingredients are cooked to perfection and beautifully presented - and the tone is invariably relaxed. Magic.

⭐

L Fri-Sun 12.30-2.30, D Tue-Sat; early D Tue-Thu 6-7pm, Fri-Sat 5.30-6pm, from about €34; also à la carte D Tue-Sat 6-10pm. Vegetarian menu. Children welcome; wheelchair accessible. Closed D Sun, all Mon; 2 wks Jan, 1 wk Jul. CC. **Directions:** Off John's Green, near the railway station.

KERNEL BAR & KITCHEN AT KILKENNY INN

5/16 VICAR STREET KILKENNY CO KILKENNY   EAT | DRINK | STAY
056 777 2828 | info@kilkennyinn.com
www.kilkennyinn.com/kernel-bar-and-kitchen

Close to St Canice's cathedral and within easy walking distance of the city's attractions, the Kilkenny Inn reopened under new ownership in 2017, and it offers comfortable, well priced accommodation and a pleasantly quirky interior. But the hotel's big USP is its food offering at respected chef Maria Raftery's Kernel Bar & Kitchen - a destination restaurant and first floor bar. Maria has a following in the region and the cooking is splendid. True to form, suppliers of her carefully sourced ingredients are respectfully listed and her boldly presented dishes are strong on flavour - the Kernel Angus Beef Burger with smoked Gubbeen cheese is a tasty house speciality. Friendly young servers too, and some local beers and craft cider on the drinks list.

Rooms 30; B&B about €115 per room. Wifi. Kernel Kitchen: Breakfast and from 12 noon daily. Parking (20). CC. **Directions:** City centre, near St Canice's cathedral.

LYRATH ESTATE HOTEL & CONVENTION CENTRE

DUBLIN ROAD KILKENNY CO KILKENNY   STAY
056 776 0088 | info@lyrath.com
www.lyrath.com

Set in 170 acres of mature parkland, this modern hotel has a 17th century house at its heart, now extended to become a large hotel with a conference centre and spa. The resulting blend has considerable character and accommodation is spacious and well appointed in a modern classic style. The range of bars and eating areas includes contemporary fine dining in the handsome La Perla restaurant; a popular oriental restaurant. Yindees; and an attractive bar with terrace. Good for business and events - or when an out-of-town base with space and wide-ranging amenities is preferred.

Rooms 137 (4 wheelchair friendly) Lift; 24 hr room service. B&B from about €75pps. Laptop sized safes in rooms, free wifi. Leisure centre (17m pool). Spa. Children welcome. Closed 20-26 Dec. CC. **Directions:** 2km from Kilkenny city on the Dublin/Carlow road

MARBLE CITY BAR

66 HIGH STREET KILKENNY CO KILKENNY   EAT | DRINK
056 776 1143 | reservations@langtons.ie
www.langtons.ie

A sister establishment to the famous Langton's Bar & Restaurant and Langton House Hotel on John Street, the Langton family's historic bar was re-designed some years ago by the internationally acclaimed Irish designer, the late David Collins - who did very little work in his native country. Although initially controversial (especially the ultra-modern stained glass window which now graces an otherwise traditional frontage), it is a wonderful space to be in and attracts a varied clientèle who enjoy the vibrant atmosphere and good bar food, including a tasty chowder. Downstairs, the Marble City Tea Rooms offers lighter fare.

Bar food, 9am–10pm; Tea Rooms, 9am-9.30pm. Breakfast, from 10am; main menus 12 noon-10 pm. A la carte. House wine about €20 (€5 per glass). Free wifi. Closed 25 Dec. Ample car parking at rear. CC. **Directions:** Main Street, city centre

RISTORANTE RINUCCINI

1 THE PARADE, KILKENNY CO KILKENNY   EAT
056 776 1575 | info@rinuccini.com
www.rinuccini.com

Antonio and Marion Cavaliere's well-known Italian restaurant is in a semi-basement in the impressive terrace opposite Kilkenny Castle and the closely packed tables are an indication of its popularity, with the room quickly filling up. The secret of its success is consistently good classic Italian cooking of fresh mainly local ingredients, together with great service and outstanding value for money. One of Ireland's best Italian restaurants.

Seats 100 (+10 outdoors; private room, 60). L daily 12-2.30pm (Sun open all afternoon, 12-9), D daily 5-10pm (Sun to 9pm). Early D Sun-Fri 5-7, Sat 5-6.30, Sun and Banh hol 5-6.30. Children welcome. Reservations accepted. A la carte. Closed 25-26 Dec. CC. **Directions:** accross the road from Kilkenny Castle.

ROSQUIL HOUSE

CASTLECOMER ROAD KILKENNY CO KILKENNY   STAY

056 772 1419 | info@rosquilhouse.com
www.rosquilhouse.com

Phil and Rhoda Nolan's handsome guesthouse is just a short walk from the city centre. Their dream was to combine the best attributes of a small hotel with the personal care and good value associated with Ireland's best guesthouses. The result is an exceptionally comfortable and hospitable place to stay, with spacious rooms, pleasant lounging spaces - and excellent breakfasts showcasing local artisan foods.

Rooms 7 (double; triple; family suite); B&B from about €45pps. Wheelchair accessible. WiFi. Self catering mews available. Terrace. Parking. CC.

ZUNI RESTAURANT & BOUTIQUE HOTEL

26 PATRICK STREET KILKENNY CO KILKENNY   EAT | STAY

056 772 3999 | info@zuni.ie
www.zuni.ie

Although Zuni is an hotel ('boutique', and with a youthful style of accommodation), the atmosphere is more restaurant with rooms. An oasis of contemporary chic right in the bustling centre of Kilkenny, this small owner-run property is well established as a dining destination - and, as well as the smart light-filled restaurant, there's a street-side café at the front which is popular for its good coffee and light fare. Compact and distinctively Irish in tone, Zuni offers something different

Rooms 13 (8 shower only, 1 wheelchair friendly). Lift. Room only from €60pps, midweek DB&B from €85pps. Children welcome. **Restaurant seats 70** (+24 outside). L daily 12.30-2.30. A la carte. Early D daily from 6pm, from about €25. D Mon-Sun 6-9.30 (Sun to 9). Toilets wheelchair accessible; children welcome before 7pm. Ho-tel closed 23-27 Dec. CC. **Directions:** On Patrick Street - leads to Waterford road; 200 meters from Kilkenny Castle.

BLANCHVILLE HOUSE

DUNBELL MADDOXTOWN CO KILKENNY

STAY

056 772 7197 | mail@blanchville.ie

www.blanchville.ie

Tim and Monica Phelan's elegant Georgian house is easy to spot - there's a folly in its grounds. A friendly, welcoming place, it has classic dining and drawing rooms and the comfortably furnished bedrooms in period style all overlook attractive countryside. There's an excellent breakfast – also dinner, if pre-arranged. There are four self-catering houses in the renovated Coach Yard and they - and / or the main house - are available for ex-clusive use, making this an ideal destination for family get-togethers and groups.

Rooms 6 (all with private bathroom, 2 shower only). B&B from about €55pps. Children over 10 yrs welcome. Residents D about €45, by prior arrangement only. Closed Nov-Feb. CC. **Directions:** From Kilkenny take N10 (Carlow-Dublin road), 1st right 1km after 'The Pike Pub'; 3km to crossroads (Connolly's pub). Take left, large stone entrance 1.5km on left.

BALLYDUFF HOUSE

THOMASTOWN CO KILKENNY

STAY

056 775 8488 | ballydhouse@eircom.net

www.ballyduffhouse.com

Set in fine rolling countryside, Brede Thomas's 18th century house overlooking the River Nore is blessed with an utterly restful location. Brede is a relaxed host who enjoys sharing her home with guests, who have the use of large well-proportioned day rooms as well as spacious bedrooms furnished with antiques. Hunting is the area's traditional country pursuit but other activities include salmon and trout fishing on the Nore and there are beautiful walks on the estate.

Rooms 5 (all with private bathrooms). B&B from about €50pps. Children welcome. Pets permitted by arrangement. Self-catering accommodation adjacent. Weddings, parties, events. Open all year. **No CC. Directions:** 5km south of Thomastown.

BASSETTS

MARSH'S STREET THOMASTOWN CO KILKENNY

056 7724916 | mijke.jansen@live.nl

www.facebook.com/BassettsThomastown/

EAT

An attractive and stylishly renovated building is the setting for John Bassett and Mijke Jansen's restaurant in Thomastown. Having had a loyal following at their much-missed Inistioge restaurant, Bassetts of Woodstock, this new venture is very welcome - and their philosophy of excellence brings top quality food and service to a town that is no stranger to the best. Combining hearty popular fare with refined cooking, their speciality of Kilkenny beef - air-dried in-house, in a unit that provides an unusual focal point in the restaurant - is a stroke of genius, and the whole experience is sure to please.

Open: L Wed–Sun 12-3 (Sun to 5), D Tue–Sat 5-9; à la carte. Wines from €23. Reservations advised. **Directions:** On the edge of Thomastown, on the Mount Juliet road - just around the corner from Market Street.

THE BLACKBERRY CAFÉ

MARKET STREET THOMASTOWN CO KILKENNY

086 775 5303 | jackiehoyne@clara.co.uk

www.theblackberrycafe.ie

EAT

Formerly a cobbler's workshop, Jackie Hoyne's café with its immaculately maintained paintwork and lovely Georgian windows presents an alluring face to the passerby. Inside, blackboard menus offer apparently familiar café fare - but tip-top ingredients, careful preparation (and the welcome aroma of home baking coming from the semi-open kitchen) make this casual dining destination stand out from the crowd.

Open: Mon-Fri 9.30-5.30pm, Sat 10-5, bank hol Mon 11-5. Closed Sun. **No CC. Directions:** On the corner of Market Street, beside turning signed Mount Juliet.

MOUNT JULIET

THOMASTOWN CO KILKENNY

056 777 3000 | info@mountjuliet.ie
www.mountjuliet.ie

EAT | STAY

One of Ireland's finest Georgian estates, beautiful Mount Juliet has a uniquely restful atmosphere, luxurious accommodation, exceptional on-site activities, pampering at the Spa & Health Club - and friendly staff who make guests feel at home. Outstanding food too, notably at the fine dining **Lady Helen Dining Room**, where Head Chef Ken Harker pays great attention to seasonal, local and speciality foods - and the same principles apply to

The Hound, a stylishly informal family friendly restaurant in Hunters Yard.

⭐

Rooms 132 (1 wheelchair friendly). No Lift. B&B from €99pps. Children welcome. **Lady Helen Dining Room**, D Tue-Sat 6.30-9.30. Closed Sun & Tue. 9-course Tasting Menu, about €99, also à la carte. Al Fresco Menu and Afternoon Tea (1-6 daily). Reservations required. **The Hound:** Tue-Sun, 12.30-9pm (closed Mon). Free wifi. Open all year. CC. **Directions:** Signed from Thomastown.

COUNTY LAOIS

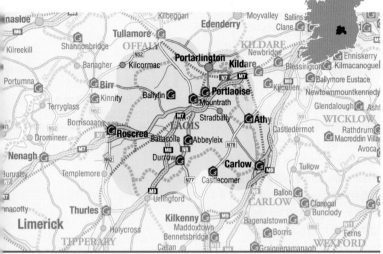

With its territory traversed by the rail and road links from Dublin to Cork and Limerick, Laois is often glimpsed only fleetingly by inter-city travellers. But as with any Irish county, it is a wonderfully rewarding place to visit as soon as you move off the main roads. For Laois is the setting for Emo Court www.emocourt.net and Heywood www.dochara.com , two of the great gardens of Ireland at their most impressive.

And it's a salutary place to visit, too. In the eastern part, between Stradbally and Portlaois, there's the Rock of Dunamase, that fabulous natural fortress which many occupiers inevitably assumed to be impregnable. Dunamase's remarkably long history of fortifications and defences and sieges and eventual captures has a relevance and a resonance for all times and all peoples and all places.

But there's much more to Laois than mournful musings on the ultimate vanity of human ambitions. With its border shared with Carlow along the River Barrow, eastern Laois comfortably reflects Carlow's quiet beauty. To the northwest, we find that Offaly bids strongly to have the Slieve Bloom Mountains www.slievebloom.ie thought of as an Offaly hill range, but in fact there's more of the Slieve Blooms in Laois than Offaly, and lovely hills they are too. And though the River Nore may be thought of as quintessential Kilkenny, long before it gets anywhere near Kilkenny it is quietly building as it meanders across much of Laois, gathering strength from the weirdly-named Delour, Tonet, Gully, Erskina and Goul rivers on the way.

LOCAL ATTRACTIONS AND INFORMATION

>Abbeyleix **Abbeyleix Heritage House**
www.abbeyleixheritage.com | 0502 31653

>Abbeyleix **Sensory Gardens** 0502 31325

>Donaghmore **Castletown House Open Farm**
0505 46415

>Donaghmore **Donaghmore Workhouse Museum**
0505 46212

>Emo: **Emo Court (Gandon house & gardens)**
www.emocourt.net | 0502 26573

>Portlaois **Dunamaise Theatre & Arts Centre**
www.dunamaise.ie | 0502 63356

>Portlaois **Tourist Information** 0502 21178

MORRISSEY'S

MAIN STREET ABBEYLEIX CO LAOIS

057 873 1281 | morrisseys16@gmail.com

DRINK

One of Ireland's finest and best-loved pubs, Morrissey's is a handsome building on the wide main street of this attractive little town. It first opened as a grocery in 1775 and, with its high shelf-lined walls and a pot belly stove to gather round on cold days, it's a great place to lift the spirits. True to the old tradition, food is not its strength - and television, cards and singing are not allowed.

Closed 25 Dec. **Directions:** In village on right heading south.

THE GALLIC KITCHEN @ BRAMLEY

MAIN STREET ABBEYLEIX CO LAOIS

086 605 8208 | galkit@gmail.com

www.facebook.com/gallickitchen/

EAT

The traditional shop windows of this interesting restaurant and deli in the centre of Abbeyleix attract the eye - and it would be a mistake to pass by, as acclaimed baker, food producer and caterer Sarah Webb is the power behind the business. Alongside her own delicious baked goods and salads, she also offers other premium delicatessen foods. There is plenty of space in this former draper's shop to enjoy small temptations such as a freshly brewed coffee and meringue roulade, and a sun-soaked space at the back for fine days. Hot and cold food to go, too.

Open Mon-Sat 10-6, Sun 11-6. CC. **Directions:** Centre of Abbeyleix.

SANDYMOUNT HOUSE

OLDTOWN ABBEYLEIX CO LAOIS STAY
057 873 1063 | sandymounthouse@gmail.com
www.sandymounthouse.com

A charming mid-19th century house set quietly in mature woodlands on the de Vesci estate, Avril Bibby's pet-friendly country house B&B is just outside Abbeyleix village and offers all the advantages of the relaxed rural life that is typical of the area, yet is within easy distance of shops, pubs and restaurants. The traditionally furnished rooms are very comfortable, with good beds, flat screen TV and power showers, and there's a cosy sitting room too, with an open fire in winter. And you'll have a really good breakfast to see you on your way, including freshly-laid eggs from their own Rhode Island Red hens.

Rooms 4 (all shower only); B&B about €40pps. Children welcome. Dogs permitted. Wifi. Camper vans welcome. Closed 20 Dec-2 Jan. CC. **Directions:** 2km down Ballacolla/Rathdowney (R433) road from Abbeyleix, on right hand side.

THE FISHERMANS THATCHED INN

FISHERSTOWN BALLYBRITTAS CO LAOIS DRINK
057 862 6488 | sean.fishermans@gmail.com
www.facebook.com/fishermans.inn.1/

All are welcome at Sean Ward's picturesque pub. With a cheering fire in the grate and the front bar packed with bric-a-brac, it's delightful. Not a daytime place, except at weekends, and it makes no pretence of being a food destination either: a range of gourmet pies is the only food served – but there's a fine pint and a great collection of whiskeys and gins to try, and to discuss with this most hospitable of landlords.

A magic spot - you'll be glad you found it. Traditional music sessions on Tuesdays, and also Sundays in summer.

Opening times: Usually open from 6pm midweek, Sat from 2pm, Sun 12.30-11.

BALLYFIN HOUSE

BALLYFIN CO LAOIS
057 875 5866 | info@ballyfin.com
www.ballyfin.com

EAT | STAY

Chicago businessman Fred Krehbiel, his Irish wife Kay and managing director Jim Reynolds put in eight years of restoration before opening this Regency mansion in the foothills of the Slieve Bloom Mountains, in 2011, as a luxurious - yet surprisingly homely - small hotel. While certainly impressive, hospitable General Manager Damien Bastiat keeps the tone relaxed and it is emphatically not stuffy. Although undeniably expensive, the nightly full board rates give good value at this treat destination, thanks to the exceptional range of extras included.

Rooms 20 (5 suites, 8 staterooms, 7 deluxe). Lift. Full board from €915, not suitable for under 12s unless booking entire property (from €14,500). D: non-residents welcome when there is room; 5.30 for 7pm, from €105. Open all year. CC. **Directions:** M7 junction 18, signposted Mountrath/Portlaoise, on entering Mountrath turn right at the traffic lights, 7km on left.

BOWES FOODHALL & CAFÉ

THE SQUARE DURROW CO LAOIS   EAT
057 874 0669 | info@bowescafe.ie
www.facebook.com/Bowes-Foodhall-Cafe-509767295762370/

With its pretty blue and white paintwork and bold signage, you can't miss Sarah and Shane Bowe's Foodhall and Café. The building has received plenty of TLC in recent years and visitors love the ambience - the classic black and white flooring and whitewashed walls, and the lovely old walled garden with its weathered stone and outdoor seating for fine summer days - but it's Chef Adrian Sheppard's good cooking, in-house baking and the can-do service provided by friendly local staff that makes this busy place such a special destination. No wonder everyone wants to return - as soon as possible.

Seats 86. Open Mon-Sat, 9am-5pm. Wheelchair accessible. Families welcome. Open all year. CC. **Directions:** Centre of Durrow, on the main square

CASTLE DURROW

DURROW CO LAOIS   EAT I STAY

057 873 6555 I info@castledurrow.com

www.castledurrow.com

Set in lovely gardens, Peter and Shelley Stokes's impressive 18th century country house offers comfort and relaxation with style. Spacious high-ceilinged suites in the main house enjoy views over the parkland, while two wings offer pleasing rooms in different styles - and, with a south-facing rural outlook, the beautiful restaurant is a fine setting for chef Graham Gallagher's carefully sourced local and home-produced 'modern country house cooking'. Bar meals are also available, and McEvoy's Steak & Wine Bar, Abbeyleix, is in common ownership.

Rooms 46 (all bath & shower). DB&B from about €195 per couple. Restaurant: D Wed-Sat 7-9, Sun 6-8. D from about €40, L Sun only 1.30-3 about €30. Bar 12-7 daily, à la carte. Children welcome. Weddings. Restaurant closed 31 Dec-15 Jan, house closed 24-26 Dec.. CC. **Directions:** Off M8, Dublin-Cork; entrance to hotel from village green.

THE HERITAGE KILLENARD

KILLENARD CO LAOIS   EAT I STAY

057 864 5500 I info@theheritage.com

www.theheritage.com

In new ownership since 2014 and operated with style by one of Ireland's most respected General Managers, Andrew Phelan, great staff and exceptional leisure facilities are the trump cards at this luxury hotel in rural Laois. Not only is there a destination spa and (next door) an 18-hole Seve Ballesteros golf course, but onsite facilities also include bowls, tennis and a floodlit jogging track. Spacious accommodation is very comfortably furnished and dining options include fine dining in the Arlington Room, Afternoon Tea in the Lobby Lounge, and informal options elsewhere in this attractive venue.

Rooms 98 (6 wheelchair friendly). B&B from about €150 per room. Children's playground; Fairy Garden. Spa; 15m pool. Arlington Restaurant (fine dining; D daily from 7, about €55); Slieve Bloom Bar 12-9pm daily. Afternoon Tea €30, 1pm/3pm (pre-book). Self catering. CC. **Directions:** M7; exit 15 to Killenard.

ROUNDWOOD HOUSE

MOUNTRATH CO LAOIS   EAT | STAY
057 873 2120 | info@roundwoodhouse.com
www.roundwoodhouse.com

Secluded in mature woodland, at the foot of the Slieve Bloom Mountains, it is hard to see how anyone could fail to love this unspoilt 18th-century house - a sense of history and an appreciation of genuine hospitality (and good food, including breakfast) are all that is needed to make the most of a stay at this magical property. Restored by Frank and Rosemarie Kennan over many years, it is now run with equal dedication and charm by their daughter Hannah and her husband Paddy Flynn. Just don't expect television or techie devices: this is the place for a digital detox.

Rooms 10, B&B from €75pps. Children welcome. D daily, about €60 (midweek €45). Non-residents welcome if there is room, reservations required. Light menu on request. House closed 24-26 Dec. CC. **Directions:** On R440, 5km from Mountrath, on left.

IVYLEIGH HOUSE

BANK PLACE CHURCH STREET PORTLAOISE CO LAOIS   STAY

057 862 2081 I info@ivyleigh.com
www.ivyleigh.com

This lovely early Georgian house is a listed building and the present owners, Dinah and Jerry Campion, have restored it immaculately and furnished it beautifully. Bedrooms are the essence of comfort and elegance - but it is at breakfast time that this superb guesthouse is at its best and it has more than once been recognised in our Breakfast Awards. Popular with business guests and an ideal base for golf and garden visits nearby.

Rooms 6 (all shower only). B&B from €55pps. Free wifi. Garden. Not suitable for children under 8. Closed Christmas period. CC. **Directions:** Centre of town; follow signs for multi storey car park, 30m from car park.

TYNANS AT THE STOREYARD

THE STOREYARD KEALEW BUSINESS PARK PORTLAOISE CO LAOIS   EAT

057 868 8343 I info@tynans.ie
www.tynans.ie

A real hidden gem tucked away in a glorious warren of rooms packed with antiques and architectural treasures, Tynan's is well signed and easy to find once you're in the know - and it has become a destination for Imelda Davitt's good home cooking. Having previously worked with her late brother, Jim Tynan, in the much-missed Kitchen and Foodhall ('Jim's Kitchen'), Imelda has a following in the area. Her philosophy is simple: she uses top quality ingredients from local suppliers, including her own garden, and cooks everything from scratch every day, from breakfast through to lunch and lighter bites. Home baking, flavour and quality are the mainstays of this thriving - and most unusual - business. Definitely worth a detour.

Open Tue-Sat 9.30am-5pm; L from 12 noon. CC. **Directions:** West of town centre, off R445 (The Storeyard is signed).

In Memory Of

Nora J. Murray

Writer and Poet
Born in this house 1888.
Died in Dublin 1955.

Little Town

*"There are silver waters lapping
Under arches grey and brown,
When the swans come up the river
To the bridge at Carrick Town."*

Carrick - on - Shannon 2016 Historical Society

COUNTY LEITRIM

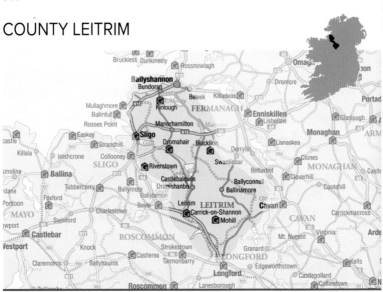

County Leitrim (www.leitrimtourism.com) sets the pace in preparing its best features to welcome the visitor. Central to the county is the River Shannon. Far from seeing it as a barrier, in Leitrim it is an asset, to be developed as pleasantly as possible for travel and relaxation. In addition to travel by boat, it offers access to walkers and cyclists with the **Shannon Blueway** (www.bluewaysireland.org), a magic route through otherwise hidden places, and part of a growing nationwide system.

Today, Leitrim quietly prospers. The county town, Carrick-on-Shannon, is one of Ireland's brightest and best, a bustling river port and gateway to the restored **Shannon-Erne Waterway** (www.waterwaysireland.org/places-to-go/shannon-erne-waterway/boating) whose vitality has contributed significantly to the county's new prosperity.

Leitrim is rightly seen as a pleasantly away-from-it-all sort of place which has many attractions for the discerning traveller, not least enthusiasts for traditional music, good food and drink - and, with a determinedly alternative bent, it's home to **The Organic Centre** (www.theorganiccentre.ie), and the beating heart of Ireland's emerging Ecotourism and organic culture.

And what a hive of culinary activity it is too. Some of Ireland's best-loved chefs and restaurants are in Leitrim, which not only boasts a great choice of restaurants, pubs and cafés but an extraordinarily energetic and diverse range of producers who make everything from the county's trademark traditional product - boxty - to the craft beers and spirits that have recently started production. Judging by the success of enterprises like the **Carrig Brewery** (www.carrigbrewing.com) and **The Shed Distillery** (thesheddistillery.com) in Drumshanbo - also home to **The Food Hub** (www.thefoodhub.com) artisan food production enterprise centre and education facility, and **The CheeseHub**, (www.thecheesehub.ie) artisan contract cheese ripening and maturing service - there is no fear of Leitrim being left behind in Ireland's great craft drinks renaissance. All this and the wonderful waterways to enjoy too - a trip to lovely Leitrim is sure to be rewarding.

THE COTTAGE RESTAURANT

JAMESTOWN CARRICK ON SHANNON CO LEITRIM   EAT

071 962 5933 | info@cottagerestaurant.ie

www.cottagerestaurant.ie

Engaging owner-chef, Shamzuri Hanifa ('Sham'), is famous for serving modern European and Asian food with real finesse at this cheerful white-washed restaurant on the edge of the pretty village of Jamestown. It has become a firm favourite with local diners and visitors, many of whom arrive by boat - from the quay, it's a pleasant half mile walk through the village, with pavement all the way and past two particularly enticing pubs. Offering great food and service, plenty of atmosphere and good value, this is an understandably popular little restaurant so it would be wise to book, especially at weekends.

Seats 40 (outdoors 16). D Thu-Sun 6-10, L Sun only 12-4-ish. Closed Mon-Wed. [Also at daytime Synergy Café, Sligo Road, Carrick-on-Shannon; Chef Sham Sauces sold; cookery classes.] CC. **Directions:** On right just before entering Jamestown village.

Carrig Brewing Company's Brazen Amber + Lager - brewed locally in Drumshanbo

Mountain Man Hairy Goat I.P.A.

Galway Hooker Pale Ale

Mc Gargles Gravy Maevy Pilsner

8 Degrees Sunburnt Red

Brú Dubh Stout

Weston's Stowford Press Cider

On bottle - over 20 craft

THE OARSMAN

BRIDGE STREET CARRICK-ON-SHANNON CO LEITRIM   EAT I DRINK

071 962 1733 I info@theoarsman.com

www.theoarsman.com

Famed for great food, atmosphere and friendly service, this characterful pub is run by brothers Conor and Ronan Maher whose family have a long history of hospitality in the town. The bar is solidly traditional, with welcoming fires and a pleasant outside seating area at the back, and there's also an attractive first floor dining area overlooking the bar. A strong kitchen team produces consistently excellent food showcasing the best of local and other Irish artisan produce - superb Andarl Farm pork from Galway, for example, and Cloonconra cheese made in Roscommon from the milk of rare breed moiled cows. One of Ireland's finest pubs - definitely worth a detour.

Bar meals Tue-Sat 12-9pm (Fri & Sat to 9.30). Restaurant: Fri- Sat from 5pm. Closed Sun, Mon, 25 Dec (possibly Good Fri). CC. **Directions:** Town centre.

ST GEORGES TERRACE RESTAURANT

TOWNPARKS CARRICK-ON-SHANNON CO LEITRIM   EAT | DRINK | LEARN
071 961 6546 | info@stgeorgesterrace.com
www.stgeorgesterrace.com

There are plenty of good eating places in Carrick-on-Shannon but this restaurant near The Dock Arts Centre brings something different to the town. With a background in fine dining, Dave Fitzgibbon offers refined but accessibly priced cooking in the rather grand surroundings of a former bank - and, backed up by the excellent front of house management and service provided by his business partner, Siobhan Smyth, it is not only a superb neighbourhood restaurant but also the go-to special occasion destination for discerning diners from a wide area. With outstanding food and service, accessible prices and relaxed Irish hospitality, this Shannonside gem is a place that food lovers will be very glad to find.

Restaurant: D Wed-Sun D 6-10pm, L Sun 12.30-3pm. Afternoon Menu Thu-Sat, 1-5pm. Closed Mon-Tue. Cookery School; catering. CC. **Directions:** Near The Dock Arts Centre.

LUNA

MAIN STREET DROMAHAIR CO LEITRIM   EAT
071 913 4332 | joegrogan2017@gmail.com
www.facebook.com/LunaRestaurantDromahair/

Tucked away behind the homely facade of a mustard-yellow cottage, well known restaurateurs Grainne Sheridan and Joe Grogan's small restaurant is introducing plenty of visitors to the unspoilt village of Dromahair. Grainne is the chef and does what she has always done so well, sourcing the best local and other (mainly) Irish ingredients and transforming them into unfussy and deliciously flavourful dishes (Donegal mussels, local steaks, pasta, gourmet pizza...). There is even a separate vegan menu, so there really is something for everyone. Suppliers are proudly credited and everything is made from scratch in-house - the quality is obvious on the plate and on the palate. Well worth seeking out.

Seats 45 (+12 outdoors) Open Tue-Sat from 4pm, Sun from 3pm. A la carte; also vegan menu. Closed first 3 wks Jan. CC. **Directions:** Centre of Dromahair village

THE COURTHOUSE RESTAURANT & ACCOMMODATION

MAIN STREET KINLOUGH CO LEITRIM   EAT | STAY
071 984 2391 | thecourthouserest@eircom.net
www.thecourthouserest.com

Owner-chef Piero Melis offers excellent contemporary Mediterranean cooking at this popular and highly-regarded restaurant with rooms. Atmospheric, with a cheering open fire on chilly days, it's a welcoming place and full of charm. Piero's philosophy is to keep it simple and allow his carefully sourced local foods to take centre stage, but this simplicity is skilfully achieved. Regular diners travel considerable distances to enjoy a meal here so booking is strongly advised, especially at weekends.

Seats 40. D Wed-Sat 6.30-9.30. L&D Sun 4-8.30. Early D Thu-Sat 6-7pm, from about €29; early D Sun 4-7; also à la carte. **Rooms 4** (shower only), B&B about €40pps; family €90. Free wifi. B&B Fri-Sat only off season (Nov-Feb). House closed Mon-Wed, Oct–Mar, also 10 days Jun or Sep. CC. **Directions:** Off main Donegal-Sligo road (N15), 5km towards Sligo from Bundoran; signed at Tullaghan.

LOUGH RYNN CASTLE HOTEL & ESTATE

LOUGH RYNN MOHILL CO LEITRIM

EAT I STAY

071 963 2700 I enquiries@loughrynn.ie

www.loughrynn.ie

Set amongst 300 acres of rolling countryside, historic Lough Rynn Castle has seen major restoration with a view to making it a perfect country haven, and no expense or effort has been spared. Opulently appointed lounges, drawing rooms and a library are remarkably intimate for public rooms in an hotel, and bedrooms include luxurious castle rooms with wonderful views of the estate and surrounding countryside. Known for sophisticated cooking showcasing local produce, the hotel's elegant **Sandstone Restaurant** is a favourite fine dining destination. A beautiful, peaceful - and homely - place.

Rooms 43. B&B from about €60pps. Children welcome. **Sandstone Restaurant:** open daily L & D (12-3, 6-9.45). Weddings. Self-catering also available. Open all year. CC. **Directions:** Signed from Mohill village.

René
Cusack   Organic Salmon
←

Fruit Farm

Milk Market
Limerick

limerick.ie

COUNTY LIMERICK

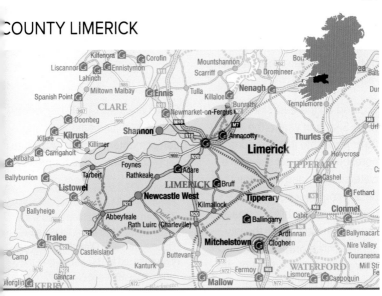

The story of **Limerick city and county** (www.limerick.ie) is in many ways the story of the Shannon Estuary, for in times past it was the convenient inland access provided by Ireland's largest estuary - it is 80 kilometres in length - which encouraged the development of life along the estuary's sea shores, and into the fresh water of the River Shannon itself.

Today, the river remains the beating heart of the city and its environs, while the area's national and global transport is served by air, sea and land through **Shannon International Airport** (www.shannonairport.ie) the port of **Foynes** - home to the **Foynes Flying Boat & Maritime Museum** and **Irish Coffee Centre** (www.flyingboatmuseum.com) - better rail links, and a modern road network including a tunnel under the Shannon Estuary near Limerick city. Within the city, the **University** (www.ul.ie) its **Concert Hall** (www.uch.ie) and the famed **Hunt Museum** (www.huntmuseum.com) are heavyweights at the centre of the city's vibrant arts and cultural life, while the produce on sale at the bustling Victorian **Milk Market** (www.milkmarketlimerick.ie) each weekend is a reminder of the city's special place at the heart of Ireland's lushly productive **Golden Vale**.

Limerick's long history of food production - notably the world famous Limerick Ham - is celebrated through the city's near legendary Food Festivals including **Pigtown** (www.pigtown.ie), **Riverfest**, the **International Food Truck Festival**, the **World BBQ Championships**, and **Culture & Chips**, to name just a few, also the Wednesday **Limerick Street Food** market that's held on Harvey's Quay boardwalk.

Inland from the river, eastern Limerick merges into Tipperary's rich farmland and, to the southwest of the city, the splendid hunting country and utterly rural atmosphere of the area around the beautiful village of Adare - and the recently re-opened **Adare Manor** (www.adaremanor.com) and its magnificent parkland golf course - offer visitors a very different experience.

ABSOLUTE HOTEL

SIR HARRY'S MALL LIMERICK CO LIMERICK

061 463 600 | info@absolutehotel.com

www.absolutehotel.com

STA

Located on the east side of the River Shannon where the Abbey River flows into it, this modern hotel enjoys a great site with a waterside bar and restaurant, decked outdoor seating area and views of the hills - a peaceful situation in what is still the city centre. Three grades of room are offered with no shortage of style at any level and, while there's only a modest premium for more spacious Superior rooms, the chic Suites are surprisingly reasonably priced. With fine amenities and complimentary parking, Absolute represents real value for money.

Rooms 99 (all shower only, 5 wheelchair friendly). Lift. B&B from about €65pps. Children welcome. Laptop sized safes in rooms. Spa, hair salon; fitness suite. Open all year. CC. **Directions:** Limerick city centre, on the N7 just north of the junction between the N7 & N20.

BOBBY BYRNE'S

3 O'CONNELL AVENUE LIMERICK CO LIMERICK

061 316 949 | info@bobbybyrnes.ie

www.bobbybyrnes.ie

EAT | DRINK

One of Limerick's best-loved sporting pubs, Bobby Byrne's has been in business for over half a century. Opened in 1963 by the original Bobby and his wife Helen, it's always been a great supporter of local teams, particularly rugby. Now operated by son Robert and family, its original character has survived refurbishment and everyone enjoys the lovely ambience. Attention to provenance lifts the wholesome fare, all freshly-cooked from scratch, and there's a great range of craft beers and speciality gins and whiskeys - and this friendly pub always has a good buzz, making it a destination of choice for many return visitors to the city.

Food Mon-Fri 8.30-9 (includes vegan breakfast), Sat 9.30-9, Sun 12-8. Carvery L daily; evening menu 3-9 (Sun 4-8). No food bank hol Mons. Bar closed 25 Dec. Beer garden. CC. **Directions:** Just off Quinlan Street

CANTEEN

30 MALLOW STREET LIMERICK CO LIMERICK   EAT
085 215 3212 | office@wearecanteen.com
www.wearecanteen.com

Close to Limerick City Gallery of Art, Canteen is a tiny but very popular street-side café in the picturesque Georgian part of town - and with its sights clearly set on sustainability and local produce. Originally opened as a 'pop-up', chef-patron Paul Williams continues to serve pared back modern food with a healthy angle from this small café. A happy marriage of two of the most popular recent food trends, the new breed of trendy pop-up style restaurants and 'food truck' cuisine, the decor is plain to the point of Spartan - but at Canteen provenance is prized above all else.

Open: Mon-Fri 8am-4pm, Sat 10.30am-4pm. A la carte. Closed Sun. **Directions:** Just off junction of Catherine Street and Mallow Street

THE CORNSTORE RESTAURANT

19 THOMAS STREET LIMERICK CO LIMERICK   EAT
061 609 000 | limerick@cornstore.com
www.cornstore.ie

A stylish mix of quality, accessibility and buzz works well in Padraic Frawley's atmospheric dining venue in the heart of his home city. Great steaks and fresh seafood are the specialities, but there is much more to The Cornstore than surf'n'turf. Locally produced organic and artisan ingredients - including seasonal produce grown in their own Ballingarry garden - is central to their wide-ranging menus and the cooking has flair. With its emphasis on atmosphere, quality and value, together with carefully selected wines, cocktails and good service, Limerick is lucky to have the Cornstore.

Seats 200. Open daily 12-10. Set menu from €35. Set Sun L from €25. Children welcome. Closed 25 Dec. CC. **Directions:** Centre of Limerick. Also at The Cornstore, Cornmarket Street, Cork

THE CURRAGOWER SEAFOOD BAR

CLANCYS STRAND LIMERICK CO LIMERICK   EAT | DRINK

061 321 788 | curragower.cian@gmail.com
www.curragower.com

Cian Bourke's atmospheric riverside bar on the County Clare side of the River Shannon is said to be one of the oldest pubs in the city; it has character by the bucketful and a splendid view across the Curragower Falls to King John's Castle from the attractive terrace. The food style is homely, which suits the surroundings perfectly; the emphasis is on freshly cooked food using local ingredients and speciality dishes are all seafood, but the offering overall is evenly balanced and there is sure to be something to please everyone at this appealing venue.

Open Mon-Sun 12.30-late (Fri-Sun from 12); food served Mon-Sun 12-9 (Mon & Tue to 8). CC. **Directions:** From the city, cross Sarsfield Bridge (the main Ennis Road), turn right and drive along the river until you see the Curragower sign on the left.

FREDDY'S BISTRO

THEATRE LANE GLENTWORTH STREET LIMERICK CITY   EAT

061 418 749 | www.freddysbistro.com

Run by sisters Liz Phelan, Caroline Kerely and Maeve Newman, the long established Freddy's Bistro is part of the fabric of Limerick dining and this friendly and atmospheric hideaway consistently delivers great food. Eclectic menus - which, unusually, include a full coeliac menu - span several continents, but local produce is highlighted and good value given. It is very popular and reservations are advised - but this Limerick gem has lots of character and is well worth seeking out.

Seats 60. D 5.30-late Tue-Sat. Early D Tue-Thu 5.30-7 from €24.50; main menu from 7pm (Sat from 6.30), from about €28. Closed Sun & Mon, incl bank hols. CC. **Directions:** Theatre lane runs parallel to - and between - O'Connell Street and Henry Street.

THE FRENCH TABLE

STEAMBOAT QUAY LIMERICK CO LIMERICK   EAT

061 609 274 | info@frenchtable.ie
www.frenchtable.ie

French chef Thomas Fialon and his Limerick-born wife, Deirdre, run this excellent, pleasingly understated quayside restaurant overlooking the River Shannon. It's the city's premier French restaurant - an airy and spacious place, with stylishly pared back décor and well-trained, welcoming staff who convey a sense of order, in preparation for the serious business of enjoying a good meal. Francophiles will be in their element here, as Thomas interprets classic French dishes with finesse - and offers outstanding value.

Seats 52. L Tue-Fri from 12; set L from €16. Sun 12.30-8pm. Set D Tue-Sun from 6pm, about €30, also a la carte. Children welcome. Closed Sat L, all Mon, 24-26 Dec, 1 Jan, Good Fri. CC. **Directions:** On riverbank by Dock Road, near the landmark Clayton Hotel

LA CUCINA CENTRO

HENRY STREET LIMERICK CO LIMERICK   EAT

061 517400 | centro@lacucina.ie
lacucina.ie

Tucked behind a smart olive-green shopfront, Lorraine Fanneran and Bruno Coppola's delightful little Italian café/deli is a family-run business that specialises in authentic Italian food, while also taking pride in using fresh Irish produce. Its friendliness and the sheer quality of both ingredients and cooking are the ingredients that make La Cucina stand out, and they have a well earned reputation for simple food that looks great, is very tasty and offers outstanding value for money in both the restaurant and the takeaway. Highly recommended.

Open Mon-Fri 10–9pm (to 10 Thu & Fri); Sat 12–10pm; Sun 12-8. No reservations. Parking: metered car parking on street. **[Also at:** La Cucina, Castletroy, near UL (061 517 405)]. **Directions:** Limerick city centre, on the R527.

LIMERICK STRAND HOTEL

ENNIS ROAD LIMERICK CO LIMERICK   EAT | STAY
061 421 800 | info@strandhotel.ie
www.strandhotellimerick.ie

Just across the Sarsfield Bridge from the main commercial heart of Limerick, this well-appointed modern hotel is especially well equipped for business travellers, but all guests also enjoy the pleasant ambience, excellent leisure facilities and - unusually for a large hotel - the opportunity to explore the foods of the region. Head chef Tom Flavin (a Failte Ireland Food Champion) makes provenance and seasonality a point of difference, especially at The River Restaurant - and his kitchen team engages closely with their carefully selected suppliers, ensuring that guests will experience a true taste of Limerick.

Rooms 184 (10 wheelchair friendly). B&B from about €60pps. Children welcome. River Restaurant: D Mon–Sun (5-9.30pm). Sun L 1-3. Bar meals daily 9am-10pm. Leisure Centre. Underground parking CC. **Directions:** City centre, on the Clare side of the River Shannon (Ennis Road).

MORTELL'S DELICATESSEN & SEAFOOD RESTAURANT

49 ROCHES STREET LIMERICK CO LIMERICK   EAT | BUY
061 415 457 | mortellcb@gmail.com
www.mortellcatering.com

A sandwich board welcomes hungry passers-by into this appealing deli and casual daytime restaurant/coffee shop in the centre of Limerick, with a tempting offer of fresh fish – Irish caught, and cooked to order in front of you by your chosen method. There is also a seafood breakfast, which is unusual, and everything served here is cooked from scratch. Run by Brian Mortell and his wife Margaret, who also have a highly regarded catering company, the business dates back to 1881, when the Mortell family opened a fish and game shop in Charleville, Co Cork - so these people have the food business in their genes. Freshness, friendly service and an interested and eagle-eyed proprietor make this a place to seek out.

Seats 30. Open Mon-Sat 8.30-4.30 (late closing Fri). Closed Sun. CC. **Directions:** 50 metres from O'Connell Street.

NO. 1 PERY SQUARE HOTEL & SPA

PERY SQUARE LIMERICK CO LIMERICK
061 402 402 | info@oneperysquare.com
www.oneperysquare.com

EAT | STAY | BUY
LEARN | PRODUCER

A stunning property on the city's most gracious Georgian square, this is Limerick's premier boutique hotel. Immaculately restored by owner Patricia Roberts in celebration of its original architectural features, the warm welcome at this luxurious hotel matches the care devoted to the building. Fine public rooms and sumptuous bedrooms are a delight and the holistic Spa @ No. 1 offers the ultimate in pampering. Memorable dining too at **Sash**

Restaurant, where Head Chef Tim Harris showcases local and seasonal produce with finesse.

Rooms 20 (2 wheelchair friendly). Lift. B&B from about €68pps Children welcome.
Sash Restaurant: Tue-Sat L&D, 12.30-6 & 6-9pm; Sun 1-6pm. Kitchen Garden Menu about €35, also à la carte. Park Room Lounge, L daily. Afternoon Tea. Bar food 9am-9pm. Wine shop. Restaurant closed Sun D, Mon; house closed 25-27 Dec CC.
Directions: 2 minute walk from O'Connell Street.

1826 ADARE

MAIN STREET ADARE CO LIMERICK

061 396 004 I info@1826adare.ie

www.1826adare.ie

EAT

Top chef Wade Murphy and his wife Elaine's rustic chic restaurant is in one of this postcard-pretty village's most charming cottages. Moving away from his fine dining background, Wade offers keenly-priced gastropub-style casual dining "but without being a pub!" Monthly-changing menus are built on seasonal local produce, with daily blackboard specials offering extras such as whole sole on the bone and braised meats. Top notch cooking in a relaxed style -

seriously delicious food, and at a very accessible price. Another must-visit destination for Adare.

⭐

Open: Wed-Sat from 6pm (Sun from 3, bank hol Sun from 4). Value menu to 7 (last reservation 6.30), about €30. D à la carte; late Sun L 3-5.30 (last reservation 5, from about €25. Closed Mon & Tue, 1 wk Nov, 2 wks mid-Jan-early Feb. CC. **Directions:** On Adare's main street, across the road from The Dunraven Arms

ADARE MANOR HOTEL & GOLF RESORT

ADARE CO LIMERICK

EAT | STAY

061 605 200 | info@adaremanor.com

www.adaremanor.com

Set in 900 acres beside the River Maigue, this magnificent neo-Gothic mansion was bought in 2015 by Limerick-born businessman JP McManus and, following closure for a multi-million euro refurbishment, re-opened late in 2017. As well as upgrading many areas of the hotel, a luxurious new 42-bedroom wing was added, along with a 350-seater ballroom and amenities including a La Mer spa (the first in Ireland or the UK), swimming pool and cinema.

The redesigned championship golf course takes pride of place among outdoor activities, but there are many more - including falconry, fishing and archery. Varied dining options include The Oak Room, a romantic restaurant lit only by candlelight.

Rooms 104 (staterooms, suites, deluxe; some wheelchair accessible); room rate from about €375. Oak Room Restaurant (fine dining) seats 70; D daily. Open all year, including Christmas. CC. **Directions:** Centre of Adare village.

DUNRAVEN ARMS HOTEL

ADARE CO LIMERICK   EAT | STAY
061 605 900 | reservations@dunravenhotel.com
www.dunravenhotel.com

Established in 1792, the Murphy family's large hotel in Adare has retained the comfortable ambience of a country inn – albeit a very luxurious one. An unrivalled reputation for the quality and value of short breaks offered, and a dedication to giving personal service, make Dunraven Arms an outstanding example of contemporary Irish hospitality. The delightfully old-fashioned Maigue Restaurant showcases the best of local produce and is set up as smartly for the excellent breakfast as it is for dinner.

Rooms 90 (some wheelchair friendly). Lift. B&B from €75pps. Children welcome. Maigue Restaurant: D daily, early D from about €22; L Sun only, about €32. Also à la carte. Light bar menu 11am-10pm, D 6-9.30pm. No children under 12 after 7pm. Leisure centre, swimming pool. Open all year (Residents only Dec 25). CC. **Directions:** First building on right from Limerick side.

THE WILD GEESE RESTAURANT

ROSE COTTAGE MAIN STREET ADARE CO LIMERICK   EAT
061 396 451 | info@thewild-geese.com
www.thewild-geese.com

In one of the prettiest cottages in Adare, David Foley and Julie Randles' atmospheric restaurant offers consistently excellent modern Irish cooking and caring service, making an irresistible package. David, a Euro-Toques chef, sources the best local ingredients with meticulous care and presents them with pride; whether for a daytime bite or a special dinner - when all the niceties, such as presenting an amuse-bouche, are observed - everything is made from scratch, and the difference is deliciously obvious on the plate.

Seats 50 (+10 outdoors). Open Tue-Sat: B'fast & brunch 9.30-11.30, L 11.30-4, D from 6. Sun L 12.30-3, from about €22; value D all evening, from €30; Early D Tue-Sat 6-7pm, from about €27. Vegetarian D menu. Children welcome. Closed D Sun, all Mon. CC. **Directions:** Top of Adare village, opposite Dunraven Arms Hotel.

COPPER & SPICE

ABOVE THE MILL BAR ANNACOTTY CO LIMERICK   EAT
061 338791 | info@copperandspice.com
www.copperandspice.com

Seema and Brian Conroy's attractive Indian-Asian restaurant is very pleasantly located in a restored mill overlooking the Mulcair River, and well away from the traffic - and agreeable staff are quick to welcome arriving guests. Indian background music immediately creates atmosphere and the ambience is very pleasing, with the spicy theme echoed in the warm tones of the stylish modern decor and some open brickwork lending a hint of rusticity. Offering consistently good cooking and a different experience from other ethnic restaurants in the area, this appealing destination gives both a sense of occasion and value for money.

Seats 75; D Mon-Sat 5-10.30, Sun 2-10. L Sun only. Early D Mon-Sat 5-7 (Sun 2-7), from about €18); also à la carte. Children welcome. Closed 25 Dec, Good Fri. CC. **Directions:** Just off the main Dublin-Limerick road, at Annacotty Village.

THE MUSTARD SEED

BALLINGARRY CO LIMERICK

069 68508 | mustard@indigo.ie

www.mustardseed.ie

EAT | STAY

Established in Adare by the original owner Dan Mullane, in 1985, The Mustard Seed later moved just ten minutes' drive away and is now in the safe hands of the former manager, John Edward Joyce. The house is set on seven acres of lovely gardens, including the organic kitchen garden and orchard that supply seasonal produce to an outstanding kitchen. When staying, choose between traditionally sumptuous rooms (old house) and contemporary style (new suites). A one-off - what a magical place this is.

⭐

Rooms 16 (4 shower only, 1 wheelchair friendly). B&B from €70pps. Children welcome. Restaurant: Early D Mon-Fri, 6-7.30. D daily 7-9.30, from €60. Restaurant unsuitable for children; reservations required; non-residents welcome. Closed 24-26 Dec and first 2 weeks Feb. CC. **Directions:** From top of Adare village take first left, 11km to Ballingarry; in village.

THE OLD BANK

BRUFF CO LIMERICK   STAY

061 389 969 | reservations@theoldbank.ie
www.theoldbank.ie

Very close to Lough Gur and the Ballyhoura Mountains (popular for cycling and walking breaks), Bruff is a lovely village within easy driving distances of a lot of interesting places and Miriam Sadlier Barry's unusual and very hospitable B&B would make a great base for exploring the area. Formerly a bank, it's an intriguing building and has been well converted to offer a high standard of accommodation at reasonable prices.

Rooms 9 (2 shower only). B&B from €35pps. Children welcome. Closed 23-27 Dec. CC. **Directions:** Bruff is located southeast of Limerick City (on the R512 road).

Richmond Harbour
at Clondra
Co Longford

COUNTY LONGFORD

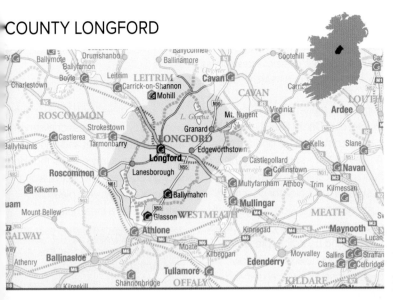

Explore & Enjoy the Heart of Ireland is the tagline for Longford Tourism (www.Visitlongford.ie), and it's a good one - this county of gently undulating farming country, lakes and bogland is a place that rewards exploration.

To the north, the beautiful **Derrycassin Woods** (www.coillte.ie/site/derrycassan) provide lovely woodland walks along the shores of intricate Lough Gowna, while Molly Hill to the east provides the best views of the lake in an area which arouses passionate patriotism: nearby **Ballinamuck** (with Visitor Centre), scene of the last battle in the Rising of 1798 in a part of Longford renowned for its rebellions against foreign rule.

By contrast, the southern part has the peaceful associations of Longford-born writer Oliver Goldsmith. The **Goldsmith Trail** begins in Longford Town, ending at his 'Village of the Roses', Glasson, Co Westmeath - and Goldsmith himself would be charmed to know that tiny **Ardagh** - a place of just 75 citizens - is so immaculately maintained that it has been the winner of the Tidiest Village in the Tidy Towns awards.

West of Longford town at Clondra, handsome Richmond Harbour is where the restored **Royal Canal** finally reconnnected with the Shannon in 2010, having been closed since 1954 - and today the **Royal Canal Way** is also a wonderful amenity. The Longford section of the 144km Dublin-Clondra walking and cycling route meanders between Abbeyshrule and Clondra and, since 2014, has included a 14km section between Clondra and Longford Town.

And it is in Longford Town itself that we find an even more inspiring work of restoration than the Royal Canal. **St Mel's Cathedral** – a truly monumental building - had its interior destroyed by fire at Christmas 2009. Yet, after a painstaking €30 million project, it was re-opened "better than ever" by Christmas 2014 and today is a beacon of hope for the Midlands and North Shannon region. And, thanks to some dedicated restaurateurs and food producers, Longford has also become famous in recent years for nourishing the body as well as the soul.

NINE ARCHES RESTAURANT

MAIN STREET BALLYMAHON CO LONGFORD   EAT

090 645 2895 | ninearchesrestaurant@gmail.com
www.facebook.com/NineArchesBallymahon

Formerly at the renowned Viewmount House, chef Daniel Skukalek and his partner Lorna Halligan opened Nine Arches in 2017 - soon making this handsome canalside town a dining destination of choice for discerning customers from a wide area. Daniel's classical training is very evident in his creative and beautifully presented cooking - but he also has a down to earth respect for local demand that ensures an exceptionally good and generous meal at an accessible price - and, under Lorna's supervision, with friendly and professional service to match. Early dinner and Sunday lunch are especially popular (booking strongly advised), and a stroll along the Royal Canal is very pleasant before or after a meal here.

D Wed-Sat 5.30-9pm, L Sun 1-4.30pm. Early D Wed-Fri 5.30-6.30pm, from about €25. CC. **Directions:** Town centre - corner where N55 joins R392 (beside O'Hanlons Pharmacy).

AUBERGINE GALLERY CAFÉ

1ST FLOOR THE WHITE HOUSE   EAT
17 BALLYMAHON STREET LONGFORD CO LONGFORD

043 334 8633 | aubergine@eircom.net

Brother and sister Stephen and Linda Devlin have been delighting Longford residents - and attracting visitors to the town - since 1998, and the popularity of this smart and buzzy café-bistro on the main street never wavers. Stephen Devlin is an accomplished chef and his Irish/Mediterranean menus feature delicious, fresh-flavoured dishes, including tasty vegetarian choices as well as creative seafood and poultry dishes - and, of course, the great steaks that are de rigeur around here. Excellent service from friendly staff, a warm relaxed atmosphere, stylish cooking and good value explain the success of this appealing restaurant – a great place to break a journey and well worth a visit at any time.

Open Tue-Sat 12-4 (Fri-Sat to 9.30) Sun 1-7, set D about €32. Closed Mon, bank hols, Dec 23-Jan 2. CC. **Directions:** First floor premises, town centre.

TORC CAFÉ & FOODHALL

NEW STREET LONGFORD CO LONGFORD

043 334 8277 | Torccafefoodhall@yahoo.ie

www.torccafe.com

EAT | BUY | PRODUCER

Chocoholics will love Ruth McGarry-Quinn's relaxed modern café as (exceptionally good) chocolate is the speciality. Seating, servery and food hall blend seamlessly, so it's tempting to pick up some treats while waiting for your order of healthy and very tasty home-made food - a steak sandwich with horseradish dip, perhaps, or a wholesome vegetarian option such as roast vegetables and goats cheese flan.

There are delicious home-baked cakes, too, while other highlights include real food for kids - and an imaginative choice of cold drinks, including traditional lemonade. A very useful place to know about.

Open Mon-Sat 9.30am-6pm; Fri & Sat also D 6-9pm (Pasta & Pizza menu). Closed Sun, bank hols, 25-26 Dec. CC. **Directions:** From Dublin direction, on the left after St Mel's cathedral.

VIEWMOUNT HOUSE AND VM RESTAURANT

DUBLIN ROAD LONGFORD CO LONGFORD   EAT | STAY
043 334 1919 | info@viewmounthouse.com
www.viewmounthouse.com

Surrounded by beautiful gardens created over two decades, the heart of James and Beryl Kearney's lovely Georgian property is its famous VM Restaurant. Opened with chef Gary O'Hanlon in 2008, they've taken the midlands by storm, making Longford a must-visit destination for food lovers. Gary (a household name) is from Donegal - proud source of his fresh fish - and the cooking is grounded in the familiar products of the region, and not overly cheffy. Like Viewmount House itself, VM Restaurant is special - and well worth a journey.

⭐

Rooms 12 (1 wheelchair friendly). B&B from about €70pps. D Wed-Sat 6.30-9, L Sun only 1-4. Early D Wed-Fri 6.30-7.30, from €35; Set D from €60, Sun L €32. Reservations advised. Weddings. Restaurant closed Mon-Tue; house closed Dec 24-27. **Directions:** Longford - R393 Ardagh, 1km; signed on right.

COUNTY LOUTH

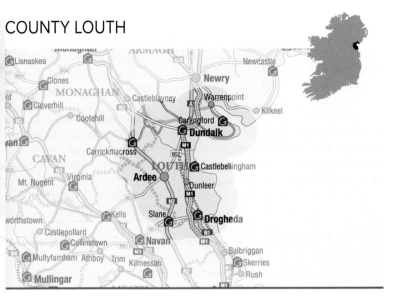

Louth www.visitlouth.ie has long been a beneficiary of Ireland's motorway system, as the transfer of through traffic to the M1 has seen what is Ireland's smallest county reassert its agricultural roots. Much of the Louth is fine farmland, but there are distinctive uplands in the southwest, whose name of Oriel recalls an ancient princedom which is also remembered in Port Oriel, the busy fishing port at Clogherhead.

In the north of the county, the Cooley Mountains www.carlingford.ie sweep upwards in a style which well matches their better-known neighbours, the Mountains of Mourne, on the other side of Carlingford Lough, with a car ferry service www.carlingfordferry.com inaugurated in 2017 Its name might suggest that this is a genuine fjord, but it isn't. However, its beauty is such that there's more than enough to be going along with, and on its Louth shore the ancient little port of Carlingford town used to be a best-kept secret, a quiet little place imbued with history, but today it is happily prospering both as a recreational harbour for the Dundalk and Newry area, and as a bustling visitor attraction in its own right.

The county's three main townships of Ardee www.thisisardee.ie, Dundalk and Drogheda www.drogheda.ie each have their own distinctive style, and all three have been finding fresh vitality in recent years. Drogheda is the main commercial port, its river valley crossed by the Boyne Railway Viaduct of 1855 vintage, a remarkable construction that is reckoned one of the seven engineering wonders of Ireland.

LOCAL ATTRACTIONS AND INFORMATION

>Carlingford **Carlingford Adventure Centre**
www.carlingfordadventure.com | 042 937 3100

>Castlebellingham **Farm Market** 0404 43885

>Drogheda **Beaulieu House and Garden**
www.beaulieuhouse.ie | 041 983 8557

>Drogheda (Tullyallen) **Old Mellifont Abbey**
www.mellifontabbey.ie | 041 982 6459

>Drogheda **Tourism Information**
www.drogheda.ie | 041 983 7070

CARLINGFORD HOUSE

DUNDALK STREET CARLINGFORD CO LOUTH

STAY

042 937 3118 | info@carlingfordhouse.com
www.carlingfordhouse.com

Discerning visitors to Carlingford will love Peter and Irene Finegan's fine 19th century house in the heart of this charming medieval village. It offers great hospitality and a stylish mix of old and new – reception rooms are smartly traditional while bedrooms have a more contemporary airy feel. No dinners, but Irene can advise on the best restaurants to suit your needs in the town - and sends guests off with an excellent breakfast.

Rooms 5 (all double, shower only & no smoking). B&B from about €60pps. Children welcome. No pets. Parking. Discount on stays of 2 or more nights. Closed Christmas. CC. **Directions:** M1 Dublin-Belfast, take Exit 18 to R173 Carlingford.

GHAN HOUSE

CARLINGFORD CO LOUTH

EAT | STAY | LEARN

042 937 3682 | info@ghanhouse.com
www.ghanhouse.com

One of Carlingford's most interesting houses, the Carroll family's 18th century property is attractively situated in its own walled grounds on the edge of the medieval village, with views across Carlingford Lough to the Mountains of Mourne. Atmospheric rooms in the main house have sea or mountain views and an adjacent building offers newer accommodation. Residents and other guests in for dinner can mingle and relax in the bar, or beside the fire in the drawing room.

> **Rooms 12** (1 shower only, 4 wheelchair friendly). B&B from €75pps; discount on 2+ nights. **Restaurant:** D 'most days' 6-9, from about €38; Sun L, when available, 1-3pm, about €30. Children welcome. Bespoke cookery classes offered (groups). Electric car charging point. Kennels. Closed 24-26 Dec & 31 Dec-2 Jan. CC.
> **Directions:** Entering Carlingford from Dundalk direction, after 50kph sign on left.

KINGFISHER BISTRO

DARCY MCGEE COURTYARD DUNDALK ROAD CARLINGFORD CO LOUTH   EAT

042 937 3716 | info@kingfisherbistro.com

www.facebook.com/kingfisherbistro

Although it is a little off the beaten track, Mark and Claire Woods' appealing restaurant at the heritage centre in Carlingford has a well-earned loyal local following. An attractive space with an open kitchen and a very pleasant outside seating area with well maintained planters and plenty of space for large groups, it packs a mighty punch, offering great cooking and modern menus including, of course, some tempting seafood specials. Pricing is very reasonable, including the interesting wine list.

Seats 42. D Mon-Sat 6-9, Sun 12.30-8.30 (maybe also Sat in summer). A la carte (minimum charge about €16 per person). CC. **Directions:** Signed on Dundalk road, in Carlingford village.

WILDWOOD CAFÉ

OMEATH ROAD CARLINGFORD CO LOUTH   EAT

086 3892027 | info@carlingfordbandbviewpoint.com

www.facebook.com/pages/Wildwood

You'll find delicious healthy eating with a stunning view at Johanna Woods and Shane Lennon's wholefood café overlooking Carlingford Lough. Offering something different from other places in the village (10 minutes walk), Eat Well Be Well! is the cheerful slogan - and they mean it. While not a vegetarian restaurant, many of the dishes are plant based and the broad theme of Shane's cooking is Mediterranean/Middle Eastern so you can expect the likes of hummus and flat breads, mezze platters, lamb kofta and couscous, with some very tasty sauces. But other things are also offered, including pizza, and many people come here just for the excellent coffee and irresistible homemade cakes and desserts... And, of course, the view.

Open Wed-Sun 12noon-6pm. Closed Mon & Tue. Accommodation available. Parking. CC. **Directions:** Entering Carlingford from Omeath, R173, signed on right after the marina.

BELLINGHAM CASTLE

CASTLEBELLINGHAM CO LOUTH **STAY**

042 937 2176 | info@bellinghamcastle.ie
www.bellinghamcastle.ie

Although used mainly as a private venue at weekends, the Corscadden family's lovely castle hotel offers midweek accommodation on a B&B basis and it would make a lovely place to take a break between Dublin and Belfast, or a base for exploring this fascinating area. Overnight guests are welcomed with complimentary tea, coffee and biscuits and there is a full bar service as well as breakfast in the dining room overlooking the lovely gardens; as other meals are not available, except to groups, individual guests are directed to local restaurants for lunch and dinner.

Rooms 19. B&B limited midweek May-Oct. Weekend B&B for wedding guests. **Directions:** Exit M1 Dublin-Belfast road at Junction 15 (Castlebellingham/Tallanstown) and follow the signs for Castlebellingham (R132). Large stone entrance tower on Main Street.

EASTERN SEABOARD BAR & GRILL

1 BRYANSTOWN CENTRE DUBLIN ROAD DROGHEDA CO LOUTH   EAT | DRINK

041 980 2570 | info@easternseaboard.ie
www.glasgow-diaz.com

Husband and wife team Reuven Diaz and Jeni Glasgow offer stylish modernity, professionalism and excellent food in this American-inspired venture on the edge of Drogheda. Quality food sourcing is very evident in Reuven's flexible and interesting menus, and the value is great for food cooked and served with such style. Just a few shops down, they have also brought their unique flair to the Brown Hound craft bakery and café, which has become a foodie destination for everything from cupcakes to pumpkin doughnuts, from rustic galettes to classy sandwiches.

Seaboard: Mon-Fri 12-10pm, Sat 11-10 (brunch to 1.30) Sun 11-8 (brunch to 1.30). A la carte. Children's menu. Wheelchair accessible. Reservations advised. Brown Hound: Tue-Fri 8-6, Sat 10-6, Sun 10-4. CC Closed 25 Dec, Good Fri. CC. **Directions:** Leaving Drogheda on Dublin road, take right at traffic lights after railway station.

FIFTY4 SEAFOOD BAR

54 LAURENCE STREET DROGHEDA CO LOUTH   EAT
041 984 5507 | fifty4restaurant@gmail.com
www.fifty4.ie

Run by the Kirwan family, who also operate the long-established Kirwan's Fish Cart fishmonger next door, this seafood restaurant is a stylish recent addition to Drogheda's town centre. Seafood is given star billing on the short menu, of course, but just in case someone in the group isn't a fish fan, there are also a couple of other dishes on offer - safe options such as chicken burger and steak sandwich, perhaps - and there's a small selection of dishes available for takeaway too. Having it alongside the family-owned fishmonger is a smart move and it quickly became a much-loved fixture in the town centre, just like its sister business.

Open Tue-Sat, 11am-7pm. A la carte. CC. **Directions:** Town centre.

THE KITCHEN RESTAURANT

2 SOUTH QUAY DROGHEDA CO LOUTH   EAT
041 983 4630 | kitchenrestaurant2@gmail.com
www.facebook.com/thekitchenrestaurantdrogheda

Unassumingly located across the road from a shopping centre, this might look like a regular bistro, but open the menu and you're in for a surprise: inspired by the travels of the owners, Glyn Schneider and Anne Brennan, the culinary style reflects Spain, Morocco, Turkey and Egypt. Glyn, a classically trained chef, offers an intriguing range of tapas, starters and mains, all based on carefully sourced local ingredients and, although the Eastern Med and Middle East theme does not extend to the desserts, which are classical - baked Alaska is a popular example - the quality remains. Staff are friendly and attentive, and this inviting restaurant is always enhanced by beautiful seasonal flowers from the owners' garden. A real find.

Seats 70. Open Wed 11-9pm; Thu-Sat 11-10, Sun 12-9. Full wheelchair access. Closed Mon & Tue. CC. **Directions:** Drogheda town centre, south quay

SCHOLARS TOWNHOUSE HOTEL

KING STREET DROGHEDA CO LOUTH
041 983 5410 | info@scholarshotel.com
www.scholarshotel.com

EAT | DRINK | STAY

Martin and Patricia McGowan's small hotel is a listed 19th-century double-fronted redbrick building and, with its fountains and broad stone steps leading up to the front door, bustling, friendly staff and a sense of individuality, it creates a good impression from the outset. Rooms are compact but thoughtfully planned, and the restaurant is an attraction in its own right, offering creative cooking with a focus on local produce, especially seafood - and attentive service. An oasis in Drogheda's busy town centre.

Rooms 16 (14 shower only, 1 family, 1 wheelchair friendly). B&B about €40pps. **Restaurant:** L & D daily 12-6pm & 6-9.30, Sun L 12-5pm; children welcome until 7pm. Set L from about €23. Gourmet D €75 including wine. Also a la carte. Gastro Lounge L 12-4 Mon-Sat; Afternoon Tea (pre-book). Restaurant closed 25-26 Dec. CC. **Directions:** Town centre, near St Laurence's Gate.

LISTOKE HOUSE

BALLYMAKENNY ROAD DROGHEDA CO LOUTH
041 984 4742 | info@listoke.com
www.listoke.com

EAT | PRODUCER
LEARN | STAY

Famed for its lovely gardens, Patrick and Patricia Barrow's fine property just north of Drogheda has moved into a new and energetic phase of late, with the involvement of their daughter and son-in-law, Juliet and Raymond Gogan, who have introduced a number of new elements to the traditional mix. These include the Listoke Distillery (listokedistillery.ie) - producer of the small batch 'sipping gin', Listoke 1777 Gin - and Gin School, and an Art Gallery'. Also charming Tea Rooms, which are a popular destination locally - and where breakfast is served to guests staying in the spacious and beautifully situated Courtyard Accommodation.

Tea Room: Thu-Sun, 11am- 5pm. Tour of Distillery & Gin School & Afternoon Tea Thu & Fri only, 3pm (must book). Vegan Fridays (with yoga classes). Weddings. Accommodation available (B&B about €135 per room). **Directions:** Due north of Drogheda, off Ballymakenny Road.

FITZPATRICK'S BAR & RESTAURANT

ROCKMARSHALL JENKINSTOWN DUNDALK CO LOUTH   EAT | DRIN

042 937 6193 | Admin@fitzpatricks-restaurant.com

www.fitzpatricks-restaurant.com

Masses of well-maintained flowers draw attention to Danny and Dympna Fitzpatrick's well-run old-world bar and restaurant on the Carlingford Road. Atmosphere aside, the secret of their success is traditional home-cooked food (sometimes with a modern twist); the wide range offered includes a good selection of local seafood. It can seem expensive, especially at lunchtime, but their tasty food is very wholesome and portions are generous.

Seats 90 (+150 outdoors). Open daily in summer, otherwise Tue-Sun 12.30 -10pm (Tue-Wed to 9pm), Sun 12.30-3.30 & 5.30-9pm). D 6-10. Daily set D about €34, Sun L from about €24. Also à la carte & vegetarian menu. Seniors menu Tue-Fri 12.30-3.30. Fitzers own brew lager. Wheelchair friendly; children welcome before 9pm. Closed Mon Oct-Apr (except bank hols), 25 Dec. CC. **Directions:** Off Dublin-Belfast road, north of Dundalk; take Carlingford road; 8km on left.

Croagh Patrick & Clew Bay
from Inishnakillew
Co. Mayo

MAYO.IE

COUNTY MAYO

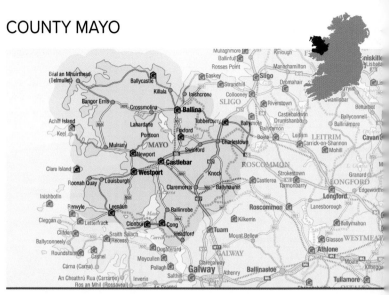

Mayo is magnificent. All Ireland's counties have their devotees, but enthusiasts for Mayo have a devotion which is pure passion. In their heart of hearts, they feel that this austerely majestic Atlantic-battered territory is somehow more truly Irish than anywhere else. And who could argue with them after experiencing the glories of scenery, sea and sky that this western rampart of Ireland puts on ever-changing display, particularly in the cloudscape over Achill Island.

Yet among Mayo's many splendid mountain ranges we find substantial pockets of fertile land, through which there tumble the pristine fish-filled streams and rivers that make this one of the world's most desirable angling destinations. And in the west of the county, the rolling hills of the drumlin country, which run in a virtually continuous band right across Ireland from Strangford Lough, meet the sea again in the island studded wonder of Clew Bay, where the neat town of Westport is a byword for hospitality, the southern end of the 42km **Great Western Greenway Walking and Cycling Track** (www.greenway.ie), and a place so pleasing that in a national poll in 2012, it was voted Ireland's Best Place to Live, and it seems that nowhere else has challenged it since.

Along Mayo's rugged north coast, turf cutting at the **Ceide Fields** (www.ceidefields. com) near Ballycastle has revealed the oldest intact field and farm system in existence, preserved through being covered in blanket bog 5,000 years ago. An award-winning interpretive centre has been created at the site, and even the most jaded visitor will find fascination and inspiration in the clear view that it provides into Ireland's distant past. A few miles eastward, the charming village of Ballycastle is home to the internationally-respected **Ballinglen Arts Foundation** (www.ballinglenartsfojndation.org), creative home-from-home for artists worldwide, and nearby, the lively town of Ballina is where the legendary salmon-rich River Moy, having emerged from the broad elegance of Lough Conn, meets the sea in the wide sweep of Killala Bay.

Lakes abound in Mayo, as in the south it has Lough Mask, and there's even a short but beautiful piece of Mayo coastline on the northeast of Lough Corrib, at the enchanting village of Cong. But although the beautiful or scenically spectacular parts of Mayo and attractions like the **Gourmet Greenway** (www.mulrannyparkhotel.ie/gourmet-greenway) around Clew Bay draw in the visitors, the engine of this large county is its administrative town of Castlebar, a bustling place of enterprise and energy which sets the pace in a region of pleasant surprises.

LOCAL ATTRACTIONS AND INFORMATION

> Mayo - **Tourism Information**
  www.mayo.ie

> Mulranny - **Gourmet Greenway**
  www.mulrannyparkhotel.ie/gourmet-greenway
  096 983 6000

> Westport - **Westport House & Children's Zoo**
  www.westporthouse.ie | 098 25430/27766

> Castlebar area - **Turlough Museum of Country Life**
  www.museum.ie/Country-Life
  094 903 1589 (Tue-Sat 10am to 5pm, Sun 2pm to 5pm, closed Mon).

> Westport - **Great Western Greenway** (42km cycle/walkway to Achill Sound)
  www.greenway.ie

> Westport - **Tourism Information**
  098 25711

> **Westport** | www.westporttourism.com
  Tourism Information 098 25711

> Ballina - **Tourism Information**
  www.ballina.ie | 096 70848

> Castlebar - **Linenhall Arts Centre**
  www.thelinenhall.com | 094 9023733

> Castlebar - **Tourism Information** 094 9021207

> Killasser (Swinford) - **Traditional Farm Heritage Centre** 094 9252505

> Kiltimagh - **Glore Mill Follain Arts Centre**
  094 82184

ACHILL ISLAND

Achill island is the largest island in Ireland so don't forget to top up with fuel as you're driving on to it; there's a large service station, Lavelle's Esso Garage, on the right - and it is open on Sundays. It is a place of great beauty, with mountains, lakes, valleys, magnificent sea-cliffs, wild moors and spectacular scenery. It has a number of small attractive villages, several unpolluted sandy beaches ideal for bathing, excellent deep sea, shore and lake angling and opportunities for all kinds of outdoor activities. An interesting place that is also useful to know about is Seasamh O'Dalaigh's workshop and gallery, **Dánlann Yawl** (www.achillpainting.com), at Owenduff (on the right coming from the mainland); it has a coffee shop during gallery hours, making a pleasant place for a break - and also offers painting courses. And don't miss the unique and stunningly located activity centre and bar/restaurant, **Pure Magic** (www.puremagic.ie/achill), overlooking Keel Lake and the dramatic cliffs, shore and sea beyond.

PURE MAGIC

SLIEVEMORE ROAD DUGORT ACHILL ISLAND CO MAYO
085 2439782 | achill@puremagic.ie
www.puremagic.ie/achill

EAT | DRINK
STAY | LEARN

In a stunning location on the lower slopes of Slievemore mountain - and overlooking Keel Lake - this aptly named lodge and restaurant/ wine bar lays claim to being one of Ireland's best-kept secrets and it is well worth seeking out. And one of the nicest things about Pure Magic is that anyone who is simply moseying around the island will feel equally welcome. It's an ideal place to drop into for a casual lunch or a snack in summer - and dinner too, although it might be wiser to book. A mix of French and Italian cuisine is the style, with authentic pizzas a speciality, and service is charming.

Restaurant open daily in summer 1-5pm & 6-9pm, Sun brunch 12-5pm. Off season open Wed night-Sun (call to check times). **Rooms 10**, all en-suite. B&B about €35pps.

THE BEEHIVE

KEEL ACHILL ISLAND CO MAYO
098 43134 | joycesbeehive@msn.com
www.facebook.com/The-Beehive-Craft-Coffee-Shop

EAT | DRINK

At their informal restaurant and attractive craft shop in Keel, husband and wife team Michael and Patricia Joyce take pride in the careful preparation and presentation of the best of Achill produce, especially local seafood. Offering great all-day self-service food - which you can have indoors, or take out to a patio overlooking Keel beach - everything is home-made and baking is a speciality. The shop is interesting also, with some quality gift items and clothing lines not found elsewhere.

Seats 100 (+60 outdoors). Food served 9.30-6pm daily, Easter-early Nov. Wheelchair accessible. Children welcome. CC. **Directions:** Situated in the centre of Keel village overlooking beach and Minaun cliffs.

BERVIE

BERVIE KEEL ACHILL ISLAND CO MAYO   EAT | STAY
098 43114 | john.barrett.bervie@gmail.com
www.bervieachill.com

The ultimate escape for its many happy guests since 1932, John and Elizabeth Barrett's magical beachside house was once a coastguard station. A little wicket gate gives direct access to the beach, and there's an other-worldliness which is very rare these days. Elizabeth was born here and, aside from the location and the charm of the house, the sense of continuity is very special - and she has the 'hotelier's gene', which makes hospitality come naturally. Comfortable, compact rooms, a cosy fire, great food (at both dinner and breakfast) and delightful staff all add to the charm.

Rooms 14 (1 shower only). B&B from about €50pps. Dining Room seats 32. D daily from 7pm, (about €40), reservations required, non-residents welcome (if availability). Afternoon Tea. Children welcome. Closed Dec-Mar. CC.
Directions: From bridge follow signs to Keel; left in village, towards beach.

BELLEEK CASTLE

BALLINA CO MAYO
096 22400 | info@belleekcastle.com
www.belleekcastle.com

EAT | STAY | PRODUCER

Situated just outside Ballina amidst 1,000 acres of woodland and forestry, on the banks of the River Moy (and near the Connacht Whiskey Distillery, www.connachtwhiskey.com), Paul Doran's castle was the ancestral home of the Earl of Arran and, with a 16th century armoury, big open fires, quirky Armada Bar and massive chandeliers, it now makes an unusual small hotel. It manages to combine old-world charm with modern comforts - and, while atmospheric, the candlelit restaurant offers much more than character, as Head Chef Stephen Lenahan's faultless cooking of local and homegrown produce has made this an impressive dining destination.

Rooms 10 (1 family, 5 shower only). B&B from €80pps. Restaurant: D only, daily from 5.30pm, about €35. Light afternoon food from 2.30pm daily. Castle tours daily. Closed Dec-Feb. CC. **Directions:** Off R314 (Killala road) into Ballina, Follow for Belleek.

THE ICE HOUSE HOTEL

THE QUAY BALLINA CO MAYO
096 23500 | chill@theicehouse.ie
www.theicehouse.ie

EAT | STAY

Bring your binoculars when heading for this quirky hotel, as the wildlife in the River Moy and its wooded banks is one of its most fascinating features. Sporting a spa and riverside hot tub, the 150-year-old building is a funky mix of traditional and bold contemporary design, with room styles varying from modern to quaint. Highly regarded Mayo native Anthony Holland heads up the kitchen team, offering destination dining in The Restaurant, a light-filled conservatory extension (with outdoor seating too), and daytime fare in the adjacent atmospheric bar.

Rooms 32 (4 shower only, 1 wheelchair friendly). Lift. B&B from about €70pps. Children welcome. Restaurant: D daily from 6pm, à la carte. L Sun only, from about €24. Bar food Mon-Sat, 12-9 (Sun from 1pm). Closed 25-26 Dec. CC. **Directions:** N59 to Ballina, through town, turn down by the river.

MOUNT FALCON ESTATE

FOXFORD ROAD BALLINA CO MAYO
096 74472 I info@mountfalcon.com
www.mountfalcon.com

EAT I STAY

Once a romantic family home, Mount Falcon is now a luxury hotel with some beautiful period features. Most of the accommodation is modern, but there are six deluxe rooms in the main house with original features. The 100-acre estate offers country pursuits, including double-bank salmon fishing on the River Moy, lovely lakeside and woodland walks and an impressive kitchen garden. The classically appointed restaurant is in the original kitchen, storeroom and pantry and, with homegrown and local produce providing the foundation for adventurous cooking, you should have a treat in store.

Rooms 32 (2 wheelchair friendly). Lift. B&B from €110pps. Children welcome. Restaurant seats 72 (+20 outdoors): L & D daily 12.30-2.30 (to 2pm Sun) & 6.30-9.30 (Sun 7-9). Bar menu daily, 12.30-7.30pm. Self-catering available. Closed 24-25 Dec, all Jan. CC. **Directions:** About 6.5km outside Ballina on the N26 to Foxford.

ENNISCOE HOUSE

CASTLEHILL BALLINA CO MAYO

STAY

096 31112 | mail@enniscoe.com

www.enniscoe.com

In the same family ownership since the 1650s, this charming Georgian mansion on the shores of Lough Conn offers crackling log fires, warm hospitality and good home cooking - and the current custodians, Susan Kellett and her son DJ, enjoy sharing their home and its surrounding parkland with guests. A very special place for anglers and anyone with an empathy for the untamed wildness of the area, its large rooms have period style, and Susan's delightfully simple dinners are served in the intimate dining room. Converted outbuildings offer a genealogy centre, small agricultural museum with working blacksmith, conference facilities, and the restored walled gardens (with tea rooms) are open to the public.

Rooms 6. B&B from about €80pps. D daily, from €50, non-residents welcome by reservation. Pets welcome. Self-catering available. Closed Nov-Mar. CC. **Directions:** 3km south of Crossmolina on R315.

MARY'S COTTAGE KITCHEN

MAIN STREET BALLYCASTLE CO MAYO

096 43361 I maryscottagekitchen@gmail.com

EAT I BUY I PRODUCER

Mary Munnelly's homely little restaurant is the perfect place to stop for some tasty home cooking. Baking is the speciality but she does "real meals" as well - a full Irish breakfast, (just the thing for walkers), home-made soups and free-range chicken dishes. If the day is chilly, it's very pleasant to get tucked in beside a real fire - and there's also a garden with sea views for fine weather.

Seats 30 (+ 12 outdoors). Open 10-6 daily in summer (may open later in high season; shorter hours off season). Children welcome. Toilets wheelchair accessible. Closed Sun off-season (Oct-Easter), & first 3 weeks Jan. **No CC. Directions:** Centre of Ballycastle.

BAR ONE GASTRO PUB

RUSH STREET CASTLEBAR CO MAYO

EAT I DRINK

094 903 4800 I baronecastlebar@gmail.com
www.barone.ie

Run by Mark Cadden - whose family have a long history of hospitality in the area - this smart gastropub is the busiest bar food venue in the area and it's easy to see why. Modern and well designed, the welcome is warm and friendly - typical of the high standards that epitomise this fine pub, where hospitality is king. Nothing is ever too much trouble for the kind and well trained staff, and the philosophy of seeking out and taking inspiration from the best local foods and drinks (proudly acknowledged) shows in the flavour and quality on the plate. And, not only is the food superb, it is Castlebar's weekend night-time hotspot too.

Meals: Mon-Sat 12-9pm. No food on Sun, bank hol Mon. Toilets wheelchair accessible. CC. **Directions:** Around the corner from the Linenhall Arts Centre (turn left).

HELENA CHOCOLATES

8 CAVENDISH LANE CASTLEBAR CO MAYO
094 902 2755 | facebook@helenachocolates.ie
www.helenachocolates.ie

As well as producing beautiful hand-made chocolates, cakes, desserts and one-off pieces (most famously including a chocolate version of the treasured Sam Maguire Cup), Dirk Schonkeren and his wife Elaine run their shop and café as 'a chocolate experience'. Now an honorary Mayo man, the Belgian chef and chocolatier was a pioneer in Irish chocolate making when they first set up business here in the 1980s, and he is Ireland's Ambassador for the renowned Swiss chocolate manufacturer Barry Callebaut. He has trained many of Ireland's best chocolatiers in their craft, and you'll find his own tempting range here - but this atmospheric cafe is also a great destination for excellent coffee, light meals and treats. Diabetics, vegetarians, vegans and coeliacs are all catered for, and you're sure to leave with some irresistible chocolates to take home.

Open Mon-Sat, 10-6. CC.

RUA CAFÉ & DELI

SPENCER STREET CASTLEBAR CO MAYO
094 928 6072 | info@caferua.com
www.caferua.com

EAT | BUY | PRODUCER

Ann McMahon's vision was very clear when she set up **Café Rua** on New Antrim Street and, while she is still involved, it must be rewarding to see her children, Aran and Colleen McMahon, carrying on and developing the philosophy - they are serious about their food, but the tone is light-hearted. Café Rua is still going strong and this, their second premises, is a brilliant deli and café serving super breakfast/brunch/lunch fare and selling a wide range of the delicious foods they have served in the café for over a decade. International speciality foods feature too, but the West of Ireland stars - and local produce includes the foods they make themselves, like their tasty range of chutneys, relishes and dressings.

Open: Mon-Sat 8.30-6. Closed Sun, bank hols, Christmas week. Children welcome CC. **Directions:** Near Courthouse and The Mall.

CLARE ISLAND LIGHTHOUSE

CLARE ISLAND CO MAYO   STAY
087 983 7662 I clareislandlighthouse@gmail.com
www.clareislandlighthouse.com

If an island stay is the ultimate escape, a stay in a lighthouse at the northern tip of a mountainous island off Ireland's rugged west coast should fulfil the dream very nicely. Renovated to a high standard and welcoming guests since 2013, Clare Island Lighthouse offers wonderful views and a stylishly simple yet cosy base to enjoy exploring the island - which is an artists', walkers' and nature lovers' heaven - and good food reflecting the seasons and the region's produce. A very unusual break. *Killadangan House (www.killadanganhouse.com), a residential Activity, Health and Learning Centre near Westport, is a sister project.

Rooms 6 (5 shower only). DB&D from about €200pps per night (min stay 2 nights, Wed/Thu & Fri/Sat). Not suitable for under 16's. Dogs permitted by arrangement. Closed Sun; Nov-mid Mar. CC. **Directions:** Ferry from Roonagh Pier near Louisburgh.

FLANAGAN'S PUB

BRICKENS, CLAREMORRIS CO MAYO
086 385 7550 I info@flanaganspub.ie
http://flanaganspub.ie

Easy to spot with its bright cream and red colour scheme and an old Austin delivery van parked outside, Luke and Caroline Flanagan's smart pub once provided the traditional village combination of bar, grocery and hardware that was common in rural Ireland up to the 1970s. The main menu of this very family-friendly venue offers plenty of crowd pleasers, but the difference is in the commitment to quality - the Flanagans are great supporters of local producers, with a list of suppliers given and many ingredients name checked throughout their menus. They also offer an appealing selection of tapas to enjoy with local beers, craft ciders or wines, and their reputation for quality and value is well deserved.

Open Wed-Sun 12.30-9pm. A la carte & tapas. Wheelchair accessible. CC. **Directions:** Midway between Ballyhaunis and Claremorris on the main road, N60.

ASHFORD CASTLE

CONG CO MAYO

EAT | STAY | BUY

094 954 6003 | ashford@ashford.ie
www.ashford.ie

Beautifully situated overlooking Lough Corrib, Ireland's grandest castle hotel dates back to the 13th century. A byword for luxury, it is owned by Beatrice and Stanley Tollman (of South Africa's Red Carnation Hotels), who have invested heavily to bring this beautiful property back to its glorious best. Extensive outdoor pursuits, a state-of-the-art spa, cinema, and impeccable service are among its many USPs - also fine food by Executive Head Chef,

Philippe Farineau, whose strong support for artisan producers and suppliers is seen across a range of dining options.

⭐

Rooms 83. Lift. Rooms from €625. George V Dining Room: D 6.30-9.30 daily. Cullen's at the Cottage (daily in summer; phone call advised off-season): L 12.30-5pm, D 6-9.30; Sat & Sun, L 1-5pm. The Dungeon D 6-9. Afternoon Tea daily (pre-book). Bakery/gift shop. Open all year. CC.
Directions: Signed from Cong.

HUNGRY MONK CAFÉ

ABBEY STREET CONG CO MAYO   EAT

094 954 5842 | info@hungrymonkcong.com
www.hungrymonkcong.com

This atmospheric café nestles in a pretty row of single storey cottages in the centre of picturesque Cong village. It has been here for many years and is thriving in the ownership of Jonathan and Aisling Byrne, who took it over in March 2014 and "don't do fast food, but do fresh, wholesome Irish food as quick as we can". If you like to know about your food, what's in it and where it came from, The Hungry Monk has all the (very tasty) answers. A cosy little establishment to recharge and refresh when exploring Cong.

Seats 30. Open Mon-Sat 10-5 & bank hol Sun. L 12-2. Toilets wheelchair accessible; children welcome. Closed Dec-Feb. CC. **Directions:** Centre of Cong village.

THE LODGE AT ASHFORD CASTLE

ASHFORD ESTATE CONG CO MAYO   EAT | STAY
094 954 5400 | reception@thelodgeatashfordcastle.com
www.thelodgeatashfordcastle.com

In common ownership with neighbouring Ashford Castle, the heart of this boutique hotel is a fine period house with views down Lough Corrib from the bar, restaurant and the best rooms. Newer accommodation - including suites - is comfortable and stylish, and at Wildes Restaurant head chef Jonathan Keane serves wonderfully imaginative cuisine based on the best seasonal local produce. In a lovely first floor space with lough views from window tables, you can expect an unusual dining experience backed up by an interesting wine list.

Rooms 64 (38 shower only, 3 wheelchair friendly). Lift. B&B from about €150 per room. Children welcome. Free wifi. Hot tub. Wildes Restaurant: D daily 6.30-9pm, from about €50. L Sun only 1-3pm. Bar food daily 12-9. Closed 24-28 Dec, midweek Nov-Feb. CC. **Directions:** Just outside Cong, on Ashford Castle estate.

FOXFORD WOOLLEN MILLS VISITOR CENTRE

PROVIDENCE ROAD FOXFORD CO MAYO   EAT | BUY
094 925 6104/7280 | info@fwm.ie
www.foxfordwoollenmills.com

Established in 1892, this is one of the last working woollen mills in Ireland and - having been rescued from threatened closure in 1987 - visitors today will find a revitalised business. Although most famous for the beautiful products woven on site (and recently some stylish contemporary products too), the first floor restaurant has also become a destination for its wholesome meals, notably salads and home bakes - and also for the charm of the place itself. Where else in Ireland can you feel the hum of looms working on the ground floor below coming up through your feet, while you enjoy an unpretentious and very tasty meal? A magic spot and well worth a detour.

Visitor Centre/shop: Mon Sat 10am-6pm, Sun 12-6pm. **Restaurant:** Mon-Sat 10am- 5pm, Sun 12- 5pm. Own food products on sale. Online shop. CC. Ample free parking.

LEONARD'S

LAHARDANE BALLINA CO MAYO   DRINK | BUY
096 51003

This unspoilt roadside traditional pub and grocery shop was established in 1897 and is very much the centre of local activities. There's a large dining area behind the pub, where all the local get-togethers take place – if only those walls could talk. And, if you get hungry when travelling, there's always the makings of a picnic on the shelves.

Closed 25 Dec & possibly Good Fri.

MULRANNY PARK HOTEL

MULRANNY WESTPORT CO MAYO

EAT | STAY

098 36000 | info@mulrannyparkhotel.ie
www.mulrannyparkhotel.ie

Set in wooded grounds, this former railway hotel dates back to 1897 (the line is now the Great Western Greenway walking and cycling route) and it has retained some of the original character. Under the caring eye of General Manager Dermot Madigan, it's a welcoming hotel, with well-appointed rooms, good amenities - and a strong focus on food. Head Chef, Chamila Mananwatta, is closely involved with the Gourmet Greenway (artisan food trail) and his commitment to local produce inspires all hotel menus, notably in the elegant Nephin Restaurant, which has stunning views across Clew Bay.

Rooms 60 (4 shower only, 3 wheelchair friendly). B&B from about €45pps. Dogs allowed in some areas. Nephin Restaurant: D daily 6-9, about €45. Bar food, 12-9pm. Leisure centre (20m pool). Closed 26 Nov-2 Dec, 7-26 Jan. CC.
Directions: In Mulranny village on the N59.

KELLY'S KITCHEN

MAIN STREET NEWPORT CO MAYO
098 41647
www.facebook.com/KellysKitchenNewport/

Next door to the famous Kelly's Butchers - an excellent traditional butchers with a licensed abattoir where they slaughter all their own and locally sourced lamb and beef, and make some great products including the famous putóg (traditional blood pudding) and Wild Atlantic puddings (black and white puddings, flavoured with seaweed) - this homely cafe is run by Sean Kelly's daughter, Shauna, whose appealing food includes many ingredients from her dad's shop. This is just the place to find a traditional mixed grill, and the house speciality is Kelly's Black Goat - a hot open baguette sandwich with black pudding and St Tola goats cheese. Lovely desserts and cakes too, to enjoy with a cup of tea or coffee.

Café open Mon-Sat, 9-6. CC.

THE BLUE BICYCLE TEA ROOMS

MAIN STREET NEWPORT CO MAYO   EAT
096 984 1145 | phillychambers@eircom.net
www.bluebicycletearooms.com

The Great Western Greenway brings a lot of people to Newport, and many visitors who are looking for a bite to eat while they're passing through the town head straight here, to Phil Chambers' delightful old-world tea room. In an impressive stone building with steps leading up to it, this atmospheric spot is a real blast from the past with its dainty china and home baking, but the focus on local and home grown ingredients is timeless. A great little place to find on your travels, and with a delightful garden for fine weather too.

Open daily, May-Oct 10.30am-6pm.
Directions: Top of the main street, opposite Kellys butchers.

NEWPORT HOUSE

NEWPORT CO MAYO

EAT | STAY

098 41222 | info@newporthouse.ie
www.newporthouse.ie

Kieran Thompson's distinctive creeper-clad Georgian house was once the home of the O'Donnells, Earls of Tir Connell. Today this riverside gem symbolises all that is best about the Irish country house, and has been close to the hearts of fishing people for many years. John Gavin, head chef since 1983, is one of Ireland's unsung food heroes; the lovely dining room makes the perfect backdrop for "cooking which reflects the hospitable nature of the house" in fine meals made with home-produced and local foods - and Kieran's renowned wine list adds an extra magic.

Rooms 10 (2 with private - non-connecting - bathrooms, 2 wheelchair friendly). B&B from about €95pps. Children welcome. **Seats 38**. D daily, 7-9; about €68, also à la carte. Non-residents welcome by reservation. House closed mid-Oct - mid-Mar. CC. **Directions:** In village of Newport.

AN PORT MOR

1 BREWERY PLACE BRIDGE STREET WESTPORT CO MAYO

098 26730 | anportmor@gmail.com

www.anportmor.com

EAT

Popular chef Frankie Mallon named his restaurant - very appropriately - after a business in his home town, Portmor House in Blackwatertown, Co Armagh. Now very much a Westport man, he delights customers with his no-nonsense cooking and enthusiasm for the superb produce - especially seafood - available locally. Acknowledged as cooking some of the best food in the area, and particularly noted for good saucing and great flavour, he aims 'to give the customer the very best in local fresh produce and value for money'. This he does well, backed up by great local staff with a knowledge of the food producers featured on his menus - where suppliers are enthusiastically credited.

Seats 34. D daily from 5pm. A la carte. Early D 5-6, from about €24. CC.
Directions: Half way up Bridge Street in laneway opposite McCormack's butchers.

CRONINS SHEEBEEN

ROSBEG WESTPORT CO MAYO   EAT | DRINK
098 26528 | info@croninssheebeen.com
www.croninssheebeen.com

Although the once-famous thatch has now gone, the Cronin family's popular old-world pub just outside Westport, is still a pleasing destination for its pleasant, almost-waterside, location overlooking Clew Bay. Inside, it's a relaxed and characterful place, with a cosy fire, several rooms and hideaway corners in the bar, and an atmospheric first floor restaurant that is used at busy times. The friendly local staff are great, extending a warm welcome to all - and they're especially accommodating to families. Food has a welcome focus on local ingredients, especially seafood, and simple dishes - like Clew Bay chowder or fish & chips - never fail to please, so it should be an enjoyable experience.

> Food served daily in summer: Mon-Thu from 5pm, Fri-Sun from 12 noon. Winter: Fri-Sun, 5-9pm. CC. **Directions:** Far side of Westport harbour.

HOTEL WESTPORT

THE DEMESNE NEWPORT ROAD WESTPORT CO MAYO   EAT | STAY
098 25122 | reservations@hotelwestport.ie
www.hotelwestport.ie

Just a short stroll from Westport town centre, this friendly modern hotel adjacent to (and now in common ownership with) Westport House makes an excellent base for both leisure and business guests - and extensive on-site amenities are a major attraction for families, who also appreciate the kids club (summer and mid-term). The spacious rooms are regularly refurbished and the hotel's Islands Restaurant serves upbeat traditional menus, which are imaginative for an hotel and take pride in promoting local ingredients.

> **Rooms 129** (33 shower only, 9 wheelchair friendly). Lift. B&B from €49pps. Children welcome. Restaurant: set D daily 6-9.30, from €35. Set L Sun only 1-2.30, from €26, children €9.50. Bar food daily, 12-9.30pm. Leisure centre (20m pool). Spa. Open all year. CC. **Directions:** Almost town centre, signed off Newport Road.

THE IDLE WALL RESTAURANT

THE QUAY WESTPORT CO MAYO

EAT | LEARN

098 50692 | info@theidlewall.ie
www.theidlewall.ie

Formerly The Quay Cottage, this well-loved and beautifully located waterside restaurant sits snugly beside the gates of Westport House. The name takes inspiration from a nearby wall where dockers once kicked their heels while waiting for casual harbour employment - and, appropriately, there's a keen young Chef/Patronne, Aine Maguire, at work here, creating a buzz in the kitchen. Aine is committed to showcasing the foods, especially seafoods, of the Western Way and Great Western Greenway areas and her menus reflect this. The cooking is admirably simple with an emphasis on provenance and flavour, so an evening spent in this atmospheric restaurant should be most enjoyable.

Seats 40 (+8 outside); D Wed-Sun 5.30–10pm, à la carte. Early D 5.30-6.30 from €22. Cookery classes. Closed Jan & Feb. CC. **Directions:** On the harbour front, at the gates to Westport House.

KNOCKRANNY HOUSE HOTEL & SPA

KNOCKRANNY WESTPORT CO MAYO

EAT | STAY

098 28600 | info@khh.ie
www.khh.ie

Set in landscaped grounds overlooking Westport town, Adrian and Geraldine Noonan's Victorian-style hotel offers spacious bedrooms, fine views of Croagh Patrick, and excellent facilities A popular short break destination and wedding venue, the hotel has a reputation for its food at La Fougère, where Euro-Toques chef Seamus Commons favours local ingredients (some from their own kitchen gardens) and classic French techniques. His showpiece special occasion meals are well known and the tasting menu is another culinary highlight, complemented by an extensive wine list.

Rooms 97 (3 shower only, 4 wheelchair friendly). Lift. B&B from about €65pps. Children welcome. La Fougère Restaurant: Set D daily 6–9.30pm (9pm midweek), from about €52; also à la carte. Set Sun L from about €26. Bar food from 12.30pm .Spa; relaxation pool. Hotel closed 22-27 Dec. CC. **Directions:** Edge of town, on Castlebar road.

MATT MOLLOY'S BAR

BRIDGE STREET WESTPORT CO MAYO

098 26655

DRIN

If you had to pick one pub in this pretty town, this soothingly dark atmospheric one would do very nicely - not least because it is owned by Matt Molloy of The Chieftains, a man who clearly has respect for the real pub: no TV (and no children after 9 pm). Musical memorabilia add to the interest, but there's also the real thing as traditional music is a major feature in the back room every night - and Matt will probably be there himself, if he's not on tour. Note that it's an afternoon into evening place, not somewhere for morning coffee.

> Open Mon-Thu 12.30-11.30, Fri & Sat 12.30-12.30. Sun 12.30-11pm. Closed 25 Dec and (maybe) Good Fri. **Directions:** Town centre, lower end of Bridge Street.

MCCORMACK'S AT THE ANDREW STONE GALLERY

BRIDGE STREET WESTPORT CO MAYO

098 25619

EAT

Above Kate McCormack's sixth-generation butchers shop in Westport this small, unpretentious restaurant showcases works by local artists and serves terrific soups, quiches, patés and home-baked cakes, the product of generations of family recipes and particularly of Annette McCormack's table. Here, her two daughters, Katrina and Mary Claire, carry on the tradition. Simple everyday dishes that might be quite ordinary elsewhere are memorable here, thanks to the quality of the ingredients used and the care taken in their preparation. Don't leave without one of the gloriously home-made desserts.

> **Seats 34**. Open Thu-Sat and Mon, 10-5. Closed Sun & Wed. CC. **Directions:** Westport town centre, on the main street - the entrance is off-street, at the side of the family butchers shop.

THE PANTRY & CORKSCREW

PETER STREET THE OCTAGON WESTPORT CO MAYO   EAT

098 26977 I info@thepantryandcorkscrew.com
www.thepantryandcorkscrew.com

Dermott Flynn and Janice O'Rourke's little café-restaurant offers 'a small food menu and some good wine selections', with everything made on the premises and plenty of local produce. Dermott's cooking is good, and so is the value and quality, while Janice's very pleasant and helpful service helps the restaurant to give off a cosy, comfortable feeling - in tune with their aim 'to bring a casual and fresh slow food dining experience to the town'. A good place that keeps getting better - well worth a try.

Seats 24. D Wed-Sun, 5-10, à la carte. Early D to 6.45, from about €22. Closed Mon & Tue. CC. **Directions:** On Peter Street just off the Octagon.

SAGE

10 HIGH STREET WESTPORT CO MAYO   EAT

098 56700 I sagewestport@yahoo.ie
www.sagewestport.ie

Chef Shteryo Yurukov and front of house partner Eva Ivanova have instilled great life into this attractive restaurant since they took on the ownership in 2013. It was formerly noted for authentic Italian cooking (and a few of the popular pasta dishes have remained on the menu) but their main focus is on seafood and contemporary Irish cooking. It's good to see local foods highlighted and Shteryo's cooking is very good - main courses, especially, are quietly impressive. A very pleasing restaurant and good value too, it has a well-earned place among the area's best dining destinations.

Seats 36. D daily 5.30-10, à la carte, also vegetarian. Early D to 6.30, from about €22. Wheelchair accessible. CC. **Directions:** Just beyond the clock at the top of the main street, up the hill on the right.

WESTPORT PLAZA HOTEL

CASTLEBAR STREET WESTPORT CO MAYO   EAT | STAY

098 51166 | info@westportplazahotel.ie
www.westportplazahotel.ie

Adjoining its larger sister property the Castlecourt Hotel in the centre of Westport, this smart, contemporary and well-managed hotel has spacious, stylishly furnished public areas, including a comfortable bar, and impressive accommodation - and guests have use of the 'Spa Sula' and the C Club leisure facilities next door. A destination for local diners, Restaurant Merlot offers consistently good modern international cooking that is always well presented and enjoyable - although, with two sittings on some nights, it may not be a place to linger.

Rooms 87 (5 shower only, 5 wheelchair friendly). Lift. Room rate from about €120. Children welcome. Restaurant seats 120. D daily 6-9.30; reservations required. Leisure Centre. Parking. Open all year. CC. **Directions:** Approaching town from the N5 (Castlebar road), hotel is on the right hand side at first set of traffic lights

THE TAVERN BAR & RESTAURANT

MURRISK WESTPORT CO MAYO
098 64060 | info@tavernmurrisk.com
www.tavernmurrisk.com

EAT | DRINK

Myles and Ruth O'Brien have been running this fine bar and restaurant just outside Westport at the foot of Croagh Patrick since 1999, and they've built up an enviable reputation. It's become the go-to place in the area for a lot of loyal customers, and the location ensures plenty of visitors too. It's a warmly atmospheric bar, known for genuine hospitality, and Myles's good cooking showcases the best of local foods (with suppliers proudly credited). Extensive menus offer something for everyone, but local seafood - everything from a great chowder to lobster - steals the show, and the welcoming and well-informed local staff know the menu and the nightly specials.

Seats 75. In summer open Mon-Thu, 12.30-9.30 (weekends to 10); off season 12.30-9 daily. Closed 25 Dec. CC.
Directions: At the foot of Croagh Patrick, 5 minutes' drive from Westport.

COUNTY MEATH

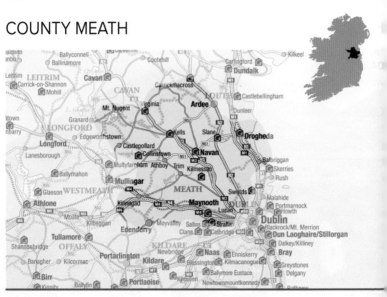

Royal Meath. Meath of the pastures. Meath of the people. Meath of many people.......its key location near Dublin means Meath www.meath.ie is one of the fastest-growing counties. The proximity of Dublin can be challenging. But it also brings benefits. With an increasingly affluent and discerning population, Meath is able to support a wide variety of hospitable establishements ranging from glossy restaurants of international quality, to characterful pubs deep in the heart of the country.

And the inevitable changes – for instance, the need to find ways through the county for new major roads - are projects which you feel Meath can absorb. There were some very vocal objections raised when the M3 was created through the valley beside the Hill of Tara www.hilloftara.org , Royal Tara, ancient seat of the High Kings. But now that the road is running smoothly and safely, and largely hidden by trees, it's appropriate to remember that Tara's power was based on being the meeting point of the six great roads of ancient Ireland. How better to honour Tara in the 21st Century than with a modern motorway which takes today's traffic harmlessly to the east, well clear of the main sacred site with its wonderful views westward?

Anyone with an interest in the remote past will find paradise in Meath, for along the Boyne Valley the neolithic tumuli at Knowth, Newgrange and Dowth are awe-inspiring, Newgrange www.newgrange.com in particular having its remarkable central chamber which is reached by the rays of sun at dawn at the winter solstice.

LOCAL ATTRACTIONS AND INFORMATION

>Donore **Bru na Boinne Visitor Centre**
www.heritageireland.ie | 041 988 0300

>Kells **Grove Gardens & Tropical Bird Sanctuary**
046 9234276

>Navan **Tourism Information**
www.meath.ie | 046 9073426

>Navan **Navan Racecourse**
www.navanracecourse.ie | 046 9021350

>**Newgrange (inc Dowth & Knowth)**
www.newgrange.ie | 041 988 0300 / 982 4488

>Oldcastle **Loughcrew Passage Tombs** (3000BC)
www.knowth.com | 049 854 2009

HEADFORT ARMS HOTEL

HEADFORT PLACE KELLS CO MEATH   EAT | STAY
046 924 0063 | info@headfortarms.ie
www.headfortarms.ie

Once the Marquis of Headfort's town house and owned by the Duff family for over 40 years, this historic three star hotel offers comfortable accommodation and true hospitality. An ideal base to explore the 'Royal County', it offers interesting packages, some of which include dinner in The Vanilla Pod (see entry). Also, thanks to the energetic leadership of Failte Ireland Food Champion, Olivia Duff, in promoting local food through the Boyne Valley Food Series (www.boynevalleyfoodseries.ie), visits to local food producers are often included. The hotel is also the hub of community activities and a popular wedding venue, so there's always a buzz. An interesting one to try.

Rooms 45. B&B from about €50pps. Spa. Café Therese (informal, French style), 7.30am-10pm daily. Closed Dec 25. CC. Off street parking. **Directions:** On main Dublin-Cavan road, centre of Kells.

VANILLA POD RESTAURANT

HEADFORT ARMS HOTEL KELLS CO MEATH   EAT
046 924 0063 | info@headfortarms.ie
www.headfortarms.ie

This consistently pleasing bistro-style restaurant is run independently of the hotel. It was the brainchild of the inspired Olivia Duff (who joined the hotel management team in 2005) and - reflecting the local food philosophy and drive that has since seen her become a leader in promoting the region's food and its producers - it has always offered good food based on carefully sourced ingredients, many of them local. Quite a few contemporary dishes are offered, including some vegetarian; the cooking is excellent, including homemade desserts, and the presentation delightful. Wine evenings are sometimes held.

Seats 80. D Mon-Sat 5-10 (Fri- Sat to 11); Sun 12.30-9.30. Early D from about €23, Set D about €35, also à la carte. Children welcome. Closed 24-26 Dec. CC. **Directions:** On main Dublin-Cavan road, centre of Kells.

THE STATION HOUSE HOTEL

KILMESSAN CO MEATH   EAT | STAY

046 902 5239 | info@stationhousehotel.ie

www.stationhousehotel.ie

The Slattery family's unique establishment is an old railway junction, and all the various buildings were converted to make a hotel full of charm and character. An interesting and unusual place to visit, with lovely gardens, it makes a pretty wedding venue and the traditional Signal Restaurant is especially popular for Sunday lunch.

Rooms 20 (1 shower only, 1 wheelchair friendly). B&B from about €65pps. Children welcome. Signal Restaurant Seats 90 (+ 100 outdoors). L daily 12.30-2.30 (Sun to 4.30); D daily 5-9.30. Set D about €30, also à la carte; Sun L about €30. Reservations advised; toilets wheelchair accessible. Bar Menu Mon-Sun 12-8. Open all year. CC. **Directions:** From Dublin, M3 to junction 6 Dunshaughlin and follow signs.

THE CENTRAL

4 TRIMGATE STREET NAVAN CO MEATH   EAT | DRINK

046 902 7999 | info@thecentral.ie

www.thecentral.ie

This big sister restaurant to The Bective in Kells is owned by respected restaurateurs Michael and Tara Gavigan, who have a long history of providing good food and hospitality in County Meath. A very family-friendly place, The Central aims to be relaxed, fun and friendly and this multi-purpose venue - café, bar & restaurant, beer garden, cool private party areas - not only serves lively modern menus, great steaks and a strong lineup of craft drinks, but there's also an ethos of 'contributing to the local community by using local produce and suppliers where possible'. Menus state that 90% of the food is sourced within the county, so this is a real taste of Meath, albeit with an international flavour. It's easy to see why it's so popular.

Food served: Mon-Fri 8am-late, Sat 10am-late, Sun 12 noon-late. CC.

LOUGHCREW ESTATE, GARDENS, CAFÉ & ADVENTURE CENTRE

OLDCASTLE CO MEATH EAT | STAY | LEARN
049 854 1356

In north County Meath, on the border with Cavan and Westmeath, the extraordinary Loughcrew Estate is the location of the largest complex of ancient passage graves in Ireland - and also home to a very modern adventure centre, complete with zipwire. And its credentials don't end there. St Oliver Plunkett was born and raised here - couples renting the property for their wedding can get married in his 17th-century church, in the gardens. Thanks to the current owner Emily Naper and her late husband, Charles, Loughcrew is now accessible to all - the gardens are open to the public and the Lime Tree Coffee Shop, which serves tasty fare, also acts as a reception centre for everything on the estate.

Gardens & café, 11-5 (shorter hours in winter), groups welcome (pre-book); wheelchair accessible. Accommodation: 1850s house, sleeps 17 (private rental).

GEORGES PATISSERIE

CHAPEL STREET SLANE CO MEATH EAT | BUY | PRODUCER
041 982 4493 | reservations@georgespatisserie.com
www.georgespatisserie.com

You're in for a real treat at this continental-style bakery, where much-admired pâtissier George Heise bakes a wide range of fresh breads and scones (the brown bread and blueberry scones are especially good) superb cakes and desserts. With just a few small tables to enjoy a coffee and a delicious bite, it's a great spot for locals and a wonderful place for visitors to know about - and travellers on the N2, to break a journey or buy goodies to take home.

Seats 20. Open Wed-Mon, 9am-6pm. Children welcome (high chair); unisex toilet wheelchair accessible. Closed Tue, 25-26 Dec. **Directions:** Centre of Slane.

ROSSNAREE

SLANE CO MEATH   STAY
041 982 0975 | info@rossnaree.ie
www.rossnaree.ie

Perched above the River Boyne, overlooking the famous megalithic passage tombs of Knowth and Newgrange, Aisling Law's handsome Victorian and Italianate house offers three individually themed bedrooms. Breakfast is a grand affair, served in the elegant dining room in front of a crackling log fire, and dinner is available by arrangement. An interesting house and the perfect place for history-lovers, (Aisling is the great-granddaughter of the Irish revolutionary, Maud Gonne), this is an enchanting bolthole too, ideal for a quick escape from Dublin.

Rooms 4 (all en-suite or with private bathrooms). B&B from about €70pps. Pet friendly. Fishing. Open Mar-Oct.
Directions: M1 north, exit for Bru na Boinne, through Donore, past Newgrange visitors centre, entrance on sharp bend on left.

SLANE CASTLE

SLANE CO MEATH   STAY
041 988 4400 | sales@slanecastle.ie
www.slanecastle.ie

Thanks to the current owner, Lord Henry Mountcharles, Slane Castle is renowned as a concert venue that has drawn some of the biggest global music names to this small Meath village. But its new state-of-the-art whiskey distillery and two food offerings, Browne's Bar and the more formal Gandon Room (named after the architect James Gandon, principal designer of the 1785 reconstruction), are putting Slane on the map for different reasons now. Atmospheric and fun - and with outside tables for fine weather - a meal here (and the house cocktail or a glass of their own Slane Irish Whiskey perhaps) can round off a visit to this special estate very nicely.

Tours (Distillery, Castle - each 1 hour). Gandon Room Restaurant: Thu-Sat 5-10pm, Sun 12-8pm; Browne's Bar: Thu-Sat 10.30-11.30pm, Sun-Wed 10.30am-8pm. CC.

TANKARDSTOWN HOUSE

RATHKENNY SLANE CO MEATH
041 982 4621 I info@tankardstown.ie
www.tankardstown.ie

EAT I STAY

Managed with style by Helen Byrne, this magnificent Georgian country house offers delightful accommodation and outstanding food: Head Chef Adrian Cassidy offers a memorable fine dining experience at the sophisticated rustic Brabazon Restaurant, and other options at weekends are all charming and serve excellent food based on local ingredients and garden produce, with good service to match.

Rooms 26 (7 in main house, 8 shower only, 1 wheelchair friendly); B&B from €105pps. Children welcome (& pets in cottages). **Brabazon Restaurant:** L Wed-Sun 12-4.30pm, (Sun to 3.30). D Wed-Sun from 6pm, Tasting D €70. Also à la carte. Afternoon Tea Wed-Fri 12-3.30pm. **Cellar Restaurant:** Sun L 12.30-5pm from about €20. **The Tea Garden:** Sat & Sun 1-4pm. Weddings, conferences (250). Open all year. CC. **Sister properties: Conyngham Arms** and **Boyne House**, Slane. **Directions:** 7km north of Slane.

O'CONNELL'S

SKRYNE HILL OF TARA CO MEATH

DRINK

046 902 5122

Four generations of O'Connells have been caretakers of this wonderfully unspoilt country pub and long-time owner, the late Mary O'Connell, delighted customers old and new for many a year until her death in 2012 at the age of 95. Now run by her daughter Marguerite and other members of the family, it's all beautifully simple - two little bars with no fancy bits, lots of items of local interest, and a welcoming fire in the grate. What more could anyone want? As for directions: just head for Skryne Castle - the tower beside the pub - which is visible for miles around.

Closed 25 Dec & possibly Good Fri. **No CC.**

Craft Brewery
Co Monaghan

monaghantourism.ie

COUNTY MONAGHAN

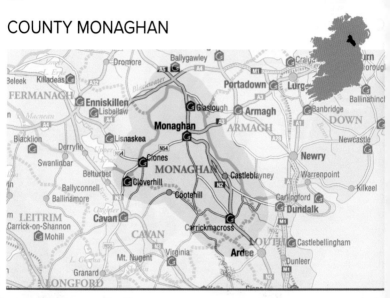

Monaghan Tourism (www.monaghantourism.com) describe the county as 'Ireland's best kept secret' - adding, for good measure, 'There's more to Monaghan...' And they could be right.

Right in the centre of the drumlin belt, that strip of pretty rounded glacial hills which runs across the country from Clew Bay in Mayo to Strangford Lough in County Down, Monaghan takes its name from *Muineachain* - "Little Hills".

Those little hills enclose many lakes, making Monaghan a coarse angler's paradise - and, with some outstanding country house destinations also tucked among them, it has become a restorative short break paradise as well. Lovely places to explore include a particularly attractive lake district with forest park and adventure centre at Castleblayney, around **Lough Muckno** (a world class angling and wakeboarding centre).

For those in search of creativity and contemplation **Annaghmakerrig House** (www.tyroneguthrie.ie), near the Quaker-named village of Newbliss, is a retreat for writers and artists, while the **Patrick Kavanagh Resource Centre** (www.patrickkavanaghcountry.com) at Inishkeen celebrates that special poet and the landscape and communities that inspired him.

The famous **Carrickmacross and Clones Lace** (seen in local museums) is still being made (www.irishlace.org) and remains highly desirable - Carrickmacross Lace (carrickmacross lace.ie) was used in the wedding gowns of both Princess Diana and the Duchess of Cambridge (Kate Middleton), and also in Prince George's christening gown.

Today's vibrant crafts culture can be explored through the fascinating **'Artisan Monaghan' Trail of Crafts & Foods**, which includes small organic food and drink producers, and the county is also home to some highly respected large scale producers, including Silver Hills Foods whose Pekin duck is internationally renowned.

A hidden gem that will soon be better known is the old Ulster Canal, which is being revived as a Greenway - and, in northeast Monaghan, there's even gold in them thar little hills. Enough to merit mining apparently, but even if it weren't, the fact that it's there at all is another of Monaghan's more intriguing secrets.

COURTHOUSE RESTAURANT

1 MONAGHAN STREET CARRICKMACROSS CO MONAGHAN   EAT

042 969 2848 | info@courthouserestaurant.ie
www.courthouserestaurant.ie

Well known chef Conor Mee and Charlotte Carr's atmospheric restaurant caters well for the daily changing needs of their local clientèle, and it's become a destination for food lovers from afar. Conor's menus combine quality and value, offering imaginative choices. The simple things like breads and soups are excellent (always a good sign), while specialities include delicious local meats and poultry - notably pork and duck - and classics such as fish and chips, which are sea-fresh and perfectly made. Well worth a detour.

D Wed-Sun, L Sun only: Wed-Fri, 5-9.30, Sat to 10, Sun to 9. Sun L 12.15-3.30 €27. Set D (Wed-Fri 5-9.30), €27; also tapas & à la carte. Vegetarian & vegan menu available. Children welcome. Bar. Closed Mon (except bank hol Mon, open from 4pm), Tue, 1st week Jan. CC. **Directions:** Main street, beside the Courthouse.

HILTON PARK

CLONES CO MONAGHAN   STAY

047 56007 | mail@hiltonpark.ie
www.hiltonpark.ie

Once described as a "capsule of social history" thanks to their collection of family portraits and memorabilia going back 250 years or more, the Madden family's wonderful 18th century mansion is set in beautiful gardens, amidst 200 acres of woodland and farmland. Johnny and Lucy Madden have handed over the reins to son Fred (a chef) and his wife Joanna, and you may expect a luxurious and very special country house stay, with great food - Lucy, a keen gardener, supplies fresh organic produce for the delicious meals served. A rare treat.

Rooms 6. B&B from €95pps; unsuitable for children under 8. Residents D Tue-Sat, 8pm (Fri, 8.30), €60 (24 hours notice). Pets in some areas (by arrangement). Self-catering accommodation available. Open Apr-Sep, weekends Mar & Oct; all year by arrangement. CC. **Directions:** 5km south of Clones on Scotshouse Road.

CASTLE LESLIE ESTATE

GLASLOUGH CO MONAGHAN
047 88100 | info@castleleslie.com
www.castleleslie.com

EAT | STAY | LEARN

Choose between rooms in the extraordinary Castle or in The Lodge, a sensitively designed and atmospheric modern hotel built around a stable courtyard, complete with an equestrian centre and Victorian Treatment Rooms. Except for Afternoon Tea at The Castle (and groups), dining options for both residents and non-residents are the hotel's informal Conor's Bar or Snaffles Restaurant, where chef Andrew Bradley has added his personal stamp to old recipes from the Castle Leslie Estate Cookbook - and a very good breakfast is served.

Castle: **Rooms 20**, B&B from €100pps. 12 seater cinema. Afternoon Tea from 2.30pm, about €25. Lodge: **Rooms 29** (1 wheelchair friendly); Lift. Children welcome. Wifi. B&B from about €90pps. D daily 6-9.30pm; set D about €65, also à la carte. Conor's Bar: food daily (seasonal). Equestrian Centre; Treatments. Closed 24-27 Dec. **Directions:** Monaghan Town -Armagh road-Glaslough (10 min).

ANDY'S BAR AND RESTAURANT

12 MARKET STREET MONAGHAN CO MONAGHAN

EAT | DRINK

047 82277 | info@andys.com
www.andysmonaghan.com

Right in the centre of Monaghan, the Redmond family's long-established bar and restaurant is a gem. A classic of its type, it offers consistently generous and tasty local food - and interesting craft drinks from Monaghan and nearby counties. Following a fire, the handsome Victorian-style bar has recently been restored to its former glory and the restaurant got a new look. Steaks are a particular speciality - very unusually, their top quality beef is dry-aged in-house for up to 40 days, and that is the secret of its stellar reputation. Continuing the family tradition, brothers Sean (chef) and Kevin (manager) offer great food, great service - and great value too.

Bar meals: Tue-Sun, 4-10.15. Restaurant: D Tue-Sun, 4-10, Sun 1.30-9.30, à la carte. Children welcome (children's menu). Closed Mon, bank hols, 25 Dec. CC. **Directions:** Town centre, opposite Market House.

HILTON PARK GARDENS

The Great Telescope
Birr Castle Gardens & Science Centre
Co Offaly

birrcastle.com
visitoffaly.ie

COUNTY OFFALY

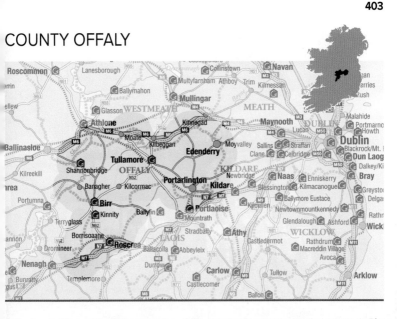

At the heart of the old Ely O'Carroll territory, Offaly is Ireland's most sky-minded county. At **Birr Castle** (www.birrcastle.com) there's the Parsons family's famous restored 1845-vintage 1.83m astronomical telescope – rated one of the Seven Wonders of Ireland - through which the 3rd Earl of Rosse observed his discovery of the spiral nebulae. Today, set in 120 acres of award-winning gardens, **Birr Castle Gardens and Science Centre** is not only home to the **Great Telescope**, but also to **Ireland's Historic Science Centre** - and the tallest tree house in Ireland. And in Tullamore, there's a thriving amateur Astronomical Society whose members point out that the wide clear skies of Offaly have encouraged the regular observation of heavenly bodies since at least 1057 AD, when astronomy was the province of moon-minded monks.

On a more modern note, the **Tullamore Dew Heritage Centre** (www.tullamoredew.com) is housed in the restored 1897 canal-side bonded warehouse which formerly stored the famous local whiskey. The Centre explores Tullamore's distilling, canal and urban history with entertaining style. Style is also the theme of the new **County Hall** in Tullamore (www.discovertullamore.com) which has been awarded the An Taisce Sustainable Building accolade.

The Grand Canal (www.waterwaysireland.org) crosses Ireland from Dublin on an away-from-it-all journey for boats and towpath travellers alike, finally meeting the great river at Shannon Harbour - and on the river itself **Clonmacnoise** (www.visitoffaly.ie), founded by St Ciaran in 544 AD, is an extraordinary place where the remains of an ancient monastic university city give pause for thought.

And forget the widely held belief that Offaly is just a vast tract of flat bogland - yes, there's plenty of precious peatland, and that's where you'll find some famous environmental attractions, including **Lough Boora Discovery Park** (www.loughboora.com), which is a must-visit when in the area.

In the south, the modest heights of the **Slieve Bloom Mountains** rise attractively above Offaly's farmland and bogs and their understated charm has particular appeal. **Visit Offaly** (www.visitoffaly.ie) market their county as **Ireland's Hidden Gem**, and they are right: the more you learn about Offaly, the more layers are revealed.

THE COURTYARD CAFÉ

BIRR CASTLE DEMESNE BIRR CO OFFALY
057 916 9735 | food@birrcastle.com
www.birrcastle.com

EAT | BUY

Birr Castle is a brilliant place to visit at any time and, tucked away in a restored stable block in the entrance courtyard, is a gorgeous café that's a destination in its own right - and you don't have to pay the entrance fee to the grounds in order to eat there, so it's accessible to all. Simple, with a lovely understated style, there are big menu blackboards offering tempting seasonal dishes and proclaiming in no uncertain style the food

philosophy upheld by Manager Mary Walsh-Kinsella and her team since opening here in spring 2013: "We promote and celebrate local producers and suppliers - we would like you to know where our food comes from". Simply delicious.

Open: Mon-Fri & Sun 10-5, Sat 10-8, in summer. (Closed late Sep-mid-Mar. Check hours off season). CC. **Directions:** in Birr Castle Demesne

EMMAS CAFÉ & DELI

31 MAIN STREET BIRR CO OFFALY   EAT, BUY
057 912 5678 | debbykenny1902@gmail.com
www.facebook.com/EmmasBirr

This delightful Heritage Town is blessed with excellent choices when it comes to local foods and casual daytime fare, and Adrian Shine and Debbie Kenny's well-known café-deli is one of the longest established and best. The specialities are simply excellent - fans come here especially to enjoy a bowl of the delicious vegetable soup with their freshly baked brown bread or a gluten-free scone, for example - and the difference is in the quality of the ingredients used, and careful preparation. Combining an attractive café and a deli counter, it offers a tempting range of artisan products, including cheeseboards and hampers that are made to order all year round.

Open: Mon-Sat 8-6, Sun 9.30-6. Wheelchair accessible. Children welcome. Vegetarian & gluten free options.

SPINNERS ON CASTLE STREET

CASTLE STREET BIRR CO OFFALY   EAT | DRINK | STAY
057 9123779 | spinnersbirr@gmail.com
www.spinnersbirr.com

Hands-on management by owner Jordan Darrah, a consistent kitchen and delightful staff, make Spinners a favourite destination for locals as well as visitors to this handsome town. An atmospheric restaurant offers fine dining on some evenings, but the bar is the heart of the everyday dining experience here. With warmly traditional decor lightened by modern touches, and access to a courtyard, it is an inviting room to enjoy good pub staples like steak sandwiches or beer-battered fish (with triple-cooked chips), and also offers wider choices. Individually decorated guest rooms include the sumptuous 'Ely O'Carroll'.

Rooms 11 (3 separate bathroom); room rate from about €99. Restaurant Fri & Sat D, 6-9 (call to check, may be open other times). Bar: Tue-Thu 5-9, Fri-Sun 9-9, (Sun to 7); Bar L & D Fri-Sun. Closed Mon, mid Feb-mid Mar. CC. **Directions:** near Birr Castle.

THE THATCH BAR & RESTAURANT

CRINKLE BIRR CO OFFALY   EAT | DRINK
057 912 0682

This pretty thatched pub and restaurant outside Birr shows just how pleasing a genuine, well-run country pub can be. Des Connole, proprietor since 1991, has a well-earned reputation for the immaculate maintenance and atmosphere of the pub, and both bar food and restaurant meals offer generous portions at a reasonable price.

Seats 50. Open: Mon-Thu 4-8.30. L Fri & Sat 12.30-3 (Sun to 2.30). Early D Fri & Sat 5-7.30, Sun 5.15-7.15. D Fri & Sat 6-9. A la carte. Establishment closed 25 Dec, possibly also Good Fri. CC. **Directions:** 1.5km from Birr (Roscrea side).

TOWNSEND HOUSE GUESTHOUSE

TOWNSEND STREET BIRR CO OFFALY   EAT | DRINK | STAY
057 912 1276 | enquiry@townsendhouse-guesthouse.com
www.townsendhouse-guesthouse.com

Martin and Lorraine Kearns's impressive guesthouse has kept original period features (and open fires), yet offers all the comforts and conveniences demanded by today's travellers. Bedrooms vary in size due to the age of the building, which is part of the charm, and all are en suite. It's a great base for exploring the town and its environs - and there's even a Wine & Tapas Bar at this atmospheric place, which makes a welcome addition to evening dining options in the area.

Rooms 12. B&B €40pps, ss €10. Discounts offered on stays of 2+ nights. Children welcome. (Pets permitted by arrangement; kennels). Tapas & Wine Bar, Thu-Sat, 6-10pm. Wine from about €20. Secure parking. Free wifi. CC. **Directions:** Centre of Birr.

ARDMORE COUNTRY HOUSE

THE WALK KINNITTY CO OFFALY   STAY
057 913 7009 | info@kinnitty.com
www.kinnitty.com

Walking holidays are a speciality at Christina Byrne's stone-built Victorian house and it offers very welcome old-fashioned comforts: brass beds, turf fires and homemade bread and preserves for breakfast. The lovely bedrooms are deliberately left without amenities to make a visit here a real country house experience and to encourage guests to mix with each other - Christina welcomes guests with home baking on arrival, and tea or coffee is available downstairs at any time in this hospitable house. She also plays the fiddle and guests can go along with her to the pub when there's a session on, to enjoy traditional music and meet the locals.

Rooms 5 (3 shower only, 1 wheelchair friendly). B&B from about €40pps; children welcome. Wi-Fi. Drying room; lock up for bikes and motor bikes. Closed 23-27 Dec. CC. **Directions:** Kinnitty village centre.

THE VILLAGE TAVERN

MAIN STREET SHANNONBRIDGE CO OFFALY   DRINK | BUY EAT
090 967 4112 | louise.killeen@ireland.com
www.facebook.com/pg/Killeens-Bar-Shannonbridge

'A real taste of Ireland from days of old' is the promise at J.J. Killeen's and it's one they deliver - anyone interested in finding a real traditional Irish country pub should head straight to Shannonbridge and see it for themselves. A visit to this wonderful pub and shop is sure to restore the weariest of travellers and, as well as enjoying great drinks, craic and wholesome fare, you can also top up on groceries, fishing bait and gas - and anything else you might need, 'including the kitchen sink'. Music six nights a week from May to September; weekends only during the off season.

Directions: On the main street of Shannonbridge, between Ballinasloe and Cloghan.

THE BLUE APRON

HARBOUR STREET TULLAMORE CO OFFALY   EAT
057 936 0106 | theblueapronrestaurant@gmail.com
www.theblueapronrestaurant.ie

This little restaurant near the canal is Tullamore's premier dining destination and well worth seeking out for owner-chef Kenan Pehlivan's interesting cooking. Behind the smart frontage lies a pleasantly understated restaurant and a warm welcome from Sarah Pehlivan and her friendly staff. Menus cover all the bases, yet also offer something different - fresh crab on a homemade pastry spoon makes a deliciously different starter, for example - and the saucing is delicate. The cooking is among the best to be found in a wide area and there's good value too. A must for food lovers when visiting Tullamore.

> Open Wed-Sat 5.30-10, Sun 12.30-9. Set D midweek from about €23, also à la carte. Vegetarian menu. L Sun only, about €27. Closed Mon & Tue, late Jan-early Feb, last 2 weeks Aug. Full wheelchair access. CC. **Directions:** Centre of Tullamore

---

ANNAHARVEY FARM

TULLAMORE CO OFFALY   STAY | LEARN
057 934 3544 | info@annaharveyfarm.ie
www.annaharveyfarm.ie

Although equestrian activities are the main attraction at Henry and Lynda Deverell's restored grain barn near Tullamore - and equestrian packages and schooling are offered for varying levels of experience - very comfortable accommodation is also offered for casual visitors at this fourth-generation working farm. Good home cooking has always been a central feature and there's a choice of full board, half board or B&B (with some meals, if required), and a lounge area with a stove, where guests can socialise. A very appealing place to stay for a real rural break.

> **Rooms 7** (6 shower only; all no-smoking); B&B about €45pps. Children welcome (under 2 free; cot available without charge). No pets. Residents' meals available, L about €15, D about €25. Stabling for guests' horses. Small conferences/events. Youth/language camps. Closed Nov-end Feb. CC. **Directions:** R420 Tullamore - Portarlington.

COUNTY ROSCOMMON

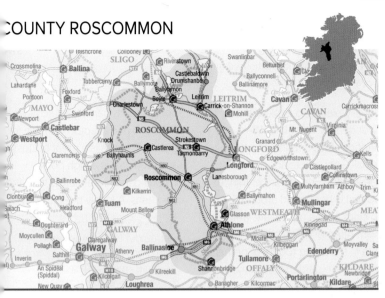

It could be said that Roscommon www.roscommon.ie is a county much put upon by the counties about it. Sometimes it seems that just as Roscommon is on the verge of becoming significant, it becomes somewhere else. In one notable example - the hotel complex at Hodson's Bay on the western shores of Lough Ree - the location is actually in Roscommon, yet the the postal service have given it to Athlone and thereby Westmeath.

But Roscommon is a giving sort of county, for it gave Ireland her first President, Gaelic scholar Douglas Hyde (1860-1949), it was also the birthplace of Oscar Wilde's father, and the inimitable songwriter Percy French was a Roscommon man.

Roscommon town itself has a population of 1,500, but it's growing, though the presence of extensive castle ruins and a former gaol tell of a more important past. The gaol was once noted for having a female hangman, today it has shops and a restaurant. Northwestward at Castlerea, we find Clonalis House www.clonalis.com , ancestral home of the O'Conor Don, and final resting place of O'Carolan's Harp.

In the north of the county, the town of Boyle near lovely Lough Key with its outstanding Forest Park www.loughkey.ie is a substantial centre, with a population nearing the 2,000 mark. Boyle is a place of unexpected interest, including the restored King House www.kinghouse.ie , a masterpiece from 1730. Reckoned to have been the most important provincial town house in Ireland, its exhibits eloquently evoke the past. Nearby, the impressive riverbank remains of Boyle Abbey, the largest Cistercian foundation in Ireland, date from 1148.

LOCAL ATTRACTIONS AND INFORMATION

>Boyle **Boyle Abbey** 071 966 2604

>Frenchpark **Dr Douglas Hyde Interpretive Centre** 0907 70016

>**Strokestown Park House, Garden & Famine Museum** www.strokestownpark.ie | 071 9633013

LOUGH KEY HOUSE

BOYLE CO ROSCOMMON

STA

071 966 2161 | loughkeyhouse@gmail.com

www.loughkeyhouse.com

Ideally placed to explore the wonderfully wild North-West, Frances McDonagh's charming small Georgian residence is just beside the Forest Park entrance. Arrival is best timed around 5 o'clock, when guests are welcomed with Afternoon Tea beside an open fire in the sitting room - or perhaps in the rose garden, in summer. Rooms are large, luxurious but all quite different and it's a happy house, with lots of animals around, books, board games, flat screen TV, piano and a laptop with Wifi for guests. Frances is a great hostess and breakfast is a high point, including freshly-laid eggs from the own hens. A lovely place to stay.

Rooms 6 (3 shower only, 1 family, 2 pet friendly). B&B from about €50pps; discount on multiple nights. Children welcome. Free wifi. Closed early Nov-Easter. CC. **Directions:** On the N4, 5km from Boyle.

CASTLECOOTE HOUSE

CASTLECOOTE CO ROSCOMMON

EAT | STA

090 666 3794 | info@castlecootehouse.com

www.castlecootehouse.com

Painstakingly restored it to its former glory by the present owner, Kevin Finnerty, this fine Georgian house is a wonderful place for individuals and groups to stay, with plenty to do on-site and attractions, including Strokestown House and Gardens, nearby. Bright and airy guest rooms have marble fireplaces and four-poster beds but, even if you aren't staying here, this Hidden Ireland property is a beautiful place to visit - cultural events are held here, including the Percy French Summer School, annually in July.

Rooms 3 (1 with private bathroom, 1 shower only); B&B from about €70pps. Children welcome; pet friendly; not suitable for wheelchairs. D by arrangement €48 (book previous day). Closed Oct-Mar. CC. Heli-pad. **Directions:** into village, cross bridge, bear right, gates are directly ahead.

CLONALIS HOUSE

CASTLEREA CO ROSCOMMON   STAY

094 962 0014 | info@clonalis.com
www.clonalis.com

Despite the grandeur, there's a warm and homely atmosphere at Pyers and Marguerite O'Conor-Nash's stunning 45-room Victorian Italianate mansion. Everything is on a huge scale: open fires burn in the vast yet comfortable reception rooms, and luxurious bedrooms have massive four-poster and half-tester beds. The beautiful dining room makes an impressive setting for Marguerite's good home cooking, but an informal alternative is also offered in a 'country kitchen' setting. History is everywhere - even in a small museum (open to the public). A magnificently rewarding place to stay.

Rooms 4 (1 with private bathroom). B&B from about €88pps. Discount for 2 night stay. Unsuitable for children under 12 years. Residents D Tue-Sat, 8pm, €50 (24 hrs notice required); kitchen supper also served €30 (same notice required). No pets. Closed 1 Oct-end Mar. CC.
Directions: N60, west of Castlerea.

GLEESONS RESTAURANT & ROOMS

MARKET SQUARE ROSCOMMON CO ROSCOMMON   EAT | STAY

090 662 6954 | info@gleesonstownhouse.com
www.gleesonstownhouse.com

Overlooking the square, Mary and Eamonn Gleeson's townhouse and restaurant provides just what every visitor hopes to find: a warm welcome, comfortable rooms and first-class food. The Gleesons place great emphasis on food, offering wholesome fare in their popular coffee shop and extensive all day menus in the Manse Restaurant. They buy local where possible, including produce from the weekly farmers' market, and take pride in offering house special-ities such as their famous chowder, and the region's great meats - in their renowned version of the classic Irish Stew, for example.

Rooms 19. B&B €60pps. Children welcome; pets permitted. Restaurant seats 55 (+ 30 outdoors). L&D daily 12.30-6 (Sun 12.30-5); 6.30-9.15 (Sun to 8.45). All Day Menu. Wheelchair accessible. Café: 8-6 daily. Closed 25-26 Dec. CC.
Directions: Town centre, next door to Tourist Office / County Museum.

KEENANS HOTEL & RESTAURANT

TARMONBARRY (VIA CLONDRA) CO ROSCOMMON

EAT | DRINK | STAY

043 332 6052 | info@keenans.ie
www.keenans.ie

Beside the bridge over the Shannon in Tarmonbarry, Barry and Annette Keenan's friendly, well-run hotel, bar and restaurant is full of character; it's a favourite watering-hole for river folk and makes a great place to break a journey between Dublin and the north-west. Informal meals are mostly quite traditional, but with more international influences in the evening dishes, while à la carte bar menus offer hearty fare that pleases all age groups – the steak sandwich is a favourite. There is also a more formal restaurant and some of the smart en-suite guestrooms overlook the Shannon.

Rooms 12 (1 wheelchair friendly); children welcome. Wifi. B&B about €60pps. Food served Mon-Sat 11-8.45, Sun & bank hols to 7.30; Set D about €35, also à la carte; Set Sun L about €28. Closed 25-26 Dec. CC. **Directions:** On N5, west of Longford town.

THE PURPLE ONION BAR & RESTAURANT

TARMONBARRY (VIA CLONDRA) CO ROSCOMMON   EAT | DRINK
043 335 9919 | info@purpleonion.ie
www.purpleonion.ie

Paul Dempsey and Pauline Roe's busy pub has an old-world feeling and doubles as an art gallery, so good original paintings add interest and charm. Quality comes first (with suppliers credited) and the choice offered is impressive for a small restaurant. Popular dishes include great 'John Stone' dry-aged steaks from County Longford, but there's plenty to tempt more adventurous diners too; it offers something different from other places in the area - and a good drinks list too, including craft beers and changing wine 'specials'.

Summer: D Tue-Thu, 5.30-9.30, Fri- Sat 12.30-9.30. Sun L 12.30-3.30, Sun D 4.30-7.30. Winter: Tue/Wed-Fri 5.30-9.15, Sat 1-9.15, Sun 12.30-7.15. Value D from about €20 (days, times vary), also à la carte. Children welcome before 10pm. Closed Mon, sometimes also Tue in Nov & Jan. CC. **Directions:** On N5, west of Longford town.

Lissadell House
Ballinfull, Co. Sligo

lissadellhouse.com

COUNTY SLIGO

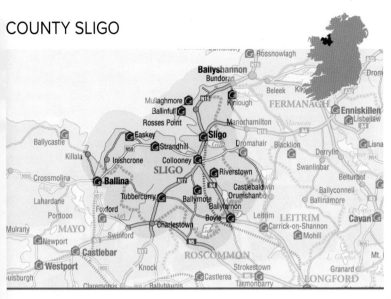

There's a stylish confidence to Sligo which belies its compact area as one of Ireland's smallest counties. Perhaps it's because they know that their place and their way of life have been immortalised through association with two of the outstanding creative talents of modern Ireland, W.B.Yeats www.yeatssociety.com and his painter brother Jack. The former's fame seems beyond question, while the latter's star was never higher than it is today.

The town and the county have many associations with Yeats, but few are more remarkable than Lissadell House www.lissadellhouse.com , the former home of the Gore-Booths, best known as the family of Constance Gore-Booth. As Countess Markievicz, she was much involved with the Easter Rising of 1916.

But whatever the reason for Sligo's special quality www.sligotourism.ie , there's certainly something about it that encourages repeat visits. The town itself is big enough to be reassuring, yet small enough to be comfortable. And the countryside about Sligo town also has lasting appeal, with its impressive scale set by the heights of Ben Bulben.

Mankind has been living here with enthusiasm for a very long time indeed, for in recent years it has been demonstrated that some of County Sligo's ancient monuments are amongst the oldest in northwest Europe. Lakes abound, the mountains are magnificent, and there are tumbling rivers a-plenty.

Yet if you wish to get away from the bustle of the regular tourist haunts, Sligo can look after your needs in this as well, for the western part of the county down through the Ox Mountains towards Mayo is an uncrowded region of wide vistas and clear roads.

LOCAL ATTRACTIONS AND INFORMATION

>**Carrowmore** Largest Megalithic Cemetry in Ireland
 071 916 1534

>Drumcliff **Lissadell House**
 www.lissadellhouse.com | 071 916 3150

>Sligo **Sligo Art Gallery**
 www.sligoarts.ie | 071 914 5847

>Sligo **Yeats Memorial Building**, Hyde Bridge
 071 914 2693

LISSADELL HOUSE

LISSADELL BALLINFULL CO SLIGO   EAT | BUY | LEARN
071 916 3150 | info@lissadellhouse.com
www.lissadellhouse.com

Lissadell is the brightest historical and cultural gem of the North-West and a must-see destination for anyone visiting Sligo or planning a trip along the Wild Atlantic Way. Former home of the Gore-Booths - notably Constance Gore-Booth who, as Countess Markievicz, was closely involved with the Easter Rising of 1916 and, in 1918, the first elected female MP - the current owners, Edward Walsh and Constance Cassidy, restored this national treasure as a family home and opened both the house and gardens to the public. It is an extraordinary place, and the café serves wholesome fare, including produce from the Kitchen Gardens and perhaps even oysters from their own oyster beds.

House & gardens open daily March-Oct 10-6. (Adults €14; children €6). Café seats 100 (+ 40 outdoors), 10-6 daily; children welcome (high chair). CC. **Directions:** 7km off the N15 (Sligo-Donegal).

TEMPLE HOUSE

BALLINACARROW BALLYMOTE CO SLIGO
071 918 3329 | enquiry@templehouse.ie
www.templehouse.ie

STAY | LEARN

A Georgian mansion situated in 1,000 acres of farm and woodland, Temple House overlooks the original lakeside castle which was built by the Knights Templar in 1200 A.D. The Perceval family has lived here since 1665 and the current owners, Roderick Perceval and his wife Helena, now welcome guests to their home - a fascinating place where everything has a history, log fires warm the huge rooms and bedrooms are furnished with family antiques. Evening meals and breakfast, served in a beautiful dining room, are a real treat. Activity breaks, cookery demonstrations, music and traditional dancing nearby.

Rooms 6 (1 shower only, 1 family; Voya organic toiletries). B&B from about €85pps. Children welcome. Wifi. House parties welcome. Helipad. Residents D (book by 1pm, not available Sun). Working farm. Closed Dec-Mar. CC. **Directions:** Signed off N17, 0.5 km south of Ballinacarrow.

NOOK CAFÉ AND RESTAURANT

MAIN STREET COLLOONEY CO SLIGO   EAT
087 352 2135 | eatatnook@gmail.com
www.facebook.com/NookCafeRestaurant

Open since 2016, Ethna Reynolds has created a seriously impressive menu in this little gem of a café, which soon became a popular spot for breakfast and lunch. The first thing you'll notice about the menu – besides how tempting every dish sounds – is the focus on fresh, local artisan ingredients, from the meat to the cheese and right down to the beautiful salad leaves. It's an absolutely delightful new addition to Collooney and well worth a stop on your way to Sligo town or even a destination in its own right.

> Open: Summer Tue-Sat B 9.30-12.30, L 12.30-5. Winter Tue-Sat 10-3.30 (Sat to 3). Closed Sun & Mon. CC. **Directions:** Off the N4 south of Sligo town, Nook is in the centre of Collooney village.

PUDDING ROW

EASKEY HOUSE MAIN STREET EASKEY CO SLIGO

096 49794 | hello@puddingrow.ie

www.puddingrow.ie

EAT | BUY | LEARN

PRODUCER

A baker by training, Dervla James deserves great praise for the high standards at this lovely family-friendly café overlooking Easkey Castle and the Atlantic and it's an ideal stopping place, especially if you have children in tow. Everything served is made in-house, using locally produced ingredients, and many ingredients are name-checked to credit the small producers that she holds in such high regard. Even on a chilly day off season there's likely to be a good buzz with plenty of locals in, and it's a terrific place to know about when exploring the Wild Atlantic Way or the Sligo Food Trail (www.sligofoodtrail.ie).

Seats 45. Open Wed-Sun 11-5 & bank hol Mon 11-6. Otherwise closed Mon & Tue. A la carte. Children welcome. CC. **Directions:** R297 (Enniscrone coast road); village centre, on the left from the Enniscrone direction.

EITHNAS BY THE SEA

THE HARBOUR MULLAGHMORE CO SLIGO   EAT | BUY | PRODUCER
071 916 6407 | info@bythesea.ie
www.eithnasrestaurant.com

A favourite destination for seafood lovers, Eithna O'Sullivan's atmospheric harbour-side seafood restaurant teems with life throughout the summer and her food is better than ever. Mainly a daytime place, she offers classic seafood and quality light meals using the best from sea and land, including seaweeds. You'll find one of Ireland's best seafood chowders here, or you could try seafood salad on brown bread with dressed salad, perhaps, or grilled mackerel with seaweed pesto. Also vegetarian options - and delicious desserts. Simply magic.

Open daily in summer, 10-5, D Sat and other evenings if booked. Off season, open weekends 'as long as there is demand'. CC. **Directions:** on the harbour front.

COOPERSHILL HOUSE

RIVERSTOWN CO SLIGO STAY | PRODUCER
071 916 5108 | ohara@coopershill.com
www.coopershill.com

Home of the O'Hara family since it was built in 1774, this sturdy granite mansion is a warm and friendly place under the management of Simon O'Hara, who runs it with the seamless hospitality born of long family experience. Rooms are sumptuous and, as well as seasonal home grown fruit and vegetables, you may well find their own venison on the dinner menu, along with other delicious dishes cooked up by Simon's partner, Christina McCauley.

A particularly perfect, superbly comfortable country house.

Rooms 8 (1 shower only); B&B from about €109pps. Unsuitable for children under 12. Dining Room Seats 30. Set D 8pm daily €56 (non-residents welcome by reservation). Wine from €25. Dogs permitted in outhouse/kennel; horses by arrangement. Closed end Oct-1 Apr. (off-season house parties of 12-16 people welcome.) CC. **Directions:** Signed from N4 at Drumfin crossroads.

EALA BHÁN

ROCKWOOD PARADE SLIGO CO SLIGO EAT
071 914 5823 | trabanstrandhill@gmail.com
www.ealabhan.ie

Following on the success of his Strandhill seafood restaurant, Trá Bán (www.trabansligo.ie), the attractive Eala Bhán ('White Swan') is well-known restaurateur Anthony Gray's town centre restaurant, beside the Garavogue River. Although strong on seafood and local meats (from Sherlocks of Tubbercurry - try the rack of Sligo lamb), menus offer plenty of choice, with upbeat versions of many crowd-pleasing dishes including vegetarian

and children's choices. Offering delicious local, seasonal food, pleasing surroundings, great staff and value for money, it's easy to see why this restaurant is so successful.

Seats 65. L 12-3, (Sun from 12.30), à la carte. Early D 5-6.20, à la carte D 5-9. Afternoon Tea 12-3, about €25; must book. Children welcome. House wine about €23. Closed 25-26 Dec & Good Fri. CC. **Also at: Hooked, Sligo** (www.hookedsligo.ie). **Directions:** Centre of Sligo Town.

HARGADONS

4 O'CONNELL STREET SLIGO CO SLIGO

EAT | DRINK

071 915 3709 | info@hargadons.com
www.hargadons.com

This famous and much-loved traditional grocery-bar in the centre of Sligo Town is a listed building dating back to 1864. A recent sensitively undertaken restoration was a great success - the renovated bar has retained all its snugs and fires and grocery shelves intact, the restored marble counter is back in place, and you'll still get the same warm welcome. The drinks offering includes many Irish craft beers and there's tasty pub fare too. The old-world ambience combined with lovely service from friendly staff make for an enjoyable drink or meal here - allow time to make the most of it.

Seats 80 (+20 outdoors). Open Mon-Sat from 11, Sun from 6. L Mon-Sat 12-3.30, D Mon-Sat 4-9. No food on Sun. No reservations (except groups of 7+). Wine shop/off-licence. CC. **Directions:** Town centre on the main street.

KNOX

32 O'CONNELL STREET SLIGO CO SLIGO
071 914 1575 I hello@knoxsligo.ie
www.knoxsligo.ie

EAT

A hit from the day it opened in 2015, Knox is the brainchild of two former bank employees, Paddy Sweeney and David Dunne, who offer a short but balanced and carefully considered menu - coffee, breakfast, brunch, lunch and treats - in a pared-back modern setting. Each and every item is tempting, but you won't go wrong with the Knox Spanish brekky, a proper sambo, the juicy chicken burger or pan-fried hake - washed down, perhaps, with a local craft beer. Freshly baked treats too, and coffee to remember. A cracking café that's doing everything right.

Open: Tue-Sat 9-5, Thu-Sat D 6-10, Sun 10-5. B'fst 9-11.30, Brunch Sat & Sun 12-4. Tapas menu. Wine from €23. Closed Mon. **Directions:** Town centre on the main street.

LYONS CAFÉ & BAKESHOP

QUAY STREET SLIGO CO SLIGO
071 914 2969 | info@garystafford.com
www.garystafford.com

EAT | BUY | PRODUCER

A visit to the magnificently traditional Lyons Department Store (est. 1835) is de rigeur when visiting Sligo; it's a joy - and, on the first floor, Chef Gary Stafford takes seasonal, local produce and transforms it into colourful, fresh-flavoured food in his delightful and deservedly popular café-restaurant. Alongside the best of Irish comfort food you'll find great salads, sandwiches and more exotic dishes too. The homemade desserts are a strong point, or grab artisan bread, pastries or sandwiches from the Bakeshop on the ground floor - and their lovely cookery books are on sale too. Simply gorgeous.

Seats 125. Open Mon-Sat 9-6 (L 12.30-3); no reservations. Children welcome. Toilets wheelchair accessible. Bakeshop (Tel: 071 913 8006; www.bakeshopsligo. com) open Mon-Sat 9-5. Closed Sun, bank hols, 25-26 Dec. CC. **Directions:** On corner of Wine Street/Quay Street between Town Hall and Post Office.

MISO SLIGO

CALRY COURT STEPHEN STREET SLIGO CO SLIGO   EAT

071 919 4986 | misosligo@gmail.com
www.facebook.com/misosligo

Sligo's first Korean-Japanese restaurant opened at a good time, with Korean food becoming increasingly popular. Head chef and owner Nae Young Jung is from South Korea, and this is strongly reflected in the menu. The Japanese element mostly comes from the sushi offering, while the Korean dishes stick to classics such as kimchi jeon, bibimbap with an egg on top and beef bulgogi. Jung often comes out of the kitchen to chat with diners and ask how they're enjoying the food, which he takes real pride in serving. Miso received an enthusiastic welcome from the day it first opened, and its continuing success is well earned.

Open Tue-Sun; Tue- Fri L 12-3 & D from 5, Sat & Sun open all day, Sat 3-10, Sun 5-10. Closed Mon. **Directions:** North of river, across from Rockwood Parade

MONTMARTRE

1 MARKET YARD SLIGO CO SLIGO   EAT

071 916 9901 | edelmckeon@eircom.net
www.montmartrerestaurant.ie

Although out of the way, this pleasant, unpretentious French-run restaurant has a strong local following and is well worth seeking out. Proprietor-chef Stéphane Magaud's varied menus offer French cuisine in a light, colourful style, with local produce featuring, especially seafood - including local Lissadell mussels, available as starter or main course. Vegetables feature more than is usual in French restaurants, including imaginative vegetarian dishes; also game in season. A good value wine list is also priced separately, to take away. This is fine dining with a light touch - and skilful cooking, attentive service and reasonable prices ensure plenty of repeat customers.

Seats 50. D Tue-Sat, 5-11, also bank hol Sun. Set menus from about €17, also à la carte. Wines from about €22, glass from around €5. Closed Mon, 24-26 Dec. CC. **Directions:** Market Yard is off Dominick Street.

OSTA CAFÉ & WINE BAR

GARAVOGUE WEIR VIEW (NEAR HYDE BRIDGE)
STEPHEN STREET SLIGO CO SLIGO
071 914 4639 | ostacafe@gmail.com | www.osta.ie

EAT | DRINK

Brid Torrades is one of the region's culinary pioneers, well-known for her ardent support of local organic food and small producers - so it should be no surprise to find that the food at her attractive riverside café has immediacy and real depth of flavour. Specialities include great coffee, homebaked breads and pastries, Irish cheeses, charcuterie and a spectacular array of homemade cakes. Other USPs include a great brunch (with full vegetarian breakfast), interesting light evening food, good wines by the glass and events, eg Irish and Spanish speaking groups, music and literary evenings. Café society, in short.

Seats 35 (+ 12 outdoors). Open Mon-Wed 8-7 (later for events); Thu-Fri to 8, Sat-Sun 8-6. (Kitchen closes an hour ahead). A la carte. No reservations; children welcome, toilets wheelchair accessible. Closed Christmas. CC. **Directions:** Town centre, beside the Garavogue River.

SWEET BEAT CAFÉ

BRIDGE STREET SLIGO CO SLIGO   EAT
071 913 879 | hello@sweetbeat.ie
www.sweetbeat.ie

Carolanne Rushe's almost-riverside café is a great place to get your healthy food fix, with tasty plant-based menus offered throughout the day. There's a relaxed youthful vibe and it's a popular meeting place, with regulars constantly calling in. When she opened in 2015, Carolanne was already well known for the Green Warrior stall at Strandhill People's Market, where her vegan salads and other raw foods and juices went down a treat.

These, and some hot specials - a Summer Risotto, perhaps, and Roast Veg Lasagna - are the mainstays here. No need to be vegan, or even vegetarian, to enjoy a visit here - just a little hungry.

Seats about 40 (some outside seats). Open Mon-Sat, 10-5. Closed Sun. **No CC. Directions:** Beside Fureys Pub; at the river end of Bridge Street, on corner with Kempten Promenade.

THOMAS CONNOLLY

1 MARKIEVICZ ROAD RATHQUARTER SLIGO CO SLIGO   DRINK
071 919 4920 | thomasconnollysligo@gmail.com
www.thomasconnollysligo.com

Although named after a Mayor of Sligo who bought the premises in 1861, there's been a pub on this site since 1780. It's one of the great old pubs that are the pride and joy of Sligo - and a particular passion of the current owner, Paul O'Donnell, who took over this magnificent property in 2016. No food but within this famously atmospheric premises, you'll find great drinks - premium whiskeys, craft gins and beers (on tap as

well as bottles), live music and all the big sporting matches too. A truly great Irish pub - with a proud sense of history and a keen enjoyment of the present.

Open Mon-Thu 12 noon-11.30, Fri-Sat 12 noon-12.30, Sun 12.30-11. Music most nights (traditional Irish, Sun 9.30). **Directions:** Town centre; entrances on Markievicz Road (R286, riverside) and (more easily accessed) Holborn Street.

SHELLS BAKERY CAFÉ

SEAFRONT STRANDHILL CO SLIGO
071 912 2938 | hello@shellscafe.com
www.shellscafe.com

EAT | BUY

Jane and Myles Lamberth's pretty little café right on the seafront has become something of a cult destination in Ireland, and it is the first port of call for many regular visitors to Strandhill. Small but mighty, there's an obvious pride in using and producing the best and the menus are surprisingly extensive. All breads and baked treats are made in-house and afternoon tea is a big treat, whether served indoors, in the cute nautically-themed café or - perfect on a sunny day - out on the terrace. They run the lovely Little Shop next door too. A great little spot worth going out of your way for.

Open daily 9-6. No reservations. Licensed. Little Shop also open from 9 daily for home bakes and freshly roasted coffee. Online shop. CC. Directions: On the sea front.

STRANDHILL LODGE & SUITES

TOP ROAD STRANDHILL CO SLIGO
071 912 2122 | info@strandhilllodgeandsuites.com
www.strandhilllodgeandsuites.com

STAY

Aimed at the discerning yet budget-conscious traveller, the Lodge has all the advantages of quality hotel standard accommodation without the price tag that goes with service. It's equally suited to couples seeking a romantic getaway, families who need the space and freedom that you don't normally find at hotels, and business guests. Rooms all have ocean views over the village and everything travellers could wish for - and, teaming up with local businesses, packages are offered with the famous Voya Seaweed Baths and The Venue (see entry). A great asset to Strandhill, and with good food, music and craic available right next door, too.

Rooms 22 (4 suites, 18 deluxe). B&B from about €50pps. Packages (DB&B,with Venue; Spa with Voya) about €120pps. CC. **Directions:** Located on the R292 road 7km from Sligo Town, well signed.

THE DRAFT HOUSE

SHORE ROAD STRANDHILL CO SLIGO
071 912 2222 | info@thedrafthouse.ie
www.thedrafthouse.ie

EAT | DRINK

With its casual food, focus on craft drinks and laid-back vibe, Daniel McGarrigle's gastropub fits in perfectly at this seaside village known for its surfing scene. Head chef Lee Mastin arrived here via The Oarsman in Carrick-on-Shannon, so he came well prepared for the house motto: 'We don't do ordinary'. While menus tick a lot of typical gastropub boxes, particular pride is taken in local suppliers and the Irish craft beers and other speciality drinks offered which partner well with the tasty food. This, plus friendly staff, a fun atmosphere, and an enviable seaside location, make The Draft House a good place to know about on the Wild Atlantic Way.

Open Wed-Sun 12-late. L12-5, D 5-9. A la carte. Families welcome; wheelchair friendly. CC. **Directions:** Centre of Strandhill village, near the shore.

THE VENUE BAR & RESTAURANT

TOP ROAD STRANDHILL CO SLIGO
071 916 8167 | info@venuestrandhill.ie
www.venuestrandhill.ie

EAT | DRINK

Shoreside properties tend to claim the attention in seaside towns, but the inquisitive visitor will find this lovely pub up the hill, overlooking Strandhill Bay. Beyond the cosy, old-world front bar, the restaurant is a big, bright room with panoramic views – a pleasant setting to enjoy good down-to-earth food, notably steaks and local seafood. Everything is wholesome and homemade which, together with the lovely location, friendly atmosphere and pocket-friendly prices, explains its well-deserved popularity. It's a great music pub too, with regular sessions (free entry).

Bar open 12.30-late. **Restaurant seats 120**. Open daily 12.30-9.30. L Mon-Sat 12.30-4. Wine from about €22. [Packages offered with Strandhill Lodge & Suites.] Closed 25-26 Dec & Good Fri. CC. **Directions**: Located on the R292 road 7km from Sligo Town, next door to Strandhill Lodge & Suites.

COILL DARA HOUSE B&B

BALLINA ROAD TUBBERCURRY CO SLIGO   STAY

071 9186095 / 087 259 7700 | patricia@coilldarahouse.ie
www.coilldarahouse.ie

Patricia and Roger McCarrick's beautiful Georgian-style family home, Coill Dara (Wood of Oak), is set in an acre of landscaped gardens on a small sheep farm on the edge of Tubbercurry. Yet, despite its wonderfully away-from-it-all rural ambience, the walk to town takes just five minutes and Ireland West Airport (Knock) is only 15 minutes. Luxurious, family-friendly, pet friendly and offering excellent food, including picnic lunches, it's an ideal centre for exploring Sligo and Mayo and - with a 9-hole golf course, walking trails, guided walks, horse riding and water sports on Lake Talt all nearby, it's perfect for activity breaks. No ordinary B&B.

Rooms 6 (double, twin, family). B&B €90; family room €120.WiFi. Pets by arrangement. Drying room. Picnic lunches available. Ample parking. CC. **Directions:** Off N17 - just outside Tubbercurry on R294.

The Rock of Cashel
Co Tipperary

COUNTY TIPPERARY

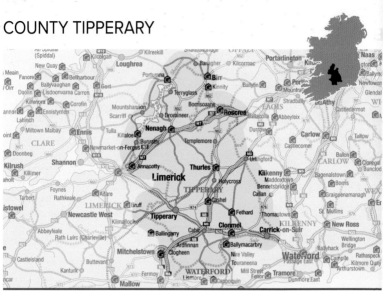

Time to take it all in is a well chosen tagline for Tipperary (www.tipperary.com), for the cup of life is overflowing in this extensive and wondrously fertile county. Describing itself modestly as 'the undiscovered heartland of Ireland', this bountiful place is 'abundant in authentic, yet-to-be discovered experiences that are rooted in a land even more ancient that the historic buildings that remain, yet fully in harmony with the modern world.'

With fertile plains, mountain ranges, lakes and rivers, it's an extraordinarily diverse county and also a great base for touring as - in addition to major attractions within Tipperary, including the **Rock of Cashel**, **Holy Cross Abbey** and **Cahir Castle** - many other destinations such as the Cliffs of Moher, Kilkenny Castle and Cork City are all accessible for a day out.

Along the great river valleys that traverse the county, the prosperous lands of the **Golden Vale** are the heart of the county's agricultural production, supplying many of the foods that members of the excellent **Tipperary Food Producers** (ww.tipperaryfoodproducers.com) take such pride in, and which are proudly showcased in the region's hotels and restaurants.

An increasingly popular destination for walking and outdoor adventure - in the Galtee Mountains, the Glen of Aherlow, the River Suir and the Knockmealdowns - Tipperary also has its own riviera, the beautiful eastern shore of **Lough Derg** (www.waterwaysireland.org). Some of the most striking views of the area are from the Arra Mountains, east of the lough, and lakeside and boating facilities are offered at Ballina, Portroe, Garrykennedy, Dromineer and Terryglass.

And, of course, Tipperary is home to some of Ireland's most famous thoroughbred stud farms, including the world leader, **Coolmore** (www.coolmore.com), and a wonderful destination for an equestrian holiday. So, the recently opened **Fethard Horse Country Experience** (www.fhcexperience.ie), 'An exploration of Tipperary's relationship between the people, the horse and the land which has produced some of the world's finest racehorses', is yet another must-visit in this most generously endowed county.

BROCKA-ON-THE-WATER

KILGARVAN QUAY BALLINDERRY NENAGH CO TIPPERARY　　　　　　　EAT

067 22038 I brockaonthewater@gmail.com

www.facebook.com/BrockaOTW

Anthony and Anne Gernon's almost-waterside restaurant in their home has attracted a following disproportionate to its size over the years. The atmosphere is very much a 'proper restaurant', but with a warm family welcome. Hens cluck around a garden stocked with the fruit and vegetables that will inspire the night's dinner - which also offers popular specialties showcasing local products.

Seats 30. D by reservation, 7-9 Fri-Sat, other nights according to demand (call to check opening times off-season). Set D about €40, also à la carte & vegetarian menu. Wine from €22. Fully wheelchair accessible. Closed Sun. CC. **Directions:** Lough Derg drive, half way between Nenagh and Portumna.

BAILEYS HOTEL CASHEL

MAIN STREET CASHEL CO TIPPERARY　　　　　　　EAT I DRINK I STAY

062 61937 I info@baileyshotelcashel.com

www.baileyshotelcashel.com

Set back from the road, with an attractive planted plaza in front, the Delaney family's fine early 18th century building in the heart of Cashel is a very pleasant place to stay and to experience Irish hospitality and good cooking. Although larger than it looks, with 19 immaculately maintained bedrooms, a Penthouse suite and a leisure centre, a spacious restaurant and cosy cellar bar give it a homely, welcoming feeling.

An appealing all-purpose stop for business people and visitors alike, with the Rock of Cashel and Hore Abbey within walking distance.

Rooms 20 (1 wheelchair friendly, 1 penthouse suite, all with underfloor heating), lift, B&B from €65pps. Restaurant 42: **Seats 60** (+15 outdoors); à la carte L&D. Children welcome before 7pm; bar food daily 12-9.30. Closed 24-28 Dec. CC. **Directions:** Centre of town, opposite post office.

CHEZ HANS

MOORE LANE CASHEL CO TIPPERARY   EAT

062 61177 | www.chezhans.net

Opening a restaurant in a church was highly original when Hans-Peter Matthia did it in 1968, providing an atmospheric setting for some seriously fine food. Still the area's leading restaurant, it's now run by son Jason and his wife Louise who make an equally formidable team. The cooking is outstanding and it merits a special journey - booking ahead is essential. Alongside, Jason's brother Hans runs the smashing little daytime destination

Café Hans (062 63660), serving terrific, flavour-filled modern food - also worth a detour.

Chez Hans: D Tue-Sat 6-10. Weekday D from about €28 (Tue-Thu 6-9.30, Fri 6-7); also à la carte. Closed Sun-Mon, 1 week each Sep, Jan & Easter. CC. **Café Hans:** Tue-Sat, 12-5.30. No reservations. **No CC.** Closed Sun-Mon, 2 weeks Jan. **Also at: Stef Hans, Thurles** (0504 58858; www.facebook.com/stefhanscafe). **Directions:** First right from N8, 50m on left; at foot of Rock of Cashel.

THE OLD CONVENT GOURMET HIDEAWAY

MOUNT ANGLESBY CLOGHEEN CO TIPPERARY   EAT | STAY

052 746 5565 | info@theoldconvent.ie
www.theoldconvent.ie

The perfect destination for couples seeking a short 'get away from it all' experience, Dermot and Christine Gannon's stylish restaurant with accommodation is in one of the most beautiful and unspoilt parts of the country. Dermot's nightly-changing tasting menus offer stunning cooking of their own and local produce, while sumptuously appointed rooms and relaxation areas have wonderful views of the gardens

and countryside. A true gourmet hideaway.

⭐

Rooms 6 (1 shower only); adult destination; B&B from €75pps. Restaurant: D Fri-Sat (& bank hol Sun); children over 12 years welcome. Set 8 course gourmet D about €65; vegetarian menu (advance notice). Closed Sun (except bank hols) & Mon-Thu; closed Christmas-end Jan except New Year. CC. **Directions:** From Clogheen take the Vee/Lismore road, 0.5km on right.

HICKEYS BAKERY & CAFÉ

WEST GATE CLONMEL CO TIPPERARY

EAT | BUY | PRODUCER

052 612 1587 | info@hickeysbakery.com
www.hickeysbakery.com

Visitors to this medieval town are delighted to find this charming fourth-generation craft bakery and café, which has been pleasing customers (including the author, the late William Trevor, who loved the place) since 1901. Nuala Hickey continues the family tradition, baking her unique traditional crusty bread, artisan bread and cakes, including the famous Hickey's barm brack, which is also available online. Beside the bakery counter, the little café is set up with closely packed tables, where locals and visitors mingle cheerfully, enjoying the wholesome food and atmosphere.

Open Mon-Sat 8.30-6. Café wheelchair accessible (1 step to toilets). Closed Sun & bank hol Mon. Online sales. CC. **Directions:** Town centre.

HOTEL MINELLA

COLEVILLE ROAD CLONMEL CO TIPPERARY

STAY

052 612 2388 | frontdesk@hotelminella.com
www.hotelminella.com

Dating back to 1863, the Nallen family's pleasant hotel is attractively located in its own grounds, overlooking the River Suir. A welcoming place where you may well be greeted by the family's friendly Old English Sheepdog, it is the main hotel in the area and, with pleasing public areas and good facilities, it's the hub of local activities. Many of the suites and (recently refurbished) rooms overlook the river and there's a welcoming tone, with complimentary local apples offered at reception - a hint of the hotel's commitment to local food producers, which is seen in the overall food offering including a good breakfast.

Rooms 90 (3 wheelchair friendly). B&B from about €70pps. Children welcome. Leisure centre (20m pool). Weddings/ events. Food available all day. Set L about €32, set D about €40. CC. **Directions:** Edge of Clonmel town.

KILMANEEN FARMHOUSE

ARDFINNAN NEWCASTLE CLONMEL CO TIPPERARY
STAY | LEARN

052 613 6231 | info@kilmaneen.com
www.kilmaneen.com

Set in two acres of garden, with many unusual trees and shrubs, Kevin and Ber O'Donnell's delightfully situated and immaculately maintained farmhouse is on a former dairy farm that has been in Kevin's family for six generations. It's surrounded by three mountain ranges - the Comeraghs, the Knockmealdowns and the Galtees - and close to the rivers Suir and Tar, making it an ideal base for walking and fishing holidays. Genuinely hospitable hosts and homely comforts add up to a real country break here, and a good breakfast will include delicious homemade treats - apple juice from their own trees, compotes with other farm-fresh fruits and freshly baked breads.

Rooms 3 (2 shower only). B&B €from about €40pps. Children welcome; dogs permitted in adjacent self-catering cottage. Closed 1 Dec-1 Jan. CC. **Directions:** In Ardfinnan, follow signs at Hill Bar.

THE WHISKEY STILL

DROMINEER NENAGH CO TIPPERARY
EAT | DRINK

067 24129 | thewhiskeystill@eircom.net
www.facebook.com/The-Whiskey-Still-112124492172236

Joe and Rita Ryan's characterful old place just up from the harbour has a big deck facing the water for fine weather, with patio heaters to extend the long summer evenings and a welcoming stove in the bar for colder days. Always a pleasure to visit and the food is good. Opening times vary, so it is advisable to phone ahead to check opening and food service times, especially off season.

Food served all year. Mon-Fri 5-9.30, Sat & Sun 12.30-8.45. Summer (May-Sep) 12.30-9.30 daily. Reservations advised - essential on Sundays. Traditional music Fri nights & bank hol Sun. CC. **Directions:** in Dromineer village.

MCCARTHY'S PUB

MAIN STREET FETHARD CO TIPPERARY   EAT | DRINK
052 6131149 | vinny@mccarthysfethard.com
www.mccarthyshotel.net

In the middle of medieval Fethard, at the heart of the Tipperary equine scene, McCarthy's is a useful place where you can get anything from a coffee to a casket. Dark and cosy, and lit by oil lamps, very little has changed at this atmospheric bar since it was established in the 1850s by Richard McCarthy, as McCarthy's Hotel. The present proprietor, Vincent Murphy (known to all as Jasper) is the fifth generation running the pub, restaurant and undertakers business with his family. The food is good, including excellent local beef, Cashel Blue cheese - and a good pint too, with Tipperary beers on tap. A real gem and a piece of old Ireland.

Open: Mon-Thu 12 noon-midnight, Fri-Sun 12 noon-1am. A la carte. CC. Closed 25 Dec. **Directions:** Town centre

LARKINS BAR & RESTAURANT

GARRYKENNEDY PORTROE NENAGH CO TIPPERARY   EAT | DRINK
067 23232 | info@larkins.ie
www.larkins.ie

You can't miss this pretty white cottage pub with its cheerful red paintwork at Garrykennedy's charming little harbour. Although not as old as it looks, it has a genuinely traditional ambience and, as the Boyle family are from farming backgrounds, the wholesome food offered by current managers, Cillian and Muireann Boyle, is firmly based in the locality, especially the area's famous meats. You'll find delicious traditional dishes - beef & Guinness stew, bacon & cabbage, Irish stew - alongside modern ones; local beef is the backbone of the evening menu, which takes things up a gear, and service is exceptionally accommodating. Full of character, it's an attractive spot, with music at weekends and on Wednesday in summer (with Irish dancing).

Summer food: Mon-Sun 10.30-9.30. Winter food: Mon-Sun 12-9. Closed 25 Dec. Closed 25 Dec. CC. **Directions:** 12km from Nenagh

COUNTRY CHOICE DELICATESSEN & COFFEE BAR

25 KENYON STREET NENAGH CO TIPPERARY
067 32596 | info@countrychoice.ie
www.countrychoice.ie

EAT | BUY | LEARN
PRODUCER

Peter and Mary Ward are among Ireland's most famous artisan shopkeepers - so plan your itinerary to take in a light meal of simple, seasonal, home-cooked food and some serious shopping. Local foods reflect the agricultural economy of Tipperary, and Peter's cheeses are legendary. Mary, an exceptional cook, quietly produces magnificent terrines from the family's saddleback pigs, thousands of jars of jam in season and vast numbers of handmade Christmas puddings. Definitely worth a detour.

Café: seats 35 (+4 outdoors), open Mon-Sat 9-4.30. Shop open Mon-Sat 9-6; picnic service. Shop & café wheelchair accessible (toilets upstairs). Children welcome. Closed Sun. May be closed Mon in winter, check social media. **Also at:** Limerick Milk Market Fri 10-3 (Sat from 8; Sun from 11); market shop fully wheelchair accessible. CC. **Directions:** Centre of town, on left half way down Kenyon Street.

THE PEPPER MILL

27 KENYON STREET NENAGH CO TIPPERARY
067 34598 | info@thepeppermill.ie
www.thepeppermill.ie

EAT

With interesting, well-sourced food, good cooking and combining value with a sense of occasion, it's no wonder Mairead and Robert Gill's restaurant, The Peppermill, is so popular. A tapas menu is served downstairs in the smart, comfortable wine bar and there's a fine contemporary restaurant on the first floor. Refreshingly straightforward menus show world influences, but there's a welcome leaning towards Irish themes and an emphasis on fish, delivered daily from West Cork. Pleasing choices and good cooking keep satisfied customers returning.

Seats 75 (+ 10 outdoors); D Tue-Fri, 5-9.30; Sat 4-10; Sun 4-9. Early D Tue-Fri 5-7, Sat & Sun 4-6; from about €22. Children welcome; toilets wheelchair accessible. Reservations recommended. Closed Mon, 24-26 Dec & Good Fri. CC. **Directions:** Nenagh town centre.

ASHLEY PARK HOUSE

ARDCRONNEY NENAGH CO TIPPERARY

067 38223 | info@ashleypark.com

www.ashleypark.com

STAY | EAT

Margaret and P.J. Mounsey's home is one of those beautiful 18th century houses where all is elegance, comfort and charm. Surrounded by woodland, and with views of Lough Ourna and the distant Slieve Bloom Mountains, it's just the place for anyone seeking peace and comfort in really splendid surroundings - and it makes a highly romantic wedding venue. Each of the handsome rooms enjoys a fine view - as does the luxurious restaurant overlooking Lough Orna where impressive modern dishes are precisely prepared with ingredients from the walled garden, the local area and the seafood fresh from the coast.

Rooms 5 (2 shower only, 2 family, 1 wheelchair friendly). B&B from €70pps. **Restaurant:** set D from €35, also à la carte. Conferences/banqueting (120). Open all year except Christmas. CC. **Directions:** On the N52, 7km north of Nenagh.

COOLBAWN QUAY LAKESHORE SPA & MARINA

COOLBAWN NENAGH AREA CO TIPPERARY   EAT | STAY

067 28158 | reservations@coolbawnquay.com
www.coolbawnquay.com

This unique resort on Lough Derg is modelled on a 19th century Irish village, with understated luxurious accommodation scattered throughout the pretty cottages. The mini spa, conference facilities, berthing for cruisers (fee applies), charming bar and restaurant all contribute to making this a destination of choice. It is a magical setting for weddings.

Rooms 48 (2 shower only, 1 wheelchair friendly). B&B from about €75pps. Children welcome. **Restaurant Seats 40** (+ 30 outdoors). Non-residents welcome by reservation (not suitable for children under 12). Set D daily in summer 7-9, about €50, also à la carte. Bar food daily in high season. Spa; beauty treatments, massage, relaxation room. Walking, fishing, garden. *Luxury 3 & 4 bed cottages available with hotel-style service. Closed Christmas. CC. **Directions:** located exactly 3.2km past Coolbawn village.

MONAINCHA HOUSE & HEALTH SPA

ROSCREA CO TIPPERARY   STAY

050 523 757 | info@monainchahouse.com
www.monainchahouse.com

Tom and Carmel Moore's 18th-century house is well situated for exploring this beautiful part of the country, but with a health spa (operated by their daughter, Niamh), tennis court, 5 acres of gardens and farmland walks on site, you might not want to venture out very much at all. The rooms are all south facing and have views over the gardens to the countryside beyond. A good choice for a short break.

Rooms 3. B&B about €40pps; group discount, spa packages and guided walking breaks available. **Directions:** 3 km from Roscrea on the N7 (Dublin road), large entrance gates between Roscrea Golf Club and Racket Hall Hotel

FIACRÍ COUNTRY HOUSE RESTAURANT & COOKERY SCHOOL

BOULEREA KNOCK ROSCREA CO TIPPERARY
0505 43017 | fiacrihouse@eircom.net
www.fiacrihouse.com

EAT | LEARN

Enda and Ailish Hennessy's country house-style restaurant and cookery school is well worth seeking out as it offers excellent cooking and the caring service that makes a special experience. Ailish showcases the food of the area and, while menus are balanced, local meats are especially good. Cookery classes are offered throughout the year and Ailish aims to teach cooking skills in an atmosphere in which students will also make new friends. A very popular restaurant – advance booking is essential.

Seats 70. D Wed-Sat, 7-9.15. Early D Wed-Fri 7-8, from about €43; 5 course D €53. Full bar licence. Toilets wheelchair accessible. Reservations required; unsuitable for children under 12. Closed Sun-Tue and 25 Dec, Good Fri. *Cookery classes run throughout the year, suitable for individuals, groups and team building packages etc; new recipes each year. **Directions:** 10km from Roscrea.

COUNTY WATERFORD

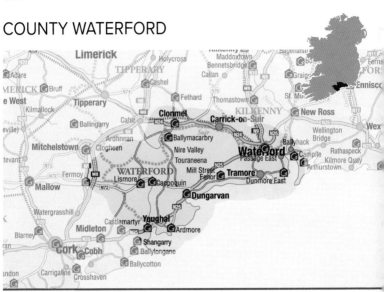

Waterford's quays www.watefordcity.ie are witness to a trading and seafaring tradition which goes back at least 1,150 years. But this sense of history also looks to the future, as Waterford is popular as a Tall Ships assembly port. Today's larger commercial ships may be berthed downstream on the other side of the river at Belview, but the old cityside quays on the south bank retain a nautical flavour which is accentuated by useful marina berthing facilities in the heart of town.

This fine port was founded in 853 AD when the Vikings - Danes for the most part - established the trading settlement of Vadrefjord. Its strategic location in a sheltered spot at the head of the estuary near the confluence of the Suir and Barrow rivers guaranteed its continuing success under different administrators, particularly the Normans, so much so that it tended to overshadow the county of Waterford, almost all of which is actually to the west of the city.

The county town is Dungarvan www.dungarvantourism.com , which is two-thirds of the way westward along Waterford's extensive southern shore – the Copper Coast. This spreading of the administrative centres of gravity has balanced the life of the Waterford region. Yet the extreme west of the county is still one of Ireland's best kept secrets, a place of remarkable beauty between the Knockmealdown, Comeragh and Monavullagh mountains, where fish-filled rivers such as the Bride, the Blackwater, and the Nire www.nirevalley.com make their way seawards at different speeds through valleys of remarkable variety and beauty, past pretty towns and villages such as romantic, castle-bedecked Lismore www.lismorecastle.com .

LOCAL ATTRACTIONS AND INFORMATION

>Tramore **Tramore House Gardens** 051 386 303

>**Waterford Airport** 051 875 589

>Waterford **Waterford Crystal Glass Centre** 051 332 500

>**Waterford Int. Festival of Light Opera** (Sept) 051 375 437

>Waterford **Theatre Royal** 051 874 402

>Waterford **Tourism Information** 051 875 823

THE CLIFF HOUSE HOTEL

ARDMORE CO WATERFORD

024 87800 | info@thecliffhousehotel.com

www.thecliffhousehotel.com

EAT | STAY

A bold modern boutique hotel overlooking Ardmore Bay, this chic bolthole draws guests as much for the culinary offerings as the setting. Dutch head chef Martijn Kajuiter strives for perfection using meticulously sourced local and seasonal produce to deliver stunning cooking that appeals to adventurous diners. General Manager Adriaan Bartels is well known for his warmth and discreet customer care, and this luxury hotel has earned a reputation for service too. The Well spa includes a stunningly positioned outdoor infinity pool overlooking the bay.

⭐

Rooms 39. Room rate about €225. L & D daily 12-5 & 6.30-10 (to 9 Sun). Set L from about €30; D menus €65-€85; also à la carte; Children welcome; reservations required; toilets wheelchair accessible. Bar food daily 12-9. Restaurant closed Sun-Mon (+Tue off season. Hotel closed 24-26 Dec. CC. **Directions:** N25-R673; end of Ardmore village.

WHITE HORSES RESTAURANT

ARDMORE CO WATERFORD

024 94040 | whitehorses@eircom.net

EAT

Christine Power and Geraldine Flavin's delightfully bright and breezy café-restaurant is open for all the little lifts that visitors need – morning coffee, afternoon tea – as well as imaginative lunches (plus Sunday lunch, which runs all afternoon) and a more ambitious à la carte evening menu. Offering a good balance between traditional dishes and more adventurous fare, it's equally good for a reviving cuppa and a sweet treat from the luscious homemade selection on display, or a full meal. The cooking is consistently excellent and the pleasant and well-organised service is another reason that happy customers keep returning to this well-run establishment.

Open May-Sep: Tue-Sun 11-'late'; L 12.30-3.30, D 6-10. Winter, weekends only: Fri from 6, Sat 11-11 & Sun 12-6. Closed Mon all year, except bank hols (bank hol opening as Sun), 1 Jan-13 Feb. CC. **Directions:** Centre of village.

GLASHA

GLASHA BALLYMACARBRY VIA CLONMEL CO WATERFORD   STAY

052 613 6108 | glasha@eircom.net
www.glashafarmhouse.com

Olive and the late Paddy O'Gorman made their hospitable farmhouse beside the river Nire into the kind of relaxed country retreat visitors to Ireland dream of finding, with rooms that are luxurious for a farm stay, and plenty of comfy lounging room too. Ideal for lovers of outdoor pursuits, it's a walkers' paradise - Glasha links the Comeragh and Knockmealdown sections of the Munster Way - and the nearest pub is just 3 minutes' walk. Olive makes a delicious home-cooked dinner for guests, by arrangement, and it's just a lovely place to stay.

Rooms 6 (4 jacuzzi bath, 2 shower only); B&B about €60pps. Children welcome. Residents' D Mon-Sat, 6.30-8.30 by arrangement, from about €25. Closed D Sun, 20-27 Dec. CC. **Directions:** Off R671 Clonmel- Dungarvan, 3.5km from Ballymacarbry.

HANORA'S COTTAGE

NIRE VALLEY BALLYMACARBRY CO WATERFORD

052 613 6134 | hanorascottage@eircom.net

www.hanorascottage.com

EAT | STAY

Equally wonderful for foot-weary walkers and desk-weary city folk in need of clean country air, this spacious and beautifully located country guesthouse is a very special place. Mary Wall and her family offer outstanding hospitality, luxurious accommodation - and a special focus on good food. Eoin and Judith Wall are both Euro-Toques chefs, using local foods from small suppliers whenever possible and crediting them on the menu. People travel from far and wide to dine in the restaurant and overnight guests begin the day with Hanora's legendary breakfast buffet - it takes some time to get the measure of this feast, so make sure you get up in time to make the most of it.

Rooms 10. Restaurant: D Mon-Sat, 7-8.45. Not suitable for children. Reservations advised. Closed Christmas week. CC. **Directions:** Take Clonmel/Dungarvan (R671) road, turn off at Ballymacarbry.

BARRONS BAKERY & COFFEE SHOP

COOK STREET CAPPOQUIN CO WATERFORD
058 54045 | info@barronsbakery.ie
www.barronsbakery.ie

EAT | BUY | PRODUCER

Esther and Joe Barron's business dates back to 1887, and this wonderfully traditional bakery still uses the original Scotch brick ovens to make breads with real flavour and an old-fashioned crust. The range is wide, but the Waterford 'blaa' is unique; made in two varieties. 'Soft' and 'Crusty', this traditional white yeasted roll is produced by only four bakeries, all in the Waterford/Kilkenny area, and has held EU Protected Geographical Indication (PGI) status since 2013 - one of only a handful of Irish products to have achieved this distinction. Alongside the bakery, the Barron family run a delightful coffee shop, which serves lunch and wholesome daytime snacks and is deservedly popular.

Seats 50 (+6 outdoors). Bakery and café open Mon-Sat 8.30-5.30. Wheelchair access. Closed Sun. **Also at:** Dungarvan Farmers' Market. CC.

RICHMOND HOUSE

CAPPOQUIN CO WATERFORD
058 54278 | info@richmondhouse.net
www.richmondhouse.net

EAT | STAY

Genuine hospitality, high standards of comfort, caring service and excellent food are all to be found in the Deevy family's fine 18th century country house and restaurant just outside Cappoquin. Claire or Jean Deevy will usually be there to welcome guests, and show you to one of the nine individually decorated bedrooms. The restaurant is the heart of Richmond House, with Paul an ardent supporter of local produce. Menus balance traditional country house cooking and more adventurous dishes inspired by international trends. Service is attentive and discreet and the Deevys make sure you will have a memorable breakfast to see you on your way too.

Rooms 9. B&B from about €60pps. D daily from 6pm (early menu Tue-Fri), set D about €55. Closed pre-Christmas to about mid Jan. CC. **Directions:** 1km outside Cappoquin on N72.

THE TANNERY RESTAURANT & TOWNHOUSE

10 QUAY STREET DUNGARVAN CO WATERFORD   EAT | STAY | LEARN

058 45420 | info@tannery.ie

www.tannery.ie

Paul and Maire Flynn's stylish contemporary restaurant in Dungarvan has been delighting discerning diners since 1997. Paul's menus are wonderfully simple yet, paradoxically, the food tastes very exciting - exceptional cooking uses the best local ingredients to produce deliciously eclectic fare with a strong Irish slant. Attentive and efficient service and an interesting, well-priced wine list enhance a standout experience. There is also an atmospheric Wine Bar, and chic accommodation at The Tannery Townhouse (beside the Cookery School), with a very good breakfast served in the restaurant.

⭐

Rooms 14 (12 shower only), children welcome. DB&B from about €140pps, D from about €33. Restaurant (reservations advised): L Fri 12.30-2.30, Sun to 3.30. D Tue-Sat 5.30-9. Wine Bar (no reservations): evenings only, closed Mon (also Sun except Jul-Aug). Closed 25-26 Dec, Good Fri, 2 wks Jan. CC. **Directions:** Beside old market house.

LEMON TREE CAFÉ

SEACLIFF COXTOWN DUNMORE EAST CO WATERFORD   EAT

051 383 164 | info@lemontreecatering.ie

www.lemontreecatering.ie

Joan Power's gem of a café is just outside Dunmore East village, but well worth the effort of seeking out for lovely fresh fish and home baking. There's a welcoming decking area and, while the décor is low-key, there's original artwork (for sale) and some entertaining notices that bring smiles to customers' faces. They do breakfast and afternoon tea, and at lunchtime spanking fresh fish, salads and very tasty soups feature, together with a tempting snack menu. Staff are very friendly and efficient and it's good to see the restaurant's suppliers chalked up on a blackboard on the wall. A very pleasant spot.

Open Jun-Aug: Mon-Thu 9-7, Fri- Sat 9-9.30, Sun 9.30-4. Early D 5-7. Sep-May: Tue-Sat 9-6, Sun 9.30-4.30. D Fri & Sat 5-9.30, all year. Closed Mon & Nov. CC. **Directions:** Past the harbour, 200m up the hill.

THE COPPER HEN

FENOR CO WATERFORD   EAT

051 330 300 | info@thecopperhen.ie
www.thecopperhen.ie

The scenery of Waterford's 'copper coast' is a treat in store for visitors – and the savvy traveller will plan to fit in a visit to The Copper Hen, run by talented chef Eugene Long and his wife Sinead Frisby. A lovely space above Mother McHugh's pub, it has put the small village of Fenor firmly on the food lover's map. Eugene is proud to name suppliers of the quality local and Irish ingredients used in his excellent and stylishly presented cooking - which may well include the delicious local Comeragh Mountain Lamb, along with fresh fish from Dunmore East - and friendly, informed service is another highlight of this appealing and wallet-friendly casual restaurant.

D Wed-Sat from 5.30. Set D from about €22. Daily specials; vegetarian & gluten-free dishes. L Sun only, 12.30-4.30. **Directions:** Coast road, about 6km from Tramore.

BALLYRAFTER COUNTRY HOUSE HOTEL

LISMORE CO WATERFORD   EAT | STAY

058 54002 | info@ballyrafterhouse.com
www.ballyrafterhouse.com

Ballyrafter House was built by the Duke of Devonshire as his estate manager's residence and overlooks the Duke's fairy tale Lismore Castle. Today Joe and Noreen Willoughby run it as a welcoming country house hotel, where fishing is a big draw but a relaxing laid-back atmosphere, log fires and good home cooking also add up to an appealing package for all guests - as many new fans have discovered in recent years. The great charm of Ballyrafter (aside from its owners) is that - while continuously upgraded - it has escaped over-energetic refurbishment and remains its characterful self.

Rooms 10 (3 shower only). Rooms from about €50pps. Restaurant: D about €44, daily in summer 7-9.30 (Mon, residents only), winter Sat only (bar & restaurant). L Sun only, 1-2.30, about €28. Bar Meals: 12.30-6 daily. CC. **Directions:** Cappoquin side of town.

THE SUMMERHOUSE CAFÉ

MAIN STREET LISMORE CO WATERFORD EAT | PRODUCER

058 54148 | info@thesummerhouse.ie

www.facebook.com/pg/The-Summerhouse-Café

This appealing all-day café is the go-to place in Lismore for food lovers - and, in a roundabout way, it's one of the most interesting food destinations in the country. Using only the best ingredients is a point of pride here, and it shows - and, not only do goodies a-plenty, including freshly baked breads, lunches and other treats please proprietor Gael Byrne's customers very much indeed, but the bakery is where the superb, distinctively packaged and eminently giftworthy Lismore Food Company (www.thelismorefoodcompany.com) biscuit range is produced by Gael's husband Owen Madden, his brother Ken, and chef Beth-Ann Smith. It's quite a place - and Gael is a gifted florist as well.

Open Tue-Sun 10-5. Closed Sun & Mon. CC. **Directions:** At the east end of Main Street, across from the Post Office and supermarket.

BAY TREE BISTRO

16 MERCHANTS QUAY WATERFORD CO WATERFORD EAT

051 858517 | thebaytreebistrowaterford@gmail.com

www.thebaytreebistro.ie

Keith and Carmel Boyle's spacious two-storey restaurant makes an atmospheric setting for some impressive cooking and its popularity is not surprising. "Locally sourced food, cooked local, by a local chef" is the mantra that has diners beating a path to the door, and Keith's seasonal cooking is a tribute to quality suppliers, including some lesser known local gems alongside the national names. They have also earned a reputation for great service, value and a good drinks list, including craft beers - and the pleasing combination of old and new gives this lovely premises a warmly welcoming feeling, conveying a sense of occasion. A treat in store.

D Tue-Sat 5-10. Early D Tue-Thu all evening, Fri-Sat 5-6.30, from about €23. D from about €35 (wine pairings from €15 extra). Closed Sun-Mon. CC. **Directions:** South quays, second block from Edmund Rice bridge.

BODÉGA!

54 JOHN STREET WATERFORD CO WATERFORD

EAT | DRINK

051 844 177 | info@bodegawaterford.com
www.bodegawaterford.com

Firmly established as a Waterford favourite that delivers quality and value, this warmly atmospheric place glows with warm Mediterranean colours and it's always busy. Proprietor Cormac Cronin has a high regard for the raw materials in the region; 85-90% of their ingredients are produced locally, suppliers are proudly name-checked on menus and the drinks list includes local craft beers. At lunchtime it attracts young people, some with children – who are made especially welcome – and, while prices rise later, the early dinner menu is a snip. Regular live music too, including big names. Burzza 'Neapolitan Pizza & Proper Burger' restaurant next door is under the same management.

Open Mon-Sat 12-10. Children welcome. Set L from about €20, D from about €23. Closed Sun except bank hol weekends, Good Fri, 25/26 Dec, 1 Jan. CC. **Directions:** City centre.

GRANVILLE HOTEL

MEAGHER QUAY WATERFORD CO WATERFORD

051 305 555 | stay@granville-hotel.ie

www.granville-hotel.ie

EAT | STAY

A former GCGuides Hotel of the Year and one of the country's oldest hotels, this much-loved quayside establishment has been owner-run since 1979 by the Cusack family, who have restored the old building to its former glory. The overall food style is proudly traditional, with some local specialities featuring, and the hotel's Bianconi Restaurant delivers good value and excellent cooking by Executive Head Chef Stephen Hooper, so reservations are essential. As elsewhere in the hotel, it is the warm Irish hospitality and service that really make a visit here memorable.

Rooms 100. B&B from €60pps. Lift. No pets. Free overnight parking for residents, 5pm-noon. Restaurant: D daily 5-9.30, L Sun only, 12-30-5; early D from about €23, Set D about €33, also à la carte. Bar food daily. 10-9.30. Closed 25-27 Dec. CC.: **Directions:** on the quays opposite Clock Tower

LA BOHÈME

2 GEORGE STREET WATERFORD CO WATERFORD

051 875 645 | labohemewaterford@gmail.com

www.labohemerestaurant.ie

EAT

Christine and Eric Thèze's elegant fine dining restaurant in the vaulted basement of Waterford's Chamber of Commerce building is smart and stylish with a lovely French vibe. Warm and friendly French waiters give one a feeling of being in expert hands and gleaming glass, silver, and crisp white linen are perfect in this room. The cooking style is modern classic French, with seasonally-changed menus offering Irish meats, seafood, rabbit and veal in dishes that typify French restaurants while giving credit to quality local produce. A strongly French wine list offers value in regional wines – and service is excellent. This restaurant is serious about its food and is a great asset to Waterford city.

Seats 60. D Mon-Sat, 5.30-late, L Fri only. Set D menus from about €26. Children welcome Wheelchair lift. Closed Sun (except bank hol weekends), 25-27 Dec. CC.

MOMO

47 PATRICK STREET WATERFORD CO WATERFORD   EAT

051 581 509 | kamila@momorestaurant.ie
www.momorestaurant.ie

Open since 2014, the cheery brightly-painted frontage of Harry O'Neill and Kamila Bystrzonowska's welcoming restaurant would be hard to miss, and they offer a great combination of lively international menus, a commitment to local sourcing, good cooking and a relaxed informal vibe. Healthily delicious just about sums up the food at Momo, as special dietary needs are anticipated in mainstream dishes, everything is homemade (right down to the stocks), and the wide range of dishes offered includes loads of gorgeous salads, wholesome slow cooked meats and fresh fish that's sourced daily from nearby fishing ports. Reasonably priced wines and local craft beers too. A smashing place all round.

Seats 60. Open Tue-Sat 12-9 (Fri-Sat to 10), Sun 1-8. Early D Tue-Sat 5-6.30 (all day Sun). Wheelchair accessible. CC.
Directions: Town centre; opposite Omniplex

WATERFORD CASTLE HOTEL & GOLF RESORT

THE ISLAND BALLINAKILL WATERFORD CO WATERFORD   EAT | STAY
051 878 203 | info@waterfordcastleresort.com
www.waterfordcastleresort.com

Serenely situated on its own wooded island (complete with 18-hole golf course) this beautiful hotel dates back to the 16th century, and is reached by a private ferry. Combining the elegance of earlier times with modern comfort, service and convenience, it also offers atmospheric fine dining in the richly panelled Munster Room restaurant where Head Chef Michael Thomas showcases local seasonal foods and, as elsewhere in the hotel, discreet staff look after guests magnificently. A very special place.

Rooms 19. B&B from about €65pps. Lift. Restaurant: D daily, 7-9 (to 8.30 Sun); Bar Menu 12.30-6. Traditional Afternoon Tea 3-5 daily, €30 (booking advised). Self-catering lodges in grounds. Open all year. CC. **Directions:** Outskirts of Waterford City just off Dunmore East road.

GROW HQ

FARRONSHONEEN DUNMORE ROAD WATERFORD CO WATERFORD   EAT | BUY,
051 584422 | hello@growhq.org   LEARN | PRODUCER
www.growhq.org

Michael Kelly is the driving force behind the Grow It Yourself (GIY) movement and it's hard to imagine anyone other than the charismatic former journalist being able to get it going at all, never mind achieve its phenomenal growth - and, most recently, the opening of the beautiful GIY headquarters and café in Ardkeen. Here, head chef JB Dubois and his talented kitchen team transform the seasonal harvest (and other organic, chemical free, free-range ingredients sourced locally) into delicious plant-based, but not entirely vegetarian, meals. A fantastic place, and well worth visiting for a delicious bite to eat and a good browse.

Seats 65. Open daily 9-5, D Fri & Sat to 8.30. Shop. Wheelchair accessible. CC. **Directions:** Opposite University Hospital Waterford.

GAULTIER LODGE

WOODSTOWN CO WATERFORD

051 382 549 | gaultierlodge@yahoo.ie
www.gaultierlodge.com

STAY

Snugged down in sand dunes for shelter beside Woodstown Strand, Sheila Molloy's early 19th century lodge offers wonderful views from the upper windows, right across the Suir estuary, to Duncannon and the Hook. Set in large gardens it has great style and, like Sheila herself, this lovely house will lift the spirits. When dinner is unavailable the restaurants of Dunmore East are just three miles away.

Rooms 3 (1 shower only). B&B from €75pps. D by arrangement (book 24 hours in advance; not always available), about €50. Dogs welcome in kennels (free). Closed end Oct-mid- Apr. **No CC. Directions:** From Waterford take R684, Dunmore East road. Take left for Woodstown after 4km. Right at beach, last house on left behind high wall.

COUNTY WESTMEATH

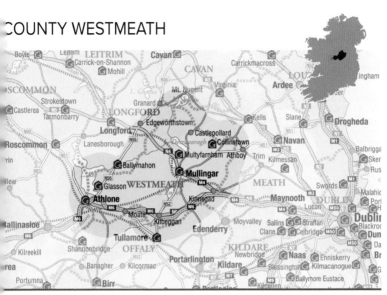

In the distant past, Westmeath tended to be ruled by whoever held Meath, or perhaps it was the other way around. But today, Westmeath www.westmeathtourism.com is a county so successfully developing its own identity that they should find a completely new name for the place. For this is somewhere that makes the very best of what it has to hand.

Its highest "peak" is only the modest Mullaghmeen of 258 m, 10 kilometres north of Castlepollard. But this is in an area where hills of ordinary height have impressive shapes which make them appear like miniature mountains around the spectacularly beautiful Lough Derravaragh, famed for its association with the legend of the Children of Lir. Turned into swans by their wicked step-mother, they were swans for 900 years until saved by the coming of Christianity.

Westmeath abounds in lakes to complement Derravaragh, such as the handsome expanses of Lough Owel and Lough Ennell on either side of the fine county town of Mullingar www.mullingar.ie , where life has been made even more watery in recent years with the restoration of the Royal Canal, which loops like a moat round the town on its way from Dublin to the north Shannon.

Meanwhile, Athlone www.athlone.ie on the Shannon to the southwest has a real buzz, and north of it there's the wide lake of Lough Ree in all its glory, wonderful for boating in an area where the Goldsmith country verges towards County Longford, and they've a monument to mark what some enthusiasts reckon to be the true geographical centre of all Ireland. You really can't get more utterly rural than that.

LOCAL ATTRACTIONS AND INFORMATION

>Athlone **Athlone Castle Visitor Centre**
090 649 2912

>Athlone **Tourism Information**
www.athlone.ie | 090 649 4630

>Castlepollard T**ullynally Castle & Gardens**
www.tullynallycastle.ie | 044 49060

>Glasson **Glasson Rose Festival** (August)
090 6485677

THE FATTED CALF

CHURCH STREET ATHLONE CO WESTMEATH

EAT

090 643 3371 | fiona@thefattedcalf.ie

www.thefatttedcalf.ie

When chef Feargal O'Donnell and his wife Fiona opened here in 2015 they brought a following from their previous business, an atmospheric gastro-pub in Glasson. It was a dramatic change of style, but excellent, stylish cooking by Feargal and chef Deirdre Adamson - matched by friendly and efficient service from Fiona and her team - ensured their chic modern restaurant soon became one of the most popular dining destinations in the town. Alongside good food, an interesting drinks list (including craft beers and cider) and a relaxed ambience, this smart restaurant offers good value too, notably on the lunch and Midweek Supper menus.

Open: D Tue-Sat 5.30-9.30, L Fri & Sat 12.30-2. L from about €15. Midweek Supper Menu from about €25, D à la carte. Closed Sun & Mon. CC. **Directions:** Beside main entrance to town centre shopping centre.

KIN KHAO THAI RESTAURANT

1 ABBEY LANE ATHLONE CO WESTMEATH   EAT
090 649 8805 | info@kinkhaothai.ie
www.kinkhaothai.ie

With its vivid yellow and red exterior making it a beacon for hungry diners, you can't miss this restaurant near the castle. Run by Irishman Adam Lyons and his Thai wife, Janya - whose family is steeped in restaurant and food tradition — this is undoubtedly one of the best Thai restaurants in Ireland, and good value for money too. It is deservedly popular and reservations are strongly advised. Well worth a detour - you're in for a real treat here.

D daily 5.30-10.30; L Wed-Fri 12.30-2.30, both a la carte. Sun L 1-3. Early D 5.30-7 Mon-Fri, to 6.30 Fri & Sat, from about €20. Children welcome. Closed 24/25 Dec, Easter Sun. CC. Directions: Castle side of town, 100 metres from Seans Bar.

THE LEFT BANK BISTRO

FRY PLACE ATHLONE CO WESTMEATH   EAT
090 649 4446 | info@leftbankbistro.com
www.leftbankbistro.com

Thanks to its understatedly pleasing surroundings, carefully sourced ingredients and smart modern cooking, Annie McNamara and Mary McCullagh's elegantly informal, contemporary restaurant is a top choice for a meal in Athlone. The keenly priced menus offer a wide range of delicious-sounding dishes with a multicultural stamp - and, for the quality of the food and cooking (and an interesting wine list), a meal here is always good value. Carefully selected small range of speciality products on sale too.

Seats 60. Open Tue-Sat from 10.30; L 12-5 & D from 5.30. Early D from about €20, (all night Tue-Fri & Sat 5-6.30), also à la carte; wine from €20. Toilets wheelchair accessible; children welcome. Closed Sun & Mon, bank hols & Christmas period. CC. **Directions:** Behind Athlone Castle, west side of the Shannon.

SEAN'S BAR

13 MAIN STREET ATHLONE CO WESTMEATH   DRINK

090 649 2358 | info@seansbar.ie
www.seansbar.ie

West of the river, in the interesting old part of Athlone town near the Norman castle, this seriously historic bar lays claim to being the pub with the longest continuous use in Ireland. All owners since 900 AD are on record and a glass case containing a section of old wattle wall original to the building highlights the age of the bar, but it's far from being a museum piece and is a legendary watering hole for Shannon boating folk. Dimly lit, with a sloping floor (to allow receding flood waters to drain), mahogany bar, mirrored shelving and open fire, it may not be a food destination, but it's an atmospheric setting for music sessions and they serve a great pint.

Closed 25 Dec & possibly Good Fri.
Directions: On the west quayside, just in front of the castle.

THYME RESTAURANT

CUSTUME PLACE ATHLONE CO WESTMEATH   EAT
090 647 8850 | info@thymerestaurant.ie
www.thymerestaurant.ie

This pleasing little restaurant is central but it could easily be missed - and that would be a pity as 'Delicious food at affordable prices' is the stated aim, and it's something that they achieve very well. Owner-chef John Coffey sources ingredients with great care and ensures that everything travels as short a distance as possible - most of the key ingredients on his imaginative, seasonally-changing menus are from Athlone and the general midlands area and his Kilmore Quay "Irish, sustainable and fresh" fish dishes are particularly interesting. Lovely food, and good value; the early dinner is a snip.

Seats 40. D Mon-Sat 5-10, Sun 1-8. Value Menu from €25, Sun-Thu 5-10, Fri- Sat 5-6.30; otherwise à la carte. Closed 2 weeks late Jan/early Feb. CC. **Directions:** Just off the main street, near the bridge on the eastern side.

LOUGH BISHOP HOUSE

DERRYNAGARRA COLLINSTOWN CO WESTMEATH   STAY
044 966 1313 I chkelly@eircom.net
www.loughbishophouse.com

In a beautifully scenic area awash with lakes, gentle hills and rich farmland, Helen and Christopher Kelly offer a warm welcome and a genuine Irish family home experience on their organic farm, famed for its moiled cattle and Irish Draught horses. Everything is spotless and gleaming, and the very comfortable rooms are TV-free zones. Dinner offers excellent home-cooked food, including some ingredients grown or reared on the farm, and there's home-baked bread, fresh fruit and apple juice from the orchard at breakfast. Magical midlands!

Rooms 3 (2 shower only). B&B about €65pps; children welcome. Residents' D 7.30pm (book before noon), about €35. Cottage also available for self-catering or B&B (2 night min stay). CC. **Directions:** Castlepollard R394, at Whitehall turn onto L5738, 3km on right hand side

---

GLASSON HOTEL & GOLF CLUB

GLASSON ATHLONE CO WESTMEATH   STAY
090 648 5120 I info@glassongolf.ie
www.glassongolfhotel.ie

Beautifully situated on a hillside overlooking Lough Ree, the Reid family's impressive hotel has been developed around their fine old family home. Although the golf club has earned an international reputation as one of Ireland's premier inland courses, the hotel is equally attractive to business guests and non-golfers, and has become a favourite place to stay for many regular visitors to this very special area. It is also popular as a wedding venue - whatever the reason for your visit, it is a lovely place to stay.

Rooms 65 (3 wheelchair friendly, 15 family rooms); Lift. B&B from about €85pps. Pets by arrangement. Killinure Restaurant: L&D daily. Bar food daily 12-9.30pm. Sauna, steam room, beauty treatments. Special breaks offered. Closed 25 Dec. CC. **Directions:** 10km north of Athlone, off the N55 Cavan-Longford road.

GLASSON VILLAGE RESTAURANT

GLASSON CO WESTMEATH   EAT

090 648 5001 | michaelrosebrooks@gmail.com
www.glassonvillagerestaurant.ie

Chef-proprietor Michael Brooks opened this attractive restaurant in 1986, making him the culinary pioneer of the area. It's an old-fashioned place in a nice way - and that is its appeal for many of his regular customers. But the cooking is imaginative – traditional French meets modern Irish – and, unusually for the midlands, fresh fish has always featured strongly. A true love of food, together with caring service and good value have earned a loyal following.

Seats 60. D Tue -Sat 5.30-9; L Sun only, set 3-course menus about €26, two sittings (1 & 3). Set D Sat about €35, also à la carte; early 3-course D from about €30, Tue-Fri, 5.30-9. Children welcome (half portions main menu). Parking (25). Closed D Sun, all Mon also Tue in winter. CC. **Directions:** 8 km from Athlone on Longford/Cavan road (N55)

GROGAN'S PUB

GLASSON CO WESTMEATH   DRINK

090 648 5158 | grogansofglasson@hotmail.com
www.grogansofglasson.com

Very typical of Goldsmith's 'Village of the roses', this pretty flower-bedecked pub is one of those proudly-run, traditional places with two little bars at the front (one with a welcome open fire in winter) and everything gleaming. Currently run by Moira and Miriam Grogan, it was established in 1750 and feels as if the fundamentals haven't changed too much since then. Wholesome food is served in the back bar and on Friday nights there's traditional music, when three generations of the same family play and visiting musicians are also welcome.

Food served Mon-Sat 12-9, (Sun to 8). Value menu from about €22 (available Mon-Sat 4-9, Sun & bank hol Mon 4-8). Children's menu. Sun L 12.30-3.30, à la carte. Monthly specials. Wines from €21. Closed 25 Dec. CC. **Directions:** Centre of village.

WINEPORT LODGE

GLASSON CO WESTMEATH   EAT | STAY
090 643 9010 | lodge@wineport.ie
www.wineport.ie

Ray Byrne and Jane English's unique shoreside lodge overlooking Lough Ree started life in 1993 as a restaurant and - although it now has thirty beautiful rooms (all with private balconies overlooking the lake), a hot tub and treatment rooms - the lovely contemporary restaurant remains its heart, serving fine meals with warmth and professionalism. The food experience has always been about seasonal local produce and a formal meal in this stunning venue is a special outing - but it's also ideal for Afternoon Tea or a casual daytime bite in the bar, and it makes a perfect journey break.

Rooms 29 (2 wheelchair accessible). Lift. B&B from about €60pps. D daily 5.30-9 (Sun 6-9), Sun L 1.30-3.30. Bar food daily 12-9. Short breaks; small conferences/meetings; weddings. Closed 24-26 Dec. CC. **Directions:** Cavan exit off the M6 at Athlone.

SHANNON PRINCESS

QUIGLEYS MARINA KILLINURE POINT GLASSON ATHLONE CO WESTMEATH   STAY

087 251 4809 | info@shannonprincess.com

www.shannonprincess.com

Discerning visitors interested in a week's luxury hotel-style barge cruise on the Shannon should check out Ruari and Olivia Gibbons' Shannon Princess, which is based near Athlone. They operate a full-board itinerary between Glasson and Killaloe on alternate weeks, with shore excursions in their own mini bus along the way - to the Kilbeggan Distillery, for example. The beautiful en-suite cabins have proper plumbing - toilets and showers, just like home - and electricity. Most of the (very good) meals are served on board - and the rate includes all meals (on board and ashore), drinks, transfers, admissions and shore excursions.

Cabins 5 (double or twin, all en-suite). Charter (groups of 6-10) or individual bookings. Children welcome with charter bookings, individual booking over 14s only; pets charter only. Guide price, from about €3,750/US$4.400 per person for the week, full board.

ANNEBROOK HOUSE HOTEL

AUSTIN FRIARS STREET MULLINGAR CO WESTMEATH   STAY | EAT
044 935 3300 | info@annebrook.ie
www.annebrook.ie

Built around a beautiful old house, with the town park on the doorstep and the River Brosna flowing through the grounds, it's all distinctly fairy tale for a town centre hotel. Bedrooms, in a new build, are comfortably furnished and impressive public rooms in the original house include The Old House Bar (complete with grand piano), which is available for private parties, and the Old House Restaurant; a series of rooms in the cellars of the original house, this atmospheric restaurant is the antithesis of the standard hotel dining room and one of the area's top dining destinations. Popular for weddings and business, this friendly hotel is also ideal for a weekend away.

Rooms 75. B&B from about €40pps. Self-catering apartments. **Old House Restaurant:** D Thu-Sat 6-9 (Sat to 10). Sun L 2-5. Berty's Bar 12-9. CC. **Directions:** On main street.

MILLER & COOK

50 PEARSE STREET MULLINGAR CO WESTMEATH   EAT | BUY | PRODUCER
044 934 0884 or **085 872 4666** | info@millerandcook.ie
www.millerandcook.ie

Formerly a bank, Mark Gavin's stylish bakery, café and food hall has been a regular haunt for food lovers in the area since it opened in 2013. 'Local Goodness' is the admirable motto of this vibrant business and it's seen in action everywhere, including the two eating areas ('The Front Room' and 'Bistro'), just inside the front and back entrances, and the quality produce - much of it local, including in-house products - on sale in the food hall. The first floor has been renovated and 'Upstairs' is open for Sunday lunch and private dining. A must-visit destination for visitors to Mullingar.

Seats 130 (+ 6 outdoors). Front Room: Tue–Sat 8.30am-9.30pm, Sun 10-5, (shop Mon-Sat to 5, Sun to 4). Bistro 8.30-3. 'Upstairs' Sun L 12.30–5. Wheelchair accessible (lift). Parking. **Directions:** Centre of Mullingar, opposite the Tourist Office.

MORNINGTON HOUSE

MORNINGTON MULTYFARNHAM CO WESTMEATH   STAY
044 937 2191 | stay@mornington.ie
www.mornington.ie

Just a meadow's walk away from Lough Derravarragh where the mythical Children of Lir spent 300 years of their 900 year exile, Warwick and Anne O'Hara's gracious Victorian house has been in the O'Hara family home since 1858, and is still furnished with much of the original furniture and family portraits. Although centrally heated, log fires remain an essential feature, and the spacious bedrooms are well appointed. Anne cooks proper breakfasts and country house dinners for residents, using fresh fruit and vegetables from the walled garden and local produce (Westmeath beef cooked in Guinness is a speciality). A tranquil and restorative place for a short break.

Rooms 4 (1 shower only); B&B from €75pps. Residents' D about €45, (book previous day). Closed Nov-Mar. CC. **Directions:** Exit N4 for Castlepollard.

WEIRS BAR & RESTAURANT

MULTYFARNHAM MULLINGAR CO WESTMEATH   EAT | DRINK
044 937 1111 | weirs@eircom.net
www.weirsmultyfarnham.ie

Pat and Una Weir's handsome stone pub and restaurant is an atmospheric place, especially the friendly front bar with its welcoming fire. Behind it is a restaurant serving home-cooked food, with their own home-smoked mackerel, Killybegs seafood chowder, steaks and roast Silverhill duckling among the specialities. It's a delightful spot, attracting regular custom from miles around, and the Weirs take pride in using as much local and organic produce as possible. A relaxed atmosphere, friendly service and good food – what more could you ask of a country pub?

Seats 60. Food served: Wed-Sat, 12.30-8.30; Sun, 12.30-8. Children welcome. All day value D from €17. No food served Mon (except bank hols) & Tue. Closed Good Fri, 25 Dec. CC. **Directions:** 2km off N4 between Mullingar and Ballinalack.

Hook Lighthouse
Hook Head
Co Wexford

visitwexford.ie

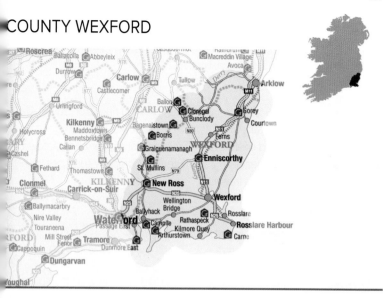

COUNTY WEXFORD

The cornerstone of **Ireland's Ancient East**, Wexford (www.visitwexford.ie) is also - for many visitors - all about beaches, sunshine and opera. Boasting the longest continuous beach in all Ireland (an astonishing 27 kilometres from Cahore Point south to Raven Point) and a genuinely generous amount of sunshine, the 'Sunny Southeast' is the family holiday destination par excellence and - with an unrivalled range of family entertainment offering everything from **Seal Rescue Ireland** and open farms, to the **Pirates Cove** (www.piratescove.ie) complex at Courtown - there is something for all ages and every conceivable interest.

And opera...? Well, the annual **Wexford Festival Opera** (www.wexfordopera.com) in October is a byword for entertaining eccentricity - as international enthusiasts put it, "we go to Wexford town to enjoy operas written by people we've never heard of, and we have ourselves a thoroughly good time."

As for the Ancient East, the county's fascinating history is certainly at the heart of many of Wexford's top activities, attractions and festivals, but it's handled with a light touch - so whether it's living history at the **Irish National Heritage Park**, just outside Wexford Town, or learning a traditional craft there's more than a hint of entertainment in the mix. A range of **Wexford Trails** offers everything from Craft, Gardens or Walking to exploring the Norman Way Trail, along the South Coast. Good food too, notably local seafood and the summer fruits the area's famous for - and, of course, the Georgina Campbell National Breakfast Meats Award winner, **O'Neills Dry Cure Bacon Co.** (www.oneillsbacon.ie), which is produced here in the county, and it's showcased in some very good eating places.

A favourite destination for many visitors is the authentic re-creation of a 19th Century emigrant ship - the impressive **Dunbrody** (www.dunbrody.com) - on the picturesque waterfront in New Ross. It has special resonance in an area with strong historical links to President John F. Kennedy – his great-grandparents sailed from New Ross to America on the original **Dunbrody**.

So, whether it's the great outdoors, cultural and historic attractions, festivals or just good family fun, so perhaps it's time you woke up to Wexford?

DUNBRODY COUNTRY HOUSE HOTEL & COOKERY SCHOOL

ARTHURSTOWN CO WEXFORD **EAT | STAY | LEARN | PRODUCER**

051 389 600 | info@dunbrodyhouse.com

www.dunbrodyhouse.com

Set in parkland on the Hook Peninsula, across the estuary from Waterford city, celebrated chef Kevin Dundon and his wife Catherine's elegant Georgian manor is a tranquil retreat and dining destination of note - **The Harvest Room** and Dundon's Champagne Seafood Bar & Terrace should both be a treat. Converted outbuildings house what must be Ireland's most stylish cookery school, with a beautiful spa beside it - also a rustic bar, The Local Pub, and a dual craft brewing operation comprising a micro-brewery and a larger commercial brewery, Arthurstown Brewing Company, that uses locally grown grains and hops.

⭐

Rooms 22 (3 wheelchair friendly). B&B from abut €75pps. D Mon-Sat from €55, L Sun only, €35. **Seafood Bar** daily, 2-10. **'The Local'**, casual food: Thu-Sat (daily in summer). House closed 19-27 Dec & early Jan-early Feb. CC. **Directions:** On R733, Wexford-Arthurstown.

GLENDINE COUNTRY HOUSE

ARTHURSTOWN NEW ROSS CO WEXFORD **STAY**

051 389 500 | ann@glendinehouse.com

www.glendinehouse.com

Ann and Tom Crosbie's large 19th-century farmhouse is approached up a driveway off the main road to Arthurstown, and has magnificent views across the estuary from the main public rooms and all bedrooms. It is a comfortable and hospitable place to stay at a reasonable price and ideal for a family holiday, as there is an enclosed playground and unusual farm animals in paddocks beside the house - and there are sandy beaches nearby. The Crosbies take pride in giving their guests personal attention, a really good breakfast and lots of advice on local amenities and attractions. The very best kind of genuine Irish hospitality experience.

Rooms 6 (1 shower only); B&B from about €49pps; children welcome. Pets allowed by arrangement. Off-season breaks offered. Self-catering cottage. Closed Christmas. CC. **Directions:** From Wexford R733, on right before village.

CLONGANNY HOUSE

BALLYGARRETT GOREY CO WEXFORD

053 948 2111 | info@clonganny.com

www.clonganny.com

EAT | STAY

Just south of Gorey lies an unusual Georgian gem offering luxurious country house accommodation - and fine dining with a distinctly French flavour. Former restaurateurs Philippe Brillant and his wife Brona opened Cloganny House as a quiet destination for adult guests in 2015. The four spacious en-suite guest rooms are in the former coach house and stables in a restored courtyard, each with French doors opening onto a walled garden; while very different, they are all furnished with style. An excellent breakfast is served in the main house, where dinner menus featuring a range of Philippe's signature French dishes are also available by arrangement - and with a good, mainly French, wine list to accompany.

Rooms 4. B&B from €80pps. D Fri-Sat, from €50 (must book); non-residents welcome by reservation. Self-catering lodge. Licensed. CC. Open all year. **Directions:** Off R742, south of Ballygarrett village.

KILMOKEA COUNTRY MANOR & GARDENS

GREAT ISLAND CAMPILE CO WEXFORD

051 388 109 | kilmokea@eircom.net

www.kilmokea.com

EAT | STAY

Garden lovers will be delighted with Mark and Emma Hewlett's relaxing late-Georgian country house. Set on an historic site in seven acres of Heritage Gardens - a key attraction in the region that includes formal walled gardens - the house is elegantly furnished, and guest amenities include a tennis court, indoor swimming pool, gym, sauna and aromatherapy treatment rooms. The lovely bedrooms have garden views, and so does the Peacock Dining Room where mainly organic dinners that include home produce are served. Daytime food is also available in the Tea Rooms, which are open to the public.

Rooms 6 (1 wheelchair friendly). B&B from €75pps. Children welcome. Self catering also available. L (12-3) & D (7.30) daily; Tea Rooms Mar-Nov, 10-5 daily. Open late Jan-early Nov (groups all year). CC. **Directions:** Signed on R733, south from New Ross to Ballyhack.

THE LOBSTER POT

BALLYFANE CARNE CO WEXFORD

EAT | DRINK

053 913 1110 | info@lobsterpotwexford.com
www.lobsterpotwexford.com

Friendly service, a relaxing atmosphere and carefully prepared fresh food promise an enjoyable visit to Ciaran and Anne Hearne's handsome country pub. Local seafood is the speciality, with daily deliveries ensuring fresh fish supplies. The catch dictates daily specials and simple but carefully prepared meals are served all day in the bar, along with an extensive evening menu - and good value too. Don't miss the house chowder.

Seats 100 (+ 20 outdoors). Bar food Tue-Sat 12-9, Sun 12.30-8.30. D Tue-Sat from 6pm. Sun 12-30-8.30. Families welcome during the day. Closed Mon except bank hols, also Tue in winter months, 25 Dec, 1 Jan-9 Feb; possibly also Good Fri. CC. **Directions:** 8 km south of Rosslare port.

ALDRIDGE LODGE

DUNCANNON NEW ROSS CO WEXFORD

EAT | STAY

051 389 116 | info@aldridgelodge.com
www.aldridgelodge.com

Billy Whitty and Joanne Harding have a well-earned following for the excellent food and warm hospitality at their restaurant with rooms overlooking the picturesque fishing village of Duncannon. Billy's fine modern Irish cooking showcases superb local produce, including crab and lobster supplied by his father, and his sister's free range pork. A super destination, offering outstanding food and lovely accommodation.

Rooms 3 (2 shower only). B&B from about €45pps. DB&B midweek €80pp, weekend €85. Not suitable for children under 7; no pets. Set D from about €40. Sun L from about €35. Closed Mon & Tue, 24-28 Dec, 3 weeks Jan. CC. **Directions:** 0.5km outside Duncannon, overlooking the beach on the Fethard-on-Sea road.

THE WILDS

23 WEAFER STREET TEMPLESHANNON ENNISCORTHY CO WEXFORD   EAT | BUY
053 9237799 | hellothewilds@gmail.com
www.thewilds.ie

Paula Asple and Simon Nelson's thriving café at the top of Weafer Street has become the place to go to in Enniscorthy for good daytime food. An attractive space in a landmark building, The Wilds serves the best local, Irish, seasonal, free-range and organic foods. It offers a wide range of home cooking, including good breakfasts, healthy salads, soup, quiches, cakes and much more - and there is also a little shop offering local produce, carefully selected homeware, kitchenware, furniture and gifts for sale. It is easy to see how they have built up such a loyal clientèle.

Seats 60 (+ 10 outdoors, private dining 14). Open Tue-Fri 9-5; Sat 10-5 (Sun to 4); weekend brunch 10-4. Closed Mon, Dec 25–Jan 1. Full wheelchair access. CC. **Directions:** sign on the gable wall as you come up the street.

MONART DESTINATION SPA

THE STILL ENNISCORTHY CO WEXFORD   EAT | STAY
053 923 8999 | info@monart.ie
www.monart.ie

Arriving at Monart's imposing gates outside Enniscorthy, you get a sense that something quite special lies inside this private estate, which boasts miles of marked walks. Despite its striking design, the hotel and spa marry seamlessly with the wonderful old trees and clever landscaping. It's a luxurious destination with spacious rooms and complimentary access to the impressive thermal suite for all guests. Despite the focus on health and wellbeing, there is no hardship here - Monart is known for its good food and the Garden Lounge offers appealing all day fare, becoming an intimate dining space by night.

Rooms 68. Restaurant seats 86; D daily from about €45. Non-residents welcome by reservation; Garden Lounge L 12.30-5.30. D 5.30-7.30. Adults only. Closed mid-Dec-27 Dec. CC. **Directions:** N11 from Dublin, then right on to N80, first left and follow the signs.

THE KITCHEN @ GOREY

1-4 NORTH PARADE GOREY CO WEXFORD   EAT
053 948 0541 | eat@thekitchengorey.ie
www.thekitchengorey.ie

"To create simple but refined dishes using only the very best local ingredients" is the philosophy of Cathy and Jane Farrell's spacious, informal and family-friendly cafe-restaurant, just off Gorey's Main Street. While the ambience and long opening hours make it popular as a drop-in daytime place, evening meals have finesse, and well-sourced ingredients are cooked with care. A place well worth seeking out.

Open Mon, Wed-Fri 12-9, Sat 12-10. Sun 12-30-8. Open bank hols. Open daily Jul & Aug. Closed Tue. CC. **Directions:** Centre of Gorey.

PARTRIDGES ARTISAN CAFÉ & FINE FOOD SHOP

93/94 MAIN STREET GOREY CO WEXFORD   EAT | BUY
053 948 4040 | info@partridges.ie
www.partridges.ie

This very popular café, at the back of a specialist food shop selling artisan foods from Ireland and beyond, features simple, unpretentious dishes that allow the high quality of the ingredients to shine. Expect the likes of good soups with home-baked bread, unusual pasta dishes, savoury tarts, flavoursome salads, an excellent farmhouse cheese and oatcake plate and an enticing selection of home-baked cakes and tarts. Everything is delicious and, although the pricing reflects the cost of quality ingredients, the discerning clientèle clearly feel the premium is merited and there are queues at busy times.

Seats 48 (+ 12 outdoors); open Mon-Sat 8.30-5 (Sat to 5.30). Deli Mon-Fri 9-5. Closed Sun. CC. **Directions:** Main Street Gorey town.

MARLFIELD HOUSE & THE DUCK CAFÉ-RESTAURANT

COURTOWN ROAD GOREY CO WEXFORD   EAT | STAY | BUY
053 942 1124 | info@marlfieldhouse.ie
www.marlfieldhouse.com

Often quoted as 'the luxury country house hotel par excellence', this impressive house was once the residence of the Earls of Courtown, and is now an elegant oasis of unashamed luxury offering outstanding hospitality and service, where guests are pampered in sumptuous surroundings. Opened as an hotel in 1978 by Mary and Ray Bowe, their daughters Margaret and Laura are now continuing - and developing - the family tradition of hospitality. As well as the main house, they now also operate a lovely informal café-restaurant, The Duck, alongside the kitchen garden - and also Duck Lodge, a contemporary self-catering cottage.

⭐

Rooms 20. Restaurant: D Wed-Sun & Sun L (June-Sep); closed Thu Jan-May. **Duck Terrace Restaurant:** Apr-Sep, daily from 11am; Oct-Mar, Wed-Sun from 12. Reservations advised; wheelchair accessible. CC. **Directions:** Exit 23 N11, left at Courtown roundabout, follow signs.

SEAFIELD HOTEL & SPA RESORT

BALLYMONEY GOREY CO WEXFORD STAY
053 942 4000 | sales@seafieldhotel.com
www.seafieldhotel.com

Set in lush parkland adjacent to the Seafield Golf Club (18-hole Peter McAvoy designed course) this stylish hotel enjoys fine views of the Irish Sea and its extensive facilities include an impressive spa and smart contemporary rooms, some with terraces. Only about an hour from south Dublin, it's a popular business, conference and wedding venue, with self-contained facilities for groups of all sizes. But it's also a desirable short break destination and offers real value too - hotel guests have free use of spa amenities, for example, including the thermal suite, steam room, 16m hydrotherapy pool and gym. Food is generally above average, and a good breakfast usually includes a freshly cooked full Irish.

Rooms 265 (5 wheelchair friendly). Lift. B&B from about €85pps. Children welcome. CC. **Directions:** signed from N11

IN A NUTSHELL

8 SOUTH STREET NEW ROSS CO WEXFORD EAT | BUY
051 422 777 | inanutshell8@gmail.com
www.facebook.com/cafenutshell

Traditional country methods, handed-down recipes and a respect for fresh produce are at the heart of Philip and Patsy Rogers' Emporium in New Ross town. The concept is a natural evolution from Philip's background in farming, and Patsy's love of cooking; everything is freshly made every day - and 'chemically treated or pre-prepared foods are not welcome'. Anyone staying in self-catering accommodation in the area should also check out the food to go, which offers the same high standards of genuinely home-cooked foods that Patsy serves in the café. A real treasure.

Seats 50. Open Mon-Sat 9-6. Children welcome (supervised). Closed Sun, Bank Hols. CC. **Directions:** town centre.

RATHASPECK MANOR

RATHASPECK CO WEXFORD

STAY

053 914 1672 | info@rathaspeckmanor.ie
www.rathaspeckmanor.ie

Surrounded by parkland and a Par 3 golf course (available to guests at very moderate cost), the Cuddihy family's handsome Georgian house is an interesting and unusual place to stay. While impressive, it's also a warm and welcoming family home and it offers very pleasing country house accommodation. No dinner is offered but Betty O'Kennedy-Cuddihy is happy to offer her personal dinner recommendations to guests - and there's a very good breakfast featuring local produce.

Rooms 4. B&B from about €70pps.
Directions: 15 minutes' drive south from Wexford Town, Rathaspeck is a couple of minutes from the N25.

ARCHWAYS B&B

ROSSLARE ROAD TAGOAT ROSSLARE CO WEXFORD   EAT | STAY

053 915 8111 | thearchways@eircom.net

www.thearchways.ie

Eileen and Chris Hadlington's smart modern B&B just outside Tagoat is an exceptional place to stay, offering superb food and genuine hospitality. They constantly find new ways to ensure a memorable stay for their guests and this includes outstanding food. Chris is an inspired chef - residents' dinner is a real treat. Seasonal, local and home-produced is the ethos and his own rare breed pork or beef may well be on the menu. It's the perfect place to overnight when arriving off the ferry and a snack can be arranged for late arrivals. Early breakfast available too.

Rooms 5 (3 shower only). B&B from about €38pps; D by arrangement. Children, bikers & dogs welcome. Wheelchair friendly. CC. **Directions:** Just off N25 main Rosslare Road.

KELLY'S RESORT HOTEL & SPA

ROSSLARE CO WEXFORD

053 913 2114 | info@kellys.ie

www.kellys.ie

EAT | STAY | LEARN

With its special brand of relaxed professionalism, the Kelly family's renowned seaside hotel sums up all that is best about the sunny south-east for many regular visitors. Family ownership spans five generations, so there's not a lot these hospitable people don't know about keeping guests happy. Its special qualities are so wide-ranging that it's hard to know where to begin. Take your pick, perhaps, from the beachside location, superb leisure and family facilities, the outstanding food served in two restaurants, the famous wine cellar, a stunning art collection... quite simply, this hotel has everything.

Rooms 118 (2 wheelchair friendly). B&B from about €88pps. Beaches Restaurant. L&D daily. La Marine: L & D daily. Kelly's Café: Mon-Sat 9.30-5.30, Sun & bank hols 12-5.30. Hotel closed early Dec-mid Feb. **Also at: Kelly's Café**, Drinagh (053 916 8800). **Directions:** Take the signs for Wexford/Rosslare/Southeast.

CISTIN EILE

80 SOUTH MAIN STREET WEXFORD CO WEXFORD   EA

053 912 1616 | warrengillencistineile@gmail.com

www.facebook.com/pg/Warren-Gillens-Cist

Warren Gillen's restaurant Cistin Eile ('another kitchen') has a following, and no wonder - he is one of the most interesting chefs in the region and a great supporter of local and artisan producers. Short, constantly-changing modern menus have a sense of place and - while every dish is richly layered with flavours - this accomplished chef never overpowers his carefully selected seasonal (and, often, less expensive) ingredients.

Serving the best of contemporary Irish food and offering great value for money (on the wine list as well as the menu), this unpretentious and very focused small restaurant merits wider recognition.

Seats 44. L Mon–Sat 12-3. D Wed-Sat 6-9. A la carte. Free wifi. Closed Sun, D Mon & Tue D, bank hols, 25-26 Dec, 1 Jan. CC. **Directions:** Main Street runs parallel to Crescent & Paul Quay.

LA CÔTE

CUSTOM QUAY WEXFORD CO WEXFORD

053 912 2122 I lacotepaulhynes@gmail.com

www.lacote.ie

EAT

Appropriately enough, the smartly presented 'Paul Hynes La Côte Seafood Restaurant' on the corner of Custom House Quay, overlooks the mussel boats in the nearby harbour. Although this is his first restaurant, Paul Hynes has a following in the area and it is easy to see why - a fine dining chef by training, he also brings down to earth informality, accessibility and connection to seasonal foods of both sea and land. A welcoming and efficient front of house team led by Paul's partner Edwina ensures that a visit to this high quality and reasonably priced restaurant will be memorable for the whole experience as well as excellent cooking.

Seats 40. D Tue-Sat 5.30-9.30. Set D from about €24. Closed Sun & Mon (except bank hol w/e). Earlier opening during the Opera Festival.

WHITFORD HOUSE HOTEL

NEW LINE ROAD WEXFORD CO WEXFORD
053 914 3444 | info@whitford.ie
www.whitford.ie

Probably the busiest hotel in the area, the Whitty family's friendly hotel is a pleasant place to stay and there's always a buzz. Several grades of room are offered - the best have balconies or private patio areas - and good facilities attract a wide clientele. It's a particularly appealing destination for family breaks with good facilities for children including a children's pool, playground and football area. Self-catering accommodation is also available, with easy access to good food in the hotel if required.

Rooms 36 (1 wheelchair friendly). Room only from about €79. Children welcome. Seasons Restaurant: D from about €34. Sun L from €25. Bar food Mon-Sat 12-9pm. No dogs. Leisure centre. Closed 24-28 Dec. CC. **Directions:** On N25 2km from Wexford Town (Rosslare direction).

KILLIANE CASTLE COUNTRY HOUSE & FARM

DRINAGH WEXFORD CO WEXFORD   STAY
053 915 8885 | info@killianecastle.com
www.killianecastle.com

Kathleen and Jack Mernagh's magical farm B&B is the perfect place for stressed townies, especially with children in tow - a real castle, a 17th century house to stay in, and lots to do. As well as offering exceptionally comfortable accommodation, plenty to read (history of castle, area, books and magazines) and garden furniture for the enjoyment of fine weather, both children and adults are sure to find plenty to interest them, including farm walks, watching the milking, and pitch & putt among a whole range of activities. All this and great food too.

Rooms 8 (1 shower only). B&B about €60pps. Evening meals by arrangement from April. Children welcome. Dogs permitted (stay in outhouse/kennel). Self-catering available (3 courtyard apartments). Closed late Dec–early Mar. CC. **Directions:** Off N11 towards Rosslare, approx 7km from central Wexford.

COUNTY WICKLOW

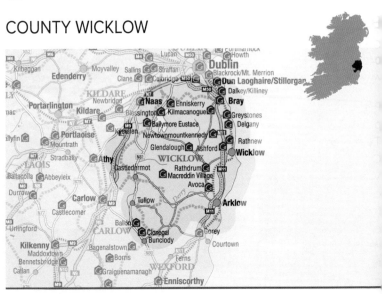

Wicklow www.visitwicklow.ie is a miracle. Although the booming presence of Dublin is right next door, this spectacularly lovely county www.wicklowmountainsnationalpark.ie is very much its own place, an away-from-it-all world of moorland and magnificent mountain, farmland and garden, forest and lake, seashore and river with its essence found in Glendalough www.glendalough.ie . It's all right there, just over the nearest hill, yet it all seems so gloriously different.

The people's sense of difference is easily understood, for even with today's traffic, it is only a short drive on notably handsome roads to transform your world from the crowded city streets right into the heart of some of the most beautiful scenery in all Ireland. Such scenery generates its own strong loyalties and sense of identity, and Wicklow folk are rightly and proudly a race apart. Drawing strength from their wonderful environment, they have a vigorous local life which keeps metropolitan blandness well at bay.

While being in a place so beautiful is almost sufficient reason for existence in itself, they're busy people too, with sheep farming and forestry and all sorts of light industries, while down in the workaday harbour of Arklow www.arklow.ie in the south of the county - a port with a long and splendid maritime history - they've been so successful in organising their own seagoing fleet of freighters that there are now more cargo ships registered in Arklow than any other Irish port.

LOCAL ATTRACTIONS AND INFORMATION

>Ashford **Mount Usher Gardens**
  www.muntushergardens.ie | 0404 40116

>Enniskerr **Powerscourt House & Gardens**
  www.powerscourt.com | 01 204 6000

>**Glendalough Visitor Centre** 0404 45325

>Kilmacanogue **Avoca Handweavers Garden**
  01 286 7466

>Rathdrum **Avondale House** 0404 46111

>Wicklow County **Gardens Festival** (May-July)
  0404 20100

>**Wicklow Mountains National Park**
  www.wicklowmountainsnationalpark.ie
  0404 45425

>Wicklow Town **Wicklow Historic Gaol**
  www.wicklowhistoricgaol.com | 0404 61599

BALLYKNOCKEN HOUSE & COOKERY SCHOOL

GLEANEALY ASHFORD CO WICKLOW   STAY | LEARN

0404 44627 | reservations@ballyknocken.com

www.ballyknocken.com

Perfectly placed for walking, playing golf, or exploring the area, TV chef and cookbook author Catherine Fulvio's charming Victorian farmhouse provides comfort, cosiness, home-cooked food and hospitality - and the option of classes at her well-known cookery school. Antique-furnished bedrooms have very good beds and pretty bathrooms, and both the excellent breakfasts and the 4-course dinners offered at weekends showcase local produce. All this plus great picnics and a relaxing atmosphere keep guests coming back for more.

Rooms 7 (1 shower only). B&B from about €59pps. Residents set D Fri-Sat at 7.30pm, about €49. Parking. Wheelchair access to cookery school only. Sep-May open Fri & Sat only. CC. **Directions:** From Dublin turn right after Tougher Oil Petrol Station in Ashford. Continue for 5.5km.

GRANGECON CAFÉ

KILBRIDE ROAD BLESSINGTON CO WICKLOW   EAT | BUY | PRODUCER

045 857 892 | grangeconcafe@eircom.net

www.grangeconcafe.blogspot.ie

People very easily get addicted to Jenny and Richard Street's smashing café - and no wonder. Even though it's more expensive than other places, it's so popular that you may have to queue but the wholesome aromas and gorgeous freshly cooked food on display will remind you why it's worth the wait. The menu is fairly brief, but that's the beauty of it, allowing the cooking to be this good. Everything on the menu is made on the premises, including the breads, pastries and ice cream. They also produce freshly-cooked meals (fresh and frozen) that are a boon to take home on a busy day. Not cheap, but good value for money. Magic.

Seats 30. Open Tue-Sat 9-4. (L 11.30-4). Toilets wheelchair accessible; children welcome. Closed Sun, Mon, bank hols & 25 Dec-1 Jan. CC. **Directions:** Off Blessington main street, Kilbride turning.

KILLRUDDERY ESTATE

SOUTHERN CROSS BRAY CO WICKLOW
01 286 3405 | info@killruddery.com
www.kilruddery.com

EAT | BUY | LEARN | PRODUCER

Killruddery has been home to the Brabazon Family (Earls of Meath) since 1618. Designed on a large scale with a view to impressing visitors, the estate is a hive of activity and very accessible to the public. The many reasons to visit include: the historic house and its beautiful gardens; farm produce supplied by Anthony Ardee (son of the 15th Earl of Meath), on sale at the weekly Farm Market; his wife Fionnuala Ardee's Tearoom, serving estate and local produce in a unique hexagonal former dairy - and the many cultural events hosted at this remarkable venue. Not to be missed.

Open: May-Sep 9.30-6 daily; April & Oct weekends only 9.30-6. Farm market, Sat 10-3. Christmas markets. House open for tours. **Directions:** Exit 7 off N11; between Bray and Greystones.

FIREHOUSE BAKERY & CAFÉ

OLD DELGANY INN GLEN ROAD DELGANY CO WICKLOW
Firehouse Bakery: **01 287 6822** | info@thefirehouse.ie
www.thefirehouse.ie/bakery.html

EAT | BUY
LEARN | PRODUCER

Stylishly renovated, the former Delgany Inn houses a varying number of independent businesses operating jointly as The Delgany. Together, they make an enticing go-to destination - you can shop at the superb Firehouse Bakery (also at Heir Island, West Cork), for example, for artisan breads and pastries, and pick up more goodies from The Delgany Grocer or other shops - and then reward yourself with a seriously tasty casual bite at the Firehouse Café, or head upstairs to the Pigeon House café. It's a great place to know about if you're visiting beautiful Co Wicklow, or as a destination in its own right.

Firehouse Bakery: Mon-Fri 8.30-5.30, weekends 9.30-5; food served 11-4.30 (woodfired pizzas available from 12.30); **Delgany Grocer:** Mon-Sun 9-6. **Pigeon House:** Daytime menus Tue-Fri 9-4 (L12-4), Sat-Sun brunch 10-4; D Thu-Sun from 5.30. CC. **Directions:** In Delgany village.

RATHSALLAGH HOUSE

DUNLAVIN CO WICKLOW

045 403 112 | info@rathsallagh.com

www.rathsallagh.com

EAT | STAY

The O'Flynn family's large, rambling country house on the Wicklow-Kildare border is just an hour from Dublin, but it could be in a different world. Insistent that it is 'not an hotel', it has a classic country house atmosphere - but it's very professionally run and has all of the expected amenities. Rooms range from spacious ones with great views in the old house to cottagey rooms in the stable yard, all very comfortable. Good food is central to Rathsallagh - starting with seasonal produce from the farm and beautiful walled garden, you will eat well here.

Rooms 35. B&B from €95pps. Restaurant: D daily 7-9.30 (to 9 Sun), à la carte. L Sun only 1-2.30 about €39. Non-residents welcome for D. Not suitable for children under 6. Reservations required. Food at Rathsallagh Golf Club 9-9 daily (to 7pm in winter). Open all year. CC.
Directions: Signed from Dunlavin.

THE POWERSCOURT HOTEL

POWERSCOURT ESTATE ENNISKERRY CO WICKLOW   EAT I STAY

01 274 8888 I info@powerscourthotel.com

www.powerscourthotel.com

Scenically situated in the beautiful Wicklow Hills south of Dublin city, this deluxe hotel's palatial public areas make the most of the wonderful location and accommodation is luxurious. Dining experiences range from afternoon tea or casual meals in McGills Pub bar or the foyer lounge area, to fine dining on the terrace. Excellent amenities include a leisure centre and destination spa, golf, and extensive conference/banqueting facilities.

Rooms 194. **Sika Restaurant: Seats 88** (+48 outdoors). D daily 6-10 from about €55. Early D daily 6-7, about €40. Children welcome before 5pm. Sugar Loaf Lounge: bistro-style food daily from 12. Afternoon Tea daily 2.30-5.30. Bar food daily 6-10 in McGills Pub. Leisure centre. Destination Spa. Wheelchair friendly. Open all year. CC. Heli-pad. **Directions:** on Powerscourt Estate.

THE WICKLOW HEATHER

LARAGH GLENDALOUGH CO WICKLOW   EAT I DRINK I STAY

0404 45157 I bookings@wicklowheather.ie

www.wicklowheather.ie

Betty and John Kenny's inviting restaurant in the heart of Laragh has been welcoming diners for over 40 years and, with consistently good locally sourced food and friendly and attentive staff, it is more popular than ever. It offers all day snacks and wide ranging lunch and evening menus, with a full bar - and a choice of dining outdoors, or in atmospheric rooms with unique historical interest (especially the Irish Writers' Room). Always buzzing with a happy blend of local families, couples and tourists, it offers something for everyone.

Seats 125 (+ 40 outdoors). Open daily B'fst 8-12, L 12.30-5.45, (Sun to 4.30), D 6-9, (Sat to 10). **Rooms 5** (all shower only; Heather House: www.heatherhouse.ie). B&B from €40pps. Closed 25 Dec. CC. **Directions:** Centre of Laragh Village.

CHAKRA BY JAIPUR

1ST FLOOR MERIDIAN POINT CHURCH ROAD GREYSTONES CO WICKLOW   EAT

01 201 7222 | info@jaipur.ie

www.chakra.ie

This delightful sister to the other successful Jaipur restaurants in Dalkey, Dublin and Malahide (www.jaipur.ie) offers the same warmly attentive service and maintains Jaipur's crisp, modern, contemporary take on traditional Indian food with colourful, delicious dishes. There are numerous vegetarian choices and old favourites are served with splendid accompaniments. Unusually for an Indian restaurant, the dessert menu is also worth exploring and wines are carefully selected to match the food.

Seats 95. D daily 5.30-11, Sun & bank hol 1-10. L Sun & bank hol only 1-3.45, about €18. Early 3 course D €24, Mon-Thu 5.30-7, Fri 5-6.45, Sat 5-6.30, Sun 4-6.45. A la carte Mon-Thu 5.30-10.30, Sat from 5, Sun 4-9.30. Wine from about €28. Toilets wheelchair accessible; children welcome. Closed 25 Dec. CC. **Directions:** Just off main street in new shopping centre, 2 minutes from DART station.

THE HAPPY PEAR

CHURCH ROAD GREYSTONES CO WICKLOW   EAT | BUY

01 287 3655 | info@thehappypear.ie
www.thehappypear.ie

Famous twins David and Stephen Flynn run this cheerfully ethical vegetable shop, smoothie bar and café - a lot for a vegetable shop, but their plant-based food is simple and tasty. The twins' younger brother Darragh runs their Living Foods sprout farm, where wheatgrass is the star; they have a production unit too, making healthy products for widespread distribution, and a range of services including catering and Happy Heart cookery courses.

Food Shop & Happy Pear: 8.30am daily (Mon-Thu to 6, Fri-Sat to 9, Sun to 7). Café **seats 40** (+30 outdoors). Vegetarian. Children welcome. Wine from about €17. Wheelchair accessible. Online shop (orders over €50). CC. **Also at: Shoreline Leisure Centre**, Mill Road Greystones (Mon-Thu 8-9, Fri to 8, Sat-Sun 10-5).**The Round Tower Centre**, Clondalkin, Dublin 22; cafe & food shop open daily, 8am-8pm. **Directions:** Main Street Greystones.

THE HUNGRY MONK

CHURCH ROAD GREYSTONES CO WICKLOW   EAT

01 287 5759 | info@thehungrymonk.ie
www.thehungrymonk.ie

Wine buff Pat Keown and his wife Sylvie opened this famously quirky restaurant in 1988 - Pat is still likely to be the host, and his warmth and enthusiasm are undimmed. Local fish is the speciality in summer and game in winter, while the famous wine list is a labour of love offering a choice of over 600 bottles - all hand picked by Pat or his son Julian (also with a wine background) who now manages the Hungry Monk with his wife Samantha. Genuine hospitality, great wines and interesting, high quality and skilfully cooked food at affordable prices explain The Hungry Monk's lasting success. A place to treasure.

Open Mon-Sat 5-11, Sun 12.30-9. A la carte. Wine from about €22. Reservations advised. Children welcome. Closed 24-26 Dec. CC. **Directions:** Centre of Greystones village near DART station.

AVOCA HANDWEAVERS, KILMACANOGUE

KILMACANOGUE BRAY CO WICKLOW

01 286 7466 I reception@avoca.ie
www.avoca.ie

EAT I BUY

The flagship premises of Ireland's most famous group of craft shops, now equally popular for their wholesome, home-cooked food, which is based as much as possible on local and artisan produce. The style at Avoca is eclectic, and although best known for great baking and traditional dishes, their salads and vegetables are also legendary. Here, the Fernhouse Café offers an elegant option with table service, in addition to the familiar high quality self-service cafe and deli. In-store butchers and fishmongers in some outlets.

Self-service: 9.30-5 daily (Sun 10-5). Fernhouse Café: Mon-Wed 9.30-5, Thu-Sat to 9.30. Summer Sun: 9.30-5. Closed 25-26 Dec. CC. **Directions:** On N11 signed before Kilmacanogue Village. **Also at**; Co Wicklow: Powerscourt, Avoca Village, Mount Usher; Dublin 2: Suffolk Street; Co Dublin: Monkstown, Rathcoole, Malahide; Co Meath: Dunboyne; Co Galway: Letterfrack; Co Kerry: Moll's Gap; Belfast: Arthur Street.

THE BROOKLODGE HOTEL & WELLS SPA

MACREDDIN VILLAGE CO WICKLOW

STAY | EAT | PRODUCER

0402 36444 | info@brooklodge.com
www.brooklodge.com

Evan Doyle and his brothers, Eoin and Bernard, built this extraordinary food, drink and leisure complex on the site of a deserted village in a Wicklow valley in 1999. Today, it is a spacious and welcoming 'green' hotel offering everything from conferences and events to a sumptuous spa and wonderful food. Its main restaurant, The Strawberry Tree, was Ireland's first certified organic restaurant and the hotel is famous for promoting organic and wild food - delicious, and good value too.

Rooms 86 (2 wheelchair friendly). Lift. B&B from €75pps. Strawberry Tree: D Tue-Sun from 7pm (daily in Aug); set D from €65. La Taverna Armento, D Wed-Sun. Actons Pub & Microbrewery: food daily, times vary. Lounge food daily 12.30-6.30. Afternoon Tea Wed-Sun 2.30- 4.30 (daily Aug). Orchard Café: weekends & bank hol Mon. Open all year. CC. **Directions:** Signed from Aughrim.

DRUIDS GLEN RESORT

NEWTOWNMOUNTKENNEDY CO WICKLOW

EAT I STAY

01 287 0800 I reservations@druidsglenresort.com
www.druidsglenresort.com

This luxurious hotel and golf resort enjoys a stunning setting in the Garden of Ireland, between the mountains and sea. Spaciousness is a key feature of the hotel, from the extensive grounds to the very comfortable suites and bedrooms, and it offers excellent amenities. Although best known for business, conferences and events, families are also very well catered for and, just a short drive from Dublin, it is an appealing short break destination.

Contemporary cooking in Hugo's fine dining restaurant has a pleasing emphasis on seasonality.

Rooms 148 (6 wheelchair friendly). Lift. B&B from about €75pps. Children welcome. Spa, health club, 18m pool. Restaurant: D daily 6-9. Early D Fri-Sat 5.30-6.30, about €35, otherwise à la carte. Reservations essential. Set Sun L 1-2.30, from €26. Afternoon Tea in The Conservatory, 2-5pm daily, €24. CC. **Directions:** Off N11, at Newtownmountkennedy.

BATES RESTAURANT

3 MARKET STREET MARKET SQUARE RATHDRUM CO WICKLOW

EAT

040 429 988 I info@batesrestaurant.com
www.batesrestaurant.com

In a pretty higgledy-piggledy row of interlinked stone cottages, Bates is a charming sight when spotted down a laneway in this small town in the Wicklow hills. And, with its whitewashed interior, oodles of atmosphere and a reputation for sound cooking, people travel long distances to this attractive restaurant for the relaxed rural ambience and good food, made with simple, quality ingredients. Seasonal menus offer an appealing range of mainstream

modern European dishes with an Italian accent, often featuring the excellent meats of the area. Warm, friendly staff and good value too, including wines.

Seats 46. D Tue-Sat 6-9 (Fri-Sat to 9.30, Sat from 5.30); Sun 12-30-8. L Sun only 12.30-3, about €20. Early D to 6.45, from about €20. D à la carte. Reservations recommended; children welcome, wheelchair accessible. Closed Mon. CC. **Directions:** Alongside the Cartoon Inn.

HUNTER'S HOTEL

NEWRATH BRIDGE RATHNEW CO WICKLOW   EAT | STAY
0404 40106 | reception@hunters.ie
www.hunters.ie

Set in lovely gardens alongside the River Vartry, this much-loved small hotel is one of Ireland's oldest coaching inns. It's run by fifth generation brothers, Richard and Tom Gelletlie, who offer old-fashioned comfort and food based on local and their own home-grown produce. There's a proper little bar and a traditional dining room overlooking the beautiful garden where their famous afternoon tea is served in summer. There's nowhere else in Ireland like it.

Rooms 16 (1 shower only, 1 wheelchair friendly). B&B from about €65pps. DB&B from €95. L daily, 1-2.30 from €19.75. Sun 2 sittings: 12.45 & 2.45, from about €34. D daily 7.30-8.45; Sun-Fri from about €30, Sat D about €48. Afternoon Tea 4-5.30pm. Closed 3 days at Christmas. CC. **Directions:** Off N11 at Ashford or Rathnew

---

ROUNDWOOD INN

ROUNDWOOD CO WICKLOW   EAT | DRINK
01 281 8107

Owners since 1980, Jurgen and Aine Schwalm have developed their own unique style at this atmospheric 17th-century inn. The ever-burning log fire in its enormous open fireplace is a welcome sight in the main bar food area, where their broadly Irish-German food is served at sturdy wooden tables - Hungarian goulash, fresh crab bisque, Galway oysters and hearty meals, notably Wicklow venison and the house Irish stew, are all favourites. Although they also do popular dishes (chicken in a basket) the food here has its special character and this, together with the place itself, has earned the inn its reputation.

Bar meals daily 12.30-8.30pm. Restaurant weekends only, reservations required. D Fri & Sat, 7.30-9; à la carte. L Sun only, 1-2. (Children welcome for lunch). Restaurant closed L Mon-Sat, D Sun-Thu. CC. **Directions:** N11, follow sign for Glendalough.

NORTHERN IRELAND - COUNTY ANTRIM

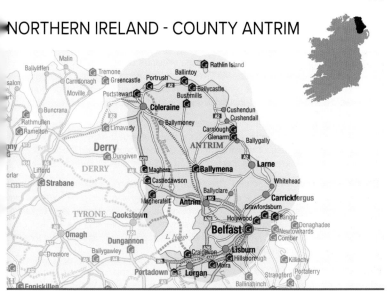

With its boundaries naturally defined by the sea, the River Bann, the extensive lake of Lough Neagh, and the River Lagan, County Antrim has always had a strong sense of its own clearcut geographical identity. This is further emphasised by the extensive uplands of the Antrim Plateau, wonderful for the sense of space with the moorland rising to heights such as Trostan (551m) and the distinctive Slemish (438m), famed for its association with St Patrick.

The plateau eases westward to fertile valleys and bustling inland towns such as Ballymena, Antrim and Ballymoney, while the coastal towns ring the changes between the traditional resort of Portrush www.causewaycoastalroute.com in the far north, the ferryport of Larne in the east, and historic Carrickfergus in the south.

In the spectacularly beautiful northeast of the county, the most rugged heights of the Plateau are softened by the nine Glens of Antrim www.causewaycoastandglens.co.uk , havens of beauty descending from the moorland down through small farms to hospitable villages clustered at the shoreline, and connected by the renowned Antrim Coast Road. Between these sheltered bays at the foot of the Glens, the sea cliffs of the headlands soar with remarkable rock formations which, on the North Coast, provide the setting for the Carrick-a-Rede rope bridge and the Giant's Causeway www.giantscausewayofficialguide.com , a World Heritage site.

From the charming little port of Ballycastle, Northern Ireland's only inhabited offshore island of Rathlin is within easy reach by ferry, a mecca for ornithologists and perfect for days away from the pressures of mainstream life.

LOCAL ATTRACTIONS AND INFORMATION

>Ballycastle **Carrick-a-Rede Rope Bridge**
  028 20 731582

>Bushmills **Irish Whiskey-World's Oldest Distillery**
  028 20 731521

>**Giants Causeway & Bushmills Railway**
  028 20 741157

>**Rathlin Island Ferries**
  www.rathlinballycastleferry.com | 028 20 769299

BELFAST

Belfast www.visitbelfast.com is much newer than Ireland's other cities. It was 1613 when it officially started to come to life where the River Lagan meanders through its increasingly deep valley into the sea at the head of a handsome lough. But it proved to be the perfect greenfield site for rapid development as the Industrial Revolution got under way.

Its rocketing growth began with linen manufacture in the 17th Century, and by the end of the 19th Century it could claim with justifiable pride to have the largest shipyard in the world, the largest ropeworks, the largest linen mills, the largest tobacco factory, and the largest heavy engineering works, all served by a greater mileage of quays than anywhere comparable.

By 1906 its population was 349,180 - the biggest city in Ireland - with an exuberant new City Hall www.belfastcity..gove.uk at its heart to express growing civic pride. While it may be on the grand scale, nevertheless it is right at the heart of a very human town which has reinvented itself with the Odyssey Arena www.odysseyarena.com and the Titanic Centre www.titanicbelfast.com which is now one the world's most popular tourist attractions, together with burgeoning film production facilities.

Modern technologies and advanced engineering have displaced the old smokestack industries in the forefront of the city's work patterns, with the Harland & Wolff shipyard ceasing to build ships in March 2003, making Bombardier Aerospace the city's biggest employer.

The energy of former times has been channeled into impressive urban regeneration along the River Lagan. Here, the flagship building is the Waterfront Hall www.waterfront.co.uk , a large concert venue which has won international praise. In the southern part of the city, Queen's University (founded 1845) www.qub.ie is a beautifully balanced 1849 Lanyon building at the heart of a pleasant university district which includes the respected Ulster Museum & Art Gallery www.nmni.com , while the university itself is particularly noted for its pioneering work in medicine and engineering.

There's a buzz to Belfast which is expressed in its cultural sporting and warmly sociable life, and reflected in the internationally-minded innovative energy of its young chefs. But there is still much to it that speaks of a country town and port strongly rooted in land and sea, and it is all the better for that.

LOCAL ATTRACTIONS AND INFORMATION

>**Belfast Castle & Zoo** www.belfastzoo.co.uk
 028 90 776277

>**Fernhill House: The People's Museum**
 www.culture24.org.uk | 028 90 715599

>**Grand Opera House**
 www.goh.co.uk | 028 90 241919

>**Kings Hall** (exhibitions, concerts, trade shows)
 www.thekingshall.com | 028 90 665225

>**Lagan Valley Regional Park**
 www.laganvalley.co.uk | 028 90 491922

>**Linenhall Library**
 www.linenhall.com | 028 90 321707

>**Lyric Theatre**
 www.lyrictheatre.co.uk | 028 90 381081

>**St Anne's Cathedral**
 www.belfastcathedral.org | 028 90 328332

>**Titanic Belfast**
 www.titanicbelfast.com | 028 9076 6399

>**Tourism Information**
 www.visitbelfast.com | 028 90 246609

AN OLD RECTORY

148 MALONE ROAD BELFAST CO ANTRIM BT9 5LH   STAY

028 90 66 7882 | info@anoldrectory.co.uk
www.anoldrectory.co.uk

Conveniently located near the King's Hall, Public Records Office, Lisburn Road and Queen's University, Mary Callan's lovely late-Victorian house is a former Church of Ireland rectory. Great attention is paid to every detail for guests' comfort, from the extras included in the bedrooms - a desk and sofa, magazines to browse, beverage trays (with fresh milk and iced water available) - to the superb breakfast which is a particular USP. Light evening meals are offered on weekdays too and organic produce is used where possible. But best of all, perhaps, is the complimentary hot whiskey in the drawing room each evening (7-8pm), encouraging guests to mingle and relax.

Rooms 7 (3 shower only, 1 wheelchair friendly). B&B from about £48pps. Children welcome. Closed Christmas-New Year & Easter. **Directions:** 3km (2 miles) from city centre, between Balmoral Avenue and Stranmillis Road.

THE BARKING DOG

33-35 MALONE ROAD BELFAST CO ANTRIM BT9 6RU   EAT

028 9066 1885 | info@barkingdogbelfast.com
www.barkingdogbelfast.com

The Barking Dog is handily located near QUB and the Botanic Gardens - the name is apparently explained by former owner Sam Spain's softness for canine companions - and the appealing theme has endured a change of regime. Chef Michael O'Connor (now co-owner, with Michael Fletcher) offers a range of well-priced, carefully thought out menus for different times and occasions, from weekend brunch to bar food to a full evening menu - and well-trained staff provide service to match the excellent, sometimes witty, food. The speciality beef shin burger is a winner for a first visit, and attention to provenance - including drinks - is impeccable. A busy, deservedly popular place.

Seats 76 (+ 24 outdoors). Open daily: L Mon-Sat 12-2.30, Sun to 4; D Mon-Thu 5-10, Fri & Sat to 11, Sun to 9. Closed 11-12 Jul, 24-26 Dec. CC.

THE BAR AND GRILL AT JAMES STREET SOUTH

21 JAMES STREET SOUTH BELFAST CO ANTRIM BT2 7GA   EAT
028 9560 0700 | info@belfastbargrill.co.uk
www.belfastbargrill.co.uk

Niall McKenna, chef-proprietor of one of the city's top fine dining restaurants, James Street South, brought a little bit of New York to Belfast when he opened this classy urban steakhouse next door. While the menu is all about straightforward, gutsy dishes and steak - elevated to lofty, smoky heights thanks to the Josper charcoal grill - customers who know their meat will note with approval the variety of cuts offered, and their varying sources; also Irish rose veal, which is good to see. There's a small but special selection of salads, pasta and risotto too, and retro desserts like Baked Alaska to finish. Belfast's top spot for a classy steak dinner.

Seats 65. Open Mon–Sun, 12-'late'. Wheelchair access. Closed 25-26 Dec, 1 Jan, 12 Jul. CC. **Directions:** City centre - behind City Hall and the Crown Bar.

BULLITT BELFAST

40A CHURCH LANE BELFAST BT1 4QN

028 9590 0600 | info@bullitthotel.com

www.bullitthotel.com

STAY

Cool, chilled out and yet nostalgic, The Merchant's younger sister - or should that be brother? - offers back to basics with a difference. The 'traditional hotel' concept is completely reimagined and pared down for maximum comfort, efficiency and fun: forget about baths, wardrobes and minibars, think big beds, flat screen TVs (full Sky package), wifi, a great range of bars, and local, seasonal food and drinks. Waygu beef from Noble House is the star of the show at Taylor & Clay restaurant, where chefs entertain customers as they rustle up big-flavoured meals on a huge Asador grill. A great place - and not just for the young.

Rooms 74, (3 wheelchair friendly, all shower only). Lift. Room rate from £100. B'fst 7-11.30, L 12-4, D 5-10. A la carte except early D. Closed 25 Dec. **Directions:** city centre.

CAST AND CREW

TITANIC QUARTER QUEENS ROAD BELFAST CO ANTRIM BT3 9DQ   EAT

028 90 451 400 | info@castandcrewbelfast.co.uk

www.castandcrewbelfast.co.uk

Offering rustic street food from the James Street South group, Cast and Crew is a clever pun on the café's near neighbours - the Titanic Visitor Centre and the Paintball Film Studios in Belfast. With quality all-day dining seven days a week, this perfectly pitched offering is bang on the dude food trend of burgers and hot dogs. It's open from breakfast onwards, serving hearty and healthy breakfasts, salads, burgers, hot dogs and sides. The USPs are superb ingredients, great cooking with plenty of eye appeal - and terrific service from smartly uniformed staff, who know their menu and the most popular options. Nice outdoor seating too.

Open Mon-Fri 8.30-5, Sat and Sun 9-5. Children welcome. Wheelchair friendly. BBQ classes in summer. Available for private hire (evenings, after 6). CC. **Directions:** Beside Titanic Centre.

CROWN LIQUOR SALOON

46 GREAT VICTORIA STREET BELFAST CO ANTRIM BT2 7 BA   EAT | DRINK

02890 279 901

www.nicholsonspubs.co.uk

Belfast's most famous pub was perhaps the greatest of all the Victorian gin palaces that once flourished in Britain's industrial cities and is now owned by the National Trust. Built in 1826, it's a rare example of the flamboyant baroque style of the era, complete with elaborate stained glass, ornamental woodwork and gaslight. A visit to one of its famous snugs for a pint and a bowl of Irish stew or a steak and Guinness pie is a must. Currently operated by Nicholson's Pubs, it's now also a speciality Sausage and Chop House.

Open 11.30-12 (Sun 12.30-11). Food served downstairs: Mon-Thu 11.30-7 (Fri & Sat to 4.30). Upstairs daily 11.30-10. Closed 25 Dec. CC. **Directions:** City centre, opposite Europa Hotel.

DEANES EIPIC

36-40 HOWARD STREET BELFAST CO ANTRIM BT1 6PF   EAT

028 9033 1134 | eipic@michaeldeane.co.uk

www.deaneseipic.com

A very grown-up Scandi-chic space - lots of grey and cream with black accents - this extremely comfortable fine dining restaurant is an elegant, refined space in which to experience the unhurried service of carefully considered menus, and a wine list that should please any wine buff. Northern Irish head chef Alex Greene worked at Gordon Ramsay restaurants in London and The Cliff House in Ardmore before returning to Belfast in 2016 to work again for his former boss - and he now works with hand picked suppliers and transforms their seasonal ingredients into delicious, perfectly cooked dishes at EIPIC. This special restaurant feels expensive, yet it offers good value.

Seats 30. L Fri only, 12-1.30, £30; D Wed-Sat 5.30-9.30. Tasting menu £65, vegetarian available (paired wines £5.95/£8.95 per shot/glass). Wheelchair accessible; children welcome. Closed Sun; bank hols. CC. **Directions:** City centre.

DEANES MEAT LOCKER & LOVE FISH

36-40 HOWARD STREET BELFAST CO ANTRIM BT1 6PF   EAT

028 9033 1134 | info@michaeldeane.co.uk

www.michaeldeane.co.uk

Deservedly hailed as Northern Ireland's premier dining destination for many years, chef Michael Deane's Howard Street site accommodates three restaurants: EIPIC (fine dining, see separate entry), Love Fish and the Meat Locker - all three are exceptional. Love Fish and Meat Locker are presided over by chef Andy Provan, who brings experience at Tom Kerridge's famous English gastropub, the Hand & Flowers. At Love Fish, they keep it casual with the freshest seafood and sharing plates; The Meat Locker combines Hannan's famous 35-day Himalayan salt-aged beef with the accuracy of the Asador grill and you can watch the chefs at work, preparing the meat as well as cooking it - and the drinks list includes Deanes 93 draft beer.

Meat Locker: L Mon-Sat 12-3, D Mon-Sat 5.30-10. Pre-theatre 5.30-7. **Love Fish:** Mon-Sat 12-10. Wheelchair accessible; children welcome. CC. Closed Sun **Directions:** City centre.

DEANES AT QUEENS

36-40 COLLEGE GARDENS BELFAST CO ANTRIM   EAT | DRINK

028 9038 2111 | info@michaeldeane.co.uk

www.michaeldeane.co.uk

One of the most attractive restaurants in the Deane empire - and in the city - this child-friendly all-day bar and grill has a large (no smoking) terrace and enjoys a lovely leafy location beside the university, and near the Botanic Gardens and Ulster Museum. Head Chef Chris Fearon - well known from the BBC's Great British Menu - puts local seasonal ingredients first and includes Deanes' classics on menus, but he has also put his own stamp on the restaurant with his gutsy, flavoursome cooking style. This stylish smart-casual venue is also perfect for a private party.

Bar food all day. Restaurant Mon Sat L 12-3, D 5.30-10, Sun L 1-6. **Directions:** Beside Queen's University, overlooking Methodist College - top of University Road, right into College Gardens at junction with Malone Road.

THE FITZWILLIAM HOTEL BELFAST

-3 GREAT VICTORIA STREET BELFAST CO ANTRIM BT2 7BQ   EAT | STAY

028 9044 2080 | enq@fitzwilliamhotelbelfast.com

www.fitzwilliamhotelbelfast.com

This smart hotel beside the Grand Opera House impresses from the outset and - like its Dublin sister - you'll find the trademark chic, modern-classic Fitzwilliam style and attention to detail throughout. Rooms have luxurious beds, sumptuous bathrooms and little extras - and especially desirable corner rooms have windows on two sides overlooking the city. The stylish restaurant offers pleasing surroundings, good cooking and slick service at affordable prices, making this a popular dining destination for non-residents.

Rooms 130. (7 wheelchair friendly; all with separate bath & shower). Lift. Room rate from about £124. D daily from 5-9.30. Pre-Theatre D 5–6.30. Bar food daily 12.30-9.30. Hotel open all year. CC. **Directions:** Centre of Belfast, left off Howard Street on to Great Victoria Street, immediately on right.

GINGER BISTRO

68-72 GREAT VICTORIA STREET BELFAST CO ANTRIM BT2 7AF   EAT

028 9024 4421 | info@gingerbistro.com

www.gingerbistro.com

Simon 'Ginger' and his wife Abby McCance's chic and cheerful bistro may be bigger these days, but in essence it doesn't change - and that's the reason it's been one of Belfast's most consistently popular restaurants since first opening on the Ormeau Road in 2000. Carefully sourced, mainly local, ingredients have always been at the centre of this likeable chef's philosophy and menus offered include a dedicated vegetarian menu, as well as appealing meat dishes and the seafood that he likes to cook best. Offering great food and wine at affordable prices in a fun atmosphere, this is one of Belfast's best.

Open Tue-Sat 12-10. L/early D Tue-Fri 12-6.45, Sat 12-4. Set L about £30. Set D about £32.50. Also à la carte. Vegetarian menu. Closed Sun-Mon. CC. **Directions:** City centre, on corner of Great Victoria Street and Hope Street.

HADSKIS

33 DONEGALL STREET COMMERCIAL COURT BELFAST CO ANTRIM BT1 2NB   EAT
028 9032 5444 I info@hadskis.co.uk
www.hadskis.co.uk

Expect locally-inspired daily specials alongside classic European offerings at this former foundry in Belfast's trendy Cathedral Quarter. Owned by Niall and Joanne McKenna of James Street South (see entry), it's a tribute to the city's great engineering and manufacturing heritage and remembers Stewart Hadski, who made pots and pans on this site in the eighteenth century. Although the long narrow space is quite stark, well-trained staff are friendly and attentive - and Chef Cathal Duncan's food is deliciously warm and comforting. Many regulars come especially for the steaks but there's plenty of interesting 'restaurant' food too, often including unusual dishes like whole baked fish or roast pheasant. Great drinks list too- and good value.

Open daily, noon-'late'; early D 4-6 from about £17; also à la carte. Brunch Sat-Sun, 11-2. Wheelchair friendly. CC. Closed 25-26 Dec, 1 Jan, 12 July.

HASTINGS EUROPA HOTEL

GREAT VICTORIA STREET BELFAST CO ANTRIM BT2 7AP   STAY

028 9027 1066 | res@eur.hastingshotels.com
www.hastingshotels.com

Particularly striking when illuminated at night, this landmark building is one of Northern Ireland's largest hotels. Service has always been outstanding and, following recent renovations and the addition of executive rooms, there is accommodation to match, with details such as Egyptian cotton sheets and Espa toiletries in all rooms - and, of course, the famous Hastings duck in every bathroom. There's a constant buzz at the lobby bar and all-day brasserie; the Piano Lounge is quieter. But this famous hotel's greatest assets are the function suites and, especially, its excellent staff.

Rooms 272 (1 Presidential Suite, 5 Junior Suites, 92 Executive, 85 shower only, 3 wheelchair friendly). Lift. B&B from about £65pps. Children welcome. Restaurant L 12.30-3, D 3-10.30 daily. Lobby Bar Mon-Sat, food 12-2.30. Piano Lounge: Light fare, Afternoon Tea daily 2-5. Closed 24-25 Dec. CC. **Directions:** City centre.

JAMES STREET SOUTH

21 JAMES STREET SOUTH BELFAST CO ANTRIM BT2 7GA
028 9043 4310 | info@jamesstreetsouth.co.uk
www.jamesstreetsouth.co.uk

EAT | LEARN

The flagship of Niall and Joanne McKenna's restaurant group - the others are The Bar & Grill at James Street, Hadskis and the cheerful little Cast & Crew in the Titanic Quarter (see entries) - this understatedly stylish restaurant conveys a welcoming sense of confidence and offers modern fine dining at its best. An excellent kitchen team led by Head Chef David Gillmore produces refined food which can be truly memorable: expect exuberant modern cooking that is innovative, with seasonal and local produce very prevalent, and a harmonious balance of fresh flavours - plus excellent service, and one of the best wine lists in town, to match.

★★

L Wed-Sat, 12.30-2.30; D Mon-Sat, 5.30-10. Set L and pre-theatre D (5.30-6.30) from £18, also à la carte. Wheelchair accessible. **Cookery School**; chef apprenticeships. Closed Sun; 25-26 Dec, 1 Jan, 12 July. CC. **Directions:** City centre.

THE MERCHANT HOTEL

35-39 WARING STREET BELFAST CO ANTRIM BT1 2DY   EAT I STAY
028 9023 4888 I info@themerchanthotel.com
www.themerchanthotel.com

The grandeur of a larger-than-life Victorian banking building is a fit setting for Belfast's most dramatic and beautiful hotel. The lobby sets the tone for the whole hotel – warmly luxurious, but not ostentatious. The elegant, opulent bedrooms and suites are available in Victorian and Art Deco styles; everything exudes indulgence and service is impeccable. The house style in the aptly named Great Room Restaurant is upbeat classic and accomplished meals showcase local ingredients; a 9-course Tasting Menu offers good value (£70), especially with matching wines (£20), and Afternoon Tea is a speciality, served in the Great Room and with vegetarian, gluten-free, and nut-free options available.

Rooms 62 (shower & bath; 2 shower only). Restaurant daily, L 12-2.30; Afternoon Tea (times vary, must book); D 6-10.30; Sun 12-9; bar food from 12 (Sun 12.30). Spa; roof garden. Closed 25 Dec. CC. **Directions:** City centre.

MOLLY'S YARD

1 COLLEGE GREEN MEWS BOTANIC AVENUE
BELFAST CO ANTRIM BT7 1LW

EAT | DRINK

028 9032 2600 | info@mollysyard.co.uk | www.mollysyard.co.uk

This atmospheric restaurant - informal ground floor bistro with a more elegant dining room above - is in the former stables of College Green House and there is nothing clichéd about it, giving an intriguing feeling that this place is a 'find'. While the food offering may seem quite limited, it should be a pleasant surprise - and the all day 5-10-5 menu gives great value. But the bar is the major USP, as Molly's Yard is owned by Ireland's oldest independent brewery, Hilden Brewing Co, in nearby Lisburn, so this is the place to enjoy their draught and bottled beers. You can take some home too, in their Ale Sack (4 bottles in a sack, £10).

Food Mon-Sat 12-9.30. Children welcome before 6. Wheelchair accessible. Closed Sun, 25-26 Dec, 1 Jan. CC. **Directions:** Beside Dukes Hotel behind Queen's University.

MOURNE SEAFOOD BAR BELFAST

34-36 BANK STREET BELFAST CO ANTRIM BT1 1HL

EAT | DRINK

028 9024 8544 | belfast@mourneseafood.com
www.mourneseafood.com

This informal restaurant owned by well-known chef Andy Rae and business partner Bob McCoubrey of the original Mourne Seafood Bar in Dundrum, Co Down, has become a Belfast institution. Andy has a great following and his passion for seafood is evident: he uses less popular local fish rather than trendy imports and, of course, mussels and oysters from their own shellfish beds in Carlingford. Everything is homemade and the menu changes daily according to the catch. An interesting drinks list includes craft beers from Whitewater Brewery, Co Down, and cocktails featuring local craft spirits such as Shortcross Gin. **HOME** restaurant and the purpose-built **Belfast Cookery School**, adjoining the Seafood Bar, are associated businesses.

L Mon-Sat 12-4 (Fri-Sat to 3.30); Sun 1-4. D daily from 5. Children welcome. Wheelchair accessible. Closed 24-26 Dec, 1 Jan, 17 Mar. CC.

MUDDLERS CLUB

WAREHOUSE LANE CATHEDRAL QUARTER BELFAST CO ANTRIM BT1 2DX   EAT

028 90313199 | info@themuddlersclubbelfast.com

http://www.themuddlersclubbelfast.com

Opened in 2015 by top chef Gareth McCaughey and tucked into an alleyway, The Muddlers Club is named after a secret society that met around here two centuries ago, yet it is the true essence of a contemporary restaurant. It feels exciting on every level - from the bespoke wooden floors and tables to the scorched herbs, smoky aromas and intense seasoning of Gareth McCaughey's food.

Based on hand-selected seasonal ingredients, the bold dishes are plated with a maturity of spirit and the flavours pack a punch - and the excellent cooking is backed up by perceptive, knowledgeable and friendly service.

Seats 52. L Tue-Sat, 12-2.45; D Tue-Sat, 5.30-10. Tasting menu (vegetarian & vegan available) £45 (with wine £70). Closed Sun, Mon. CC. **Directions:** City centre, off Hill Street - back of Duke of York pub.

NATIVE BY YELLOW DOOR AT THE MAC

ST ANNE'S SQUARE CATHEDRAL QUARTER BELFAST CO ANTRIM BT1 2NJ   EAT

028 9023 5053 I native@themaclive.com

www.yellowdoordeli.co.uk/native

Food and theatre are a happy marriage at this café-bar and restaurant in Belfast's MAC arts venue. As expected of any enterprise that The Yellow Door puts its name to, it's big on local, sustainable and home-grown produce (and the famed Yellow Door baking of course), and the food is vibrant and packed full of flavour. Open for breakfast, lunch, dinner (on show nights) and light bites, the menu at NATIVE changes according to the seasons but there are some constants, including the Doran's beef burger - which also features in miniature on the NATIVE Bites menu - and pairings with local craft beers and ciders. Well worth a visit, theatre or not.

Open 9.30-7 (on show nights D 5-7.30; 2/3 course £13/17.50). Vegan & vegetarian menus; children's menu. Closed 25 Dec. Wheelchair accessible. CC. **Directions:** St Anne's Square.

OX

1 OXFORD STREET BELFAST CO ANTRIM BT1 3LA
028 9031 4121 | info@oxbelfast.com
www.oxbelfast.com

EAT

The opening of Stephen Toman and Alain Kerloc'h's ambitious yet relaxed Lagan-side restaurant in 2013 marked a sea change in Belfast dining. Describing itself simply as 'A restaurant with seasonal creativity', it combines stylish modern ingredients-led food with a casual vibe; its immediate success inspired a lot of re-thinking and it remains one of the most consistently exciting dining rooms in the country. OX's short (and reasonably priced) menu is a model of pared-down promise and Stephen Toman's cooking is exquisite, with great attention to detail - a standard mirrored by impeccable service. A great team and a wonderful, affordable restaurant - and with an atmospheric bar, Ox Cave, next door.

★★

L Tue-Sat 12-2.30 (Sat 1-2.30), D Tue-Sat 6-9.30. Tasting Menu (also Vegetable) from £50, wine pairing £30. **Ox Cave:** Tue-Sat 4-late, music Sat from 9. Closed Sun-Mon. CC.

RAVENHILL HOUSE

690 RAVENHILL ROAD BELFAST CO ANTRIM BT6 0BZ
028 9020 7444 | info@ravenhillhouse.com
www.ravenhillhouse.com

STAY

Roger and Olive Nicholson's late-Victorian redbrick house has a sense of seclusion despite being on a busy road. It's a very welcoming house and the bedrooms are comfortable and stylishly furnished, with lots of little extras such as fresh milk kept handy in a fridge for guests' use. But it is breakfast that is sure to be the highlight of a stay here. The Nicholsons buy all their fresh goods from local farmers and producers at the weekly St George's Market, and they make everything possible on the premises, even grinding the flour for their breads. And they are very helpful with guests' daily itineraries - an excellent base for a stay in Belfast.

Rooms 4 (2 shower only). B&B from about £45pps, free wifi. No pets, no wheelchair access. Closed Christmas. CC.
Directions: Two miles from city centre.

SALT BISTRO

SAINT ANNE'S SQUARE BELFAST CO ANTRIM BT1 2LR   EAT
028 9023 8012 | info@saltbistrobelfast.com
www.saltbistrobelfast.com

Donal and Teresa Cooper (previously well known in Limerick), run this quietly excellent restaurant in Belfast's exciting cultural quarter right beside the Metropolitan Arts Centre (MAC). It's a polished operation and, while offering predictable-sounding food, it's the cooking that makes a difference - you can take the fine dining out of the menu, but you can't take the classical training out of the cook. Smart service, good wine list - and fair value too. Well worth a visit.

L Mon-Fri 12-2.30 (Sat to 3.30); D Mon-Wed 5-9, (Thu-Sat to 9.30). Pre-theatre from about £16, also à la carte. Children welcome. Wheelchair accessible. Outdoor seating. Closed Sun. CC.

SAPHYRE

135 LISBURN ROAD BELFAST CO ANTRIM BT9 7AG   EAT
028 9068 8606 | dining@saphyrerestaurant.com
www.saphyrerestaurant.com

Swanky, sophisticated and not a bit stuffy sums up the sumptuous Saphyre restaurant. This is one of the city's best restaurants and multi-talented Dutch chef Joery Castel's dishes are a delight to the eye and on the tongue. Given the exceptional quality of the food, service and setting (created by leading interior designer Kris Turnbull), Saphyre offers value, especially at lunch time. And don't forget to smarten yourself up for this treat - everyone else does.

⭐

Open Wed -Sat 11-10, Sat 1-10 (music Sat 1-3), Aft Tea Sat 2pm, from £24. L Wed-Fri 12-3, D Wed-Sat 5-10. Brunch Wed-Fri, 11-3. Set L from about £30; Tasting L from £40. 5/7/9-course Tasting menus £50/£65/£85, wine pairings £30/£45/£60; Vegetarian 5-course Tasting £50, wine pairing £30, also à la carte. Closed Sun-Tue. CC. **Directions:** Lisburn Road, near junction with Wellesley Avenue.

SHU

253 LISBURN ROAD BELFAST CO ANTRIM BT9 7EN

EAT

028 9038 1655 | eat@shu-restaurant.com

www.shu-restaurant.com

The tall arched windows and smartly painted Victorian frontage of Alan Reid's much-admired restaurant exude warmth. Restaurant manager Julian Henry and his staff are very welcoming, and the open kitchen adds interest to the large and atmospheric room. Since 2004, former Great British Menu star Brian McCann has headed up a talented team of chefs here and McCann's unwavering enthusiasm for uncomplicated quality food is unmistakable; they are in pursuit of excellence - there is something to suit every taste and pocket, notably a crowd-pulling lunch menu that offers exceptional value. With great food, service, value and atmosphere, Shu continues to be a leader in the Belfast restaurant scene.

Open Mon-Sat, L12-2.30, D 5.30-9.30; Set D from about £20, also à la carte. Closed Sun, 24-26 Dec, 1 Jan, 11-13 Jul. CC. **Directions:** Half mile south on Lisburn Road.

CLENAGHANS

48 SOLDIERSTOWN ROAD AGHALEE CO ANTRIM BT67 0ES   EAT | STAY
028 9265 2952 | restaurant@clenaghans.com

Located at the meeting of three counties - Antrim, Armagh and Down - this delightful rural restaurant was re-opened in November 2017 by Stevie and Cristina Higginson of the popular Square Bistro (see entry) in nearby Lurgan, in partnership with leading chef Danni Barry, formerly of Deanes Eipic, Belfast. The premises, a former pub dating back to the 17th century, is full of rustic charm, making a dream setting for good food. True to form, menus are produce driven and the promise from the famous fine dining chef is 'there will be something for everyone' - so this will be just the place to find those gutsy, deeply-flavoured soups and rustic pies...

Open: L Tue-Sat 12-3, D Tue-Sat from 5, Sun 12-6. Accommodation available. CC. Directions: Halfway between Moira and Aghalee, at junction of Soldierstown Road and Drumbane Road.

RED DOOR TEA ROOM

14A HARBOUR ROAD BALLINTOY CO ANTRIM BT54 6NA   EAT
028 2076 9048 | thereddoortearoom@yahoo.co.uk
www.facebook.com/thereddoortearoom

Near the quaint little fishing harbour of Ballintoy and its iconic whitewashed church, Joan and Nigel McGarrity's little red-doored tea room opened in 2012 and it was such a hit that it gradually developed into a small restaurant. While still offering snacks and afternoon tea, they now have a drinks licence and also offer a short but tasty menu of locally sourced traditional dishes, including a great seafood chowder and a hearty Irish stew, along with lighter fare such as toasted ciabattas and desserts. Right in the middle of the Causeway Coast, it's ideally placed for both locals and tourists - from the coast road, you'll spot the name painted on the roof.

Seats 50 (+75 outside). Open daily in summer 11-4, also occasional evenings in high season; off season weekends only. CC. **Directions:** up a lane near Ballintoy harbour.

WHITEPARK HOUSE

150 WHITEPARK ROAD BALLINTOY BALLYCASTLE CO ANTRIM BT54 6NH   STAY

028 2073 1482 | bob@whiteparkhouse.com

www.whiteparkhouse.com

On the A2 between the Giant's Causeway and Carrick-a-Rede Rope Bridge, Bob and Siobhán Isles's pretty old house is tucked away in a sylvan setting, well back from the road. It enjoys stunning views of Whitepark Bay, and a path just across the road leads down to the beautiful beach. Famous first and foremost for the warm welcome extended by the chatty and well-informed hosts, it's an exceptional place to stay - stylish, cosy and luxuriously comfortable, and with Bob's lovely gardens to enjoy as well. Gorgeous food too, including an immaculately presented afternoon tea on arrival as well as delicious breakfasts (vegetarian, vegan options) - and all the low-down on the best local dining spots. A one off.

Rooms 3. B&B from £65pps. Unsuitable for children under 12. Wifi. Closed Dec-Feb. CC. **Directions:** Coast road, 6m east of Bushmills.

CENTRAL WINE BAR

12 ANN STREET BALLYCASTLE CO ANTRIM BT54 6AD   EAT I DRINK

028 2076 3877 I info@centralwinebar.com
www.centralwinebar.com

Dating back to 1861, this family business has been run by Phillip and Gemma McHenry since 2000 and is now an extensive food and entertainment complex. While a large, modern bar and restaurant may not be an obvious destination for food lovers, the Central Wine Bar is a Taste of Ulster member and talented head chef, Ciaran Sansome, and his team are committed to showcasing local and Irish ingredients on seasonal menus that offer something for everyone. Local meats and fish are highlights, also a traditional Irish dish of the day - and there are some great vegetarian choices. An all-round winner.

Food 12-9 daily. Set Sun L about £14, also à la carte. Music Fri & Sat night (5 nights weekly in summer). CC. **Directions:** Ballycastle town centre.

THYME & CO CAFÉ

5 QUAY ROAD BALLYCASTLE CO ANTRIM BT54 76J   EAT

028 2076 9851 I info@thymeandco.co.uk
www.thymeandco.co.uk

With its welcoming, informal atmosphere, this is just the kind of place visitors to Ballycastle will be happy to find. Run by Tom and Eimear Mullin, who take great pride in doing the important things right, this café has earned a following for the delicious homemade flavours of the food, which is based on locally sourced ingredients, and especially the home baking (including gluten-free). The locals have known all along that there was something special about the breads here and in 2017 it became official, when their 'Ballycastle Wheaten' won the Irish Wheaten Loaf category in the World Bread Awards. Very much the hub of the community, they also sell local crafts.

Open: Tue-Fri 8.30-4, Sat 9-9, Sun 10-3.30, sometimes open evenings. **No CC. Directions:** Centre of Ballycastle, beside park on A2 Quay Road.

GALGORM RESORT & SPA

136 FENAGHY ROAD BALLYMENA CO ANTRIM BT42 1EA   EAT I STAY
028 2588 1001 I sales@galgorm.com
www.galgorm.com

This former gentleman's residence is now one of Northern Ireland's most luxurious country house hotels, and the region's premier wedding venue. Yet, while larger and more contemporary following major redevelopment, it has retained its pleasant tranquil atmosphere. Spacious rooms and excellent facilities (including equestrian, and thermal spa) are matched by outstanding food, notably in the River Room where accomplished chef Chris Rees's cooking of seasonal food and local specialities is a memorable experience - as is the renowned 'Galgorm breakfast'.

Rooms 122 (3 wheelchair friendly). B&B from about £100pps. Choice of restaurants; **River Room** (fine dining): D Wed-Sat, Sun 12.30-10; Afternoon Tea daily; Cocktail & Gin Bar. Open all year. CC. **Directions:** At Galgorm roundabout, third exit for Cullybackey (Fenaghy road); 2 miles, on left.

MARLAGH LODGE

71 MOORFIELDS ROAD BALLYMENA CO ANTRIM BT42 3BU   EAT | STAY
028 2563 1505 | info@marlaghlodge.com
www.marlaghlodge.com

Robert and Rachel Thompson's restored early-Victorian house now makes an unusual and comfortable haven for guests and, although close to the A36, surrounding gardens (where hens cluck contentedly) and thick walls keep traffic noise at bay. The Lodge is a classic of its era, double fronted with spacious, high-ceilinged reception rooms on each side of the entrance hall, and large, comfortably furnished bedrooms. Good food is at the heart of their ethos, and interesting dinners showcasing local produce are offered, as well as an excellent breakfast - and Afternoon Tea (by reservation) on some Sundays, too.

Rooms 3. B&B from about £50pps. Residents' D Fri-Sat, 8pm (book by noon). 'Closed occasionally', ring ahead off-season. Afternoon Tea monthly (2nd or 3rd Sun) £25. Private dining. CC. **Directions:** On A36, 1/2m from Larne Road roundabout.

BUSHMILLS INN

9 DUNLUCE ROAD BUSHMILLS CO ANTRIM BT57 8QG   EAT | STAY
028 2073 3000 | mail@bushmillsinn.com
www.bushmillsinn.com

Originally a 19th century coaching inn, the traditional tone of Alan Dunlop's famously interesting and well-run hotel is set by the turf fire and country furniture in the hall. Public rooms include an atmospheric gas-lit bar and a unique circular library and bedrooms are furnished in a cottage style that suits the building. Known for its wholesome food, pride in Irish ingredients and tradition is most obvious in day menus that include dishes like Brotchan ('an old name for "aitin n drinkin" soup'). A great base for playing the famous golf courses of the area, or exploring this beautiful coastline.

Rooms 41 (2 wheelchair friendly). B&B from £90pps. Children welcome. L&D daily; Mon-Sat 12-5 & 6-9.30. Sun L 12.30-3, D from 5. Bar food Sun only 12-4. Closed 24-25 Dec. CC. **Directions**: A4 Antrim coast road, in Bushmills village.

THE FRENCH ROOMS

45 MAIN STREET BUSHMILLS CO ANTRIM BT57 8QA
028 2073 0033 | mail@thefrenchrooms.com
www.thefrenchrooms.com

EAT | STAY | BUY

Well-known host Roy Bolton and family are behind this atmospheric enterprise. A slice of French ambience, it offers interesting interior and dining accessories, a gourmet grocery featuring 'Local Hero' products and very tasty French-inspired café food and drink, sourced in France and locally. Expect tasty bistro classics and interesting drinks (craft beer and cider, cocktails), served in a surprisingly convincing and relaxed rural French setting, at affordable prices. This is the most elegant and stylish restaurant on the Causeway Coast, and good value too. *Also 'Maison', offering 2 high-spec self-catering suites and oodles of charm.

Seats 60 + outside tables. Open Wed & Sun 10-4, Thu-Sat 10-11, D from 6. Closed Mon-Tue, also D Thu Hallowe'en-Easter. Closed 5 weeks Jan/early Feb. Wheelchair accessible. Accommodation min 2-night stay, no pets, breakfast optional. CC.
Directions: Centre of Bushmills.

LONDONDERRY ARMS HOTEL

20 HARBOUR ROAD CARNLOUGH CO ANTRIM BT44 0EU   STAY
028 2888 5255 | lda@glensofantrim.com
www.glensofantrim.com

Originally a coaching inn, this traditional hotel was formerly owned by Sir Winston Churchill and has been in the caring hands of the O'Neill family since 1948. Many of the comfortably furnished bedrooms have sea views and this is a place where visitors enjoy dropping in for good home-made bar meals or a fireside afternoon tea - and chef Manus Jamison's restaurant meals may include the local speciality, Lough Neagh Eel, which was awarded the prestigious EU Protected Geographical Indication (PGI) status in 2011. A delightful place in a lovely village - allow time for a walk around the little harbour.

Rooms 35. B&B from about £50pps. L, D and bar meals daily. Closed 24-25 Dec. CC. **Directions:** On the A2 Antrim Coast road. |

GLENARM CASTLE TEA ROOM

2 CASTLE LANE GLENARM CO ANTRIM BT44 0BQ   EAT
028 2884 1203 | info@glenarmcastle.com
www.glenarmcastle.com

Glenarm Castle, ancestral home of the McDonnell family, Earls of Antrim, offers much of interest including The Walled Garden. The Castle itself is also open several times a year and the famous Glenarm Beef and Glenarm Salmon are produced on the estate. The Tea Room is a charming setup in the old Mushroom House beside the kitchen garden and, following a recent revamp, it now has several very pleasant rooms to choose from - and a choice of outside seating too, one is in the inner gardens for customers with tickets. They offer tasty snacks, including many organic ingredients, brunch and cream teas - it makes a lovely stopping off place when touring on the coast road.

Seats 59 (+ 2 patio areas 56). Gift shop; artisan produce. Gardens & Tea Room open: April-mid-Dec, Mon-Sat 10-5, Sun 11-5. Closed 3pm Nov-Dec.

SQUARE BISTRO

18 LISBURN SQUARE LISBURN CO ANTRIM BT28 1TS   EAT
028 9266 6677 | info@squarebistro.co.uk
www.squarebistro.co.uk

Opened by chef Stephen Higginson and his wife Cristina in 2006, the Square Bistro has been Lisburn's most consistently popular restaurant for over a decade. It's a warm, friendly and atmospheric venue, with a loyal clientèle who keep coming back for the terrific service given by well-trained staff as much as for the excellent, carefully sourced food - and great value. (Who wouldn't want to pop in for a delicious weekday lunch at £16 for two?). Steaks from Peter Hannan are a speciality, also their themed nights (Tapas, Curry, Seafood) which have a keen following. In 2017 the Higginsons teamed up with top chef Danni Barry to re-open the much-loved Clenaghans restaurant near Moira (see entry).

> Open Mon-Sat 9.30-3, Tue-Thu 5-8.30, Fri-Sat 5-9. Children welcome; wheelchair accessible; wifi; vegetarian & vegan choices; bar. Closed Sun. CC. **Directions:** Moira Road; town centre.

MADDYBENNY FARMHOUSE

LOGUESTOWN ROAD PORTRUSH COLERAINE CO ANTRIM BT52 2PT   STAY
028 7082 3394 | beds@maddybenny.com
www.maddybenny.com

An exceptionally hospitable place to stay, the White family's Plantation-era farmhouse dates back pre-1650 and has since been extended many times. It is very comfortable and relaxed, with plenty of seating areas, indoor and outdoor games areas for children, and even stabling for guests' horses. The bedrooms are all en-suite, with all sorts of thoughtful extras, and Karen White's breakfasts are legendary, so allow plenty of time to start the day with one of her feasts. Eight excellent self-catering cottages are also offered, all fitted out to high specifications and three are wheelchair friendly; perfect for families and groups.

> **Rooms 3** (all shower only). B&B £35pps (child discount); no pets. Wifi. Snooker table. Horse livery. 3* & 5* self-catering (no pets); attractively sited serviced caravan/camping field (pets allowed). Closed 25-26 Dec. CC. **Directions:** Signed off A29 Portrush/Coleraine road.

RAMORE RESTAURANTS

1 THE HARBOUR ROAD PORTRUSH CO ANTRIM BT56 8BN   EAT | DRINK
028 7082 6969 | ramore@btconnect.com
www.ramorerestaurants.co.uk

The McAlpin family's Ramore was once a leading light of cosmopolitan fine dining in Northern Ireland - today they offer a very different style, where informality goes hand in hand with quality and value. Likened to a cruise ship, the Ramore Complex - comprising five individual restaurants, The Ramore Wine Bar, Coast Pizzeria, The Harbour Bar & Bistro, The Mermaid Kitchen & Bar and Neptune & Prawn - is by far the region's most popular dining destination. On a busy day they may feed a thousand here, yet the cooking is as good as ever, presentation classy, service quick and attentive. A one-off.

Ramore Wine Bar: L&D daily. Coast Pizzeria: D Wed-Sat. Harbour Bistro: Sun L&D Wed-Sun. The Mermaid Kitchen & Bar: D daily. Neptune & Prawn: D daily. Closed Mon-Tue, bank hols, 24-26 Dec. CC. **Directions:** At Portrush harbour.

SHOLA COACH HOUSE

110A GATESIDE ROAD PORTRUSH CO ANTRIM BT56 8NP   STAY
028 70825925 / +44 (0) 7565427738 | sholabandb@gmail.com
www.sholabandb.com

Tucked away in lovely gardens above Portrush town, Sharon and David Schindler's quietly located boutique B&B is away from the crowds yet handy to local attractions and good restaurants. Afternoon tea with home-baked goodies is served beside an open turf fire in the elegant guest sitting room and, while bedrooms are very different in style, the same high standards apply across the board; all have super king-size beds and good facilities, with lovely toiletries in the smart bathrooms. A highly desirable adult destination - and good value too.

Rooms 4 (1 power shower only). B&B from £50pps. Unsuitable for under 18s. Wifi. Closed Dec. CC. **Directions:** A2 to Portrush; at roundabout, 1st exit (Crocknamack Road/A2); 1st L (Ballywillan Road); 1 mile up hill, through crossroads (now Gateside Road); 50 yards, 1st R at stone wall; sharp L - gravel driveway.

THE MANOR HOUSE

RATHLIN ISLAND CO ANTRIM BT54 6RT   EAT | STAY
028 2076 0046 | info@manorhouserathlin.com
www.manorhouserathlin.com/

This handsome late Georgian gentleman's residence overlooking Church Bay dates back to the 1760s. Owned by the National Trust and managed by local hospitality duo Genevieve and Brian McLernon, it has recently been completely restored and refurbished; each bedroom reflects an era of the building, and most have wonderful sea views. The charming Lighthouse Café offers daytime food and the Island Restaurant serves evening meals for residents - also non-residents, by reservation, at weekends. The view out over the little harbour is lovely, and you need never miss the ferry as you can see it arrive and saunter down just as they slip the ropes.

Rooms 11 (all shower only, 1 wheelchair friendly), B&B from about £50pps. Lighthouse Café: Mon-Sat 12-4. Island Restaurant: residents' D nightly, non-residents Sat 6.30-8.30 & Sun 12-4, booking essential. Licensed. Open all year. CC. **Directions:** Ferry from Ballycastle.

COUNTY ARMAGH

Mention Armagh www.armagh.co.uk , and most people will think of apples and archbishops. In the more fertile northern part of the county, orchards are traditionally important in the local economy, with the lore of apple growing and their use a part of County Armagh life. And the pleasant cathedral city of Armagh itself is of course the ecclesiastical capital of all Ireland, and many a mitre is seen about it.

But in fact Armagh city's significance long pre-dates Christian times. *Emhain Macha* - Navan Fort- to the west of the town, was a royal stronghold and centre of civilisation more than 4,000 years ago. Marking the county's northern coastline, the inland freshwater sea of Lough Neagh provides sand for the construction industry, eels for gourmets, and recreational boating of all sorts. In times past, it was part of the route which brought coal to Dublin from the mines in Coalisland in Tyrone, the main link to the seaport of Newry being the canal from Portadown which, when opened in 1742, was in the forefront of canal technology.

That County Armagh was a leader in canal technology is only one of its many surprises. The discerning traveller will find much of interest, among the undulating farmland and orchards, the pretty villages, or the handsome uplands rising to Carrigatuke above Newtownhamilton, and on towards the fine peak of Slieve Gullion www.ringofgullion.org in the south of the county, down to Forkhill and Crossmaglen and the Gaelic football heartlands.

LOCAL ATTRACTIONS AND INFORMATION

>Armagh **Observatory & Planetarium** www.armaghplanet.com | 028 37 523689

>Armagh **Palace Stables Heritage Centre** 028 37 529629

>Bessbrook **Derrymore House** 028 30 830353

>Loughgall **Loughgall Country Park** 028 38 892900

>Markethill **Gosford Forest Park** 028 37 551277

>Newry **Derrymore House** 028 30 830353

>Portadown **Moneypenny's Lock** (Newry Canal) 028 37 521800

>Slieve Gullion **Forest Park** www.ringofgullion.org | 028 30 848226

THE MOODY BOAR RESTAURANT & BISTRO

PALACE STABLES PALACE DEMESNE   EAT | DRINK
ARMAGH CO ARMAGH BT60 4EL

028 3752 9678 | bookings@themoodyboar.com | www.themoodyboar.com

The picturesque Palace Stables Heritage Centre in Armagh city provides a great setting for Sean and Ramune Farnan's delicious food based on their holistic philosophy for 'sustainability, value, local produce and, most of all, flavour'. Local produce, including Lough Neagh Eel (PGI) and Fivemiletown cheese, features in appealing Small Plates and Big Plates - and the plates themselves, made by Sean's brother Stephen, are for sale along with other crafts. Original, unpretentious, tasty, fresh and good value - highly recommended.

Seats 65 (+bar 20, outside 40). Breakfast: Sat only, 10-12; L & D Tue-Sat, 12-3 & 5-9.30 (no food 3-5, tea & coffee only); Sun all day 12-7. Early D Tue-Fri 5-6.30, from about £18, otherwise à la carte. Children's menu. Wheelchair accessible. Closed Mon. CC. **Directions:** At the Palace Stables Heritage Centre (short walk from Armagh City Hotel).

4 VICARS

4 VICAR'S HILL ARMAGH CO ARMAGH BT617ED   EAT

028 3752 7772 | contact@4vicars.com

www.4vicars.com

Gareth and Kasia Reid opened this delightful restaurant in a Georgian terrace beside Saint Patrick's Church of Ireland Cathedral in 2014 - and it has been a-buzz with lucky locals and visitors to Armagh ever since. A back terrace has views over ancient Navan Fort but, inside the listed building, it's refreshingly smart and youthful. Gareth's 'source local and seasonal' food philosophy informs every aspect of the business, down to the carefully selected teas, coffees, local ciders and craft beers that lend interest to drinks lists. It's a true taste of Armagh and the constants are sound cooking, modern presentation, food with oodles of flavour - and, under Kasia's direction, great service. Good value, too.

Open Wed-Sun 10-3 & Fri-Sat 6-8.30. Sun L from about £23, otherwise à la carte. Closed Mon-Tue. Wheelchair access. CC. **Directions:** Off Castle Street.

NEWFORGE HOUSE

58 NEWFORGE ROAD MAGHERALIN CRAIGAVON CO ARMAGH BT67 0QL   STAY
028 9261 1255 | enquiries@newforgehouse.com
www.newforgehouse.com

In the Mathers family for six generations, John and Louise Mathers's lovely Georgian country house is only a short drive from Belfast yet, set in mature trees, gardens and green fields, it feels like worlds away. Stylishly furnished throughout, it offers luxurious accommodation in individually decorated rooms with beautiful bathrooms and has become one of Northern Ireland's most desirable destinations. John's excellent meals showcase local and organic produce and hens clucking around the productive orchard provide your breakfast eggs. It's a lovely spot for a short break, with many activities nearby, and makes a perfect setting for special occasions.

Rooms 6 (1 shower only). B&B from about £70pps. D Tue-Sat 8, (non-residents 7.30), about £45, reservations only. Sun & Mon light dinner only. Closed mid Dec-end Jan CC. **Directions:** M1 Belfast-Craigavon; A3 to Moira; Moira-Magheralin; L at Byrnes Pub; signed.

YELLOW DOOR DELI, BAKERY & CAFÉ

74 WOODHOUSE STREET PORTADOWN CO ARMAGH BT62 1JL

028 3835 3528 | deli@yellowdoordeli.co.uk

www.yellowdoordeli.co.uk

EAT | BUY
PRODUCER

The energetic and hugely talented Simon Dougan is one of the luminaries of the Northern Ireland food scene, and his Yellow Door Deli - a destination for discerning customers for two decades - is now at the centre of one of the region's biggest and best food operations, with several branches and excellent outside catering. Their breads and speciality foods are legendary and discerning customers home in on this smashing shop from a wide area, to top up with goodies and have a tasty bite to eat. Interesting and keenly priced wine list too. Also at: Lisburn; Belfast (Lisburn Road; Ulster Museum; Native at the MAC - see entry).

Open: Mon–Sat 9-5. Closed Sun, 12-13 Jul, 25-26 Dec, "some" bank hols. CC.
Directions: Off Main Street, on left - only street on left as the traffic flows one way.

BLACKWELL HOUSE

33 MULLABRACK ROAD SCARVA CO ARMAGH BT63 6BP

028 3883 2752 | enquiries@blackwellhouse.co.uk

www.blackwellhouse.co.uk

STAY

Complimentary cream tea for guests arriving between 3 and 4pm is just one of the nice little extras offered by Stephen and Joyce Brownless at their splendid guesthouse near Banbridge. Open since 2014, it is set in lovely rolling drumlin country on the Armagh-Down border, and makes a great base for exploring a wide area - including Belfast and Dublin which are both easily accessible for day visits. Local and homemade food is central to life at Blackwell (griddle bread baking class offered) and dinner is available, enjoyed communally around a fine big table.

Rooms 3 (1 separate bath & shower, 1 shower only). B&B from about £120 double (single from £78). D by reservation, 7-7.30pm; 3-course Seasonal Menu, about £35. Mainly an adult destination; no dogs. CC. **Directions:** West of Banbridge, north of Scarva; off A27, on Mullabrack Road.

COUNTY DOWN

County Down rings the changes in elegant style, from its affluent shoreline along Belfast Lough - the "Gold Coast" of which Bangor is the focus - through the rolling drumlin country which provides Strangford Lough's www.visitnorthernireland.com many islands, and on then past Slieve Croob, with the view southward being increasingly dominated by the purple slopes of the Mountains of Mourne www.visitmournemountains.co.uk .

The Mournes soar to Northern Ireland's highest peak of Slieve Donard (850m), and provide excellent hill-walking and challenging climbing. Yet when seen from a distance they have a gentleness which is in keeping with the county's well-groomed style. In the same vein, Down is home to some of Ireland's finest gardens, notably Mount Stewart on the eastern shore of Strangford Lough, and Rowallane at Saintfield, while the selection of forest and country parks is also exceptional.

The coastline is so indented that County Down provides more than half of Northern Ireland's entire shoreline. Within it, the jewel of Strangford Lough is an unmatched attraction for naturalists and boat enthusiasts, while Portaferry has one of Ireland's longest-established saltwater aquariums in Exploris.

In the south of the county, the increasingly prosperous town of Newry on the river and Ship Canal inland from Carlingford Lough is one of Ireland's newest cities under a re-designation of 2003. Newry is responding with enthusiasm to its enhanced status, and the urban regeneration of this interesting canalside centre is heartening, though for those who wish to stay with the coast route, a ferry now runs from Greencastle in County Down across the mouth of Carlingford Lough to Greenore in Louth www.carlingfordferry.com

LOCAL ATTRACTIONS AND INFORMATION

>Bangor **North Down Heritage Centre**
028 91 271200

>Cultra **Ulster Folk & Transport Museum**
028 90 428428

>Hillsborough **Hillsborough Castle Gardens**
028 92 681300

>Mourne Mountains **Guided Wildlife Walks**
028 43 751467

BULL & RAM

1 DROMORE STREET BALLYNAHINCH CO DOWN

028 9756 0908 | info@bullandram.com

www.bullandram.com

EAT

Opened in 2016 by well-known chef, Kelan McMichael, this former butchers shop is a listed building, sympathetically restored with original features intact - how appropriate for this master of meat cooking, whose bone-marrow gravy, huge Yorkshire puddings and moreish pork scratchings are the stuff of local legend. The beef (including 55-day aged Glenarm Shorthorn steaks) is from Hannan Meats, the lamb is from the Mourne Mountains and the sustainable fish is brought in fresh from Kilkeel every day. The menu majors on protein with the Sunday Toast to the Roast epitomising what this place is about - informal dining where flavour is king.

Food daily: Mon-Tue 12-8.30; Wed-Thu 12-9; Fri- Sat 12-9.30; Sun 12-8. Sun L about £25, also à la carte. Children's Menu. Parking. CC. **Directions:** Town centre. **Also at: Bull & Ram Belfast** University Road, Belfast.

QUAILS AT THE GALLERY

200 NEWRY ROAD BANBRIDGE CO DOWN BT32 3NB

028 4062 9667 | info@quailsfinefoods.co.uk

www.quailsfinefoods.co.uk

EAT | BUY
PRODUCER

This is an interesting place to visit and easily accessed off the M1 without having to go into the town. Everyone who visits the F.E. McWilliam Gallery praises the café and you can enjoy a pleasant lunch here looking out through big glass walls onto the sculpture garden. Operated by Joe Quail, who has a long-established (1898) butcher's shop and café in the town, this excellent family-run food hall and deli serves breakfast and lunch as well as lots of scones, muffins, tray bakes and luscious desserts. Well worth a visit.

Seats 55 (+30 outdoors). Café Mon-Sat 8.30-5. Sun (Jun-Aug only) 1-5. Closed 25-26 Dec, 1 Jan, Easter Sun. Online shop. CC. **Directions:** M1- Junction for Banbridge & Bridgewater Park.

CAIRN BAY LODGE

278 SEACLIFF ROAD BANGOR CO DOWN BT20 5HS   STAY
028 9146 7636 I info@cairnbaylodge.com
www.cairnbaylodge.com

An attractive, detached house overlooking Ballyholme Bay and set in extensive gardens, Chris and Jenny Mullen's friendly guesthouse is a pleasant base in a desirable area of this popular seaside town. A large yet cosy house dating back to 1914, Cairn Bay Lodge is full of character and its numerous USPs include lovely rooms, a pretty back garden, treatments (using gorgeous Voya organic products from Co Sligo, no less), a little gift shop - and an excellent breakfast served in The Starfish cafe - which is a popular haunt with discerning locals as well as resident guests. The beautiful Ards peninsula and Strangford Lough are very near Bangor – and well worth a visit.

> **Rooms 7** (all shower only). B&B from about £50pps. Children welcome. Starfish Café 9-2.30. Open all year. CC. **Directions:** A2 Belfast - Bangor.

CLANDEBOYE LODGE HOTEL

10 ESTATE ROAD CLANDEBOYE BANGOR CO DOWN BT19 1UR   EAT I STAY
028 9185 2500 I info@clandeboyelodge.co.uk
www.clandeboyelodge.com

Quietly set in woodland on the edge of the Clandeboye Estate (you can buy their beautiful yoghurt from the milking parlour next door), this comfortable privately-owned hotel just outside Bangor makes a good impression with its neat grounds, stylishly furnished public areas and especially friendly and helpful staff. Offering a pleasing alternative to the town, it is a popular wedding venue and convenient to Belfast for business guests. Suites sport whirlpool baths and all the spacious, modern bedrooms have ample work space. Seasonal ingredients-led meals are served in the destination brasserie, Coq & Bull, and in the very attractive adjoining lobby bar - a pleasant place to relax after a long day.

> **Rooms 43** (2 wheelchair friendly). Lift. B&B from £55pps. L & D daily. CC. Closed 24-26 Dec. CC. **Directions:** In outskirts of Bangor, off A2.

GUILLEMOT KITCHEN CAFÉ & WINE BAR

2 SEACLIFF ROAD BANGOR CO DOWN BT20 5EY   EAT
0044 78 0085 8821 I rachel@theguillemot.com
www.facebook.com/theguillemot

With its fun decor - a lively blend of maritime themes and vintage that's very easy on the eye - and constant buzz, Rachel Armstrong's super café is just a great place to be, and the friendly, well-trained staff couldn't be more accommodating. Quality was the name of the game from the outset: delicious food, simply cooked is what you will find here and who could ask for more? The Guillemot Omelette (pale smoked haddock and Gruyère cheese) is a great favourite with regulars, and the Vegetarian Breakfast of herb-roasted mushrooms & tomato with egg and guacamole on soda bread is also highly recommended. Terrific coffee, loose-leaf teas and infusions too. No wonder The Guillemot is one of Bangor's most popular cafés.

Seats about 40. Open daily 9-5, D Thu-Sat 6-11. Children welcome. CC. **Directions:** Harbour front, near the marina.

THE SALTY DOG HOTEL & BISTRO

10-12 SEACLIFF ROAD BANGOR CO DOWN BT20 5EY

028 9127 0696 | info@saltydogbangor.com

www.saltydogbangor.com

EAT | DRINK | STAY

Two Victorian townhouses in a choice corner location overlooking Belfast Lough and Bangor Marina serve as Ken Sharp's delightfully quirky boutique hotel. Popular with locals as a casual dining destination, or for a drink (they stock an exceptional range of craft beers and gins), it's a pleasant place to stay within a waterside stroll of Ballyholme Bay. Rooms vary, but most have sea views (the supplement is well worth paying) and a very good breakfast is served. The nearby restaurant, **The Boat House** (www.boathousebangor.com) is common ownership, with Chef Tim Brunton wowing fine-dining customers and private groups at this famously atmospheric venue.

Rooms 15 (all en-suite). B&B from £45pps. Children welcome. Dogs permitted (in bedroom). L&D Mon-Sat 12-3 & 5-9 (Fri & Sat to 10). Sun 12-8. CC. **Directions:** Seafront.

THE WHEATHILL

7 GRAYS HILL BANGOR CO DOWN BT20 3BB   EAT
028 9147 7405 I info@thewheathill.com
www.thewheathill.com

An impressive first venture for husband and wife team Cameron and Amée Carter, who have both worked with some of Northern Ireland's most interesting restaurateurs - experience that shows in a quietly welcoming air of confidence. 'Fine dining without the fuss' is the style here, so expect deep, gutsy flavours in food that seems simple yet has real finesse. Menus evolve with the season - and with the day, as this is an equally appealing venue for lunch or dinner - and have a broadly modern European/Mediterranean tone. Outstanding wine and drinks list, great service - and good value too. Bangor is well served with good eating places and The Wheathill is up there with the best.

L Wed-Sat, 12-2.30, D Wed-Thu 5-9, Fri-Sat 5-9.30; Sun L 12-3. Children welcome. CC. **Directions:** Bottom of Gray's Hill.

THE OLD SCHOOLHOUSE INN

100 BALLYDRAIN ROAD CASTLE ESPIE
COMBER CO DOWN BT23 6EA

EAT | DRINK | STAY

028 9754 1182 | info@theoldschoolhouseinn.com | www.the-schoolhouse.com

Tucked away on a quiet road near Strangford Lough, this substantial restaurant with rooms is run by chef Will Brown, who spent a decade honing his skills abroad before returning home in 2012 to transform this long-established family business to a place of old school hospitality and modern British cooking. Well known as a competitor on BBC's 'Great British Menu', he soon earned a following for his creative use of seasonal local ingredients (including home grown produce - you can see the kitchen garden beside the car park) and accomplished cooking. Now a favourite food destination, it's also a good base for exploring this beautiful area.

Rooms 8. B&B from about £35pps. Children welcome. Open Wed-Sun 12.30-3.30; 5.30-10 (Sun to 6.30). Open all year. CC. **Directions:** 3 miles south from Comber village - 1 mile past Castle Espie (signed).

THE OLD INN

11-15 MAIN STREET CRAWFORDSBURN CO DOWN BT19 1JH   EAT | DRINK | STAY
028 9185 3255 | info@theoldinn.com
www.theoldinn.com

The pretty village setting of this famous and hospitable 16th century inn - the oldest in continuous use in all Ireland - belies its convenient location close to Belfast. A welcoming fire and friendly staff in the cosy reception area set the tone for the whole hotel, which is full of charm, very comfortable - and always well presented. It is a popular dining destination too, offering pleasing cooking at the comfortably smart Lewis Restaurant, named after author C. S. Lewis, and in The Parlour. Rooms have traditional charm and, with Crawfordsburn Country Park, the Ulster Folk & Transport Museum and golfing all nearby, it's a great short break destination.

Rooms 32. B&B from about €50pps. Food all day. D daily from 6.30. Sun L 12-4. Closed 25 Dec. CC. **Directions:** Off A2 Belfast-Bangor (after Holywood; exit B20 for Crawfordsburn).

PIER 36

36 THE PARADE DONAGHADEE CO DOWN BT21 0HE   EAT | DRINK | STAY
028 9188 4466 | info@pier36.co.uk
www.pier36.co.uk

A pub of character beside a picturesque harbour, the Waterworth family's lively, warmly-traditional place has long been a local favourite. And no wonder, since this Donaghadee stalwart has everything that a good pub should offer: a welcoming fire in winter, a good buzz, friendly staff - and great food. Seafood lovers will enjoy treats like fresh Portavogie prawns, hand-dived Copeland Island scallops and comforting Pier 36 fish pie - but their famous 28-day dry-aged locally reared beef, which is hung and butchered on site, makes it a meat lovers destination as well. Comfortable en-suite rooms too - some with sea and harbour views. Small weddings (35).

Food 9am-9.30pm. A la carte. Rooms 6 (3 shower only). B&B about £35pps. Wheelchair accessible. Closed Dec 25. CC. **Directions:** Exit one way system towards Donaghadee Lighthouse, 200m - on harbour front

DUNNANELLY COUNTRY HOUSE

26 ROCKS CHAPEL ROAD CROSSGAR DOWNPATRICK CO DOWN BT30 9BA   STAY

077 1277 9085 | sally@dunnanellycountryhouse.com
www.dunnanellycountryhouse.com

Although it is just three miles from Downpatrick, Sally King's gorgeous Georgian-style house lies secluded in gardens, fields and woodland, with views of the Mourne Mountains to the south. Offering all the benefits of a Georgian house with the comfort of mod cons too, it would make a wonderful base for experiencing the St Patrick Story and exploring this beautiful county. The six bedrooms are beautifully furnished with great attention to detail and every comfort you could wish for - and the Kings also take pride in sourcing the best local products for breakfast, with Sally's jams among the treats, made with home-grown fruit. An absolute gem.

Rooms 6 (2 shower only). B&B from £50pps. Euro accepted. Phone to check off-season opening. Kennels. Boules. CC. **Directions:** 1/2 mile off A7 between Crossgar and Downpatrick.

MOURNE SEAFOOD BAR

10 MAIN STREET DUNDRUM CO DOWN BT33 0LU
028 4375 1377 | dundrum@mourneseafood.com
www.mourneseafood.com

EAT | BUY

The best bet for seafood in the Mourne area, you can't miss Bob and Joanne McCoubrey's lively and informal seafood restaurant in the centre of Dundrum village. In common with their Belfast sister restaurant and cookery school (in partnership with chef Andy Rae), they specialise in fresh fish from the local ports and, especially, mussels, oysters and cockles from their own shellfish beds in Carlingford Lough. As they use local fish that is not under threat, their extensive menu changes according to what is caught - and they offer local craft beer too, made at the Whitewater Brewery in Castlewellan, to accompany it.

Food Thu-Mon from 12.30 (daily in high season). Children welcome before 8pm. Wheelchair accessible. Free wifi. Closed Mon-Wed off peak, 25 Dec. CC. **Directions:** Main street. **Also at:** Mourne Seafood Bar Belfast, Bank Street (028 9024 8544).

THE PARSON'S NOSE

48 LISBURN STREET HILLSBOROUGH CO DOWN BT26 6AB   EAT | DRINK
028 9268 3009 | info@theparsonsnose.co.uk
www.theparsonsnose.co.uk

Previously named after its original owner, The Marquis of Downshire, this charming 18th century pub and restaurant is a sister establishment to that great dining pub, Balloo House in Killinchy and its stylish younger sibling, The Poacher's Pocket in Lisbane (see entries). Following a major revamp, it re-opened in mid-2017 with all its character and style intact - think old world with a distinctive modern twist - and a much more spacious and comfortable dining area on the garden level. A real coal fire welcomes customers arriving in the bar and famous local meats and poultry are a highlight at this cosy venue. 'Honest Food and Ales' is the mantra, and it shows in their good food and drink, including a selection of local beers.

Food daily from noon. Children welcome. Closed 25 Dec. CC. **Directions:** On right, entering Hillsborough

THE PLOUGH INN

3 THE SQUARE HILLSBOROUGH CO DOWN BT26 6AG   EAT | DRINK

028 9268 2985 | info@theploughhillsborough.co.uk
www.ploughgroup.com

Established in 1752, this former coaching inn is owned by the Patterson family, who have built a reputation for hospitality and good food, especially seafood and great steaks. In a setting that combines old world charm with contemporary style, they manage to please a varied clientèle and run several separate food operations successfully each day, including a new area, the Vintage Rooms, which is Hillsborough's only lounge bar experience. Replacing the former BarRetro it offers a dedicated range of food and includes a Gin Bar, spirit and wine library and whiskey cellar.

The Bar: food 12-4.15 daily. Bistro Mon-Sat from 5. Sun 12-8. Simply Seafood Fri & Sat 6-9.30. Vintage Rooms Bar: small & large sharing plates Wed-Sat evenings. Closed 25 Dec. CC. **Directions:** On village square. **Also at:** The Pheasant, Annahilt (028 9263 8056), The Tannery, Moira (028 9261 1409).

CAMPHILL ORGANIC FARM SHOP & BAKERY

8 SHORE ROAD HOLYWOOD CO DOWN BT18 9HX   EAT | BUY

028 9042 3203 | info@camphillholywoodco.uk
www.camphillholywood.co.uk

Run by the Holywood branch of the international Camphill Movement, who aim to provide a community for people with special needs and to produce organic food, this lovely shop stocks a wide range of organic products including locally sourced fresh vegetables and fruit, dried foods and dairy produce and speciality chocolates. Gluten-free, dairy-free and sugar-free options are offered, and excellent bakery products are also available in the very popular café ('Always organic and always vegetarian'), where wholesome lunches are served and 'cakes, pies and other sweet indulgences' are on offer all day, during shop hours.

Open Mon-Sat, 9-5.30 (Café to 4.30). Children welcome, wheelchair accessible. Vegan friendly. Breads and takeaway lunches can be ordered. Closed Mon. CC. **Directions:** Holywood High Street towards Bangor, left at Maypole, on the left hand side.

HASTINGS CULLODEN ESTATE & SPA COMP IMAGE

BANGOR ROAD HOLYWOOD CO DOWN BT18 0EX   EAT I STAY

028 9042 1066 I res@cull.hastingshotels.com

www.hastingshotels.com

Formerly the official palace for the Bishops of Down, the region's premier hotel is romantically set in beautifully maintained gardens and woodland overlooking Belfast Lough and the Co. Antrim coastline; it is a lovely place to stay, with many of the sumptuous rooms and suites overlooking the lough, and makes an impressive wedding venue. The Culloden has always taken pride in the food served and its provenance: fine dining with a view in The Mitre Restaurant can be memorable, while the 'Cultra Inn', in the grounds, offers an informal alternative. An outstanding Irish Breakfast experience is also provided in the restaurant, backed up by informative menus and labelled displays of local produce.

Rooms/suites 105 (2 wheelchair accessible). Lift. B&B from about £70pps. Children welcome. Mitre: D daily, L Sun only. Bar food from 11. Open all year. CC. **Directions:** A2 Belfast-Bangor.

NOBLE

27A CHURCH ROAD HOLYWOOD CO DOWN BT18 9BU   EAT

028 9042 5655 | info@nobleholywood.com
www.nobleholywood.com

A genuinely warm welcome, terrific seasonal cooking and superb service are the reasons for the success of this quietly stylish first floor restaurant in the heart of Holywood. Space is at a premium in the L-shaped room but, once tucked comfortably in at your table, everything feels just right - and, from a corner window, you might even glimpse ships heading up the lough to dock in Belfast. The first solo venture for business partners Pearson Morris (Chef, formerly of Eipic at Deanes) and Saul McConnell (Manager, formerly of Deanes) there's an air of quiet customer-focused confidence to every aspect of Noble and it's easy to see why it has become one of the hottest meal tickets in Northern Ireland. Well worth a detour.

⭐

Seats about 30. D Wed- Sat 5-10, L Thu-Sat 12-3, Sun 1-7.30. CC. **Directions:** Town centre.

RAYANNE COUNTRY HOUSE

60 DEMESNE ROAD HOLYWOOD CO DOWN B18 9EX   EAT | STAY

028 9042 5859 | info@rayannehouse.com
www.rayannehouse.com

Near Holywood Golf Club and Redburn Country Park - and just 5 minutes from Belfast City Airport – second-generation owners Conor and Bernie McClelland have built on Rayanne's long-standing reputation as a relaxing place, known for its friendly staff and excellent breakfasts. Some of the very comfortable bedrooms have views of Belfast Lough and all have thoughtful little extras. Conor's food is a highlight. Cooking for up to 30 guests, his menus showcase local produce: the pièce de résistance is a 9-course Titanic Menu, which gives a fascinating insight into life on board. A great place to stay - and to dine.

Rooms 11 (1 wheelchair friendly). B&B from £70pps. Restaurant D £65, Titanic menu £69 (booking essential). Open all year; room only 23-27 Dec & 1 Jan. CC. **Directions:** Top of My Ladys Mile, Holywood; turn right.

BALLOO HOUSE

1 COMBER ROAD KILLINCHY CO DOWN BT23 6PA
028 9754 1210 | info@balloohouse.com
www.balloohouse.com

EAT | DRINK

Ronan and Jennie Sweeney's famous 19th century coaching inn has oodles of genuine character and the old kitchen bar, with its flagstones and traditional range, makes a great setting for excellent bistro fare. Having achieved their ambition to restore Balloo's reputation as one of the finest country dining pubs in Northern Ireland, the group - now including The Poacher's Pocket, Lisbane, and The Parson's Nose, Hillsborough - has raised the bar.

Group chef Danny Millar has had a lot to do with this; as one of the region's leading champions of local seasonal produce, his philosophy is seen everywhere - and the weekend restaurant here, Upstairs at Balloo, shows him at his memorable best.

Food daily from 12. High Tea Sun-Fri 5-7. Upstairs at Balloo: D Fri & Sat from 6. Closed 25 Dec. CC. **Directions:** Comber-Killyleagh road, Balloo crossroads.

THE POACHER'S POCKET

181 KILLINCHY ROAD LISBANE COMBER CO DOWN BT23 5NE
028 9754 1589 | info@poacherspocketlisbane.com
www.ballooinns.com/the-poachers-pocket

EAT | DRINK
BUY

When Ronan and Jennie Sweeney of Balloo Inns took over the old Lisbarnett House pub in Lisbane in 2014, they kept the old-fashioned front bar, and it remains the centre of local activities. But an area behind the bar was developed with the Sweeney's special brand of country chic, creating a dining area that has a sense of occasion while also being very comfortable and relaxing - and you can watch the chefs creating delicious dishes with local produce in the open kitchen. And there's even a 'farm shop', The Poacher's Pantry, where you can buy a range of local foods (including meats for the barbecue), wines and craft beers. Delightful.

Seats 90 (+ 15 outdoors) Food daily from 12. B'fst Sat-Sun 9-11.45am; CC.
Directions: Lisbane village, main street. Also at: Balloo House, Killinchy; The Parson's Nose, Hillsborough (see entries).

WINE & BRINE

59 MAIN STREET MOIRA CO DOWN BT67 0LQ   EAT
028 9261 0500 | info@wineandbrine.co.uk
www.wineandbrine.co.uk

A first restaurant for returning natives, the renowned chef Chris McGowan and his wife Davina. The arrival of this talented duo in 2015 marked a new shift of interest from the city to its environs, and a change of style. It's fine dining with a casual vibe; big flavours, innovative combinations and inspired accompaniments characterise the cooking, which has all the finesse that would be expected of a chef of this calibre - and there are details that give great pleasure, such as the seaweed butter that comes with the Comber potatoes... There's huge enthusiasm for everything they do here, and the prices are for the most part very reasonable - with Sunday lunch, in particular, a real snip.

Open L Wed-Sat 12-2.30, D Wed-Sat 6-9.30 (Fri-Sat to 10), Sun 12-6. Closed Mon-Tue. CC. **Directions:** Centre of Moira village.

BRUNELS RESTAURANT

32 DOWNS ROAD NEWCASTLE CO DOWN BT33 0HJ   EAT
028 4372 3951 | info@brunelsrestaurant.co.uk
www.brunelsrestaurant.co.uk

Having moved from their original small but cosy home above The Anchor Bar to a much more central location, Brunel's may no longer be hidden but it is still a real gem in this famous seaside town. Named (and themed) to honour the pioneering Victorian engineer Isambard Kingdom Brunel's connections with Newcastle, the new restaurant is much bigger but it has retained the quirky charm that always made it such a delightful place to visit. Head Chef Paul Cunningham has earned a following for creative, ingredients-led cooking and those in the know travel from a wide area to enjoy his flavoursome food and the friendly service.

Seats 70. Open daily. Mon-Sat 10-2.30, Wed-Sat 5.30-9.30, Sun 10-8. Brunch Mon-Sat 10-2, Sun 10-12. Early D from about £18, also à la carte; Sun L about £25.CC. **Directions:** Near the Slieve Donard Hotel.

HASTINGS SLIEVE DONARD RESORT & SPA

DOWNS ROAD NEWCASTLE CO DOWN BT33 0AH   STAY
028 4372 1066 | res@sdh.hastingshotels.com
www.hastingshotels.com

This famous hotel stands beneath the Mourne Mountains in six acres of public grounds, adjacent to the beach and the Royal County Down Golf Links. The Victorian holiday hotel par excellence, the Slieve Donard first opened in 1897 and has been the leading place to stay in Newcastle ever since. Furnished to a high standard and immaculately maintained, the 'grand old lady' of the Hastings group is perfectly positioned for exploring the Mournes, or walking in Tollymore Forest Park, and is well known for its wide range of special short breaks, which can be very good value - excellent on-site facilities include the hotel's Elysium health club and Spa.

> **Rooms 180**. B&B from about £68pps. Oak Restaurant D 6.30-9. The Percy French Mon-Wed 4-9.30, Thu–Sun 12-9.30. Sun L 12-5. Open all year. CC. **Directions:** North end of Newcastle.

VANILLA RESTAURANT

67 MAIN STREET NEWCASTLE CO DOWN BT33 0AE   EAT
028 4372 2268 | info@vanillarestaurant.co.uk
www.vanillarestaurant.co.uk

A smart contemporary restaurant at the golfing end of Newcastle's long main street, Vanilla has become a dining destination of choice for many visitors to this famous Victorian holiday town - and many discerning local diners too. When he opened here in 2009, owner-chef Darren Ireland had a clear vision of the creative modern food and great service that he wanted to bring to his home town - and, thanks to hard work and a good team, it has paid off with plenty of happy customers spreading the word, and growing critical recognition. For a fine dining restaurant, the ambience is very relaxed and it's a welcoming place where walk-ins are encouraged, especially at lunch time.

> Mon-Sat L 12-3.30, a la carte. D Mon-Sun 5-9, (Fri–Sat to 9.30, Sat from 5.30). Tapas menu Fri-Sat 5-10. CC. **Directions:** North end of main street.

EDENVALE HOUSE

130 PORTAFERRY ROAD NEWTOWNARDS CO DOWN BT22 2AH   STAY

028 9181 4881 I edenvalehouse@hotmail.com

www.edenvalehouse.com

Diane Whyte's charming Georgian house is set in seven acres of garden and paddock, with views over Strangford Lough to the Mourne Mountains and a National Trust wildfowl reserve. Sensitively restored and modernised for the comfort of guests, Edenvale offers outstanding accommodation and hospitality and it has won a lot of friends for its consistently high standards over many years. Guests are warmly welcomed with afternoon tea and freshly baked scones - and well fed in the morning too, when excellent traditional breakfasts, including their own eggs, home baked bread and local bacon, are served at a communal table. A lovely base for exploring this beautiful and interesting area.

Rooms 3 (1 shower only, 1 family). B&B from £55pps. Children welcome. Wifi. Garden. Closed Christmas and New Year. CC. **Directions:** 2 miles from Newtownards on the Portaferry road, A20.

THE CUAN LICENSED GUEST INN

6-10 THE SQUARE STRANGFORD VILLAGE   DRINK I STAY
CO DOWN BT30 7ND

028 4488 1222 I info@thecuan.com I www.thecuan.com

Over a century old, Peter and Caroline McErlean's immaculately-maintained village inn has lots of character, with open fires, cosy lounges and a homely bar. Peter's seasonal menus have a strong emphasis on local provenance; almost every dish includes information on provenance and the cooking lets the top-rate produce do the talking: honest, simple and delicious. The inn is an old, charming, slightly cottagey building and room standards are high following recent upgrades. Hospitality is the trump card here, also Game of Thrones themed meals. An ideal base for enjoying the many attractions and activities in the area.

Rooms 9 (1 wheelchair friendly, 3 shower only). B&B from £45pps. Food daily to 8 (Fri & Sat to 9). Cuan Chip Shop (next door; hours vary). Closed 25 Dec. CC. Self-catering cottage available. **Directions:** On the square, near the ferry.

COUNTY FERMANAGH

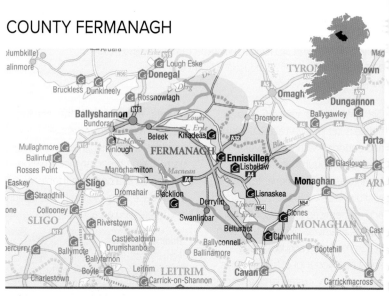

Ireland is a watery place of many lakes, rivers and canals. So it's quite an achievement to be the most watery county of all. Yet this is but one of Fermanagh's many claims to distinction. It is the only county in Ireland through which you can travel the complete distance between its furthest extremities entirely by boat.

Southeast of the historic county town of Enniskillen, Upper Lough Erne is a maze of small waterways meandering their way into Fermanagh from the Erne'e source in County Cavan. Northwest of characterful Enniskillen, the channels open out into the broad spread of Lower Lough Erne, a magnificent inland sea set off against the spectacular heights of the Cliffs of Magho. Through this broad lake, the River Erne progresses to the sea at Ballyshannon in Donegal by way of a rapid descent at Belleek in Fermanagh.

It's a stunningly beautiful county with much else of interest, including the Marble Arch caves, and the great houses of Castle Coole and Florence Court, the latter with its own forest park nestling under the rising heights of Cuilcagh (667m) – beyond it, the River Shannon emerges to begin its long journey south

For those who think lakes are for fishing rather than floating, in western Fermanagh the village of Garrison gives access to Lough Melvin, an angler's heaven which is noted particularly for its unique sub-species of salmon, the gillaroo. You just can't escape from water in this county, and Fermanagh is blessed as much of the rest of the world contemplates water shortages.

LOCAL ATTRACTIONS AND INFORMATION

>Belleek **Porcelain and Explore Erne Exhibition**
www.belleek.com | 028 68 659300

>Enniskillen **Castle Coole House & Parkland**
028 66 322690

>Enniskillen **Enniskillen Castle** 028 66 325000

>Enniskillen **Waterways Ireland**
www.waterwaysireland.org | 028 66 323004

>Florencecourt **Marble Arch Caves** 028 66 348855

>Kesh **Castle Archdale Country Park**
028 68 621588

BLAKES OF THE HOLLOW AND CAFÉ MERLOT

6 CHURCH STREET ENNISKILLEN CO FERMANAGH BT74 6JE EAT | DRINK
028 6632 0918 | blakesofthehollow@hotmail.co.uk
www.blakesofthehollow.com

One of the great classic pubs of Ireland, Blakes has been in the same family since 1887 and the classic Victorian front bar remains unchanged - somewhere to enjoy a good pint and put the world to rights. The three-storey building includes other bars, a private venue and the atmospheric **Café Merlot**, which is one of the region's most consistently popular food destinations; thanks to the great teamwork of co-owners chef Gerry Russell and front-of-house/wine man Johnny Donnelly, it's famed for creative modern cooking, a relaxed atmosphere and a great wine list. A must-visit when in Enniskillen - and Game of Thrones fans will find one of the ten doors carved from Dark Hedges trees here.

Café Merlot (casual dining): L daily 12-3; D daily 5.30-9 (Fri-Sat to 9.30), à la carte. Open all year. CC. **Directions:** Town centre.

THE JOLLY SANDWICH BAR

3 DARLING STREET ENNISKILLEN CO FERMANAGH BT74 7DP EAT | BUY
028 6632 2277 | jollysandwichbar@hotmail.co.uk PRODUCER
www.thejollysandwichbar.co.uk

With its jaunty blue and white awning, pretty pavement tables and a cheerful window display themed for the season, the Johnston family's Jolly Sandwich Bar is hard to pass by. A beacon of simple excellence, it's a lunch place of choice for discerning shoppers and has been even better since Hazel Johnston's Ballymaloe-trained daughter, Carina Cutler, joined the team. Much more than just a sandwich bar (their gorgeous cakes are renowned) - everything is home-made and personal service with attention to detail is key to the success of this super-efficient place, with Hazel Johnston overseeing everything at all times. They also make an excellent gluten free range and their own JSB jams and chutneys, known for their genuine homemade flavour.

Open Mon-Sat, 7.30am-4.15pm. Closed Sun. Directions: Town centre on the main street.

LOUGH ERNE RESORT

BELLEEK ROAD ENNISKILLEN CO FERMANAGH BT93 7ED   EAT | STAY
028 6632 3230 | info@lougherneresort.com
www.lougherneresort.com

Famously selected as the venue for the G8 Summit in 2013, this beautifully located hotel in County Fermanagh's rolling lakelands is a world-class resort with two championship golf courses and an impressive spa. Accommodation is luxurious, with some rooms having lovely views across water, and service is attentive and courteous. It's a popular dining destination for non-residents and Head Chef Noel McMeel showcases the Tastes of Lough Erne, notably in the fine dining **Catalina Restaurant**. Good informal dining is also available in a number of areas, and Afternoon Tea overlooking the lough is a popular indulgence.

⭐
Rooms 120 (some wheelchair accessible); Lift. Spa. B&B from about £75pps. Catalina Restaurant: D nightly from £45, L Sun; Blaney Bar menu 12-10 daily; Loughside Bar & Grill 12-9.30 daily; Garden Hall Afternoon Tea: 2-4 daily. Self-catering available. **Directions:** North of Enniskillen.

MANOR HOUSE COUNTRY HOTEL

KILLADEAS CO FERMANAGH BT94 1NY   EAT | DRINK | STAY
028 6862 2211 | info@manorhousecountryhotel.com
www.manorhousecountryhotel.com

An ideal base for exploring the lovely Lough Erne area, this attractive and immaculately maintained, privately owned property overlooks a marina and the impressive Victorian-Italianate house makes a fine hotel, with luxurious furnishings and décor and excellent leisure amenities. Spacious accommodation includes romantic suites, and front rooms have stunning views - as does the **Belleek Restaurant**, where excellent fine dining is offered. Informal meals are also served in the atmospheric Cellar Bar and in summer the Lady of the Lake cruiser operates dining cruises from the nearby Inishclare Harbour.

Rooms 78. B&B from about £50pps. Children welcome. **Belleek Restaurant:** D daily from 6, from £30, Sun L from 1. Bar meals 12.30-9 daily. L & D cruises (details from hotel). Open all year. Conferences, weddings. Leisure Centre. CC. **Directions:** 7 miles from Enniskillen on the B82.

WATERMILL LODGE

KILMORE QUAY LISNASKEA CO FERMANAGH BT92 0DT   EAT | STAY

028 6772 4369 | water.lodge@yahoo.com
www.watermillrestaurantfermanagh.com

Spectacularly situated on the shores of Lough Erne, this unusual restaurant with rooms is run by French chef Pascal Brissaud - a keen fisherman who decided to put down roots here - and his partner, Valerie Smith. A picturesque thatched building, it is full of French character and the lakeside rooms offer good value. Local produce includes vegetables from Pascal's garden, and lobster, scallops and Angus beef are among the specialities in cooking that's 'Irish with a French twist'. A visit to the Watermill is sure to be memorable.

Open Mon-Sat from 5; Sun from 12. Early D 5-6.30 from £20. Sun Menu from £21; also à la carte specials. Children welcome. **Rooms 7**. B&B from about £43pps, midweek DB&B from £49.50pps. Self-catering also available. Wheelchair accessible. Check hours off season. CC. **Directions:** B127 from Lisnaskea south towards Tully, 3km.

COUNTY LONDONDERRY

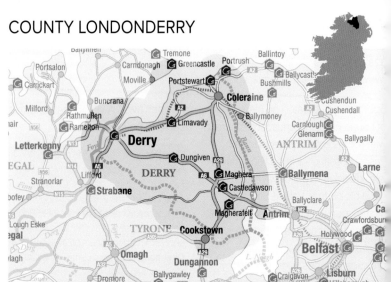

When first defined for "modern" times, this was the County of Coleraine, named for the port on the River Bann near the Atlantic coast. It was an area long favoured by settlers, for Mountsandel - on the salmon-rich Bann a mile south of Coleraine - is where the 9,000 year old traces of the site of some of the oldest-known houses in Ireland have been found.

The county was re-named after the City of Derry on the River Foyle became Londonderry in 1613, and it offers a fascinating variety of places and scenery, with large areas of fine farmland being punctuated by ranges of hills, while the rising slopes of the Sperrin Mountains dominate the County's southern boundary.

The lively seaport of the City of Derry on the Foyle could reasonably claim to be the most senior of all Ireland's contemporary cities, as it can trace its origins directly back to a monastery of St Colmcille, otherwise Columba, founded in 546AD. Today, the historic city, its ancient walls matched by up-dated port facilities and a cheerfully restored urban heart, is moving into a vibrant future in which it thrives on the energy drawn from its natural position as the focal point of a larger catchment area which takes in much of Donegal County to the west in addition to County Londonderry to the east.

The area eastward of Lough Foyle is increasingly popular among discerning visitors, the Roe Valley through Dungiven and Limavady being particularly attractive, with the summer ferry between nearby Magilligan Point and Greencastle in Donegal across the narrow entrance to Lough Foyle adding a welcome travel alternative.

LOCAL ATTRACTIONS AND INFORMATION

>Bellaghy **Bellaghy Bawn** (Seamus Heaney centre)
www.seamusheaneyhome.com | 028 79 386812

>Castlerock **Hezlett House** 028 70 848567

>Derry City **Foyle Arts Centre** 028 71 266657

>Derry City **The Guildhall**
www.derrystrabane.com | 028 71 377335

>Draperstown **Plantation of Ulster Visitor Centre**
028 79 627800

DITTY'S HOME BAKERY

44 MAIN STREET CASTLEDAWSON CO LONDONDERRY BT45 8AB
028 7946 8243 | dittyscastledawson@gmail.com
www.dittysbakery.com

EAT | BUY
PRODUCER

This friendly and atmospheric shop and café is the home base for second generation artisan baker and real food campaigner Robert Ditty's famous range of traditional breads, oatcakes and many other wonderful bakes that are Northern Ireland's pride and joy. The most famous products are the delicious Ditty's Irish Oat Biscuits and Shortbread, which are distributed to speciality stores in Ireland and abroad. The café is in the bakery, mainly serving baked treats to have with a tea or coffee, although several hot dishes are also served every day.

Food Mon-Sat 7am-5pm. Closed Sun.
Directions: On Main Street. **Also at:** Ditty's Home Bakery & Coffee Shop, Magherafelt; (028 7963 3944)

BEECH HILL COUNTRY HOUSE HOTEL

32 ARDMORE ROAD DERRY CO LONDONDERRY BT47 3QP EAT | STAY
028 7134 9279 | info@beech-hill.com
www.beech-hill.com

Beautifully set in peaceful woodland and gardens, this charming hotel dates back to 1729 and proprietor Patsy O'Kane (very deserving recipient of an MBE in 2014, in recognition of her service to the tourism and hospitality industry) is a caring hostess who loves her hotel to bits. History matters here - US Marines had their headquarters here in World War II (a small museum of the US Marine Friendship Association still attracts interest) and the comfortable rooms feature her ever-growing collection of antiques. Good food is also central to Patsy's ethos and the handsome, restored walled gardens supply seasonal produce for the **Ardmore Restaurant**, overlooking water features. A lovely place to stay.

Rooms 30 (2 wheelchair friendly). Lift. B&B from about £50pps. Children welcome. **Restaurant:** L&D daily. Afternoon Tea (must book), daily 1-5. Closed 24-25 Dec. CC. **Directions:** A6 Belfast-Londonderry.

BISHOPS GATE HOTEL

24 BISHOP STREET DERRY CO LONDONDERRY BT48 6PP   EAT | DRINK | STAY

028 7114 0300 | sales@bishopsgatehotelderry.com

www.bishopsgatehotelderry.com

Formerly a Gentlemen's Club, this atmospheric boutique hotel is an interesting place to stay within the historic city walls. It brings luxury, style and service to the Cathedral Quarter and offers a choice of dining options on site. Although a popular meeting place and at the heart of everything - just a short walk to the impressively restored Guildhall, and then over the Peace Bridge to the stunning Ebrington Square Parade Ground - it's also a luxurious retreat from the everyday and the charming staff are full of warmth, enjoying nothing better than sharing the hotel's history with guests. A very special destination - and a great asset to Derry City.

Rooms 30 (27 shower only). B&B from about £60. **Gown Restaurant** D 5-9. Bar food daily 10.30-7. Open all year. CC. **Directions:** City centre - behind the Guildhall.

BROWNS RESTAURANT & CHAMPAGNE LOUNGE

1-2 BONDS HILL LONDONDERRY CO LONDONDERRY BT47 6DW   EA

028 7134 5180 | eat@brownsrestaurant.com

www.brownsrestaurant.com

The city's most highly-regarded restaurant over several decades, Browns is enjoying an exciting phase in Ian Orr's ownership. A leading chef who is renowned for his dedication to fresh, seasonal produce and support for local suppliers, he cooks with a deft hand and a light touch. Some of the finest cooking in the land is on offer here, and very reasonably priced – visitors keen to experience the best that this fulsome area has to offer will not be disappointed; the range of menus offered is impressive and the Tasting Menu in particular is highly recommended. A must-visit when in Derry.

⭐

L Tue-Fri & Sun 12-3. D Tue-Sat from 5.30, tasting menu £45, vegetarian & vegan menus. Children welcome. CC. **Directions:** Opposite the old Waterside railway station. **Also at:** Browns in Town, Strand Road; Browns on the Green, Letterkenny (see entry).

GUILD CAFÉ

GROUND FLOOR THE GUILDHALL GUILDHALL SQUARE
LONDONDERRY CO LONDONDERRY BT48 6DQ   EAT
028 7136 0505 | info@guildcafe.co.uk | www.guildcafe.co.uk

Tables set up on the terraced steps outside this imposing building overlooking the Peace Bridge flag the presence of this appealing café and tempt passers-by in to the Guildhall. The red sandstone neo-gothic building dates back to 1887 and it's well worth a visit for its amenities, and to see the magnificently restored interior, before having a bite in Claire McGowan's café. Here you'll find a tempting display of freshly prepared foods -

simple fare, but all the better for that when everything is lusciously fresh and based on the best ingredients. A friendly and atmospheric spot to enjoy a daytime bite with an aromatic coffee or a Suki loose leaf tea.

Open Mon-Sat 9.30-5 (Sun from 10) and bank hols. Outside seating. **Directions:** Inside the Guildhall building, overlooking the Foyle Embankment and Peace Bridge.

PRIMROSE

53-55 STRAND ROAD LONDONDERRY CO LONDONDERRY BT48 7BN   EAT | BUY
028 7137 3744 | primrosecafe@hotmail.com
www.primrose-ni.com/strand-road

The little Primrose Café moved to bigger premises in 2017 and - with a kitchen team led by top chef Derek Creagh, and his longtime colleague, Monto Mansour, as Head Pastry Chef - Melanie and Ciaran Breslin's Strand Road restaurant and in-house bakery became the hottest ticket in town. Melanie's true love of cooking is the foundation of the business and Ciaran's family butchers supply quality meats - but they've always taken pride in all of their sourcing, using quality seasonal ingredients and making everything from scratch. Derek Creagh shares that philosophy - but moving into evening dining was a real change of direction, bringing lucky Derry diners a new and very tempting option for a night out.

Mon-Sat 8am-10pm, Sun 10-6pm. CC. Directions: Behind Tesco / Quayside Shopping Centre. **Also at:** Primrose on the Quay (Atlantic Quay; 028 7126 4622).

THE SOOTY OLIVE

160/64 SPENCER ROAD DERRY CO LONDONDERRY BT47 6AH   EAT
28 7134 6040 | sharrigan1@me.com
www.thesootyolive.com

Very good cooking of local foods by a dedicated owner-chef and great service are the USPs that tempt those in the know across the Peace Bridge, to Sean Harrigan's popular informal restaurant in the Waterside area. Named in honour of the 'sooty olive' fly that was used when Sean Harrigan's older brother (and business partner) caught his largest brown trout, everything about The Sooty Olive is an absolute delight. Sean is totally committed to showcasing the best local (and Irish) foods and supporting small producers: expect delicious seasonal food including produce from their own polytunnel, run in association with Derry charity, the HOPE project - and great value.

Mon-Sat 12-2.30, 5-9 (Fri & Sat to 10), Sun 1-9. D from about £19, also à la carte. CC. **Directions:** Waterside area (east of river).

WALLED CITY BREWERY

70 EBRINGTON SQUARE AND PARADE GROUND
DERRY CO LONDONDERRY BT47 6FA

EAT | DRINK
BUY | PRODUCER

028 7134 3336 | info@walledcitybrewery.com | www.walledcitybrewery.com

Launched at the Culturetech Craft Beer Festival in 2014, owner and master brewer James Huey's venture is an ambitious one and the first craft brewery in the city centre for over 100 years. Handsomely located in the old military pay office on Ebrington Square, which dates back to 1890, this is a craft brewery and restaurant in the same building – which is another first for Northern Ireland. And, with its original beer-themed decor and terrific 'local tapas' food to match the beers (all thanks to talented family members), the atmospheric bar-restaurant is a destination in itself. For a complete taste of Northern Ireland, Walled City Brewery is a must-visit.

Open Tue-Thu from 5; Fri-Sat 12.30-3.30 & 5-late, Sun from 2. CC. **Directions:** Just across the Peace Bridge from the old city, opposite the Guildhall

---

WAREHOUSE NO.1 BISTRO AND CAFÉ

1-3 GUILDHALL STREET DERRY COUNTY LONDONDERRY BT48 6BB

EAT | BUY

+44 28 7126 4798 | info@thewarehousederry.com
thewarehousederry.com

A relatively recent addition to the city's excellent choice of casual dining venues, this quirky café and bistro is famed for its coffee, very tasty hearty artisan food and an interesting drinks menu, including craft beers. Everything is top quality - and with well-known chef Ivan Taylor (former owner of Browns) leading the kitchen team, that is a given. And there are more treats in store upstairs too, where you'll find an excellent art gallery (contemporary and traditional works) and a shop offering unusual home and gift ideas. An interesting destination all round.

Café: Mon-Fri 8-8, Sat 9-6, Sun 11-6; Bistro Thu-Sat 6.30-9.30. Children welcome. Wheelchair accessible. Wifi. Outside seating. Shop.CC. **Directions**: Alongside the Guildhall building

LIME TREE RESTAURANT

60 CATHERINE STREET LIMAVADY CO LONDONDERRY BT49 9DB   EAT

028 7776 4300 | info@limetreerest.com

www.limetreerest.com

On the handsome wide main street of this attractive town, Stanley and Maria Matthews' long-established restaurant is a favourite destination for a discerning clientèle, who are happy to travel for the pleasure of dining here. And no wonder, as Stanley is a fine chef who is always keen to keep learning, and to bring fresh ideas to his menus - and Maria is a welcoming and attentive hostess. Stanley's generous menus are inspired by the seasonal, mainly local, ingredients that he sources with great care and, working from a classical base, he gives popular dishes a new twist. You'll find good cooking, good value and warm hospitality here – The Lime Tree's following is well deserved.

Seats 30. L Thu-Fri 12-1.30, D Tue-Sat, 5.30-8.30 (Fri-Sat to 9). Closed Sun-Mon, 25 Dec, 12 Jul. CC. **Directions:** Outskirts of town, Derry-Limavady road.

CHURCH STREET RESTAURANT

23-25 CHURCH STREET MAGHERAFELT CO LONDONDERRY BT45 6AP   EAT
028 7932 8083 | info@churchstreetrestaurant.co.uk
www.churchstreetrestaurant.co.uk

Just across the road from Laurel Villa (see entry), highly regarded chef Roly Graham's restaurant has been the place to go in Magherafelt since 2012, with seasonally-led menus and an emphasis on quality ingredients from hand-picked local suppliers - fish and seafood feature strongly among a varied offering, also very good beef. A major revamp in 2016 saw the opening of a new lounge and cocktail garden, providing an atmospheric place to relax before or after a meal. Friendly and engaging staff, together with attention to detail and assured cooking at attractive prices, make this a popular destination.

Seats 80 (+10 outdoors). Open: Wed & Thu 5-9, Fri & Sat: 5-10, Sun 12-8. Also SC apartment (2 doubles, shower only), room only from about £70. Closed Mon & Tue; 1 wk Jan, 1 wk Jul. CC.

LAUREL VILLA

60 CHURCH STREET MAGHERAFELT CO LONDONDERRY BT45 6AW   STAY
028 7930 1459 | info@laurel-villa.com
www.laurel-villa.com

Gerardine and Eugene Kielt's supremely comfortable Victorian townhouse exudes charm and instils a sense of curiosity within the many guests who travel here from far and wide to experience their hospitality and the unique cultural experience they offer. They host a permanent exhibition of the late Seamus Heaney, the Nobel Poet, who was born nearby; Eugene conducts heritage and cultural tours, and special poetry reading evenings and Seamus Heaney events are held – which the poet himself often attended in his lifetime. No dinner is offered but Church Street Restaurant (see entry) is just across the road – and delicious breakfasts featuring local produce have freshly-baked wheaten bread among the treats. An absolute gem.

Rooms 4 (all en-suite); B&B from £45pps. Children welcome. CC. Directions: Church Street is on the main Castledawson Road (A31).

HARRY'S SHACK

118 STRAND ROAD PORTSTEWART CO LONDONDERRY BT55 7PG   EAT
028 7083 1783 I harrysshack@gmail.com
www.facebook.com/pg/HarrysShack

Older sister of Donal Doherty's smart café in Derry city, this unique casual-dining spot hit the fame button from the day it opened in 2014. A beachside National Trust office has been transformed to create a vibrant dining space with a superb outdoor bar and eating area, with big picture windows looking out over the strand and the pounding waves - and the simple cooking of local fare (notably Greencastle fish and produce from their own walled garden at Burt) is memorable for its freshness, flavour and colour.

Beach parking (£4.50 in summer, free off season). Open Tue-Sun from 10.30, D from 5. May close 4-5. Licensed. Closed Mon, hours vary off-season. CC. *Also operates Sunny Ices van on the beach. **Directions:** At entrance to Portstewart beach. **Also at:** Harry's at the Craft Village in Derry (028 7137 1635).

STRANDEEN B&B

63 STRAND ROAD PORTSTEWART CO LONDONDERRY BT55 7LU   STAY
028 7083 3159 I strandeen@btinternet.com
www.strandeen.com

Debbie Blaney's friendly B&B overlooking Portstewart Strand is one of the most popular places to stay in this very desirable area, and it is easy to see why so many guests are keen to return. Rooms have all the details that make for a really comfortable stay, for a start, and there's a welcoming big sitting room with comfy seating, picture windows over the bay and a real fire. But most of all, there is Debbie herself – the ultimate can-do host, she obviously enjoys nothing better than spoiling her guests with afternoon tea in the sitting room and giving everyone a really good Northern Irish breakfast. Picnic lunches can also be arranged.

Rooms 5 (all shower only, 2 ground floor). B&B from about £55pps. Unsuitable for children. Parking. Wifi. Open all year. CC. **Directions:** 0.5m from town.

ARDTARA COUNTRY HOUSE

8 GORTEADE ROAD UPPERLANDS MAGHERA
CO LONDONDERRY BT46 5SA

EAT I STAY

028 7964 4490 I info@ardtara.com I www.ardtara.com

Former home to the Clark linen-milling family, this friendly Victorian country house is owned by Browns Restaurants Northwest (of Derry City and Letterkenny) and, with Executive Chef and part owner Ian Orr overseeing the kitchen team, there's a real buzz about the restaurant - the former snooker room, with original skylight and hunting frieze provides an unusual setting for excellent cooking showcasing seasonal local foods, and service is warm, friendly and relaxed. Guest rooms are luxuriously furnished in period style, with working fireplaces. Informal meals are offered in the bar or conservatory A destination in itself and an excellent base for exploring this beautiful and unspoilt area.

Rooms 9 (1 shower only, 1 wheelchair friendly). B&B from about £50pps. D Wed-Sun 5-9, Sun 12-8. CC. **Directions:** M2 from Belfast to A6. A29 to Maghera. B75 to Kilrea.

COUNTY TYRONE

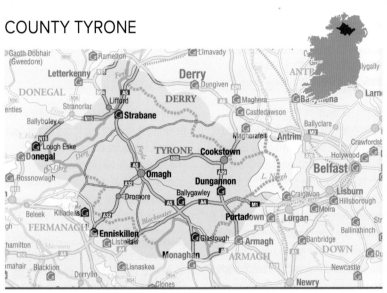

Tyrone is Northern Ireland's largest county, so it is something of a surprise for the traveller to discover that its geography appears to be dominated by a range of mountains of modest height, and nearly half of these peaks seem to be in the neighbouring county of Londonderry.

Yet such is the case with Tyrone and the Sperrins www.sperrinstourism.com . The village of Sperrin itself towards the head of Glenelly may be in Tyrone, but the highest peak of Sawel (678 m), which looms over it, is on the county boundary. But much of the county is upland territory and moorland, giving the impression that the Sperrins are even more extensive than is really the case.

In such a land, the lower country and the fertile valleys gleam like jewels, and there's often a vivid impression of a living - and indeed, prosperity - being wrested from a demanding environment. It's a character-forming sort of place, so it's perhaps understandable that it is the ancestral homeland of a remarkable number of early American Presidents, and this connection is commemorated in the Ulster American Folk Park www.nmni.com/uafp a few miles north of the county town of Omagh.

Forest parks abound, while attractive towns like Castlederg and Dungannon, as well as villages in the uplands and along the charming Clogher Valley, provide entertainment and hospitality for visitors refreshed by the wide open spaces of the moorlands and the mountains.

LOCAL ATTRACTIONS AND INFORMATION

>Ardboe **Kinturk (Lough Neagh) Cultural Centre** 028 86 736512

>Benburb **Benburb Castle and Valley Park** 028 37 548241

>Cookstown **Drum Manor Forest Park** 028 86 762774

>Cookstown **Wellbrook Beetling Mill (Corkhill)** 028 86 748210

>Dungannon **Tyrone Crystal** 028 87 725335

>Gortin **Ulster History Park** 028 81 648188

>Newtownstewart **Baronscourt Forest Park** 028 81 661683

SUITOR GALLERY TEA ROOM

17 GRANGE ROAD BALLYGAWLEY CO TYRONE BT70 2LP   EAT I BUY
028 8556 8653 I sales@suitorgallery.com
www.suitorgallery.com

Despite its location beside Ballygawley Roundabout, a converted barn in a small orchard provides an attractively rustic setting for this long-established business. It is an excellent gift shop - way above the average, with lots of gift ideas including lovely things for children and unexpected extras for the house - and also a simple teashop, serving teas, coffees, snacks and light lunches. And what a good little place it is. Everything is home-made and tasty, including lovely home baking – and you can sit outside in the garden in fine weather. The perfect place for a journey break.

> Shop open Tue-Sat 9.30-5.30. Food served 9.30-5.15 (light hot food 10-2.55, tea coffee, soft drink & home bakes all day). Wheelchair accessible. Parking. Online shop. CC.

THE BREWER'S HOUSE

73 CASTLECAULFIED ROAD DONAGHMORE   EAT I DRINK
DUNGANNON CO TYRONE BT70 3HB
028 8776 1932 I info@thebrewershouse.com I www.thebrewershouse.com

Ciaran and Vicki McCausland's 18th century hostelry offers perfect pub food – straightforward, hearty plates served by friendly staff. No formal supplier list (and imports like the ubiquitous tiger prawn feature), but interesting menus include great local produce like Lough Neagh eel, Strangford rope mussels and Cloughbane 28-day dry-aged steaks. Expect confidently simple, well-cooked and attractively presented food, with a vegetarian menu offered and real food for kids. Well worth a visit.

> **Seats about 130**. Open Mon-Thu 4.30-8.30, Sat 12-10, Sun 12-8. Express L Fri & Sat 12-4.30. 2/3 course Early D Mon-Fri 4.30-7 from about £15. Hours may change during holiday seasons. CC.
> **Directions:** Centre of Donaghmore.

OYSTERS RESTAURANT

37 PATRICK STREET STRABANE CO TYRONE BT82 8DQ   EAT

028 7138 2690 | oystersstrabane@yahoo.co.uk
www.oystersrestaurant.co.uk

Owned by Kevin and Caroline Clarke, Strabane's leading restaurant is an attractive building near the courthouse and the town theatre, with pretty hanging baskets to welcome arriving guests, and menus displayed on each side of the front door. A great all-rounder, with plenty to please at different times of every day; you can expect confident contemporary cooking and stylish presentation, sometimes with quirky details. As a Taste of Ulster member, menus reflect the availability of local foods, such as 28-day hung Northern Ireland beef, game in winter, and seasonal vegetables; vegetarians are well looked after, with a good choice of interesting dishes, and retro favourite Baked Alaska is a speciality among the delicious homemade desserts. Well worth a visit.

> Open daily 12-9.30 (Sat to 10). L 12-4, High Tea Mon-Fri 4-7, (from £13.50), à la carte 4-9.30 (Sat to 10). Closed 25/26 Dec. CC.
> **Directions:** Near the Courthouse.

INDEX

4 Vicars, Armagh	524
777 Restaurant, Dublin 2	14
1826 Adare, Adare	344
Abbey Tavern, Howth	61
Absolute Hotel, Limerick	338
Adare Manor Hotel & Golf Resort, Adare	345
Aghadoe Heights Hotel & Spa, Killarney	276
Aldridge Lodge, Duncannon	470
Allo's Restaurant, Bar & Bistro, Listowel	291
Amuse, Dublin 2	14
Andy's Bar and Restaurant, Monaghan	401
An Fear Gorta (Tea & Garden Rooms),	
Ballyvaughan	88
Anglers Return, The, Roundstone	250
Aniar Restaurant, Galway	208
Annaharvey Farm, Tullamore	408
Annebrook House Hotel, Mullingar	464
Anocht Restaurant Kilkenny, Kilkenny	311
An Old Rectory, Belfast	495
An Port Mor, Westport	383
Aqua Restaurant, Howth	61
Arbutus Hotel, Killarney	276
Archways B&B, Rosslare	476
Ardagh Hotel & Restaurant, Clifden	232
Ard Bia at Nimmo's, Galway	208
Ardmore Country House, Kinnitty	407
Ard na Breátha, Donegal	190
Ard na Sidhe Country House, Killorglin	288
Ardtara Country House, Maghera	561
Ariel House, Dublin 4	40
Aroma, Donegal	191
Arundels by the Pier, Ahakista	133
Ashford Castle, Cong	376
Ashley Park House, Nenagh	439
Asian Tea House Restaurant, Galway	209
A Slice of Heaven, Kilkenny	312
Aubergine Gallery Café, Longford	352
Avalon, Dublin 4	41
Avoca Handweavers, Kilmacanogue	489

Baileys Hotel Cashel, Cashel 433

Ballinalacken Castle Country House &
Restaurant, Doolin 94

Balloo House, Killinchy 541

Ballyduff House, Thomastown 318

Ballyfin House, Ballyfin 324

Ballygarry House Hotel & Spa, Tralee 293

Ballykine House, Clonbur 236

Ballyknocken House
& Cookery School, Ashford 483

Ballymaloe House, Midleton 178

Ballymore Inn, The, Ballymore Eustace 297

Ballynahinch Castle Hotel, Recess 246

Ballyrafter Country House Hotel, Lismore 448

Ballyvolane House, Fermoy 163

Bantry House & Garden, Bantry 142

Bar and Grill at James Street South, The,
Belfast 496

Barberstown Castle, Straffan 305

Barking Dog, The, Belfast 495

Bar One Gastro Pub, Castlebar 372

Barrons Bakery & Coffee Shop, Cappoquin 446

Barrow House, Tralee 293

Barrowville Townhouse, Carlow 76

Barrtra Seafood Restaurant, Lahinch 106

Bassetts, Thomastown 319

Bastible, Dublin 8 49

Bastion, Kinsale 167

Bates Restaurant, Rathdrum 491

Bay Tree Bistro, Waterford 449

Beara Coast Hotel, Castletownbere 149

Beaufield Mews Restaurant
& Gardens, Stillorgan 69

Beech Hill Country House Hotel, Derry 552

Beehive, The, Achill Island 366

Belleek Castle, Ballina 368

Belle's Kitchen / Salt n Batter, Rathmullan 202

Bellingham Castle, Castlebellingham 359

Bervie, Achill Island 367

Bewley's Grafton Street, Dublin 2 15

Bishops Gate Hotel, Derry 553

Blackberry Café, The, Thomastown 319

Black Pig Winebar & Café, The, Kinsale 167

Blackwell House, Scarva 526

Blairscove House & Restaurant, Durrus 160

Blairs Inn, Blarney 147

Blakes of the Hollow and Café Merlot,
Enniskillen 547

Blindgate House, Kinsale 168

Blue Apron, The, Tullamore 408

Blueberry Tea Room, The, Donegal 191

Blue Bicycle Tea Rooms, The, Newport 381

Blue Haven Hotel, The, Kinsale 169

Boathouse Winebar
& Bistro, The, Kenmare 268

Bobby Byrne's, Limerick 338

Bodéga!, Waterford 450

Bon Appetit, Malahide 64

Bowes Foodhall & Café, Durrow 325

Brewer's House, The, Dungannon 563

Brigit's Garden & Café, Roscahill 244

Brocka-on-the-Water, Ballinderry 433

Brook Lane Hotel, Kenmare 269

BrookLodge Hotel & Wells Spa, The,
Macreddin Village 490

Brooks Hotel & Francescas Restaurant,
Dublin 2 15

Brownes, Tuam 251

Browns on the Green, Letterkenny 197

Browns Restaurant
& Champagne Lounge, Londonderry 554

Brunels Restaurant, Newcastle 543

Budds, Ballydehob 135

Bullitt Belfast, Belfast 497

Bull & Ram, Ballynahinch 528

Burren Fine Wine & Food, Ballyvaughan 89

Burren Glamping and
Free Range Pork, Kilfenora 102

Burren Perfumery and Tea Rooms, Carron 93

Burtown House, Gardens and Green Barn,
Athy 296

Bushmills Inn, Bushmills 516

Butler Arms Hotel, Waterville   294
Butler House, Kilkenny   312
Byrnes Wine Dine & Stay, Ennistymon   100

Café Carleton, Newbridge   303
Café Paradiso, Cork   120
Cahernane House Hotel, Killarney   277
Caifé na Caoloige
    @ Louis Mulcahy Pottery, Dingle   259
Cairn Bay Lodge, Bangor   529
CakeFace, Kilkenny   313
Campagne, Kilkenny   314
Camphill Organic Farm Shop
    & Bakery, Holywood   538
Canteen, Limerick   339
Canteen Celbridge, Celbridge   298
Carbery Cottage Guest Lodge, Durrus   161
Carlingford House, Carlingford   356
Carrig Country House
    & Restaurant, Killorglin   289
Carrygerry Country House,
    Newmarket-on-Fergus   114
Carton House Hotel, Maynooth   302
Cashel House Hotel, Cashel   231
Cast and Crew, Belfast   498
Castlecoote House, Castlecoote   410
Castle Durrow, Durrow   326
Castle Grove Country House Hotel,
    Letterkenny   198
Castle Hotel & Leisure Centre, The,
    Macroom   173
Castle Leslie Estate, Glaslough   400
Castlemartyr Resort, Castlemartyr   148
Castle Murray House, Dunkineely   194
Castle, The, Castletownshend   151
Castlewood House, Dingle   259
Cava Bodega, Galway   209
Cavistons Seafood Restaurant
    & Food Emporium, Dun Laoghaire   59
Celtic Whiskey Bar & Larder, Killarney   277
Central, The, Navan   392

Central Wine Bar, Ballycastle   514
Chakra by Jaipur, Greystones   487
Chameleon Indonesian Restaurant,
    Dublin 2   16
Chapter One Restaurant,
    Dublin 1   9
Cherry Tree Restaurant, Killaloe   105
Chez Hans, Cashel   434
China Sichuan Restaurant, Dublin 18   55
Church Street Restaurant, Magherafelt   559
Cill Rialaig Café, Ballinskelligs   255
Cistin Eile, Wexford   478
Clandeboye Lodge Hotel, Bangor   529
Clare Island Lighthouse, Clare Island   375
Clarence, The, Dublin 2   16
Clashganny House Restaurant, Borris   74
Clenaghans, Aghalee   512
Cliff at Lyons & The Orangery Restaurant,
    Celbridge   299
Cliff House Hotel, The, Ardmore   443
Cliff Town House
    & Urchin Seafood Bar, The, Dublin 2   17
Cloister Restaurant & Bar, The, Ennis   98
Clonalis House, Castlerea   411
Clonganny House, Ballygarrett   469
Clontarf Castle Hotel, Dublin 3   38
Coill Dara House B&B, Tubbercurry   430
Connemara Sands Hotel, Ballyconneely   230
Conrad Dublin & The Coburg, Dublin 2   17
Coolanowle Country House, Carlow Area   73
Coolbawn Quay Lakeshore Spa
    & Marina, Nenagh Area   440
Coopershill House, Riverstown   421
Copper Hen, The, Fenor   448
Copper & Spice, Annacotty   347
Cornstore Restaurant, The, Limerick   339
Cornucopia, Dublin 2   18
Corrib House Tea Rooms & Guest
    Accommodation, Galway   210
Cottage Restaurant, The,
    Carrick on Shannon   331

Counter, The, Letterkenny 199
Country Choice Delicatessen
   & Coffee Bar, Nenagh 438
Courthouse Restaurant, Carrickmacross 399
Courthouse Restaurant
   & Accommodation, The, Kinlough 334
Courtyard Café, The, Birr 404
Coynes Bar & Bistro (Tigh Chadhain),
   Kilkerrin 239
Craft, Dublin 6W 48
Crawford Gallery Café, Cork 120
Cronin's Pub, Crosshaven 159
Cronins Sheebeen, Westport 384
Crookhaven Inn, The, Crookhaven 158
Crotty's Pub, Kilrush 105
Crowne Plaza Dublin Airport Hotel, Santry 66
Crown Liquor Saloon, Belfast 499
Cuan Licensed Guest Inn, The,
   Strangford Village 545
Curragower Seafood Bar, The, Limerick 340
Currarevagh House, Oughterard 243

Da Mimmo, Dublin 3 38
Daniel Finnegan, Dalkey 58
Danny Minnie's Restaurant, Annagry 188
Dax Restaurant, Dublin 2 19
Deanes at Queens, Belfast 500
Deanes EIPIC, Belfast 499
Deanes Meat Locker & Love Fish, Belfast 500
Dean, The, Dublin 2 20
Deasy's Harbour Bar
   & Seafood Restaurant, Clonakilty 156
Dela, Galway 211
Delahunt, Dublin 2 20
Delphi Lodge, Leenane 240
Dillon's, Skibbereen 184
Ditty's Home Bakery, Londonderry 551
Diva Boutique Bakery, Café
   & Deli, Ballinspittle 134
Dolphin Beach Country House, Clifden 232
Doonmore Hotel, Inishbofin Island 238

Dough Bros, The, Galway 211
Draft House, Strandhill 429
Dromoland Castle Hotel,
   Newmarket-on-Fergus 115
Druids Glen Resort,
   Newtownmountkennedy 491
Dunbrody Country House Hotel
   & Cookery School, Arthurstown 468
Dunloe, The, Killarney 278
Dunmore House Hotel, Clonakilty 153
Dunnanelly Country House, Downpatrick 535
Dunne & Crescenzi, Dublin 2 21
Dunne & Crescenzi Blackrock, Blackrock 57
Dunraven Arms Hotel, Adare 346
Dylan Hotel Dublin, Dublin 4 41

Eala Bhan, Sligo 421
Eastern Seaboard Bar & Grill, Drogheda 359
Eccles Hotel, Glengarriff 164
Edenvale House, Newtownards 545
Eithnas by the Sea, Mullaghmore 420
ely bar & brasserie, Dublin 1 10
ely winebar, Dublin 2 22
Emmas Café & Deli, Birr 405
Emmet Hotel, The, Clonakilty 154
Enniscoe House, Ballina 370
ETTO, Dublin 2 23
Europe, The, Killarney 279

Fallon & Byrne, Dublin 2 23
Fallons of Kilcullen, Kilcullen 301
Farmgate, Midleton 176
Farmgate Café, Cork 121
Farmhill Café and Restaurant, Dublin 14 54
Farm Restaurant, Clonakilty 154
Farnham Estate Spa & Golf Resort, Cavan 83
Fatted Calf, The, Athlone 456
Fergus View, Corofin 93
Ferrit & Lee, Midleton 176
Fiacrí Country House Restaurant & Cookery
   School, Roscrea 441

Fifty4 Seafood Bar, Drogheda 360
Finn's Table, Kinsale 170
Firehouse Bakery & Café, Delgany 484
Fishermans Thatched Inn, The, Ballybrittas 323
Fish Kitchen, Bantry 143
Fish Shop, Dublin 1 11
Fishy Fishy, Kinsale 170
Fitzpatrick Castle Hotel Dublin, Killiney 63
Fitzpatrick's Bar & Restaurant, Dundalk 362
Fitzwilliam Hotel, The, Belfast 501
Fitztilliam Hotel, The , Dublin 2 24
Flanagan's Pub, Claremorris 375
Fleet Inn, The, Killybegs 197
Flemings Restaurant, Cork 121
Forest Avenue, Dublin 4 42
Fortview House, Goleen 164
Fota Island Resort, Cobh 157
Foxford Woollen Mills Visitor Centre,
    Foxford 379
Foyles Hotel, Clifden 233
Freddy's Bistro, Limerick 340
French Rooms, The, Bushmills 517
French Table, The, Limerick 341
Frewin, Ramelton 202
Fumbally, The, Dublin 8 50

Gaby's Seafood Restaurant, Killarney 280
Galgorm Resort & Spa, Ballymena 515
Gallan Mor, Durrus 162
Gallic Kitchen @ Bramley, The, Abbeyleix 322
Garryvoe Hotel, Garryvoe 134
Gaultier Lodge, Waterford 454
Georges Patisserie, Slane 393
Ghan House, Carlingford 357
G Hotel & Spa, The, Galway 212
Ginger Bistro, Belfast 501
Glasha, Ballymacarbry 444
Glasson Hotel & Golf Club, Glasson 460
Glasson Village Restaurant, Glasson 461
Glebe House Gardens, Baltimore 138
Gleesons Restaurant & Rooms, Roscommon 411

Glenarm Castle Tea Room, Glenarm 518
Glendine Country House, Arthurstown 468
Glenlo Abbey Hotel
    & Pullman Restaurant, Galway 213
Global Village, The, Dingle 260
Good Things
    @ Dillon's Corner, Skibbereen 182
Gorman's Clifftop House & Restaurant,
    Ballydavid 267
Gougane Barra, Gougane Barra 166
Goya's Bakery, Galway 214
Grangecon Café, Blessington 483
Granville Hotel, Waterford 451
Granville's Bar & Restaurant, Macroom 174
Great Southern Killarney, Killarney 281
Greenery, The, Dublin 4 42
GreenHouse, The, Dublin 2 24
Greenmount House, Dingle 261
Gregans Castle Hotel, Ballyvaughan 90
Grogan's Pub, Glasson 461
GROW HQ, Waterford 453
Guild Café, Londonderry 555
Guillemot Kitchen Café
    & Wine Bar, Bangor 530
Guys Bar and Snug, Clifden 233

Hadskis, Belfast 502
Half Door, The, Dingle 261
Hanora's Cottage, Ballymacarbry 445
Happy Pear, The, Greystones 488
Hargadons, Sligo 422
Harry's Shack, Portstewart 560
Hartes Bar & Grill, Kildare 302
Harts Coffee Shop, Clonakilty 155
Harvey's Point, Lough Eske 201
Hastings Culloden Estate & Spa,
    Holywood 539
Hastings Europa Hotel, Belfast 503
Hastings Slieve Donard Resort & Spa,
    Newcastle 544
Hayfield Manor Hotel, Cork 122

Hazel Mountain Chocolate, Bellharbour 91
Headfort Arms Hotel, Kells 391
Heatons House, Dingle 262
Helena Chocolates, Castlebar 373
Herbert Park Hotel, Dublin 4 43
Heritage Killenard, The, Killenard 326
Heron and Grey, Blackrock 56
Heron Gallery Café & Gardens, Ahakista 133
Heron's Cove, The, Goleen 165
Heron's Rest B&B, The, Galway 215
Hickeys Bakery & Café, Clonmel 435
Hilton Park, Clones 399
Hooked, Galway 216
Hotel Doolin, Doolin 95
Hotel Isaacs & Greenes Restaurant, Cork 122
Hotel Meyrick, Galway 216
Hotel Minella, Clonmel 435
Hotel Westport, Westport 384
Hungry Monk Café, Cong 377
Hungry Monk, The, Greystones 488
Hunter's Hotel, Rathnew 492
Huntington Castle & Gardens, Clonegal 78

Ice House Hotel, The, Ballina 368
Idaho.Café, Cork 123
Idás, Dingle 262
Idle Wall Restaurant, The, Westport 385
Il Vicolo Restaurant & Bácaro, Galway 217
Imperial Hotel, Cork 123
Inchydoney Island Lodge & Spa, Clonakilty 155
Inis Meáin Restaurant & Suites, Aran Islands 228
Intercontinental Dublin Hotel, Dublin 4 44
Island Cottage, Skibbereen 183
Ivyleigh House, Portlaoise 328

Jack's Coastguard Restaurant, Killorglin 290
Jacques Restaurant, Cork 124
Jam, Kenmare 269
James Street South, Belfast 504
John J. Burke & Sons, Clonbur 237
John Keoghs, The Lock Keeper, Galway 218

Jolly Sandwich Bar, The, Enniskillen 547

Kai Restaurant, Galway 219
Kathleens Country House, Killarney 280
K Club, The, Straffan 306
Kealys Seafood Bar, Greencastle 195
Keenans Hotel & Restaurant, Tarmonbarry 412
Kelly's Kitchen, Newport 381
Kelly's Resort Hotel & Spa, Rosslare 477
Kernel Bar & Kitchen at Kilkenny Inn,
   Kilkenny 315
Kilbaha Gallery & Crafts, Kilbaha 101
Kilcooly's Country House, Ballybunion 255
Kilgraney House, Bagenalstown 72
Killarney Lodge, Killarney 282
Killeen House Hotel
   & Rozzers Restaurant, The, Killarney 283
Killiane Castle Country House
   & Farm, Wexford 481
Killruddery Estate, Bray 484
Kilmaneen Farmhouse, Clonmel 436
Kilmokea Country Manor
   & Gardens, Campile 469
Kinara Restaurant, Dublin 3 39
Kingfisher Bistro, Carlingford 358
King's Head, The, Galway 224
King Sitric Fish Restaurant
   & Accommodation, Howth 62
Kingsley Hotel, Cork 125
Kin Khao Thai Restaurant, Athlone 457
Kitchen @ Gorey, The, Gorey 472
Kitchen Restaurant, The, Drogheda 360
Kitty Kellys, Killybegs 196
Knockeven House, Cobh 157
Knockranny House Hotel & Spa, Westport 385
Knox, Sligo 423
Kylemore Abbey, Mitchell's Café
   & Garden Tea House, Letterfrack 240

La Bohème, Waterford 451
La Bouche, Portumna 245

La Côte, Wexford	479
La Cucina Centro, Limerick	341
Lake Hotel Killarney, The, Killarney	284
La Reserve, Dublin 6	46
Larkins Bar & Restaurant, Nenagh	437
Las Tapas de Lola, Dublin 2	26
L'Atitude 51, Cork	125
Laurel Villa, Magherafelt	559
L'Ecrivain, Dublin 2	25
Left Bank Bistro, The, Athlone	457
Lemon Tree Café, Dunmore East	447
Lemon Tree Restaurant, Letterkenny	200
Lennons @ VISUAL, Carlow	77
Leonard's, Ballina	379
Le Petit Pois Restaurant & Wine Bar, Galway	223
Les Gourmandises Restaurant, Cork	126
Levis Bar Corner House, Ballydehob	136
Limerick Strand Hotel, Limerick	342
Lime Tree Restaurant, Kenmare	270
Lime Tree Restaurant, Limavady	558
Linnanes Lobster Bar, New Quay	111
Lir Restaurant & Bakery, Kilkee	103
Lissadell House, Ballinfull	416
Listoke House, Drogheda	361
L Mulligan Grocer, Dublin 7	48
Loam, Galway	219
Loch Lein Country House Hotel, Killarney	285
Lodge at Ashford Castle, The, Cong	378
Londonderry Arms Hotel, Carnlough	518
Long Dock, The, Carrigaholt	92
Longueville House, Mallow	175
Lord Baker's Restaurant & Bar, Dingle	263
Lorum Old Rectory, Bagenalstown	72
Lough Bishop House, Collinstown	460
Loughcrew Estate, Gardens, Café & Adventure Centre, Oldcastle	393
Lough Erne Resort, Enniskillen	548
Lough Inagh Lodge, Recess	247
Lough Key House, Boyle	410
Lough Rynn Castle Hotel & Estate, Mohill	335
Luna, Dromahair	333
Lyons Cafe & Bakeshop, Sligo	424
Lyrath Estate Hotel & Convention Centre, Kilkenny	315
MacCarthy's, Castletownbere	150
MacNean House & Restaurant, Blacklion	82
Maddybenny Farmhouse, Portrush	519
Mallmore Country House, Clifden	234
Mannings Emporium, Bantry	136
Manor House Country Hotel, Killadeas	548
Manor House, The, Rathlin Island	521
Marble City Bar, Kilkenny	316
Market Lane Restaurant & Bar, Cork	126
Marlagh Lodge, Ballymena	516
Marlfield House and The Duck Café-Restaurant, Gorey	473
Martinstown House, Curragh	300
Mary Ann's Bar & Restaurant, Castletownshend	152
Maryborough Hotel & Spa, Cork	127
Mary's Cottage Kitchen, Ballycastle	371
Matt Molloy's Bar, Westport	386
McCambridges, Galway	220
McCarthy's Pub, Fethard	437
McCormack's at The Andrew Stone Gallery, Westport	386
Merchant Hotel, The, Belfast	505
Merrion Hotel and the Cellar Restaurant & Bar, Dublin 2	27
Mews Restaurant, Baltimore	138
Mews, The, Kenmare	275
Michael's, Mount Merrion	65
Miller & Cook, Mullingar	464
Mill Restaurant & Accommodation, The, Dunfanaghy	193
Mimosa Wine & Tapas Bar, Carlow	77
Miso Sligo, Sligo	425
Mitchell's Restaurant, Clifden	234
Mitchelstown, Mitchelstown	179
Miyazaki, Cork	127

Molly's Yard, Belfast 506
Momo, Waterford 452
Monaincha House & Health Spa, Roscrea 440
Monart Destination Spa, Enniscorthy 471
Monk's Lane, Timoleague 185
Montenotte Hotel, Cork 128
Montmartre, Sligo 425
Moody Boar Restaurant
    & Bistro, The, Armagh 523
Moorings & The Bridge Bar, The,
    Portmagee 292
Moran's Oyster Cottage, Kilcolgan 238
Mornington House, Multyfarnham 465
Morrissey's, Abbeyleix 322
Morrissey's Seafood Bar & Grill, Doolin 97
Mortell's Delicatessen
    & Seafood Restaurant, Limerick 342
Mount Falcon Estate, Ballina 369
Mount Juliet, Thomastown 320
Mount Vernon, New Quay 112
Mourne Seafood Bar, Dundrum 536
Mourne Seafood Bar Belfast, Belfast 506
Moy House, Lahinch 107
Mr Fox Restaurant, Dublin 1 11
Muckross Park Hotel & Spa, Killarney 286
Muddlers Club, Belfast 507
Mulberry Garden, Dublin 4 45
Mulcahy's Restaurant, Kenmare 270
Muldowneys B&B, Arranmore 189
Mullichain Café, Grainstore 80
Mulranny Park Hotel, Mulranny 380
Mulvarra House, Graiguenamanagh 80
Murphy Blacks, Kilkee 104
Murphys Ice Cream & Café, Dingle 264
Mustard Seed, The, Ballingarry 348
Muxnaw Lodge, Kenmare 271

Nancy's Bar, Ardara 188
Nash 19 Restaurant, Cork 129
NATIVE by Yellow Door
    at the MAC, Belfast 508

Newforge House, Craigavon 525
Newport House, Newport 382
Nicholas Mosse Irish Country Shop
    & Café, Bennettsbridge 309
Nightmarket, Dublin 6 47
Nine Arches Restaurant, Ballymahon 352
No. 1 Pery Square Hotel & Spa, Limerick 343
Noble, Holywood 540
Nook Café and Restaurant, Collooney 418
Nox Hotel, Galway 220
Number 31, Dublin 2 28

Oak Room Restaurant, Cavan 83
Oar House, The, Howth 63
Oarsman, The, Carrick on Shannon 332
O'Callaghan-Walshe, Rosscarbery 181
O'Connell's, Tara 396
O'Connells Restaurant, Dublin 4 45
O'Dowds Seafood Bar
    & Restaurant, Roundstone 249
O'Grady's on the Pier, Barna 226
Old Bank House, The, Kinsale 171
Old Bank, The, Bruff 349
Old Convent Gourmet Hideaway, The,
    Clogheen 434
Olde Castle Bar
    & Restaurant, The, Donegal 192
Olde Glen Bar, The, Carrigart 190
Olde Post Inn, The, Cavan 84
Old Ground Hotel, Ennis 99
Old Inn, The, Crawfordsburn 534
Old School B&B, The, Loop Head 110
Old Schoolhouse Inn, The, Comber 533
Old Street Restaurant, Malahide 64
Olive Delicatessen & Café, Skerries 66
O'Loclainn, Ballyvaughan 91
O'Neills - The Point Bar, Cahirciveen 257
One Pico Restaurant, Dublin 2 28
On The Pig's Back, Cork 130
Organico Cafe Shop Bakery, Bantry 143
Oscars Seafood Bistro, Galway 221

Osta Café & Wine Bar, Sligo 426
Osteria Lucio, Dublin 2 29
Out of the Blue, Dingle 265
Ouzos, Dalkey 58
Overends at Airfield, Dublin 14 54
OX, Belfast 509
Oysters Restaurant, Strabane 564

Packie's, Kenmare 271
Paddy Coynes Pub, Renvyle 248
Pantry & Corkscrew, The, Westport 387
Pantry, The, Kilkee 104
Papa Rich Street Food Kitchen, Galway 222
Park Hotel Kenmare, Kenmare 272
Park House Hotel, Galway 222
Parknasilla Resort & Spa, The, Parknasilla 292
Parson's Nose, The, Hillsborough 537
Partridges Artisan Café
    & Fine Food Shop, Gorey 472
Pax House, Dingle 266
Pearl Brasserie, Dublin 2 30
Pepper Mill, The, Nenagh 438
Perryville House, Kinsale 172
Petit Délice, Cahirciveen 257
Pichet, Dublin 2 31
Pickle, Dublin 2 31
Pier 26 Restaurant, Ballycotton 135
Pier 36, Donaghadee 534
Pigeon House, The, Dublin 3 39
Piglet, Dublin 2 32
Pig's Ear, The, Dublin 2 32
Pilgrims, Rosscarbery 181
Plough Inn, Hillsborough 538
Poachers Inn, The, Bandon 141
Poacher's Pocket, The, Comber 542
Portmarnock Hotel & Golf Links,
    Portmarnock 65
Powerscourt Hotel, Enniskerry 486
Primrose, Londonderry 556
Pudding Row, Easkey 419
Puffin Café, The, Clonakilty 156

Pupp, Dublin 8 51
Pure Magic, Achill Island 366
Purple Onion Bar & Restaurant, The,
    Tarmonbarry 413

Quails at the Gallery, Banbridge 528
Quay House, The, Clifden 235
Quinlan & Cooke Boutique Townhouse
    & QCs Seafood Restaurant, Cahirciveen 258

Rachels, Cork 131
Radisson Blu Hotel & Spa
    & RAW - Sushi in the Sky, Galway 223
Ramore Restaurants, Portrush 520
Rasam, Dub Laoghaire 60
Rathaspeck Manor, Rathaspeck 475
Rathmullan House, Rathmullan 203
Rathsallagh House, Dunlavin, Kildare 301
Rathsallagh House, Dunlavin, Wicklow 485

Ravenhill House, Belfast 509
Rayanne Country House, Holywood 540
Red Bank House & Restaurant, Skerries 67
Red Cliff Lodge, Spanish Point 116
Red Door Tea Room, Ballintoy 512
Renvyle House Hotel, Recess 248
Restaurant Patrick Guilbaud, Dublin 2 33
Rhonwen's Eyeries Bistro, Beara 146
Richmond House, Cappoquin 446
River Lee Hotel, The, Cork 132
Roadside Tavern, The, Lisdoonvarna 109
Roganstown Hotel & Country Club, Swords 69
Rolf's Country House
    & Restaurant, Baltimore 139
Rosa Madre, Dublin 2 34
Rosleague Manor Hotel, Letterfrack 241
Rosquil House, Kilkenny 317
Rossnaree, Slane 394
Ross, The, Killarney 286
Roundwood House, Mountrath 327
Roundwood Inn, Roundwood 492

Rua Cafe & Deli, Castlebar 374
Russell Gallery, The, The Burren 113

Saba, Dublin 2 34
Sage, Westport 387
Sage Restaurant, Midleton 177
Salt Bistro, Belfast 510
Salty Dog Hotel & Bistro, The, Bangor 531
Sand House Hotel, Rossnowlagh 204
Sandymount House, Abbeyleix 323
Saphyre, Belfast 510
Scholars Townhouse Hotel, Drogheda 361
Seafield Hotel & Spa Resort, Gorey 474
Sea Mist House, Clifden 236
Sean's Bar, Athlone 458
Sea Shore Farm Guest House,
 Kenmare 273
Seaview House Hotel, Bantry 137
Shannon Princess, Glasson 463
Sha-Roe Bistro, Clonegal 79
Sheedys Country House Hotel
 & Restaurant, Lisdoonvarna 109
Sheen Falls Lodge, Kenmare 273
Shelbourne Hotel, The, Dublin 2 35
Shelburne Lodge, Kenmare 274
Shells Bakery Café, Strandhill 428
Sheridans Cheesemongers and Wine Bar,
 Galway 224
Shola Coach House, Portrush 520
Shu, Belfast 511
Slane Castle, Slane 394
Slipway, Baltimore 140
Snug, The, Bantry 144
Sooty Olive, The, Londonderry 556
Spa Seafoods Deli & Cafe, Tralee 294
Spinners On Castle Street, Birr 405
Square Bistro, Lisburn 519
Square Table, The, Blarney 148
Station House Hotel, The, Kilmessan 392
Stephen Pearce Pottery, Shanagarry 179
Step House Hotel, The, Borris 75

St Georges Terrace Restaurant, Carrick on
 Shannon 333
St Kyrans Country House & Restaurant,
 Virginia 85
Stone Cutters Kitchen Family Restaurant,
 Doolin 96
Stoop Your Head, Skerries 67
Strandeen B&B, Portstewart 560
Strandhill Lodge & Suites, Strandhill 428
Strawberry Field, The, Killarney 275
Stuffed Olive, The, Bantry 145
Suesey Street, Dublin 2 35
Suitor Gallery Tea Room, Ballygawley 563
Summerhouse Café, The, Lismore 449
Sweet Beat Café, Sligo 427

Tankardstown House, Slane 395
Tannery Restaurant & Townhouse, The,
 Dungarvan 447
Taste at Rustic by Dylan McGrath, Dublin 2 36
Taste Matters, Loughrea 241
Tavern Bar & Restaurant, Westport 389
Teach an Tae Tea Rooms
 & Café, Aran Islands 229
Teach de Broc & Strollers Bistro, Ballybunion 256
Teach Nan Phaidai, Aran Islands 229
Temple House, Ballymote 417
Thatch Bar & Restaurant, The, Birr 406
The Cake Café, Dublin 8 50
The Chart House, Dingle 260
The Gallery Café, Gort 237
The Lobster Pot, Carne 470
The Winding Stair, Dublin 1 13
Thomas Connolly, Sligo 427
Thyme & Co Café, Ballycastle 514
Thyme Restaurant, Athlone 459
Tig Congaile, Aran Islands 230
Tigh Neachtain, Galway 225
Toddies at The Bulman, Kinsale 173
Toons Bridge Dairy
 & The Real Olive Co, Macroom 174